International Political Economy Series

Series Editor

Timothy M. Shaw, University of Massachusetts Boston, Boston, MA, USA;
Emeritus Professor, University of London, London, UK

The global political economy is in flux as a series of cumulative crises impacts its organization and governance. The IPE series has tracked its development in both analysis and structure over the last three decades. It has always had a concentration on the global South. Now the South increasingly challenges the North as the centre of development, also reflected in a growing number of submissions and publications on indebted Eurozone economies in Southern Europe. An indispensable resource for scholars and researchers, the series examines a variety of capitalisms and connections by focusing on emerging economies, companies and sectors, debates and policies. It informs diverse policy communities as the established trans-Atlantic North declines and 'the rest', especially the BRICS, rise.

NOW INDEXED ON SCOPUS!

More information about this series at
https://link.springer.com/bookseries/13996

Diana Barrowclough · Richard Kozul-Wright ·
William N. Kring · Kevin P. Gallagher
Editors

South–South Regional Financial Arrangements

Collaboration Towards Resilience

palgrave
macmillan

Editors
Diana Barrowclough
Division on Globalization and Development Strategies
United Nations Conference on Trade and Development
Geneva, Switzerland

Richard Kozul-Wright
Division on Globalization and Development Strategies
United Nations Conference on Trade and Development
Geneva, Switzerland

William N. Kring
Global Development Policy Center
Boston University
Boston, MA, USA

Kevin P. Gallagher
Global Development Policy Center
Boston University
Boston, MA, USA

ISSN 2662-2483 ISSN 2662-2491 (electronic)
International Political Economy Series
ISBN 978-3-030-64575-5 ISBN 978-3-030-64576-2 (eBook)
https://doi.org/10.1007/978-3-030-64576-2

This Palgrave Macmillan imprint is published by the registered company Springer Nature Switzerland AG
The registered company address is: Gewerbestrasse 11, 6330 Cham, Switzerland

Preface—About This Book

This book was written in response to calls from both academia and the development community for more information about one of the most interesting and potentially significant new trends in global financial architecture since Bretton Woods. It brings together research from different corners of the globe commissioned by the United Nations Conference on Trade and Development (UNCTAD), in response to a request from its member states for more information about South–South financial and monetary integration—new trends and their potential promise but also limitations. The growth of Southern-led regional financial arrangements (RFAs) has been one of the most interesting and potentially significant trends of recent decades and there was little information about the wide variety of mechanisms being established or their impact. Countries were aware of efforts within their respective regions but not further afield; and policy analysis and advice on regional financial and monetary integration efforts across the Global South was scarce. Working closely with leading international academics, policymakers, and practitioners in the mechanisms themselves, an informal network of experts began sharing research findings at major United Nations intergovernmental meetings and regional commissions and at international academic seminars and workshops, including with experts from Boston University Global Development Policy Center, the University of Geneva, the South African Institute for International Affairs, and the Institute of World Economics and Politics (IWEP) of the Chinese Academy of Social Sciences (CASS). The luxury of long-term research, carried out over several years and building upon prior and ongoing activities by all collaborators in this book, coupled with its global reach, has allowed the network to share increasingly broadly and deeply our data, experiences, and learning, thereby we hope considerably enriching our contribution to the development debate. The fact that it brings together academics and policymakers, sociologists and bankers, and original evidence gleaned from interviews as well as empirical studies, from all parts of the globe, adds further value to the diversity of experiences and views. This book was written before the economic and health shocks of 2020 and 2021 caused by coronavirus, however the lessons it highlights are particularly apt. Some countries were able to benefit from their membership of the RFAs described in these pages; a few could benefit from direct and ad hoc arrangements such as credit swaps; many had few choices; all experienced the kinds of issues relating to short-term and emergency finance covered in this book.

The book aims to present in accessible and readable format discussions relating to different aspects of the financial architecture and parts of the world that are not usually brought together. Because it is written by academics, practitioners, and policymakers, each bringing their different expertise and perspective, it hopes to be a useful source as much for undergraduate and postgraduate courses on political economy, finance, and development, as for the interested lay reader looking to plot a path through debate in the financial and mainstream media. Chapters cover both the broad sweep of monetary history—describing the history of the United States Federal Reserve, the Central Bank of Japan, and the West African Economic and Monetary Union—as well as more granular analysis of the most recent developments, such as Latin America's "virtual" currency the Sucre, alongside the Chiang Mai Initiative, and the rise of Sovereign Wealth Funds. The book also aims to highlight the fact that, while these institutions have (deservedly) garnered a great deal of attention they still need a great deal of support from the international community and cannot be seen in themselves as a final nor perfect answer—we still need a well-functioning and truly universal multilateral solution alongside the rise of regional and partial solutions to a problem and source of vulnerability that—given rising levels of debt and foreign exchange risks—is only likely to increase in the near future.

Geneva, Switzerland Diana Barrowclough
Geneva, Switzerland Richard Kozul-Wright
Boston, USA William N. Kring
Boston, USA Kevin P. Gallagher

Acknowledgments

This volume acknowledges with gratitude the financial support from the Development Account of the United Nations General Assembly. Papers associated with the project have been presented and discussed at workshops and seminars around the world, including at Boston University's Global Development Policy Centre's Global Economic Governance Initiative; the Freie University of Berlin; the Graduate Institute University of Geneva; the Institute of World Economics and Politics (IWEP) of the Chinese Academy of Social Sciences (CASS); UNCTAD intergovernmental meetings in Geneva as well as a high-level round table at UNCTAD 14 in Nairobi, Kenya; the South African Institute of International Affairs, Johannesburg and a conference hosted by the Union of South American Nations and the Ministry of External Relations and Human Resources, Ecuador. UNCTAD statistican Lyubov Chumakova contributed research findings to the introductory chapter. Jason McSparren provided editorial assistance. Any omissions and faults remain the authors' and editors' own.

Contents

Editors and Contributors

About the Editors

Diana Barrowclough is a senior economist at the United Nations Conference on Trade and Development, where she is a co-author of the *Trade and Development Report* and leader of research on finance and development. She has a B.A. and M.A. degree in economics and political science from University of Auckland and M.Phil. and Ph.D. in Economics from University of Cambridge. She was a Scholar of the Royal Economic Society and elected a Fellow of St John's College Cambridge. Prior to this, she worked in the financial sector and international consultancy in London and New Zealand.

Richard Kozul-Wright is Director of the Globalisation and Development Strategies Division in UNCTAD. He has worked at the United Nations in both New York and Geneva. He holds a Ph.D. in Economics from the University of Cambridge, UK, and has published widely on economic issues including, inter alia, in the *Economic Journal*, the *Cambridge Journal of Economics*, *The Journal of Development Studies*, and the *Oxford Review of Economic Policy*. His latest book is the *Resistible Rise of Market Fundamentalism* (with Paul Rayment) and he has also edited volumes on*Transnational Corporations and the Global Economy*, *Economic Insecurity and Development*, *Securing Peace*, and *Climate Protection and Development*.

William N. Kring, Ph.D. is the Assistant Director of the Global Development Policy Center, a university-wide center housed at the Frederick S. Pardee School for Global Studies and a Research Fellow at the Global Economic Governance Initiative.

Dr. Kevin P. Gallagher is a Professor of global development policy at the Frederick S. Pardee School of Global Studies and the Director of the Global Development Policy Center (GDPC). The mission of the GDPC is to advance policy-oriented research for financial stability, human wellbeing, and environmental sustainability.

Dr. Gallagher is the author of *The China Triangle: Latin America's China Boom and the Fate of the Washington Consensus*, *Ruling Capital: Emerging Markets and the Reregulation of Cross-border Finance*, *The Dragon in the Room: China and the Future of Latin American Industrialization* (with Roberto Porzecanski), *The Enclave Economy: Foreign Investment and Sustainable Development in Mexico's Silicon Valley*, and *Free Trade and the Environment: Mexico, NAFTA, and Beyond.*

Dr. Gallagher served on the U.S. Department of State's Investment Subcommittee of the Advisory Committee on International Economic Policy and the International Investment Division of the United Nations Conference on Trade and Development. He has served as a visiting or adjunct professor at the Paul Nitze School for Advanced International Studies at Johns Hopkins University, the Fletcher School of Law and Diplomacy, Tufts University, El Colegio de Mexico in Mexico, Tsinghua University in China, and the Center for State and Society in Argentina. He has a B.A. from Northeastern University, Boston, and an M.A. and a Ph.D. from Tufts University. Dr. Gallagher is co-editor of the *Review of International Political Economy* and writes regular columns in *The Financial Times* and *The Guardian*. You can follow him on twitter @KevinPGallagher.

Contributors

Joerg Bibow is a professor of economics at Skidmore College, United States. His main research areas are international finance and European integration, as well as international trade and development and the history of economic thought. Prof. Bibow has lectured at the University of Cambridge, University of Hamburg, and Franklin University Switzerland

and was a visiting scholar at the Levy Institute. He received a bachelor's degree with honors in economics from the University of the Witwatersrand, a diplom-volkswirt from the University of Hamburg, and M.A. and Ph.D. degrees in economics from the University of Cambridge.

Esteban Pérez Caldentey has a Ph.D. in Economics from The New School for Social Research. He is currently Chief of the Financing for Development Unit (Economic Development Division), ECLAC (Santiago, Chile), coeditor of the Review of Keynesian Economics (ROKE), and coeditor of the fourth edition of the New Palgrave Dictionary of Economics.

Barbara Fritz is a Professor of Latin American Studies at the Freie University of Berlin, Germany, where she has been leading research on financial and monetary integration for several years. Important publications include "Development Or Growth Cum Debt? Reflections on Latin America's Economic Strategy in a Time of International Financial Instability."

William W. Grimes is Associate Dean for Academic Affairs and Professor of International Relations & Political Science at the Frederick S. Pardee School of Global Studies at Boston University.

Jan Kregel is the Program Director for the Master of Science in Economic Theory and Policy of the Levy Economics Institute of Bard College and Director of the Monetary Policy and Financial Structure Program, as well as holding positions of Distinguished Research Professor at the Center for Full Employment and Price Stability of the University of Missouri–Kansas City and Professor of Development Finance at the Tallinn University of Technology. During 2009 he served as Rapporteur of the President of the United Nations General Assembly's Commission on Reform of the International Financial System.

Hechely Dzidzogbé Lawson has a Ph.D. in Economics from the University of Lome-FASEG, Togo; and is currently employed at the Centre de Recherche et de Formation en Science Economique et de Gestion (CERFEG) of the Faculty of Economic Sciences and Management (FASEG) of the University of Lomé, Togo.

Dr. Mah Hui Lim has a multidisciplinary background in finance, economics, and politics. He has a B.A. (Honors) in Economics from the University of Malaya, and an M.A. in International Affairs, an M.A. in

Sociology, and a Ph.D. in Development Studies from the University of Pittsburgh. He taught and researched at Duke University, Temple University, and the University of Malaya prior to becoming a banker, working in major international banks in New York, Tokyo, Hong Kong, Singapore, Jakarta, and Manila. These international banks included Chemical Bank (now JP Morgan Chase), Credit Suisse First Boston, Deutsche Bank, Standard Chartered Bank, and the Asian Development Bank. He is a Senior Fellow in the Asian Public Intellectuals Program of the Nippon Foundation.

Laurissa Mühlich is an academic at the Latin American Studies Institute at the Freie University of Berlin Germany; she was previously a Fox International Scholar at the Yale University Macmillan Centre, United States.

Kako Kossivi Nubukpo is currently a Global Leader Fellow at the Global Economic Governance Programme, University of Oxford. Previous experiences include his appointments as former Minister of Long-term Planning for the Government of Togo, and former Chief of research for the West African Economic and Monetary Union. He has a Ph.D. in economics from University of Lyon.

Ampiah Sodji is member of the Faculty of Economic Sciences and Management, of the University of Lomé, Togo.

Georgina Cipoletta Tomassian is United Nations Economic Affairs Officer at the Economic Commission for Latin America and the Caribbean (ECLAC). She is an economist from the University of Buenos Aires, with postgraduate studies in a Ph.D. in economics from the Argentine Catholic University and a Master's in Economic Relations and International Negotiations from the University of Barcelona and FLACSO. She has 19 years of experience in academic research on economic development, financing for sustainable development, infrastructure and logistics, trade, and regional integration.

Fernando Villanueva Melo is Associate professor of the faculty of business and administration at the University of Santiago, Chile.

Abbreviations

ABF1	Asian Bond Fund
ABI	Asian Bond Markets Initiative
ACF	Anti-Crisis Fund of the Eurasian Economic Community
ACM	Eurasian Anti-Crisis Fund
AFC	The Asian Financial Crisis
AfDB	African Development Bank
AIIB	Asian Infrastructure Investment Bank
ALADI	Reciprocal Payments and Credits Agreement
ALBA	Bolivarian Alliance of the Peoples of Our America
ALBA-TCP	Bolivarian Alliance for the Peoples of Our America-Trade Treaty
ALLAC	Latin American Free Trade Association
AMF	African Monetary Fund
AMF	Arab Monetary Fund
AMRO	ASEAN+3 Macroeconomic Research Organization
AMRO	The ASEAN+3 Macroeconomic Research Organization
ARF	Andean Reserve Fund
ArMF	Arab Monetary Fund
ASEAN+3	Association of South East Asian nations plus China, Japan and Republic of Korea

ASP	ASEAN Surveillance Process
Bank Quest Africaine de Devéloppement, BEOA	West African Development Bank
BCB	PTAX of the Central Bank of Brazil
BCEAO	Central Bank for West African States
BCIE	Banco Centroamericano de Integración Económica (CABEI)/Central American Bank for Economic Integration
BCRA	Central Bank of Argentina
BEAC	Banque des États de l'Afrique Centralee/Bank of the Central African States
BIS	Bank for International Settlements
BNDES	Brazil's National Bank for Economic and Social Development
BOP	Balance of Payments
BRICS	Brazil, the Russian Federation, India, China and South Africa
BSAs	Bilateral Swap Agreements
BWIs	Bretton Woods Institutions
CAF	The Development Bank for Latin America
CAF	Corporación Andina de Fomento/(Andean Development Corporation)
CAFM	Council for Financial and Monetary Affairs of ALADI
CARICOM	Caribbean Community
CASS	The Institute of World Economics and Politics (IWEP) of the Chinese Academy of Social Sciences
CDB	China's Development Bank
CEMAC	Central African Economic and Monetary Community
CEMAC	Economic and Monetary Community of Central Africa/Communauté Economique et Monétaire d'Afrique Centrale
CEMLA	The Centro de Estudios Monetarios Latinoamericanos
CIS	Commonwealth of Independent States
CMCP	COMESA Monetary Co-operation Program
CMI	Chiang Mai Initiative
CMIM	Chiang Mai Initiative Multi-lateralization fund
CMIM	Chiang Mai Multilateralization Initiative

CMIM-PL	Precautionary Line
CMU	CARICOM Currency Unit
COMESA	Common Market for Eastern and Southern Africa
CPCR	Agreement on Reciprocal Payments and Credits
CPCR	Reciprocal Payments and Credits Agreement
CPCR—LAIA	Latin American Agreement on Reciprocal Payments and Credits
CRA	Contingent Reserve Arrangement
CSME	Caribbean Community (CARICOM) Single Market and Economy
CSME	CARICOM Single Market and Economy
DBSA	South Africa's Development Bank of Southern Africa
EAC	East African Community
EAMU (planned)	East African Monetary Union
ECA	Economic Cooperation Administration
ECB	European Central Bank
Economic and Monetary Community of Central Africa, CAEMC	Communauté Économique et Monétaire de l'Afrique Centrale CEMAC
ECOWAS	Economic Community of West African States
EDB	Eurasian Development Bank
EMCP	ECOWAS Monetary Co-operation Programme
EMDs	Emerging Market Developing Countries
EMEAP	Executives' Meeting of East Asian and Pacific Central Banks
EMU	Economic and Monetary Union
EMU	Europe's Economic and Monetary Union
EPU	European Payments Union
ERP	European Recovery Programme
ERPD	Economic Review and Policy Dialogue
ESCB	European System of Central Banks
ESM	European Stability Mechanism
ESM	European Stability Mechanism
ESSF	Chile's Economic and Social Stabilization Fund
FCL	Flexible Credit Line
FED	Federal Reserve Bank
FEF	Fondo de Estabilizacion Fiscal
FINPRO	Fund for Productive Industrial Revolution

FLAR	and the Latin American Reserve Fund
FLAR	Latin American Reserve Fund
FOCEM	Fondo para la Convergencia Estructural del Mercosur
FONASUR	Fondo Monetario del Sur
FONPLATA	Fondo Financiero para el Desarrollo de los Países de la Cuenca del Plata FONPLATA
G20	Group of 20 countries
GCC	Gulf Cooperation Council
GDP	Gross Domestic Product
GFSN	Global Financial Safety Net
IFC	*International Finance Corporation*
IMF	International Monetary Fund
LAIA	The Latin American Integration Association
LICs	Least Industrialized Countries
LTRO	Long-Term Refinancing Operations Programme
MBS	Mortgage-Backed Security
MDGs	Their Millennium Development Goals
MERCOSUR	Common Market of the South/Mercado Común del Sur
MFSC	Monetary Financial Stability Committee
NICs	Newly Industrializing Countries
OCA	Optimum Currency Area
or SUCRE	Unified System for Regional Compensation
PER	CEMAC Programme Economique Regional
PRF	Pension Revenue Fund
RCF	Rapid Credit Facility
REPSS	Regional Payment and Settlement System
RFAs	Regional Financial Arrangements
RFI	Rapid Financing Instrument
RISDP	Regional Integration Strategic Development Programme
RMU	Regional Monetary Unit
RTGS	Real-Time Gross Settlement
SADC	Southern African Development Community
SADCC	Southern African Development Community Conference
SARB	South African Reserve Bank
SBAs	Stand-by Agreements
SCF	Stand-by Credit Facility

SDGs	Sustainable Development Goals
SDRs	Special Drawing Rights
SIP	Regional Interlinked Payment System in Central America (SIP)/Sistema de Interconexión de Pagos
SMEs	Small and Medium-Sized Enterprises
SML	Local Currency Payment System
SQS/NF	Non-Financial Corporations and Quasi-Corporations
SWFs	Sovereign Wealth Funds
TAF	Term Auction Credit Facility
TCI	Taxe communautaire d'intégration
TPSs	Transnational Payment Systems
TRT	Term Repurchase Transaction
TSLF	Term Securities Lending Facility
UDPPP (PG 77)	BOAD Public Private Partnership Development Unit
UMOA	West African Economic and Monetary Union
UNCTAD	United Nations Conference on Trade and Development
URR	An Unremunerated Reserve Requirement
VAT	Value Added Tax
WACB	West African Central Bank
WAEMU	West African Economic and Monetary Union
WAEMU	Economic Community of West African States zone
WAMI	West African Monetary Institute
WAMU	West African Monetary Union
WAMZ	West African Monetary Zone
ZMAO	Zone Monetaire de l'Afrique de l'Ouest

List of Figures

List of Tables

CHAPTER 1

South–South Regional Financial Arrangements in the Twenty-First Century—Promise and Potential

Diana Barrowclough and William N. Kring

As the world comes to grips with the devastating economic and public health consequences of the COVID-19 Coronavirus, Southern-led alternative institutions for finance and development seem more important

This book brings together research commissioned by the United Nations Conference on Trade and Development (UNCTAD), in response to a request from member states for more information about South–South financial and monetary integration. This has been one of the most interesting and potentially significant

D. Barrowclough (✉)
Division Globalization and Development Strategies, United Nations Conference On Trade and Development, Geneva, Switzerland
e-mail: Diana.Barrowclough@unctad.org

W. N. Kring
Global Development Policy Center, Boston University, Boston, MA, USA
e-mail: WKRING@BU.EDU

D. Barrowclough et al. (eds.), *South–South Regional Financial Arrangements*, International Political Economy Series,
https://doi.org/10.1007/978-3-030-64576-2_1

than ever. This volume charts the dramatic change in the global financial and monetary landscape that has unfolded over the last few decades, in particular, through the expansion of Southern-led and Southern-oriented institutions and mechanisms. The change is profound, and it has moreover not stopped; the evolution of the Southern-led financial architecture is likely to continue, as the South not only adapts to changing global economic conditions, but changes them—increasing its role in global economic governance.

This book takes stock of some of the most interesting adaptations and institutions led by the South with respect to short-term foreign liquidity and emergency finance. It focuses on common currency areas and payment systems designed to avoid exposure to volatile international currencies and to promote a more resilient pattern of interregional trade; the potential for the newly emergent Sovereign Wealth Funds (SWFs) to play a more developmental role; and, the better known short-term liquidity mechanisms that pool foreign exchange reserves or serve as multilateralized swap arrangements that can provide countercyclical finance or liquidity to member countries, oftentimes more quickly and more generously than the International Monetary Fund (IMF). As noted in the preface and below (footnote 1), the book is a response to requests from experts in many countries for more information about these new

trends of recent decades and there was little information about the wide variety of mechanisms being used or their impact. Countries were aware of efforts within their respective regions but not further afield; and policy analysis and advice on regional financial and monetary integration efforts across the Global South was scarce. Working closely with leading international academics, policymakers, and practitioners in the mechanisms themselves, an informal network of experts has been created, sharing research findings at major United Nations intergovernmental meetings and regional commissions and at academic seminars and workshops, including with experts from the Boston University Global Development Policy Center, the University of Geneva, the South African Institute for International Affairs, and the Institute of World Economics and Politics (IWEP) of the Chinese Academy of Social Sciences (CASS). The luxury of this long-time frame and global reach has allowed the network to share increasingly broadly and deeply our data, experiences, and learnings, thereby we hope considerably enriching our contribution to the development debate. This chapter in particular acknowledges with thanks statistical inputs from UNCTAD statistician, Lyubov Chumokova.

initiatives because some have been more successful than others, and many are not well known outside of their immediate borders or regions.

The different experiences described in this volume show that while these Southern-led initiatives offer many and significant benefits to broaden and diversify the global financial architecture, they are only partial and imperfect solutions to the challenges that remain. The institutions that constitute the Southern-led architecture of global financial institutions stand ill-equipped to deal with a truly systemic global crisis—with the added concern that their Northern-led counterparts are just as ill-prepared. Further, many of these new institutions remain untested. That said, they illustrate the promise and underappreciated capacity of Southern-led institutions at the present moment. To fully realize the potential of a Southern-led architecture, further efforts are needed to help these new mechanisms contribute in ways that significantly alter the global financial landscape and the behavior of the institutions within it. Hopefully these alternative institutions can further ignite the evolution of existing institutions to improve lending decisions and expand access to vital resources to contribute to an inclusive and sustainable economic transformation.

1.1 Origins of Alternative, Southern-Led Institutions

The 2007–2008 financial crisis reinvigorated criticism of the global financial order. That said, calls for reform to the global financial architecture for payments and liquidity support were not new and indeed for more than a decade, scholars and practitioners alike had pointed to the increasing frequency and costs of financial crises.

While there is extensive literature on the shortcomings of the current global financial system and Bretton Woods Institutions (BWIs), there are three key factors explored that particularly motivated the Global South in developing and capitalizing alternatives. First, the increasing scale and volatility of capital flows, which was accompanied by an increasing frequency of financial crises over the past decades, led states to self-insure. Through the accumulation of foreign exchange reserves and creation of new multilateral institutions to provide alternative sources of crisis financing and trade support, countries looked beyond the traditional global financial architecture. Second, the IMF misdiagnoses and accompanying procyclical policy prescriptions of the Asian Financial Crisis and the Argentinian Crisis diminished its legitimacy, as the IMF has subsequently acknowledged. Finally, significant changes to the composition of the global economy have yet to be reflected via a rebalancing of the international financial architecture. Reinforcing these three essentially external factors was a more endogenous trend supporting South–South initiatives and South–South trade, as local and regional markets appeared ever more attractive alongside the steady downturn in global trade and stagnating global economy. This section briefly unpacks these motivating factors in order to provide context to the emergence of these Southern-led alternatives.

The first driver of institutional innovation in the South is the increasing economic volatility that has accompanied the deregulation of capital flows on a global scale. As a result, financial crises have become more frequent since the end of the Bretton Woods fixed exchange rate system. Financial crises have occurred more than once per decade since the fall of Bretton Woods (IMF 2017) and the pain of IMF conditionality imposed in return for Fund support has made many countries, especially in Asia, determined to avoid the pain of the past. The credit crunch that followed the 2007–2008 financial crisis, and then the excessive liquidity caused by Quantitative Easing policies in the North, reinforced the gyrations of global capital markets and showed that the current financial architecture was more, and not less, unstable than ever. While some of the institutions explored in this book have roots that predate the 2007–2008 financial crisis, many of the Southern-led efforts represent defensive efforts to deal with the fallout from excessive and volatile capital flows, fluctuating exchange rates, and the dramatic drop in global trade. Further, the 2007–2008 crisis led many countries to redouble efforts to strengthen existing alternative institutions through a variety of means, such as an expansion of institutional capacity and resources.

The second driver of institutional innovation in the Global South was the legacy of IMF missteps in both Latin America and Asia. In the wake of the 2007–2008 financial crisis, as then Managing Director of the IMF Dominique Strauss-Kahn toured Asia, he noted that while the IMF did some things right during the Asian Financial Crisis, it "also did things wrong, and [the IMF has] to accept this." (See for example VOA 2011; and IMF internal evaluation reports, e.g., IMF 2003). While the IMF's

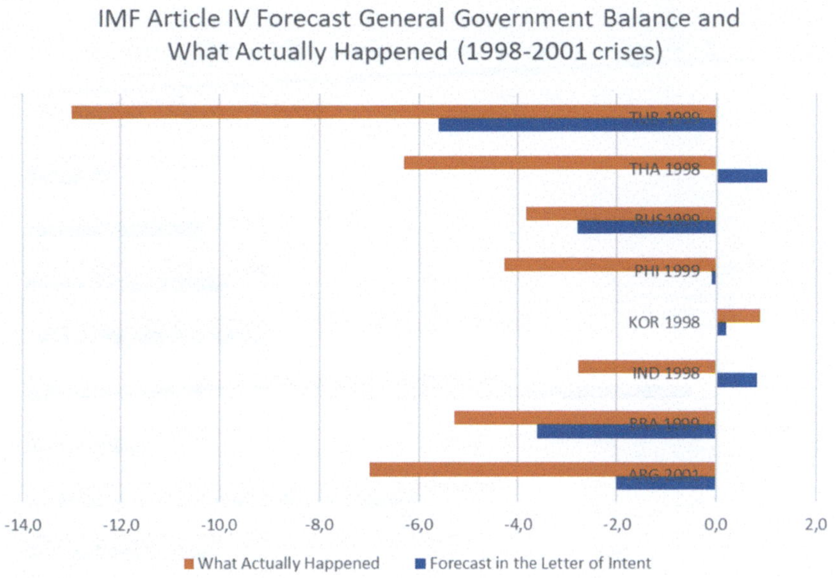

Fig. 1.1 The Disappointment Gap—Crisis the first time around (*Source* UNCTAD, derived from forecasts taken from IMF and country Article IV Letters of Intent; actual data taken from IMF database, year t+1; see UNCTAD 2011:64 for further details)

mea culpa on its past approaches to crises resulted in some subtle shifts,[1] there is considerable evidence that the rhetoric on how its conditionalities have changed is a bit misleading. For example, Kentilikenis et al (2016) identify a fundamental mismatch between the IMF's word on how it has changed and the actual nature of its austerity policies.[2] The policies applied in the wake of the 2007–2008 crisis in practice were still very similar to those used in the previous decade (see UNCTAD 2011: 63–65). Both times, as shown in Figs. 1.1 and 1.2, the actual economic impact of fiscal tightening on Gross Domestic Product (GDP)

[1] Some frequently cited examples include the Fund's acknowledgment of the need for countercyclical fiscal policies in certain types of crises and its rethink on capital controls.

[2] Recent IMF programs in Argentina and Ecuador also follow the same path as taken in the past.

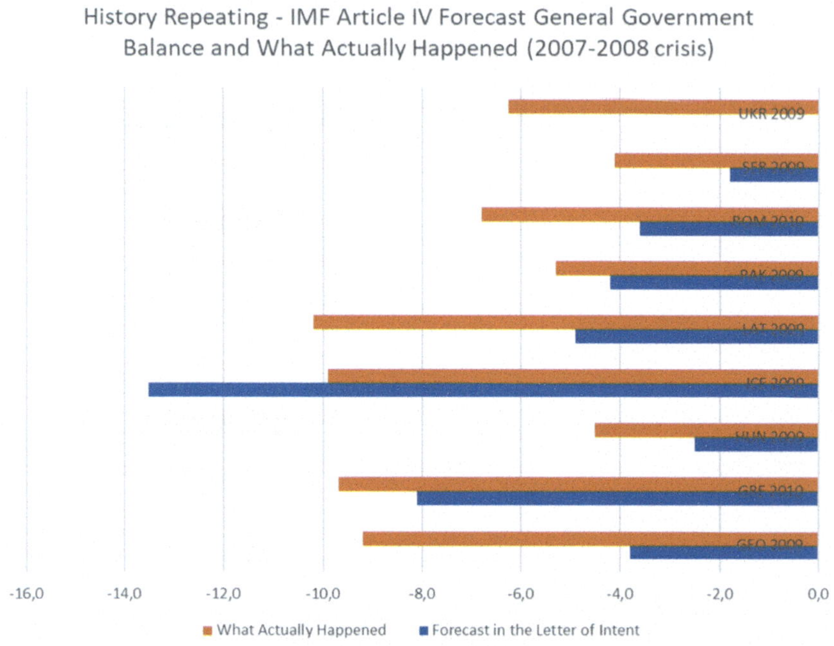

Fig. 1.2 History Repeats Itself (*Source* As above)

growth and the government budget balance was far worse than forecasted in the Letters of Intent signed between the IMF and countries receiving their emergency assistance. Actual outcomes were considerably worse than promised, and often for a long time, with only two exceptions: the Russian Federation in the late 1990s and Iceland in the late 2000s.[3] The gap between predicted and actual GDP growth was most dramatic for countries in the Asian Financial Crisis. For example, a GDP growth rate of 5% was forecast for Indonesia in 1998, but in fact it experienced minus 13%; Thailand was expected to achieve 3.5% growth, but growth actually contracted by 10.5%; and the Republic of Korea was predicted to achieve 2.5% growth but actually suffered minus 5.7% GDP growth. In the case of Thailand, it took four years for GDP to return to the levels that

[3] In the case of Iceland, the IMF followed different rules even supporting the use of capital controls as part of Iceland stand-by arrangement.

had been forecasted immediately following the bailout, for Korea it was at least a quicker recovery, taking just two. Indonesia took six. Unsurprisingly, these disappointing economic performances translated further into low levels of fiscal returns for the government in addition to the weak GDP performances, meaning that budget deficits ballooned.

With those years of struggle still in memory, many in these countries were surprised to see history then repeat itself (Fig. 1.2). The European countries in the 2007–2008 adopted similar packages and experienced similar consequences to IMF bailout conditions that overestimated growth outcomes by more than 5% points (Georgia, Hungary, Latvia, Serbia and Ukraine). Many countries took six to seven years to recover their precrisis conditions, and for two at least (Greece and Ukraine) they are still in a worse situation than whence they started. Developing country delegates discussing the crisis at United Nations meetings professed themselves surprised, amazed even, to see the tough medicine meted out by the IMF to advanced economies, having believed that these countries would be able to insist on different measures.[4] Seeing the replay of these twenty-first-century experiences further fueled the desire of a number of countries in the Global South to create alternative institutions—building on the incipient traces of the (then unsuccessful) idea for an "IMF of the South" that followed the Asian Financial Crisis, but which eventually unfurled today in regional initiatives such as Chiang Mai Initiative and the European Stability Mechanism.

In addition to this, countries in the Global South were further motivated by the realization that finance would not likely come in any sufficiently reliable manner from the private sector, and actually short-term capital flows were making things worse. As shown in Fig. 1.3, countries were reeling under a combination of excessive and then insufficient capital flows which not only unsettled financial markets but also brought exchange rate uncertainty and volatility.

The volatility of exchange rates led, particularly in Latin America, to some highly innovative new mechanisms designed to shield the region from exposure. During the early 2000s, on the back of quantitative easing in the North, some countries were deluged by a tsunami of capital flooding into and then back out of their markets through the "carry trade." Coming on the back of a global downturn in trade, some felt

[4] Comments from Ambassadors and delegates to UNCTAD conference proceedings and expert meetings, at the Palais des Nations, Geneva, during the years 2008–2010.

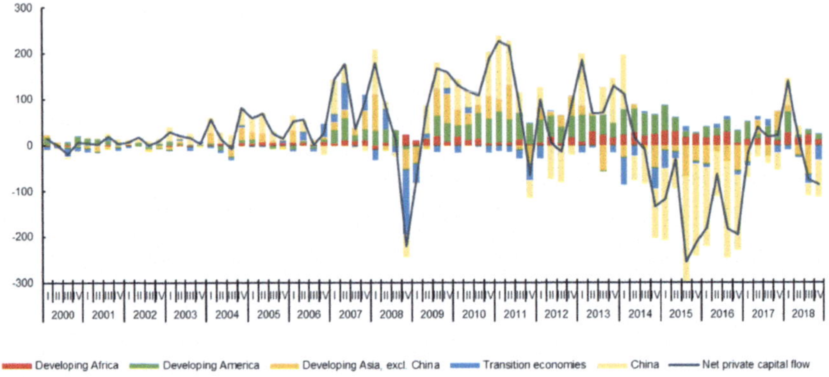

Fig. 1.3 No Lack of Short-Term Capital ... But Catch Me If You Can (*Source* UNCTAD *Financial Statistics Database* based on IMF, *Balance of Payments* database; and national central banks)

it as a "currency war," claiming that countries were intervening to make their currencies cheaper in order to promote trade. In Brazil, the real appreciated sharply against the US Dollar,[5] and in Argentina currency volatility was as high as 100% simply during the months January to August 2018 alone. Even for those countries that tried various forms of capital management, the amounts were too large and no country could act alone to save themselves, provoking extreme currency movements and raising fears of exactly the kind of balance of payments (BOP) crisis they hoped to avoid. On the other hand, for countries that were not standing alone, such as members of the West African common franc zone, their peg to the Euro was providing some stability—and the Euro crisis meant they even benefitted from a depreciating effect for the first time in decades.

Finally, accompanying the stigma of the IMF in many regions around the world due to past experiences, was the recognition by many countries in the Global South that the institutional financial architecture, most especially the Bretton Woods Institutions, were failing to adapt to a rebalancing global economy. In addition to research that reflects the extent to which the IMF largely continues to offer the same conditionalities as it

[5] E.g., Brazil in "currency war" alert, by Jonathan Wheatley in São Paulo and Peter Garnham in London, September 27, 2010https://www.ft.com/content/33ff9624-ca48-11df-a860-00144feab49a

did before the crisis, other scholars have also evaluated the extent to which changes to voting weights and representation of the Global South at the IMF more adequately reflect the changing nature of the global economy. Vestergaard and Wade (2015) find that the equity of the Global South in the IMF changed minimally after governance reform. The Bretton Woods Institutions were designed with mechanisms for future rebalancing, such as the Quota reform process. However, an assessment of changes to voting weights and representation of the Global South at the IMF and World Bank finds that "countries continue to vary widely in their share of votes relative to share of world GDP; in both organizations some countries have six times or more the votes relative to GDP of others" (Vestergaard and Wade, 2015: 1).

In summary, the need for alternative and/or supplementary institutions to long-standing Bretton Woods Institutions and payment systems is deeply rooted in the experiences of the past and the not unrelated imbalances of the present. In the context of procyclical capital flows, depressed commodity prices, and rising US interest rates, emerging and developing economies face significant and increasing risks. Similarly, as they have increased their share of the global economy, they have justifiably sought more voice and influence in the international system. This book therefore surveys exchange rate and payment systems, Sovereign Wealth Funds and closely related mechanisms for short-term liquidity support to identify the opportunities that new mechanisms present for emerging economies and developing countries to strengthen their voice and bargaining power, rebalance the power balance, establish new financing instruments with no conditionality or countercyclical conditionality, and new forms of institutional governance.

1.2 The Landscape of Southern-Led Institutions

In response to the various financial crises and developing regions' experiences with the IMF, many countries began to self-insure themselves against further vulnerability by the accumulation of foreign exchange reserves. Setting aside the economic costs of excessive foreign exchange reserve accumulation and the imbalances that can result in the global financial system, the accumulation of foreign exchange reserves brings three key capabilities. First, accumulated foreign exchange reserves can and have been utilized by countries as a first line of defense against currency depreciation, and also be lent to other countries in the region via bilateral swaps. Second, especially in the case of Asia, foreign exchange reserves in East Asia could underpin the multilateralized swap arrangement across ASEAN+3 countries known as Chiang Mai Multilateralization Initiative (CMIM)—which can now provide more resources to members than the IMF. Thirdly, some countries used these reserves to bankroll the creation of Sovereign Wealth Funds, investing for the most part in countries in the North.

Alongside these efforts based on the use of foreign reserves, countries have also created exchange rate and payment systems that to varying degrees of success, deepen regional integration and reduce vulnerability to volatile exchange rates. While many of these emerged in the immediate context of the 2007–2008 crisis, they are still constantly evolving—as evident with a new agreement between Brazil and Paraguay to trade in local currencies.

While recent events and imbalances stimulated many of the new institutions and mechanisms in this landscape, Jan Kregel in this volume shows that the roots of the problem lie in the interlinking between trade and payment systems, laid down decades earlier from the birth of the modern international financial system. Taking a broad sweep of history from the end of World War II, Kregel argues that the system of convertible currencies may have been appropriate for some developed countries but it was an impediment from the outset for many developing ones, who would face persistent and inherent imbalances between imports and exports and would be always vulnerable to the use of the dollar, including dollar financing of regional trade. Starting from Keynes' Clearing Union proposal, which proposed that any divergence between imports and exports be automatically financed by creditor countries via a global clearing house or settlement system, he sketches out some broad varieties of regional systems and shows why the limits to symmetrical adjustment continue to challenge them.

1.3 Exchange Rate and Payment Systems

As most developing countries had liberalized their exchange rates and financial markets in recent decades, they were—as Kregel's chapter explains—extremely vulnerable to the impact of a hyper volatile US Dollar and other key currencies in the postcrisis years. Latin America has been particularly experimental, as described in the chapter by Caldentey, Tomassian, and Melo, with a number of different mechanisms emerging

Table 1.1 Short- and Long-Run Financing Arrangements in the Global Economy

Short and Long-Run Financing Arrangements in the Global Economy			
Liquidity Support		*Development Banks*	
Instituition	*Size (millions)*	*Instituition*	*Total Assets (millions)*
Multilateral instituitions		Multi-lateral Development Banks	
International Monetary Fund	653,000	Advanced economies	936,310
People's Bank of China	480,000	EMD-led MDBs	257,049
Chiang Mai Initiative Multilateralization	240,000		
Contingent Reserve Arrangement*	100,000	Sub-total	1,193,359
European Stability Mechanism	90,600		
Eurasian Fund for Stabilization and Development	8,513		
Arab Monetary Fund	3,530		
Latin American Reserve Fund	2,880		
Sub-total	1,578,523		
National Reserve Holdings		National Development Banks	
Advanced economies	3,900,000	Advanced economies	1,087,152
EMDs	7,400,000	EMD NDBs	3,768,774
Sub-total	11,300,000	Sub-total	4,855,926
EMD-led	8,158,123	EMD-led	4,025,823
Advanced economy-led	4,720,400	Advanced economy-led	2,023,462
Total	12,878,523	Total	6,049,285

Source Kring and Gallagher (2019), annual reports of various institutions, IMF 2017, and McDowell 2017.

at different levels in the region, involving different and sometimes the same countries, and reflecting different responses to very similar problems and aspirations. One old idea that had been initiated in the 1960s was reformed in the new post-liberalization world of the 1980s, namely the

11-country membership of a Reciprocal Payments and Credits Agreement (CPCR); and, two completely new regional mechanisms were initiated within just a few years following the crisis. The Local Currency Payment System (SML) was created between Argentina and Brazil in 2008 and extended to Paraguay and Uruguay in 2015, while, the Unified System for Regional Compensation (or SUCRE) was created by Bolivia, Cuba, Ecuador, and Venezuela in 2010 in a developing country application of Keynes' proposal following WWII for a clearing union. All three of these regional systems share in common the aim to reduce the need for foreign exchange transfers, and to manage liquidity and credit risks. They also aimed to promote interregional trade and to deepen integration. The Sucre, in particular, had the important objective of being a step in the path to consolidate an area of Economic Complementation. In all of these mechanisms countries retained their own currencies and hence monetary policies, but looked for ways to reduce vulnerability and to build resilience—resilience coming through both changes in the productive structure and trade, and also in the mechanics of the foreign exchange system.

A very different approach is examined in the chapters by Bibow and Nubukpo. These authors launch from the experience of the Eurozone area, which remains the pinnacle of ambition for many countries. This includes countries currently planning to merge existing currency zones in West Africa with Central, East, and Southern Africa to form a single franco-anglophone union for the entire subcontinent. Both the European and African models have a long history of many decades and a rich and complex institutional framework to draw on, with myriad institutions and levels of governance at the national and regional levels reflecting their wider political and social contexts and goals.

The West African CFA, for example, was designed at a time of independence from colonial rule in Africa but with terms of South–North trade that still reflected the colonial past and are very different today. The concept of a common currency has long been integral to regional cooperation and integration in West Africa; however, it is be better formed to fit of the past more than the future according to the chapter by Dr. Nubukpo. He argues that the forms of deep regional cooperation and integration pursued over the last 70 years are no longer ideal and must be significantly reformed. He shows that the West African Economic and Monetary Union (WAEMU) and the Central African Economic and Monetary Community (CEMAC)'s use of the single currency CFA is more of a hindrance than a help. The single currency area as designed, which initially pegged to the French franc and then to the Euro, largely ties the hands of member countries in terms of their flexibility in macroeconomic policies. While such macroeconomic constraints may be suitable for wealthy, industrialized European countries, this is not the case for under industrialized, poorer countries in Africa. While the peg to the Euro has provided some benefits in terms of stability and cohesion, the CFA has frequently been overvalued and revised rarely over the course of its five-decade history. The chapter concludes with a series of fundamental proposed reforms that aim to enhance the CFA in Western Africa and promote economic growth, but will likely reverberate beyond France and West and Central Africa. Complementing debate that is taking place elsewhere about the role of Central Banking generally, Nubukpo argues that the goal of economic growth and flexibility for the coordination of fiscal and monetary policy should be accorded priority over inflation targeting.

Expanding beyond common currency arrangements, Dr. Bibow analyzes key shortcomings and failures of Europe's Economic and Monetary Union (EMU) to distill key lessons for both Europe and the African context. In particular, this chapter focuses on insights that are relevant for the large number of West and Central African countries also examined by Nubukpo.

The West African Economic and Monetary Union (WAEMU) and the Central African Economic and Monetary Community (CEMAC) are very closely linked to the EMU both in terms of philosophy and concretely through a peg with the Euro. Now, Africa is moving ahead with long-standing plans for much wider and deeper monetary and financial integration, first bringing in the Anglophone countries in West and Central Africa, and eventually aiming to cover the whole of Africa in a single union. Bibow argues that Europe's experience affirms that a fiscal union must go alongside monetary union, that market integration needs to occur alongside broader policy integration, and that persistent divergences between the competitiveness of member countries (in particular with respect to very large new members) must be prevented. He also lays out a plan for establishing a new regional bond, as a source of development finance and an appropriate use of foreign reserves.

1.4 Short-Term Liquidity: Reserve Funds and Club Mechanisms

The second main category of mechanisms and institutions examined in this volume are also not a new phenomenon, but are potentially even more significant today. Regional institutions that provide financial support for balance of payments or liquidity support during times of crisis, such as the Latin American Reserve Fund (FLAR) and Arab Monetary Fund (ArMF), have existed since the 1970s. That said, the scale of financing for financial stability has increased massively in scale in the post-2007–2008 financial crisis period. (Kring and Gallagher, 2019; UNCTAD 2011: 71–75). While some of this form of liquidity financing has emerged in the global North, such as the creation of the European Stability Mechanism (ESM), the majority of financing has been spearheaded by emerging market and developing economies.

This rise of regional solutions to global problems now accounts for new or adapted institutions that wield more than ten trillion dollars, and far outweighs the support available from traditional multilateral institutions. In addition to the financial firepower now available, the mechanisms also embody different institutional and governance characteristics which may be less tangible than finance but could be just as significant. This is not to assume that all the new forms of collaboration and cooperation have, or will, automatically succeed, nor that the process is in any way complete. Some of the new mechanisms that emerged have been very innovative in their forms and function; others rather tweak if not re-engineer more conventional instruments. Taken together, however, it is clear they change profoundly the financial, economic, and geopolitical landscape.

This section of the book begins with a chapter by Drs. Fritz and Muhlich who are among the first authors to document these trends. This chapter takes understanding further through its focus on evolution of the global financial safety net (GFSN), which they describe as a constellation of sources of liquidity funding in the global economy. In addition to the introduction of new facilities and resources at the global level from the IMF, new regional financial arrangements (RFAs) were created, and bilateral swap agreements emerged as a key component of crisis response. In this chapter, the authors assess the implications of changes to the GFSN. The authors created a database on the instances in which RFA members utilized a component of the GFSN to analyze the various options available to a member country, and to analyze how the respective volume, timeliness, and policy conditionality of these instruments affected their use. The authors find today's global financial safety net to be not global but rather a geographically and structurally scattered net with unequal access for three different groups of countries. Small countries can draw on their RFAs. Only few countries can count on a bilateral swap line. The majority of the countries do not have several options to choose from. They have the IMF as their only source. The authors find that volume alone does not explain why countries choose a certain source of emergency liquidity. Even if "the big new" voluminous swap arrangements replaced RFAs in some cases, they find a complex pattern of complementary and substitutive use of the regional and other elements of the global safety net.

To deepen understanding of how this landscape of the global financial safety net has evolved, and reasons behind its current components, the chapter by Dr. Lim takes us back to the Asian Financial Crisis and the push for a regional financial architecture that followed. Reiterating the argument that globalization in the post-Bretton Woods international financial system has led to greater economic and financial instability, both domestically and globally, Lim describes how the failure of the traditional international financial architecture prompted efforts among East Asian countries to create an Asian regional financial architecture. Under this *defensive* objective, as compared to the more developmental objectives of institutions such as the new development banks and the Asian Infrastructure Investment Bank (AIIB), the ASEAN+3 countries set up mechanisms for crisis prevention, management, and resolution. The most visible and significant achievements in this area are the establishment of the Chiang Mai Initiative Multi-lateralization (CMIM) fund and the ASEAN+3 Macroeconomic Research Organization (AMRO). The first is a \$240 billion multilateral swap arrangement among the ASEAN + 3 economies to provide liquidity support to member countries with balance of payment problems. The second shows that South–South integration embodies technical knowledge and shared expertise as well as money, indicating a broader vision for regional integration. AMRO is the economic research and surveillance organization to monitor the economic health of member countries and the region, and to provide logistic support to the CMIM. AMRO plays a critical role in the success of the CMIM fund; the more it is able to build up its capacity and credibility, the more the region is able to wean itself from IMF conditionality when accessing CMIM funds.

Building upon the previous chapter's analysis, Drs. Grimes and Kring compare two long-standing RFAs, the CMIM and the Latin American Reserve Fund (FLAR) to draw lessons for other established regional financial arrangements, as well as emerging ones such as the Contingent Reserve Arrangement (CRA). This chapter begins by providing the background and history of each RFA, an analysis of their governance model, and evaluation of their economic impact. While the CMIM and FLAR emerged for distinct reasons and in different time periods, their structure and capabilities reflect the characteristics and needs of the member economies. RFAs designed to serve economies that are very open to trade and capital flows need to be much larger than ones that cater to less-open economies. In contrast, when the economies of the members of an RFA are more symmetrical in terms of size and vulnerability, an independently managed revolving fund can be quite successful, as seen with the FLAR. The authors find that, depending on scale, RFAs may offer their members a credible exit option from status-quo governance. The FLAR could be scaled up to more fully displace the IMF as a provider of emergency funding in Latin America through increases in paid-in capital, establishment of swap agreements, issuance of debt under its AA credit rating, or solicitation of deposits from nonmember central banks. The CMIM, whose credit facilities are currently 70% linked to IMF programs, could reduce that linkage or even completely delink from the IMF if members were to choose that route.

The final chapter of this section of the book moves beyond traditional models of liquidity provision to explore the emergence of Sovereign Wealth Funds (SWFs) and their role as a countercyclical and stabilizing feature. Dr. Barrowclough chronicles the dramatic increase in this mechanism—which is at once both old, having first begun in the United States in the 1890s, and new in the sense that the majority of funds were borne in the last decade. Today these funds manage assets totaling nearly US $8 trillion, counting just the largest funds alone. Similar to the composition of development and liquidity finance institutions described in this volume, the majority of SWF growth has unfolded in the developing world to the extent that two-thirds of the 80 largest SWFs are owned by developing countries. Barrowclough argues that despite the majority of these public assets being owned by governments in the "South," the support they could potentially offer is not currently oriented toward the South or South–South cooperation. SWFs could rebalance themselves to play a more defensive and developmental role in enhancing their distinctiveness compared to, as well as complementarities with, the BWIs and regional financial institutions and contributing to a more diverse and competitive offering of global development finance. Not only can SWFs invest more in long-term developmental projects that support the South in a practical and tangible sense, their very presence in Southern markets provides an indirect benefit in terms of providing additional liquidity for regional and local debt and equity markets which may reduce reliance on international capital. However, to achieve this, Funds need to have a more public-oriented and developmental mandate.

1.5 Experiences and Lessons Learned

The chapters assembled for this book provide a number of insights into the changing nature of architecture and lessons for a variety of emerging initiatives. There are six main lessons to draw. First, the most immediately apparent is that there has been a fundamental restructuring of the GFSN over the past decade. While there was roughly US $5 billion in short-term liquidity finance available across the globe via the IMF, swaps, RFAs, and national reserves, that number has more than doubled to US $12.8 trillion since the 2007–2008 financial crisis. As shown in Table 1.1, 63% of the growth in liquidity finance has come from emerging market.

The second insight highlighted in the chapters in this volume is the increasing diversity across the architecture of alternative institutions to the traditional BWIs. In addition to continued reserve accumulation, a number of new RFAs have been introduced, existing institutions have evolved, and alternative institutions have been increasingly used by their member countries for both borrowing purposes and also as part of narratives concerned with the rebalancing of the global financial order. Further, the institutional structure of these institutions varies considerably across different contexts, which is in part a function of the diversity of member country needs and regional needs.

Thirdly, this collection finds that regionally embedded institutions can function as effective first lines of defense, as recognized by their lending history. Of all the regional mechanisms outlined in this edited book, one of the most high-profile successes has been RFAs. Through the provision of liquidity from a variety of alternatives sources to the IMF, some countries have had the benefit of turning to Southern-led alternatives for balance of payments or other short-term liquidity crises. As older institutions, such as CMIM and FLAR have been bolstered through significant increases to their resources and the development of technical capacities, and new institutions such as the CRA have emerged, a multitiered GFSN has emerged, including a myriad of bilateral swap arrangements across the globe and a robust network of RFAs. What is more, new institutions such as the CRA and proposed institutions such as the African Monetary Fund (AMF) provide further promise of a multilayered GFSN in which countries can have more options for crisis finance, depending on the circumstance (Dagah et al. 2019).

The fourth insight however, is that these are first defenses not last ones, and several writers in this volume warn that progress should not be overstated, as there are significant gaps in protection where countries and regions are not covered, in addition to there being the potential for fragmentation and instability due to the poor degree of global financial safety net integration. Further complicating the predictive value of accounts of emerging Southern-led institutions is diversity of their history and experiences. The existence of an institution is not the same thing as proven efficacy—some of the reserve funds have a long history of frequent use; others have immense resources in theory without having been called upon to use them yet—either way, other developing countries are looking at these with interest.

Moreover, while the various forms are all very diverse, they share some of the same questions about governance structures—including the benefits of differing governance structures; debates about optimal size, optimal lending rules, challenges of homogeneous and heterogeneous membership, etc. The volume reiterates a message highlighted in other publications (including Kring and Grimes (ibid) and Barrowclough and Gottschalk [2018]) regarding the essential role that solidarity plays in the effectiveness of the mechanisms—for example, the FLAR and its perfect repayment history by members. That said, the FLAR is constrained in terms of its lending capacity due to the resource constraints that its developing member country economies face. Proposed Southern-led institutions, such as the African Monetary Fund and the Melanesian Reserve Fund, face similar resource constraints, prompting numerous writers to examine the feasibility for an expanded FLAR with larger members and increased resources (e.g., Ocampo and Titleman [2012]). That said, such changes to the design of the membership base of the FLAR would dramatically rebalance the membership and risk compromising the solidarity between member countries. More generally, Volz (2016) finds that the governance structure of the RFAs is decentralized, fragmented, and lacks coordination with the IMF. This, in turn, poses a significant threat to stability of the global financial safety net (Fig. 1.4).

Contributing vitally to this limitation is the fact that some of the most widely used mechanisms are in fact not really regional, but rather depend on bilateral swaps, as opposed to multilateralized agreements as seen with CMIM. The extraordinary predominance now of bilateral swaps, especially since the 2007–2008 financial crisis, is incredibly salient as their use exceeds the use of RFAs and the IMF, as noted, in particular, by Fritz and Muhlich in this publication. Not all countries are able to negotiate such special, one-to-one arrangements; much depends on political will and wider economic relationships. That said, the authors do not contend that this points to the end of regionalism. Apart from the provision of liquidity resources for crisis response, regional mechanisms provide forums for cooperation and deliberation that can be key to effective crisis response.

The fifth lesson that emerges from the chapter is the need for mechanisms to adapt as conditions change. The chapter by Nubukpo, a former Minister with day-to-day experience of managing the financing challenges of developing countries, and Lawson and Sodji argues that after fifty years of the Common Franc Arrangements in West and Central Africa, reform is needed to meet new challenges and needs. West Africa's situation is almost unique in the world, in that it is poor and underdeveloped but also

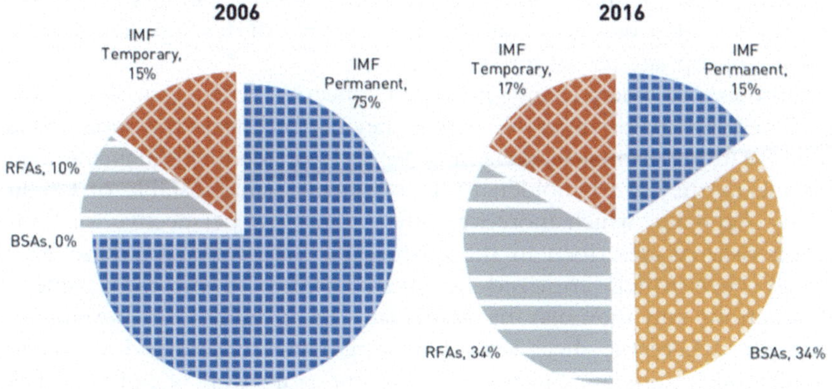

Fig. 1.4 Share of IMF Resources Before and After the Global Financial Crisis (*Source* IMF and Bank of England)

features a group of countries that have, for more than 70 years, practiced a very deep form of regional cooperation and integration. Dr. Nubukpo argues that its use of the single currency CFA is a hindrance more than a help. First pegged to the French franc and now to the Euro, he argues that it forces member countries into a straitjacket of macroeconomic policies that are appropriate for rich industrialized European countries but not for poor, yet to industrialize, African ones.

One issue currently receiving a lot of attention is the fact that the present system requires that members deposit half of their foreign reserves with the French Central Bank. This system has been credited with providing some stability and cohesion, but it has also deterred the evolution of the kinds of regional models emerging in other developing regions, or even the use of SWFs. These issues have become increasingly topical and important given Africa's wider vision for continent-wide monetary union and Dr. Nubukpo recommends a number of fundamental reforms and changes that will likely have reverberations beyond simply France and the West and Central African economies directly involved.

Similar lessons can be shared from the experiences of Europe's Economic and Monetary Union (EMU), as shown in the chapter by Dr. Bibow. He uses the European experience to argue that fiscal union must go alongside monetary union; that market integration needs to occur alongside broader policy integration; that persistent divergences between the competitiveness of member countries (in particular with respect to very large new members) must be prevented. Bibow also lays out a plan for establishing a new regional bond, as a source of development finance and an appropriate use of foreign reserves.

Another area where change is needed concerns the fact that all the new mechanisms remain vulnerable is that they depend upon retaining access to international capital markets in order to have adequate financing, and this means they are beholden to an extremely narrow stable of Credit Rating Agencies, which moreover reflect a narrow perspective for evaluating risk. As described in the chapter by Barrowclough, these have already been widely criticized for short termism in the most general of situations and they may be particularly inappropriate for developing countries, where the sheer lack of existing infrastructure and large and young populations are cause for a different evaluation of potential risk and return. Countries where there is great economic potential and unmet demand could be judged on a very different risk profile compared to those with, for example, older populations and where basic infrastructure needs are already met. There is also evidence of a systematic bias in terms of national policy choices—empirical studies show that credit rating agencies appear to positively favor the use of policies that are "Washington Consensus conventional" and more highly rate countries following those policies and less positively rate countries following more heterodox policies—regardless of the underlying economic fundamentals (UNCTAD 2015: 106–107). Some of the new Southern-led mechanisms have already indicated they may avoid the use of capital markets because of this, which because it will impact on their scale could thereby reduce their potential effectiveness, especially for the neediest countries that have few other sources of finance. The existence of SWFs can help provide extra liquidity for regional and local capital markets which can help to reduce reliance on international capital markets and potentially reduce exposure to foreign exchange volatility, however at present many are not allowed to invest in their own countries.

Finally, as argued by several authors in this volume, and elsewhere, while these essentially short- to medium-term mechanisms play a vital role, they need to be seen within a broader macroeconomic framework that also considers long-term development finance and a more equitable and resilient distribution of productive capacities, given that these determine long-term trends of employment, consumption, and trade. The chapter by Lim shows that developmental policies lead by development banks and infrastructure funds are needed to transform the basic economy in ways that will make it less vulnerable to liquidity crises in the first place; similarly, the chapter by Caldentey et. al. shows that currency and payment systems designed to promote interregional trade cannot of themselves bring this about—what is also needed is the creation and expansion of new industries with greater value added and productivity, and oriented to local and regional needs. Hence the mechanisms cannot be considered alone and an integrated approach is needed that brings together macroeconomic policy as well as the specific monetary and financial policies, or "real economy" policies at the same time. Short-term liquidity financing needs therefore also to be considered in relation to employment, production, and trade patterns, for example, which are in turn a function of long-term public and private investment capacities. Crisis prevention takes many forms, including efforts to reduce the likelihood of crisis in the first place.

1.6 Opportunities for the Future

This volume highlights the variation across the landscape of Southern-led institutions. Such variation provides valuable lessons and information for existing institutions that are expanding their mandates and/or capacities, as well as proposed institutions or those that in the process of being implemented. For example, while the African Monetary Fund has a comprehensive charter, the experience of other RFAs in the operationalization of their institutions could provide valuable insight for policy makers in kick-starting it. Further, the lessons of existing institutions such as FLAR and CMIM-AMRO can help show their value to policy makers and the general public in their respective regions, including the benefits for regional economic stability and trade integration.

In addition to RFAs learning from each other, the experiences described in this volume show that both the IMF and the RFAs have an opportunity to learn from one another. In part due to engagement with the RFAs that was mandated by the G20 and requested by the RFAs themselves, the IMF has come to understand the full extent of their liquidity firepower and the need for substantive engagement with them and other components of the GFSN over the course of the last decade. Further, the IMF appears keen to offer, and some RFAs keen to embrace, opportunities to observe, train, and engage with IMF staff, as part of their ongoing efforts at capacity building. At a minimum, the IMF appears more open to listening and engaging with outside actors than in the past. However, the extent to which this represents a genuine desire for constructive engagement is yet to be determined.

RFAs can also learn operational lessons from other RFAs and the IMF. As demonstrated by institutions such as the FLAR and ArMF, even with limited resources, RFAs can be incredibly successful in helping member countries navigate short-term balance of payments pressures or to leverage short-term liquidity financing as bridge funding to other solutions. Beyond funding, RFAs of all sizes can provide regional forums for engagement and interaction between countries, including the possibility of regional surveillance as observed with AMRO.

1.7 Conclusion

The pages above, and indeed the rest of the pages in this volume, describe an international financial and monetary architecture that has changed fundamentally in the last few decades—with these changes being driven by the South, and oriented toward the South. As this volume shows, some of these changes were presaged decades earlier—in the years immediately following World War II, when Keynes suggested an international accounting currency to manage the international monetary system and enable balance between importing and exporting nations, and while this was not a South–South mechanism one did follow quite soon afterward with the recommendation for a payments union for all developing countries that was put forward in 1968, at the second international conference of UNCTAD. In both these cases, the dominating vision was one of trade, physical trade, and how to promote it and how to avoid debilitating or costly imbalances between deficit and surplus countries. This vision of promoting regional trade continues to drive more modern initiatives, especially given the gloomy prognosis for global trade and the realization on the part of many developing countries that they have not benefited from trade as much as they had hoped for. Nonetheless, today the dominating force behind South–South initiatives is rather more related to issues of finance, reflecting the growing financialization of the global economy, the global transactions of currencies in a magnitude that has gone way beyond that which physical trade in goods requires, and the dominance of the US Dollar.

Today's developing country fears and concerns are therefore are less related to actual physical trade and more to the risks and costs associated with foreign exchange exposures on the back of hyperglobalization, open capital accounts, floating exchange rates, financial deregulation, an economic system that is characterized by boom and bust episodes, and, in particular, a massive build-up of debt. The seeds of many South–South innovations may have been sown in the Asian and Latin American crises last century but they are perhaps even more intense today given the lack of any significant reform of the international financial architecture and, in particular, ongoing limitations and concerns associated with the International Monetary Fund. The authors in this volume show there is still no real change in policy conditionalities which means that countries are reluctant to call for support; at the same time, the IMF is under-financed for what is needed. Coupled with massively rising debt levels that make the prospect of requiring a bailout sometime in the future more than just hypothetical, the fact that Southern-led regional payment systems and reserve funds now have a long history of providing liquidity and allowing settlement of trade obligations in domestic currencies suggests this is likely to continue to expand as long as there are no changes to the current system.

However, while the chapter has painted the dramatic changes in this landscape and highlighted its potential benefits and advantages for developing countries, this is not to say they can sufficiently meet the needs either. It is a real concern, as global debt soar to record levels, that most countries are not covered at all by the regional reserve funds that have emerged and remain completely exposed. Several authors have highlighted serious gaps in coverage and "knots" in these regional systems: most are simply too small for what is needed, meaning that larger countries in the regions cannot be included and even for small members, the funds would not be sufficient if several countries required support at once. Bilateral agreements such as swaps have proved to be much more significant, in volume terms at least, than the regional agreements and clubs which started the first wave of liquidity solutions and this brings with it a different set of limitations and potential problems, including the fact that only a few countries are able to attract or negotiate such support. They are also not particularly transparent, and are ad hoc by nature rather than regular. And finally, even if the IMF were to significantly change its policy direction, the fact remains that more than half the finances of the IMF are not core budget but need to be renegotiated. There is therefore still far too little financing in the so-called "safety net" to stem the next global financial crisis, let alone go the further step of providing finance for infrastructure and other structural transformations needed for a more stable, equitable, and inclusive world.

In conclusion, despite the great deal of attention these institutions have (deservedly) garnered, they still need a great deal of support from the international community and cannot be seen in themselves as a final nor perfect answer. At the same time, the challenge is that countries need to be able to prioritize and privilege regional interests over immediate and national ones. This is always a challenge but until this is realized, there is the danger of limiting not only regional and collective goals but national ones as well (Table 1.2).

Table 1.2 Some mechanisms and institutions included in this book

Objective	*Mechanism*	*Examples in this book*
Resolving short-term balance of payments	Regional liquidity pools of foreign exchange, SWAPS and credit lines	FLAR loans Chiang Mai Initiative swaps Arab Monetary Fund loans Eurasec anti-crisis fund loans
Reducing exposure to exchange rate volatility, reducing the currency costs of trade	Local and regional Currency and payment systems	Latin American agreement on reciprocal payments; SUCRE, SML between Argentina and Brasil West African currency agreement and CFA Euro
Promoting structural transformation and development	Macroeconomic cooperation at the level of the region	Sovereign Wealth Funds Southern Africa Common Monetary Area, Southern Africa Development Community, West African Monetary Zone, Economic and Monetary Community of Central Africa, European Community MERCOSUR Gulf Cooperation Council

References

Barrowclough D and Gottschalk R (2018). Solidarity and the South: Supporting the New Landscape of Long-term Development Finance. UNCTAD Research Paper No. 24, UNCTAD/SER/.RP/2018/6.

Bo-yeon, Hwang (2010). "IMF Admits Mistakes in 1997 Crisis Countermeasures." *HANKYOREH*, https://english.hani.co.kr/arti/english_edition/e_business/430107.html.

Dagah D, Hadiza, Kring W.N and Bradlow D (2019), "Jumpstarting the African Monetary Fund." GEGI Policy Brief 008

Fritz B and Muhlich M (2018). Safety for Whom? The Scattered Global Financial Safety Net and the Role of Regional Financial Arrangements. *Open Economies Review*, 2018, 29(5): 981–1001

Grabel I (2018). Toward a Pluripolar Global Financial Architecture? The Bretton Woods Institutions and the New Landscape of Developmental Finance. *Journal of Radical Political Economics*, 50(4): 653–659. Sage Publications.

IMF (2003). Evaluation Report: Fiscal Adjustment in IMF-Supported Programmes. Washington, DC, Independent Evaluation Office.

IMF (2017). "Collaboration Between Regional Financing Arrangements and the IMF." *IMF Policy Paper.* https://www.imf.org/en/Publications/Policy-Papers/Issues/2017/07/31/pp073117-collaboration-between-regional-financing-arrangements-and-the-imf.

Kentilikenis, A.E, Stubbs T. H and King L.P (2016). "IMF conditionality and development policy space, 1985–2014." Review of International Political Economy 23(4):543–582.

Kring, W. N. and Gallagher K. P. (2019). "Strengthening the Foundations? Alternative Institutions for Finance and Development." *Development and Change*, 50(1): 3–23.

McDowell, D (2017). *Brother, can you spare a billion? The United States, the IMF, and the international lender of last resort*. Oxford: Oxford University Press.

Ocampo J.O and Titleman D (2012). "Regional Monetary Cooperation in Latin America," ADBI Working Papers 373, Asian Development Bank.

Reid J and Nicol C (2018). GFC 10 Years on—More Debt and Money Printing has Covered Up a Debt Crisis. Deutsche Bank Thematic Research. https://www.dbresearch.com/PROD/RPS_EN-PROD/PROD0000000000476994/GFC_10_years_on_-More_debt_%26_money_printing_has_c.PDF.

UNCTAD (2011). Trade and Development Report. Post-Crisis Policy Challenges in the World Economy. United Nations: Geneva and New York.

UNCTAD (2015). Making the International Financial Architecture Work for Development. Trade and Development Report 2015. United Nations: Geneva and New York.

UNCTAD (2019). Financing a Global Green New Deal. Trade and Development Report 2019. United nations: Geneva and New York.

Valencia, F and Laeven L (2010). Resolution of Banking Crises: The Good, the Bad, and the Ugly. United States, INTERNATIONAL MONETARY FUND, 2010.

Vestergaard J and Wade R.H. (2015). Protecting Power: How Western States Retain Their Dominant Voice in the World bank's Governance, in Lesage D and van de Graaf T (Eds), Rising Powers and Multilateral Institutions (pp. 175–196). Springer Publications.

VOA (2011). "IMF Chief Acknowledges Errors During Asian Financial Crisis", VOA News, 1 February 2011. https://www.voanews.com/a/imf-chief-acknowledges-errors-during-asian-financial-crisis-115092654/166986.html.

Volz, U. (2016) ."Toward the Development of a Global Financial Safety Net or Segmentation of the Global Financial Architecture?" *Emerging Markets Finance and Trade*, 52(10) 2221–2237.

Wheatley J and Garnham P. (2010). Brazil in 'Currency War' Alert, Financial Times September 27, 2010. https://www.ft.com/content/33ff9624-ca48-11df-a860-00144feab49a.

PART I

Exchange and Payment Systems

CHAPTER 2

A Critical Analysis of Transnational Payment Systems in Latin America

Esteban Pérez Caldentey, Georgina Cipoletta Tomassian, and Fernando Villanueva Melo

2.1 Introduction

As in the case of other developing countries, Latin American economies face a binding external constraint to their long-run growth performance and economic development. One of the main ways in which these countries can soften or overcome the external constraint is through

E. P. Caldentey (✉)
Financing for Development Unit (Economic Development Division), United Nations Economic Commission for Latin America and the Caribbean, Santiago, Chile
e-mail: esteban.perez@cepal.org

G. C. Tomassian
United Nations Economic Commission for Latin America and the Caribbean, Santiago, Chile

F. V. Melo
Faculty of Business and Administration, University of Santiago, Santiago, Chile

D. Barrowclough et al. (eds.), *South–South Regional Financial Arrangements*, International Political Economy Series,
https://doi.org/10.1007/978-3-030-64576-2_2

structural change. Yet Latin American development strategies, especially since the implementation of Washington Consensus type policies, have led to a laggard productivity performance. In the past three decades, Latin America and the Caribbean exhibit the worst labor-productivity performance of all developing regions.

This is partly the result of a productive and extra-regional export structure anchored in natural resource-based products with little technological change and value added. Contrarily the intraregional market is home to the bulk of traded manufacturing products of Latin American origin. Also, intraregional trade has, for the most part, a higher value-added content than extra-regional trade.

However, intraregional trade remains underdeveloped and below its potential. The share of intraregional trade in Latin America and the Caribbean stands currently at 16.6% of the total and is below that registered for most regions of the world.

The promotion of intraregional trade and in general intraregional integration can improve productivity and the growth performance of the region. It could also help to bolster extra-regional trade. Latin American countries have at their disposal a mechanism to promote the development of intraregional trade: transnational payments systems. Transnational payment systems (TPSs) are agreements between countries, through their central banks, to coordinate financial actions that facilitate the transfer of funds linked to payments essentially from international trade in goods between these countries.

There are currently three payments systems in Latin America: *The Reciprocal Payments and Credits Agreement* of ALADI (CPCR) (created in 1965 and reformed in 1982); the *Local Currency Payment System* (SML) between Brazil and Argentina (2008); and *the Unified System for Regional Compensation* (SUCRE) created in the Framework of the initiative of the Bolivarian Alliance for the Peoples of Our America—Trade Treaty (ALBA-TCP) (2009).

These payments systems have been associated with intraregional trade and are one of the most long-standing regional financial cooperation mechanisms in the region. Their main objective is to promote trade and regional integration through a series of mechanisms including the reduction in the use of foreign currency transactions, promoting payments in local currency and the reduction of transaction costs and improved risk management.

The empirical evidence shows that, with a few exceptional periods, these mechanisms have not delivered their promise. The three existing payment mechanisms channel, but a small, and sometimes insignificant volume of trade flows. This is due to different reasons depending on the type of payment mechanism under consideration.

The *Reciprocal Payments and Credits Agreement* of ALADI was created for a time of scarcity of foreign exchange due in part to stringent regulations. This mechanism has not been able to adapt to a changing environment consisting of greater liquidity and access to foreign exchange. The *Unified System for Regional Compensation* (SUCRE) was designed on the basis of John Maynard Keynes post-WWII Clearing Union, which does not necessarily apply to developing countries and its workings relied on one country, Venezuela, who is facing a very serious economic and political situation. Without Venezuela, The SUCRE ceases to be operative. The *Local Currency Payment System* (SML) between Brazil and Argentina has been more successful but it centered on a few products. Also, all these payment systems do not provide the required incentives for people to use them to channel their trade transactions.

In order to contribute for transnational payment mechanism to be an effective tool for the growth of intraregional trade and integration, payment mechanisms must, on the one hand, adapt the rules of payment systems to encourage their use by member countries through their respective monetary institutions. On the other hand, they must generate incentives to increase the participation of private actors (importers and exporters) in payment systems.

This chapter is divided into seven sections. The first section argues that the external constraint faced by Latin American economies and the absence of structural change provides a justification for the need to promote intraregional trade. The second section describes the main features of the three transnational payments systems (CPCR, SML, and SUCRE). Sections three to five provide greater detail on each of these in terms of their regulations and working mechanisms. The sixth section analyzes the tools that the TPSs use to reinforce and expand trade between its member-states and also highlights their limitations. The last section concludes with an assessment of these payment mechanisms to foster greater intraregional trade and intraregional integration, the lessons learned, and their future challenges.

2.2 Latin America External Constraint and Intraregional Trade

The economic performance of developing countries (i.e. the countries of the periphery) such as those of Latin America and the Caribbean is largely determined by the international financial architecture. The current financial and monetary system is anchored in the US dollar as the reserve currency, and countries which do not issue the international reserve currency (such as the countries of the periphery, including those in Latin America and the Caribbean), need to acquire and have access to this currency that they cannot issue (for example through an international reserves accumulation policy) in order to be able to import (and develop) and conduct international financial transactions.

Consequently, the domestic policy of the periphery countries is in large part permanently delimited and restricted by external conditions. It is in this sense that the growth efforts of these economies are confronted with an external constraint. More specifically, countries face an external constraint when their performance (current and expected) in external markets and the response of the financial markets to this (current and expected) performance delimit and restrict their scope for conducting domestic policies, including fiscal, exchange rate, and monetary policy.[1]

The external constraint implies that an economy (especially on the periphery) is unlikely to be able to maintain a current account deficit for a long period, except in the case of countries that usually receive substantial amounts of foreign direct investment or official assistance flows (McCombie and Thirlwall 1999). In the long run, countries have to keep their current account or basic balance (the current account plus long-term financial flows) in equilibrium.

The binding nature of the external constraint is determined by the trend in external demand, the real exchange rate, financial flows, and by the state of structural change. In the case of Latin America, the growth of external demand (proxied by world GDP growth) has remained below

[1] This definition is based on McCombie and Thirlwall (1999, p. 49), according to whom countries face an external constraint when their performance in foreign markets and the response of the financial markets to this performance restrict growth to a rate lower than external conditions require. This definition assumes that countries grow at a rate lower than the one compatible with full employment. Consequently, the organization of the global economic system, including its financial architecture, has a restrictive bias and prevents countries subject to external constraints from realizing their growth potential.

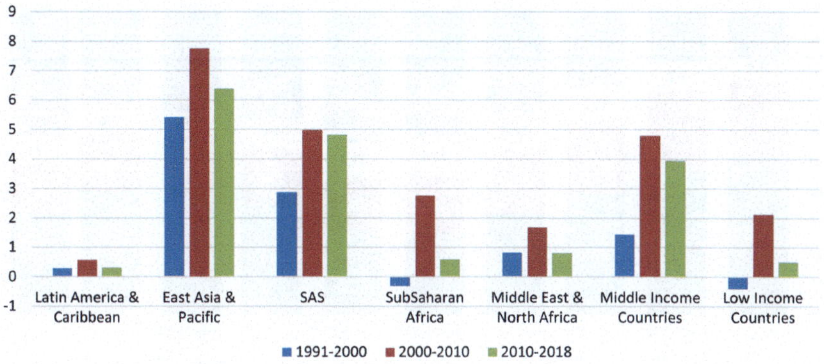

Fig. 2.1 Labor productivity growth for selected regions and country groupings (1991–2018) (GDP Per capita, 1990 PPP) *Note* SAS = South Asia (*Source* Paus [2019])

2% in per capita terms since 2011 making it one of the slowest growth periods at the global level since the 1960s. Also, Latin America's average real effective exchange rate has shown a tendency toward appreciation since the 1990s. In addition, the region can count less on the more stable type of foreign funding (foreign direct investment) to close its current account deficit, soften its external constraint, and as a means to promote growth and development.

Available empirical evidence for the periods 2000–2009 and 2010–2017 show a decline in the share of FDI as a percentage of total financial flows (60% to 41% of the total).[2] In fact, the bulk of foreign flows are short-term portfolio flows reflecting to a great extent the rise of nonfinancial corporate debt.

A more permanent way to overcome the external constraint is through structural change. However, Latin America's development strategies, in particular, those adopted following the Washington Consensus based on liberalization, privatization, and stabilization have not been conducive to structural change. This is illustrated in Fig. 2.1, which shows that the rate of growth of labor productivity in Latin America has lagged over the past thirty years behind that of all developing regions.

[2] Here FDI flows do not take into account intercompany loans which we consider to be similar to short-term capital flows.

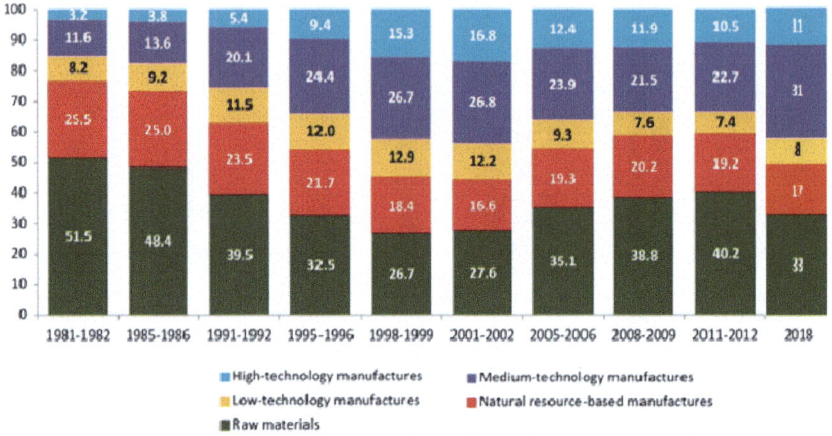

Fig. 2.2 Latin America and the Caribbean: export structure by technology intensity, 1981–2018 (*Percentages of the total*) (*Source* CEPAL [2019] Economic Survey of Latin America and the Caribbean 2019, PowerPoint presentation)

The absence of structural change is also reflected in Latin America's export structure which has over time remained anchored in natural resources. Available evidence for the period 1980–2018 shows that the share of raw materials and natural-based manufactures represented 77%, 63%, 44%, (roughly) 60%, and 50% of the total at the beginning of the 1980s, 1990s, 2000s, 2010s, and by 2018 (Fig. 2.2).

Faced with these limitations, Latin America and the Caribbean could foster intraregional trade, as a means, to raise productivity to soften its external constraint. In this sense fostering intraregional trade is a means to the improvement of the overall trade structure and composition of Latin America's exports.[3]

An analysis of the composition of intraregional trade indicates that it constitutes the export market for the highest value-added products, that is manufacturing products, within the Latin American region. On average for the period 2008–2016 the share of manufacturing exports represents on average 55.9% of the total and more than half of the countries have a greater export share (Guatemala, 57.2%; Nicaragua, 58.5%; Peru, 62.5%;

[3] This obviously implies that intraregional trade can be a way to improve the ratio between income export and import elasticities.

Uruguay, 68.3%; Colombia, 69.8%; Argentina, 72.5%; Panama, 75.7%; Chile 76.1%; Paraguay, 78.2%; and Ecuador 89.5%). This contrasts with the export of manufacturing products to the rest of the world which accounts for only 7.3% of total exports (Table 2.1 and Fig. 2.3).

Intraregional trade can also be a source of aggregate demand, employment generation, and could also provide a basis to generate spillovers. A study conducted by Blanco Estévez (2015) for Chile, Colombia, Mexico,

Table 2.1 Latin America and the Caribbean: manufacturing exports for selected destinations, average 2008–2012 (percentages of total)

Country	*Latin America and the Caribbean*	*United States*	*European Union*	*Pacific Asia*[a]	*Rest of the World*
Ecuador	89.5	5.3	1.8	0.9	2.5
Paraguay	78.2	2.8	9.3	8.2	1.4
Chile	76.1	7.2	6.8	5.5	4.4
Panama	75.7	19.8	0.4	2.2	1.8
Argentina	72.5	5.3	12	4	6.3
Colombia	69.8	12.2	6.9	6.4	4.7
Uruguay	68.3	3.2	12	8.9	7.5
Peru	62.4	25.4	7.3	2.1	2.7
Nicaragua	58.5	21.5	15.6	2.3	2.1
Guatemala	57.2	38.1	2.4	0.4	1.9
Venezuela	49.9	19	15	8.9	7.2
Bolivia	46.4	28.4	19.8	3.4	2.1
Brazil	45.5	15.6	18	11	9.8
Honduras	44.8	50.5	1.1	2.9	0.7
El Salvador	40.9	57.5	0.9	0.2	0.5
Costa Rica	27.1	38.8	10.8	13.2	10.1
Dominican Republic	20.1	65	5.9	4.1	4.9
Mexico	7.9	81.3	4.4	2.1	4.4
Latin America and the Caribbean	25.7	56.9	7.6	4.3	5.5
Latin America and the Caribbean (ex Mexico)	53.9	18.4	12.7	7.7	7.3

Source International Trade and Integration Division (ECLAC), on the basis of COMTRADE
NOTE The region Asia Pacific corresponds to ASEAN member countries: Australia, China, Japan, India, the Republic of Korea, and New Zealand.

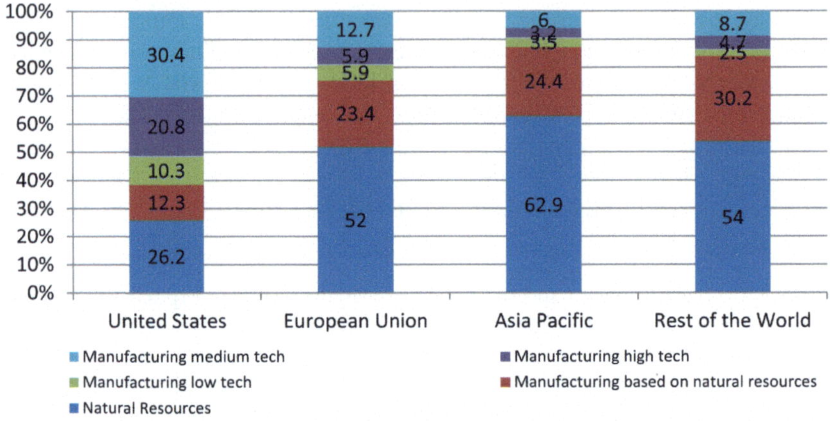

Fig. 2.3 Latin America and the Caribbean: degree of technology in exports for selected regions, 2008–2012 (As percentage of total exports per region or country) (*Source* International Trade and Integration Division (ECLAC), on the basis of COMTRADE)
Note The region Asia Pacific corresponds to ASEAN member countries: Australia, China, Japan, India, the Republic of Korea, and New Zealand

and Peru shows that the Gruber–Lloyd Index (IGL), which reflects the intensity of the exchange of products for the same industry, can be high for Latin American countries (as in the case of Chile–Colombia, Chile–Peru, and Peru–Colombia). In fact, according to the thresholds chosen by this author (see note to Table 2.2), Chile has an intra-industrial relationship with these two countries.

However, the analysis of the evolution of intraregional trade shows that it has represented historically a small percentage of total trade. In fact, since at least the beginning of the 1990s the share of intraregional trade has never surpassed 20% and it currently stands lower at 16.6% of the total. For 2017, in comparison with other regions of the world, the share of intraregional trade in Latin America fell below that of other regions with the exception of Africa and Oceania (16.7% and 7.0% of the total) (Fig. 2.4).

Table 2.2 Intra-industry trade between selected Latin American countries (2015)

	Mexico	*Colombia*	*Chile*	*Perú*
Mexico	-	0.2	0.27	0.14
Colombia	0.2	-	0.59	0.42
Chile	0.27	0.59	-	0.43
Perú	0.14	0.42	0.43	-

Note The values correspond to the Gruber–Lloyd Index (IGL). According to the estimates of this index, an IGL value of less than 0.1 indicates the presence of inter-industrial trade. An IGL value between 0.1 and 0.33 implies the existence of a potential for intra-industrial trade. Finally, an IGL value greater than 0.33 indicates the existence of an intra-industrial relationship
Source Blanco Estévez (2015), p. 9

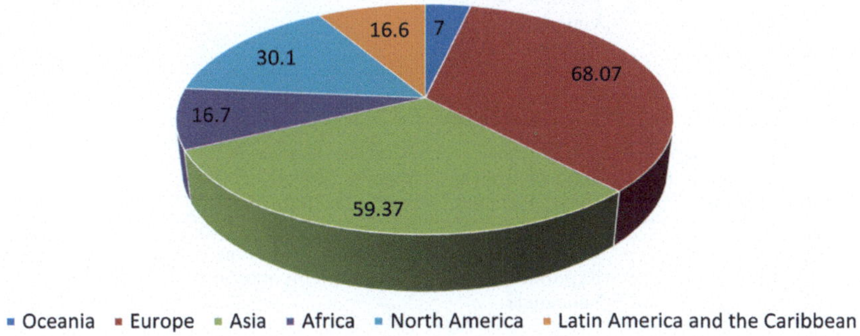

Fig. 2.4 Intra-regional trade share for selected regions of the world (In percentage. 2017) (*Source* On the basis of UNCTAD (e-handbook of statistics, 2019) https://stats.unctad.org/handbook/MerchandiseTrade/ByPartner.html)

2.3 Transnational Payment Systems in Latin America: Some General Features

Transnational payments systems associated with intraregional trade are the most long-standing regional financial cooperation mechanism. Their main objective is to promote trade and regional integration through a series of mechanisms including the reduction in the use of foreign currency transactions, promoting payments in local currency, and the reduction of transaction costs and improved risk management.

Table 2.3 Payments systems: country members, objectives, and common functions

Payment Systems	*Country members*	*Objectives*	*Common functions*
Reciprocal Payments and Credits Agreement (CPCR) of ALADI (1982) Local Currency Payment System (SML) (2008)	Argentina, Brazil, Plurinational State of Bolivia, Chile, Colombia, Ecuador, Mexico, Paraguay, Peru, Dominican Republic, Uruguay, and the Bolivarian Republic of Venezuela Argentina, Brazil (2008), Paraguay, and Uruguay (2018)	All payments systems have common objectives: • To promote reciprocal trade between member countries. • To deepen financial integration.	The reduction of foreign exchange transfers between central banks through compensation systems The reduction of transaction costs The management of credit risk and liquidity risk
Unified System for Regional Compensation (SUCRE) (2010)	Plurinational State of Bolivia, Cuba, Ecuador, and the Bolivarian Republic of Venezuela	SUCRE also has a specific objective: • To facilitate the consolidation of an area of Economic Complementation	

Source own elaboration based on official data

Transnational payment systems in Latin America were originally established to strengthen the cooperation between central banks and to foster intraregional trade payment systems constituted a key pillar of regional cooperation within a context of foreign exchange scarcity, and restrictive trade and finance (Table 2.3).

2.4 The Reciprocal Payments and Credits Agreement of ALADI (CPCR)

The CPCR is the successor to the "Reciprocal Credit and Payment Agreement" (also called the "Mexico Agreement"). It initiated the operation of the multilateral mechanism for clearing payments in convertible and freely transferable currencies between the central banks of the region. It was established within the framework of the Latin American Free Trade Association (ALLAC) regional body, which was subsequently replaced by the existing ALADI with the signing of the 1980 Montevideo Treaty.

The Mexico Agreement resulted from many attempts made in the region to achieve commercial integration, especially within the Latin American Free Trade Association (ALALC), which faced a scenario that combined the scarcity of foreign exchange with disequilibrium in the balance of payment. Its core goal was to develop mechanisms facilitating and improving the payments related to international trade in order to deepen the commercial integration of Latin America. It also sought to overcome the macroeconomic problems related to international trade.

The debt crisis and the scarcity of foreign exchange led to the demise of the Mexico Agreement, the replacement of the ALALC by ALADI (Latin America Association of Integration) in 1981, and also the creation of the CPCR in 1982. The CPCR agreement was signed in the city of Montego Bay, in August 1982, within the framework of the Council for Financial and Monetary Affairs (CAFM) of ALADI, by 12 of its central banks (Spanish-speaking South America, Brazil, Mexico, and the Dominican Republic). Brazil exited the agreement in April 2018.

The CPCR provides for a voluntary agreement between the central banks of participating member countries for the creation of reciprocal dollar credit lines and a multilateral payment clearing mechanism or net of unilateral balances of the banks quarterly. The amounts of the credit lines are established according to the importance of bilateral trade flows between the countries. Credit lines allow the accounting record of payments made between central banks and coverage of daily balances between the central banks of the member countries.

The multilateral clearing system operates in the following ways: (i) it consolidates the creditor and debtor balances (including the interests that are incurred) of the accounts in which authorized transactions carried out between the residents of the different member countries; and (ii) establishes a net balance for each member central bank every four months. This net balance is canceled in foreign currencies (US dollars). In this way, the multilateral clearing system minimizes the use of foreign exchange by central banks by using them only to cancel the net balance resulting from operations carried out through the agreement.[4]

The agreement provides for the possibility for financial institutions to receive payments in local currency from the importer. However, they make their dollar payments to the central bank of their respective country for their operations. In this case, the CPCR establishes a guarantee of convertibility and transferability that allows mitigation of uncertainty regarding the evolution of exchange rate variations that may affect the financial institution. The convertibility guarantee is that central banks ensure the immediate convertibility to dollars of local currencies received by such financial institutions for payments channeled through the agreement. This would not happen if the central bank did not intervene and simply processed the transaction through the trading banking system, as the parties would buy or sell the currency through them. For its part, the transferability guarantee assures such entities the effective dollar equivalent for payments received in local currency.

The volume of trade channeled through the CPCR increased during the 1966–1991 period and declined abruptly thereafter. As shown in Fig. 2.5, the transactions channeled through the CPCR as percentage of total regional imports were 90.9% in 1989 collapsing to 1.5% in 2003 and remaining around that level thereafter.

For its part, the volume of transactions increased by 7.1% yearly from the early 1980s until 1995. But afterward these registered a decline until the early 2000s recovering prior to the Global Financial Crisis (2008–2009). Thereafter the volume of transaction has been declining at a rate of 20% annually on average until 2016 (See Table 2.4).[5]

The steep increase in the use of the CPCR from the 1960s until the 1980s is partly due to the existence of significant restrictions, including exchange controls, on foreign exchange transactions. Most important, with rare exceptions (i.e. Uruguay) the use of CPCR for intraregional trade transactions was made compulsory by most government in the region.

[4] Net multilateral balances among central banks are recorded at the Operations Center located at the Central Reserve Bank of Peru through the Computerized System of Support to the ALADI Reciprocal Payments and Credits Convention (SICAP/ALADI). The funds are settled to the Federal Reserve Bank of New York, which is the joint correspondent bank.

[5] The year 2016 is the latest available year.

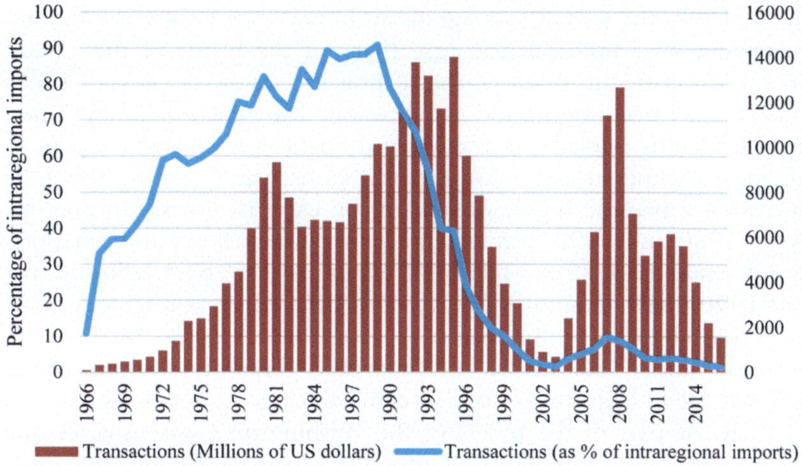

Fig. 2.5 Trade operations channeled through the CPCR (1966–2016) (*Source* Own elaboration based on ALADI data)

The 1980s' Debt Crisis plunged the whole region into a deep financial collapse. Indeed, following the onset of the crisis in 1980, Latin American GDP per capita growth contracted in 1981, 1982, and 1983 by 1.8%, 3.6%, and, 4.7%, respectively. The varying intensity of the debt crisis within Latin America produced large disparities of GDP per capita variation at the country level. In 1981, eight out of eighteen Latin American countries suffered contractions, including three of the largest economies of the region: Argentina, Brazil, and Venezuela (where GDP fell 7.1%, 6.6% and, 3.4%, respectively). In 1982, all the Latin American economies, with the exception of Panama, experienced contraction. In 1983, the region contracted once again with the exceptions of Argentina and three Central American countries (Costa Rica, El Salvador, and Nicaragua). In spite of the slow recovery process which began in 1984, these three consecutive years of massive downturns produced the worst decadal growth performance in Latin America.

The 1980s' crisis provoked a fall in intraregional trade and a decline in the trade operations channeled through the CPCR (US$ 9.3 to 6.5 billion from 1981 to 1983) as countries began to carry out foreign exchange transactions outside the framework of ALADI including through bilateral trading arrangements (Damico 2010).

In the 1990s the CPCR lost significant importance for several reasons. First, relying on a political discourse that put the blame of the 1980s' crisis on government interventionist policies followed in the 1960s and 1970s (termed import industrialization, ISI policies), Latin American governments implemented trade and financial liberalization policies simultaneously known as the Washington Consensus.[6] During this time Latin America became highly dependent on external flows. On average, between 1980 and 1990, foreign direct investment flows and net portfolio flows reached US$ 5.3 billion increasing to US$ 64.4 billion in the period 1990–1999. A similar behavior is exhibited by remittances (US$ 3.1 and 5.4 billion in both periods).

Second, under conditions of improved liquidity central banks suppressed the obligation to carry foreign exchange transactions through the CPCR. As part of the tenets of the Washington Consensus, central banks (especially under conditions of easier access to foreign exchange) did not believe they should provide financial guarantees to private transactions. Third, due to some abuses in the use of the CPCR, some central banks in the region decided to restrict its use for foreign transactions (Ibid). Finally, private financial intermediaries gained prominence in the financing of intraregional trade which also undermined the use of the CPCR (Ibid).

The CPCR never recovered its previous importance and prominence. The frequency of use of the CPCR increased mildly in the 2000s decade until the start of the Global Financial Crisis (2008–2009). Between 2002 and 2008, the percentage of transactions channeled through the CPCR increased from 2.2% to 8.9% (see Fig. 2.5). That is, in spite of the increase in its importance, 90% of all transactions were not carried under the ALADI framework during this time.

[6] Free trade policies were defended using the arguments traditionally espoused in its favor. These are first that by free trade improves resource allocation and stimulates employment and growth. Second free trade is fair trade as it provides equal trading opportunity to all countries according to their respective capacities and endowments. Third, free trade helps countries to achieve development rewarding economic agents and sectors with comparative advantage. Fourth, free trade benefits households and firms by widening the supply of products and lowering their costs. Finally, free trade prevents rent seeking behavior and promotes good government. Between 1987 and 1990, Argentina, Brazil, Chile, Colombia, México, and Venezuela liberalized their stock markets.

Table 2.4 Value of the operations channelized and its relationship with total imports

Year	*Millions of US$*	*Yearly variation (%)*	*Quantity of operations*	*% of intraregional imports*
2012	6134.6	-	22,735	3.9
2013	5630.3	−8	17,345	3.6
2014	4005.0	−29	12,285	2.8
2015	2206.8	−45	8345	1.9
2016	1570.0	−29	4174	1.5

Source own elaboration based on ALADI data

2.5 The Local Currency Payment System (SML)

The SML between Argentina and Brazil is an agreement signed in the city of Brasilia, in September 2008, by the central bank of the Argentine Republic (BCRA) and the central bank of Brazil (BCB), under the Common Market of the South/*Mercado Común del Sur* (MERCOSUR) in order to create a voluntary and bilateral system of payments in local currencies.

The SML allows the importers and exporters from Argentina and Brazil to make payments and charges in their respective currencies with the principal aim to integrate the small and medium firms in interregional trade. Its chief advantage is the reduction in administrative and financial cost associated with transactions linked to the elimination of foreign exchange operations (i.e. avoid the Argentine peso-US dollar and US dollar—Brazilian real operation).

In the SML the transaction between importer and exporter is agreed in the currency of the exporting country (e.g. in real Brazil) and the exporter receives payment in its local currency. In this sense, in the SML the exporter does not participate in any foreign exchange market.

On the other hand, this is not the case with the importer. The importer makes payments in his local currency (e.g. in Argentine pesos) so he does not have to go to the foreign exchange market (US dollars). However, since the transaction is agreed in the exporter's currency (Brazilian reals), the importer has to make the equivalent payment in his currency (e.g. Argentine pesos) and may therefore be affected by changes in the exchange rate of both currencies.

To minimize this possibility, the SML provides for legislation in which transactions are settled in real time and at a rate set out in the SML agreement. More specifically: (i) the importer records the transaction and simultaneously executes the payment with the financial institution authorized by the transaction in its own currency at an exchange rate set by the central banks (SML rate) or at an agreed exchange rate between the importer and the financial institution; (ii) the authorized financial institution registers the transaction in the currency of the exporting country with its central bank on the same day; (iii) on the same day the SML rate is disclosed, which is composed of the reference rates of the central bank of Argentina (BCRA) and that (PTAX) of the central bank of Brazil (BCB). Financial institutions are also nodded in the amount in local currency to be turned to their central banks on the following business day; (iv) payments are made the next day. Note that this procedure also takes care of the possibility of change in the exchange rate between the dates on which payment is made to the exporter and foreign currency balances are cleared.

The empirical evidence regarding the relevance of the SML shows that the bulk of operations and more precisely, more than 95% of the total, are undertaken by Brazilian companies. Also, the companies using the SML are mainly small- and medium-sized firms. Finally, as in the case of ALADI´s CPCR, the foreign transactions channeled through the SML represent a small percentage of the total. Available data between 2009 and 2018 show that its use has never surpassed 4% of total trade between both countries (Fig. 2.6).

It should be noted that the exchange rate of the agreement is uniform and independent of transaction volumes. It is also a favorable rate for agents as it is determined in the interbank market and is representative of the wholesale market. These characteristics favor small and medium-sized enterprises (SMEs).

In the case of the SML, in addition to channeling the corresponding payments, the authorized financial institution of the importer's country may jointly and directly with the importer define a weight/actual exchange rate for each transaction or carry out the operations following the SML Rate disclosed by the BCRA. The central banks of Argentina and Brazil do not charge financial institutions for the use of the payment system. All payments made are "subject to all payments made provided

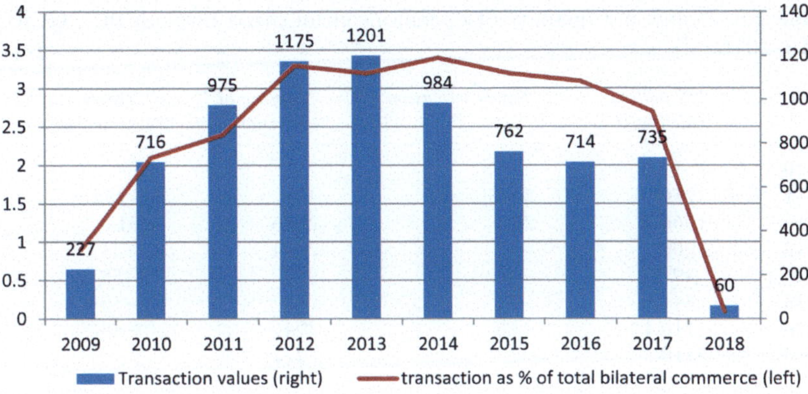

Fig. 2.6 Trade operations channeled through the SML (2009–2018) (*Source* Own elaboration based on official data)

that they are prior to and fully paid by the Importer's Authorized Entities or by the other central bank" (SML Tenth Clause).[7]

2.6 The Unified System for Regional Compensation (SUCRE)

SUCRE is a multilateral payment system whose Constitutional Treaty was signed in the city of Cochabamba in October 2009 within the framework of the VII Summit of Heads of State and Government of the Bolivarian Alliance for the Peoples of Our America—Trade Treaty of (ALBA-TCP) by Bolivia, Cuba, Ecuador, Honduras, Nicaragua, and the Bolivarian Republic of Venezuela. The objective of the Treaty was the creation of a system of regional payment compensation complemented by a fund

[7] In the case of the SML, the central banks are granted on a reciprocal basis an Eventual Margin of 10 million which is defined as an operational limit to enable the deferred payment of the bilateral balance. The regulations provide that in the event that the eventual Margin is not recomposed in the manner provided for in the Regulation or an insufficient amount is transferred to settle the debtor bilateral balance not covered by the Eventual Margin, the noncompliance central bank you must pay the amount due (you could not exceed the $120 million limit) within 120 days in four (4) equal and consecutive installments. Interest will accrue at the 2% rate on the four-month LIBOR rate, valid for the date the noncompliance is set up.

Table 2.5 Value and quantity of operations channelized through the SUCRE 2010–2016

Year	*US dollars (Millions)*	*Yearly variation (%)*	*Number of operations*	*Yearly variation (%)*
2010	12.6		21	
2011	270.3	2045	431	1952
2012	1065.9	294	2646	514
2013	909	−15	2094	−21
2014	497.2	−45	884	−58
2015	344.9	−31	752	−15
2016	110.1	−68	394	−48
Total	3210		7222	

Source Own elaboration based on the Monetary Council of the Sucre

of reserves and commercial convergence based on the use of a unit of common account, the "SUCRE" (XSU).[8] In this sense the SUCRE not only provided for a unit of account but also promote the consolidation of a zone of economic complementation, through the transformation of the economic structure and reducing the gap among the member states.

SUCRE began operating in January 2010 between Cuba and the Bolivarian Republic of Venezuela, joining Bolivia and Ecuador in the middle of the same year. The Treaty establishing this system contemplated the accession of other regional and extra-regional countries on request, subject to the approval of the Heads of State and/or Government of the countries currently members.[9][10] However, since the economic and political crisis in Venezuela the SUCRE has been rarely used (Table 2.5).

[8] The rate of exchange of the SUCRE is determined with respect to the US dollar and its value is established on the basis of a basket of national (including that of its state members) and international currencies. The distribution of XSU for each member state was supposed carried out every two years, taking into account the exports and imports value of each member state. Venezuela was the country with the biggest stock of SUCREs, with a share of 70% of the total.

[9] The Treaty has as its background the Presidential Mandate of the ALBA countries in November 2008—of establishing a monetary zone, a common account unit (SUCRE), a regional payment clearing system, and a central clearing house—and the Agreement SUCRE Framework, signed by the presidents of ALBA-TCP in April 2009 in Cumaná, which reflects the general guidelines for the operation of the system.

[10] Honduras withdrew from ALBA in January 2010.

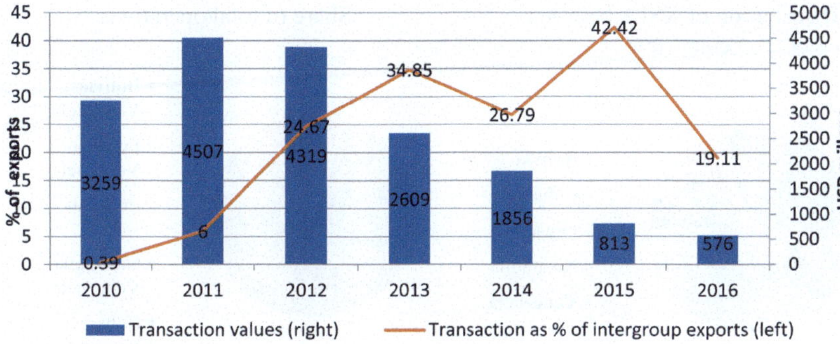

Fig. 2.7 Trade operations channeled through the SUCRE (2010–2016) (*Source* Own elaboration based on official data)

According to its design the use of the XSU (SUCRE's unity account code) allowed a lower volatility in the exchange rate in relation to the use of foreign exchange, since the exchange rate variation impact on each economy will depend on the proportion of this currency inside the basket. Actually, during the first seven year period since the start of the operations of SUCRE, it accumulated a devaluation of 0.61%. The stability of the XSU was assumed to be guaranteed by an adjustment mechanism contemplated in the agreement in cases where the member states implemented a monetary or exchange rate policy that caused a variation larger (in absolute terms) than 5%. In that case, the proportion of currencies that compose the SUCRE was supposed to be modified.

Since 2010 and until 2016, 7,222 operations equivalent to US$ 3.210 million were undertaken using the SUCRE (See Table 2.5) In spite of the strong increase in the value and number of operations channelized through the SUCRE in 2011 and 2012, in 2013 there was a steady drop in the number of transactions, as well as in the value of these transactions until 2016. Actually, the value and number of operations made in 2016 are lower than the values registered in 2011. SUCRE seemed for a period of time to be more successful in channeling foreign exchange operations as following its creation, these reached 40% of the total in 2015. However, SUCRE´s dependence on Venezuela proved to be detrimental to the agreement due to the grave and ongoing social and political crisis facing this country since 2014 (Figs. 2.7 and 2.8).[11]

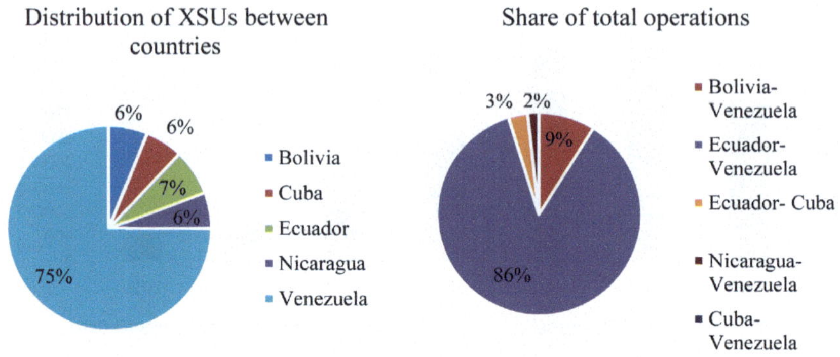

Fig. 2.8 Distribution of XSU and share of trade operations by countries (mean between 2011 and 2016) (*Source* Own elaboration based on the Monetary Council of the Sucre)

In relation to the commercial relationship between the member states, the trade between Venezuela and Ecuador represented more than 80% of total operations followed by that between Bolivia and Venezuela with a share of almost 10% and to a lesser extent by Cuba and Ecuador with a 5% of the total share.

The intraregional trade among these countries has evolved from mainly manufactured products to commodities. Table 2.6 shows the three main products exchanged through the agreement since 2011 until 2016. We can see that until 2013 the main products exchanged were vehicles, prefabricated buildings, and mechanical and orthopedic devices. Since 2014 the main products exchanged were tuna, sugar, and crude palm oil which become the main traded product for 2015 and 2016.

2.7 Tools for Fostering Commercial Integration

The tools that the TPS use focus on the generation of foreign exchange savings, the reduction in transaction costs, and in risks involved in commercial trade.

[11] The country has experienced growing contraction in GDP growth since 2014 (−5.1%, −7.4%, −18.1%, −16.7% in 2014, 2015, 2016, 2017 and more than −20% in 2018).

Table 2.6 Three main products exchanged, as percentage and millions of Sucres

	2011	*2012*	*2013*	*2014*	*2015*	*2016*
Product	Tuna	Vehicles	Tuna	Tuna	Crude palm oil	Crude palm oil
Percentage	20%	22%	18%	50%	28%	18%
Sucres	42.7	190.8	134.4	199	77.1	16.3
Product	Granular urea	Mechanical and orthopedic devices	Prefabricated buildings	Crude palm oil	Tuna	Pharmaceutical products
Percentage	13%	15%	18%	9%	13%	15%
Sucres	29.1	131.1	133.4	34.7	34.6	13
Product	Vehicles	Tuna	Vehicles	Sugar	Sugar	Tires
Percentage	11%	13%	11%	6%	7%	11%
Sucres	23.5	111.7	77.3	22.9	18.8	9.5
Cumulative percentage	44%	50%	47%	65%	48%	44%

Source Own elaboration based on the Monetary Council of the Sucre

The saving of foreign exchange is achieved through three key instruments. The first is multilateral or bilateral compensation mechanisms, which aim to compensate the debtor/creditor position of the counterparts of international trade, funneling only the net global account of each country with their commercial partners at the end of a determined period. This enables the prospect to swap foreign exchange between the central banks when the agreed period is over, allowing the savings of foreign exchange.

The exchanges are not paid individually by each country; nonetheless, only the net account is paid. The foreign exchange is not required continually but only at an established date. These two factors allow the creation of foreign exchange savings. Furthermore, the multilateral compensation mechanisms make it easier to transact payments for international trade, generating incentives to boost intraregional trade.

The second instrument related to the use of multilateral or bilateral compensation mechanisms is the use of local currency in trade. This allows the importers and exporters to make payments and charges in their respective local currencies. This is possible through the operation of an exchange rate between both currencies, in order to avoid the exchange of local currency to US dollars. This device could imply a reduction in the transaction cost of international trade due to the simplification of the foreign currency trade.

The third instrument is the use of a regional common currency. Its purpose is to set aside the use of the US dollar or Euro in intraregional trade through the creation of a common currency between countries. This currency is used as an artificial "unit of account" which creates greater foreign currency savings and while promoting stronger linkages and the interdependence of the economies of the region through commercial cooperation.

Besides the generation of foreign exchange savings, the TPS has as an additional goal, namely the reduction in the transaction costs and risks involved in commercial trade, i.e. the reduction in the administrative cost and the length of trade operations, and the reduction in the exchange rate volatility.

The tools of TPS seek to simplify the administrative procedures for exporters and importers and streamline international payments and transactions. This target is often associated with the reduction in the length of procedures, the waiting time for clearing international payments, the removal or reduction in costs and commissions charged by the agents, and helping to promote the use of local currency which can reduce exchange rate volatility between countries.

2.8 Transnational Payment Systems: An Evaluation, Challenges, and Lessons Learned

Overall, transnational payments systems have not fully lived-up their promise. Although it can be said that they have somewhat reduced transaction costs they have been unable to promote intraregional trade or to become an important mechanism for channeling foreign trade transactions. The factors that account for this fact are both specific to the particular transnational payment system taken into consideration, and common to the three types of mechanisms analyzed in this chapter.

As mentioned in Sect. 2.3, three of the main features of the CPCR which provided an incentive to use this framework for channeling foreign exchange transactions are the convertibility, transferability, and reimbursement guarantee. The convertibility and transferability guarantee proved useful only under conditions of foreign exchange restrictions or scarcity. This guarantee ensured the required foreign exchange coverage to carry out all trade operations under the CPCR. However, under conditions of increased financial openness and international integration to financial markets and of abundant foreign exchange, the convertibility and transferability guarantee lost its importance. Under current conditions there is no reason for the absence of foreign exchange coverage in intraregional transactions.

For its part, the reimbursement guarantee is a mechanism that places the burden of nonpayment by the importer on the central banks. In other words, the central banks guarantee and cover private risk. It is, in part, for this reason that central banks have discouraged the use of the CPCR. The question here is whether as part of their mandates, central banks should seek to cover private risks.

Contrary to the CPCR, the SML does not guarantee private risks. It also includes shorter periods for the completion of transactions and corresponding reimbursements. The intraregional trade channeled through the SML covers a wide variety of sectors including energy, metallurgical, automotive and auto parts, textiles, foodstuff, and cosmetics. However, the bulk of the trade is concentrated on the Brazilian side and includes low transaction volumes. This scale problem affecting the SML was identified from its very beginning. According to a MERCOSUR study in 2009 (one year after the entry into force of the SML) more than 50% of total operations were below US$ 100,000 and 80% of total operations were comprised between US$ 100,000 and 500,000 thousand dollars.

The limited use of the SML is also related to the fact that the availability of credit to pre-finance export operations and also working capital for international trade are linked to funding that is generally provided in dollars. As a result, the expansion and more intense use of the SML would require a greater expansion of credit lines and funding for international trade denominated in local currency. Also, the existing surveys point to the fact that exchange rate risks (especially in a context of high nominal exchange volatility as is the current case) and the perception of small net benefits limits the use of the SML. In addition, the SML competes with the traditional system of commercial banks to extend credit for private sector operations. Moreover, banks can lower the costs of their loans thus undermining the potential significance of the SML.

The success of the SUCRE has been dependent on the fate of Venezuela. Hence its current economic and political situation undermines the very foundations of this intraregional trade mechanism. The SUCRE was conceived along the line that resembles Keynes's Clearing Union proposal in the early 1940s. The design and logic of the SUCRE went further than that of the CPCR or the SML as it contemplated explicitly economic growth and economic complementation through the expansion of aggregate demand as an explicit objective of the agreement. In line with Keynes's ideas that surplus countries must increase spending, the arrangement provided the possibility for SUCRE surplus central bank members to contribute to the creation of a reserve fund and transfer funds to deficit countries in order to stimulate the latter's investment, production, and exports. Unfortunately, this required a degree of economic coordination and financial development that the country members belonging to the SUCRE arrangement did not have.

All three transnational payment systems were created as a first step to eventually achieve monetary and financial integration. Most recently Uruguay joined the SML (June 2015) and Paraguay and Brazil signed an agreement (which entered in force in August 2018) to trade in local currency. In this sense, all three transnational payments systems have the objective of increasing the savings of foreign currency in order to foster the use of local currency in intraregional trade transactions. And this is, in turn, a prerequisite for fostering intraregional trade and in general intraregional integration.

However, a close analysis of these three mechanisms does not indicate how they could promote foreign exchange savings. All exchanges in the SML are conducted in real time and thus no foreign exchange savings is possible. The SUCRE is a unit of account tied to the dollar and thus the accumulation of foreign exchange reserves is required to maintain the stability of the SUCRE. Thus, in this regard, the SUCRE arrangement fosters a greater demand for foreign exchange and not savings in foreign exchange. As a corollary, for these reasons, both the SML and the SUCRE do not foster the use of local currency. The CPCR provides a short span of time (four months) to settle transactions in foreign exchange. As a result, it cannot be said either that the CPCR saves foreign exchange or encourages the use of local money.

In a similar way, the chain of causality between the use of domestic current and intraregional trade and or intraregional integration has never been made explicit in the legislation of the three transnational payment systems. If a domestic currency is used only as a unit of account to settle intraregional transactions, the intensity of its use simply reflects greater intraregional trade and not the other way around. Indeed, the greater use and development of transnational payments systems can in fact be endogenous to increased intraregional trade.

Moreover, the fact that a unit of account is in greater use as a reference currency does not, necessarily, have an impact on the depth of intraregional integration. When a domestic currency is used as a means of payments, as in the cases of the CPCR and the SML, in intraregional trade through central banks, this only reflects an internal procedure of these agreements with no necessary impact on the fostering of trade or integration. Finally, central banks hold mainly reserves in US dollars or euros, currencies that are not Latin American currencies. This is the result of a given external context rather than that of a low volume of intraregional trade or a low level of economic integration.

Countries can implement policies to improve the use of intraregional payments systems. This implies on the one hand, adapting the rules of payment systems to encourage their use by member countries through their respective monetary institutions. This involves, in turn, rethinking central banks' management of credit risk. In some cases, and depending on the context, it is also worth making compensation periods more flexible and reduce transaction costs.

On the other hand, incentives must be generated to increase the participation of private agents (importers and exporters) in payment systems. This implies providing better risk coverage for trade transactions. As is well known, the risk of a cross-border business transaction is greater than that of a domestic business transaction (greater uncertainty) and the average time of a cross-border transaction is longer than that of a domestic transaction. It also means increasing the provision of liquidity and financing to trade (credits, insurance, and guarantees) and ensuring that this covers all the different stages of the production and export processes.

More importantly the development of intraregional payments systems should be accompanied with structural policies to foster the productive diversification based on the permanent transformation of the export structure of its economies. This includes promoting the creation and expansion of new industries with greater added value and productivity, the transfer of workers from traditional sectors to modern activities and a better absorption of new technologies. As mentioned in the first section, during different economic cycles of the last century, Latin American export specialization has been anchored in static comparative advantages, characterized by abundance of raw materials and low wages, which resulted in a poor export performance. Even with the improvement of the terms of trade for several years during the commodities price super-cycles (e.g. 2003–2011), the economies of the region have placed the focus of their prodution efforts on primary products, and have not improved their technological capabilities or diversified their exports, and, as a result, once the boom period ended, the effects on a lower growth became noticeable. This has had a negative effect on intraregional trade and integration.

References

ALADI (2012a): "Convenio de pagos y créditos recíprocos". Manual Divulgativo, en https://www.aladi.org, accedido el 21 de mayo de 2012.

ALADI (2012b): "Reglamento del Convenio de pagos y créditos recíprocos". Manual Divulgativo, en https://www.aladi.org, accedido el 21 de mayo de 2012.

ALADI (2012c): "Convenio de pagos y créditos recíprocos. Evaluación del funcionamiento del sistema de pagos de la ALADI en el año 2008". ALDI/SEC/di 2228, Montevideo, 14 de abril.

ALADI (2009a): "Convenio de pagos y créditos recíprocos: Reflexiones sobre su funcionamiento y algunos temas que podrían ser objeto de discusión para su dinamización". ALDI/SEC/di 2233, Montevideo, 24 de abril.

ALADI (2009b): "Convenio de pagos y créditos recíprocos. Evaluación del funcionamiento del sistema de pagos de la ALADI en el año 2011". ALDI/SEC/di 2468, Montevideo, 29 de marzo.

ALADI - Secretaría General (2002): "Convenio de pagos y créditos recíprocos", en https://www.aladi.org, Montevideo, octubre.

Al Bassam, Khalid (2003): "The Gulf cooperation council monetary union: A Bahraini perspective". In 'Regional currency areas and the use of foreign currencies'. BIS Papers vol. 17, Bank for International Settlements, Basel.

Alkhater, Khalid Rashid A. (2012): "The monetary union of the Gulf cooperation council and structural changes in the global economy: Aspirations, challenges, and long-term strategic benefits". Research Paper Series, Arab Center for Research and Policy Studies, Doha, May.

Aragao, José María (1984): "Los sistemas de pagos latinoamericanos". Estudios Económicos, Integración Latinoamericana, septiembre.

Ayuso, Juan; Ignacio Fuentes; Juan Peñalosa Y Fernando Restoy (1999): "El Mercado Monetario Español en la Unión Monetaria". Estudios Económicos, n° 67; Banco de España, Madrid.

Banco Interamericano de Desarrollo (BID) Informe mercosur N° 14 - Diciembre 2009. Segundo Semestre 2008 - Primer Semestre 2009 Argentina: BID-INTAL.

BCRA-BCB (2008): "Convenio del sistema de pagos en moneda local entre la República Argentina y la República Federativa del Brasil". Brasilia, septiembre.

BCRA (2008a): "Comercio exterior en monedas locales". Comunicación "A" 4848 – CAMEX 1 – 618, Buenos Aires, 26 de septiembre.

BCRA (2008b): "Sistema de pago en moneda local (SML) Argentina Brasil". Comunicación "A" 4847 – COPEX 1 – 270, Buenos Aires. 26 de septiembre.

Bocco, Arnaldo (2009): "Argentina – Brasil: Sistema de pagos en monedas locales". BCRA. Presentación. Marzo.

Borja, Diego (2012): "Panorama General del SUCRE". Taller SUCRE GT2-GTIF-UNASUR. Presentación. Lima, 8 de junio.

Calvo Hornero, Antonia (1999): "Organización de la Unión Europea". Editorial Centro de Estudios Ramón Areces, 2da. Edición, Madrid.

CEI (2011): "Integración económica y moneda común: reflexiones en torno del Euro"; Notas del CEI No. 30, Centro de Economía Internacional, Secretaría de Comercio y Relaciones Económicas Internacionales, MRE, CIyC, República Argentina; Julio.

CEPAL (1990): "La cooperación regional en los campos financiero y monetario". Serie Financiamiento para el Desarrollo # 5, Proyecto CEPAL/PNUD. Santiago de Chile, diciembre.

CEPAL (2011): "Eliminando barreras: El financiamiento a las pymes en América Latina". Carlo Ferraro (compilador). Santiago de Chile, Noviembre.

CEPAL (2019): "Economic Survey of Latin America and the Caribbean 2019". PowerPoint presentation. Santiago de Chile, July.

Damico, A. (2010) El Convenio de Pagos y Créditos Recíprocos de ALADI como una Herramienta de Facilitación del Comercio ante la crisis internacional. Revista de Derecho de la Universidad de Montevideo. Pp. 185–225.

EUROPEAN COMMISSION (2010): "The Road to EMU". https://ec.europa.eu

FRED (2012): Federal Reserve Economic Data. Federal Reserve Bank of St. Louis. https://research.stlouisfed.org/fred2/

Frtiz, B; Biancarelli, A; & Mühlich, L. (2014) Sistemas Regionales de Pago. Una perspectiva comparativa sobre Europa y el mundo en vías de desarrollo. El Trimestre Económico. Vol. LXXXI(4). Núm. 324, octubre-diciembre, pp. 875–908.

GCC (2012): "Process of the customs union of the cooperation council for the Arab States of the Gulf", Secretariat General. www.gccsg.org.

INTAL (2009): "Países de América Latina exploran alternativas para impulsar el comercio en monedas locales". INTAL Carta Mensual 153. Buenos Aires, abril.

INTAL (2011): "Sistema de pagos en moneda local en el MERCOSUR". INTAL Carta Mensual 175. Buenos Aires, marzo.

Jimenez, Luis F. Y Raquel Szalachman (1992): "Las monedas comunes y la creación de liquidez regional". CEPAL, Serie Financiamiento para el Desarrollo # 12, Proyecto CEPAL/PNUD. Santiago de Chile, noviembre.

López Ríos, Vladimir (2010): "Sistemas de pago y complementación regional: Estrategias para Latinoamérica frente a la crisis económica mundial". Banco Central de Venezuela, Serie Documentos de Trabajo 115, Caracas, julio.

López Ríos, Vladimir (2008): "Área monetaria óptima: un pretexto entre integración y desarrollo". Serie Documentos de Trabajo, N° 97, Caracas.

Mata, Gustavo (2012): "Hacia la consolidación de la arquitectura financiera regional: La experiencia del Sistema Unitario de Compensación Regional de Pagos (SUCRE)". Secretaría Permanente del SELA, Caracas, febrero.

Ocampo, José A. (2012): "La arquitectura financiera mundial y regional a la luz de la crisis". MIMEO. CEPAL, Santiago de Chile, junio.

Ocampo, José A. (2006): "Cooperación financiera regional". Libros de la CEPAL #91, CEPAL, Naciones Unidas, Santiago de Chile.

Paus, E. (2019) Latin America's Dismal Productivity Growth: Firm-level Innovation and Government Policies. Presentation at LASA. May 24–26. Boston.

Pérez Caldentey, E., Cipoletta Tomassian, G. & Titelman, D. (2013) Sistemas de pago transnacionales en América Latin. ALADI, SML y SUCRE. Serie Financiamiento para el Desarrollo. No. 245. Santiago, Chile: CEPAL:

Rosales, Antulio; Manuel Cerezal Y Ricardo Molero (2011): "SUCRE: A monetary tool toward economic complementarity". Research on Money and Finance. Discussion Paper no 31, Department of Economics, SOAS. Britain, August.

Rosales, Antulio (2010). "El Banco del Sur y el SUCRE: (Des)Acuerdos sobre una arquitectura financiera alternativa". MIMEO, Caracas.

SELA (2009a): "El Sistema Unitario de Compensación Regional (SUCRE): Propósitos, antecedentes y condiciones necesarias para su avance". Secretaría Permanente del SELA. Caracas, enero.

SELA (2009b): "Experiencias de Cooperación Monetaria y Financiera en América Latina y el Caribe. Balance Crítico y Propuestas de Acción de Alcance Regional". Secretaría Permanente del SELA. Caracas, septiembre.

SUCRE (2009): "Acuerdo Marco del Sistema Único de Compensación Regional de Pagos (SUCRE)". www.sucrealba.org, Caracas.

SUCRE (2011): "Informe de Gestión 2010". Consejo Monetario Regional del SUCRE. www.sucrealba.org, Caracas.

SUCRE (2012): "Informe de Gestión 2011". Consejo Monetario Regional del SUCRE. www.sucrealba.org, Caracas.

SUCRE (2013): "Informe de Gestión 2012". Consejo Monetario Regional del SUCRE. www.sucrealba.org, Caracas.

SUCRE (2014): "Informe de Gestión 2013". Consejo Monetario Regional del SUCRE. www.sucrealba.org, Caracas.

SUCRE (2015): “Informe de Gestión 2014”. Consejo Monetario Regional del SUCRE. www.sucrealba.org, Caracas.

SUCRE (2016): “Informe de Gestión 2015”. Consejo Monetario Regional del SUCRE. www.sucrealba.org, Caracas.

SUCRE (2016): “Informe de Gestión 2016”. Consejo Monetario Regional del SUCRE. www.sucrealba.org, Caracas.

UN Comtrade (2012): United Nations Commodity Trade Statistics Database. United Nations Statistics Division. https://comtrade.un.org.

CHAPTER 3

Monetary Policy and Emergence: What Lessons Can WAEMU Learn?

Kako Kossivi Nubukpo, Hechely Dzidzogbé Lawson, and Ampiah Sodji

3.1 Introduction

For the last 20 years, the world economic landscape has seen profound change marked by financial globalization and the rising power of emerging countries shaking up the world economic orthodoxy. One of the essential drivers of this mutation has been growing economic integration, with international commercial and financial ties multiplying (Kose et al 2008). Emerging countries constitute an indisputable player with growing economic power and faster growing wealth than the leading developed countries.

The concept of the "emerging country" was born in the 1980s with the development of stock markets in developing countries. The expression

K. K. Nubukpo (✉)
University of Oxford, Oxford, England

H. D. Lawson · A. Sodji
University of Lomé, Lomé, Togo

D. Barrowclough et al. (eds.), *South–South Regional Financial Arrangements*, International Political Economy Series,
https://doi.org/10.1007/978-3-030-64576-2_3

was first coined in 1981 by Antoine van Agtmael, a Dutch economist at the *International Finance Corporation* (IFC) in reference to developing countries offering opportunities for investors.

Long classified "third world", a denomination that alluded to seemingly insoluble obstacles to development, the concept of emerging countries was attributed to newly industrialized countries. But this concept has progressively evolved to give the term a new semantic connotation. Today, the term designates countries on a fast track to industrialization. These countries are characterized by the volume of industrial and tertiary sector activities within their productive system and by a growing share of their exports in world trade, with strong economic growth.

Initially characterizing the Newly Industrializing Countries (NICs), especially with reference to the "four dragons" of Asia: South Korea, Taiwan, Singapore and Hong Kong, it subsequently came to include a second generation of newly industrialized countries in South-East Asia: the "tigers", namely Thailand, the Philippines and Malaysia. Today, the category also includes China, India and Indonesia, as well as Latin American countries such as Brazil and Argentina. Among these emerging countries, the BRICS: Brazil, Russia, India, China and South Africa, are prominent figures. The first four (4) countries are the drivers of world economic growth, representing 25% by the middle of the decade.[1] Brazil is a formidable agricultural exporter. Russia is counting on its energy assets. India is specializing in IT services. China is a hypercompetitive manufacturer-exporter. The emerging nature of these four countries is due to effective integration into the world economy by exporting more goods and achieving a positive balance of trade.

Emergence is a systemic and multidimensional concept embracing economic, political and strategic criteria. In a rapidly changing world, the notion of emergence refers to the quest for economic power, at the heart of which lies the redefinition of the role of the state. The state thus plays the leading role in redefining the lines of development and in implementing the process. This central role of the state features among the eight (8) criteria proposed by Philippe Hugon[2] for a developing country to become emergent. These are as follows: (i) rate of economic growth,

[1] Jim O'Neill.

[2] Emeritus professor and researcher at the French Institute for International and Strategic Affairs (IRIS).

(ii) population size, (iii) diversification of production, (iv) degree to which it is open, (v) integration into the international financial world, (vi) the strategic role of the state in development, (vii) investment in research and development and (viii) the capacity to protect the territory.

CEPII[3] (1996), defines the concept of an emerging country through three criteria: (i) growing participation in international trade in manufactured products (growth in exports of manufactured products 2% greater per year than the growth in world trade); an attraction (ii) affecting international capital flows (role of financial centres) and (iii) a level of wealth. To date, there is no consensual definition of the notion of emergence, the fact remains that emerging countries are not one global entity: they have all developed differently historically and have different economic and social structures.

Consequently, the defining criteria for emergence differ from one institution to another. Even if there is no clear definition, a recognition of the dynamic of globalization, a development strategy centred on the mobilization of internal and external resources and structural transformation of the economy are all prerequisites for a dynamic of future convergence between a developing country and the rich countries.

Ricardo Hausmann, Lant Pritchett and Dani Rodrik (2005) observed examples of acceleration supported by economic growth. They found that accelerations in growth tended to correlate with increases in investment and trade, as well as with a depreciation in the exchange rate.

For Kaldor, monetary policy, like any economic policy, aims to act on economic variables: prices (control of inflation), level of activity (high growth), level of employment (low unemployment) and external balance (see review in Ottavj, 1993). Given the difficulty of simultaneously achieving these four objectives, Kaldor coined the term "magic square". The ultimate objectives of monetary policy are: economic growth, control of inflation and defence of the value of the national currency relative to that of other currencies. There are two conflicting schools of thought concerning the most important objective of monetary policy: Keynesians favour growth in national revenue, while monetarists give priority to controlling inflation.

Just as the "Tulip Crisis" was able, in 1637, to open the door to 150 years of formidable growth in the United Provinces of the Netherlands,

[3] *Centre D'Etudes Prospectives et d'Informations Internationales.*

the sub-prime crisis laid the foundations for challenging the worldwide financial orthodoxy through the implementation of unconventional monetary policies.

Faced with the financial and monetary crises and successive changes undergone by those countries having developed into market economies, what was the reaction of their various central banks? Even if the extent of any financial crisis seems to have been mitigated in African countries, particularly WAEMU countries, given their low degree of integration into the financial market, analysis urgently needs to be made of the crisis therapy represented by the responses given by the various central banks, in order to shed light on the optimum choice of monetary policy for the WAEMU zone.

The central question is this: given foreign exchange market volatility and even claims of currency wars over the last decade, what role does currency play in the emergence of countries? In other words, what monetary policy would be best for the emergence of Togo?

The aim of our study is to revisit monetary policies in developed countries, in emerging countries and in developing countries, in order to learn lessons for the WAEMU zone and Togo.

The value of this study lies in its contribution to the debate on the appropriate bases for the emergence of the economies of the West African sub-region in a context of international economic crisis following the sub-prime crisis, in which the competitiveness of the various economies is resurfacing. After analysing monetary policy in developed market economies (Sect. 1), and in emerging countries (Sect. 2), Sect. 3 will be dedicated to developing countries, more specifically the countries in the Economic Community of West African States (ECOWAS) and WAEMU zones. This last section will draw lessons for the viability of monetary policy in the WAEMU zone based on the most recent developments following the worldwide financial crisis.

3.1.1 Monetary Policy in Developed Market Economies

At the end of the Second World War and in the light of the economic crisis of 1929, Keynesian thinking inspired western economic policies up until the economic crisis of the 1970s, marked by a combination of accelerating inflation and rising unemployment, which stimulated a return to "orthodox" monetary practices.

After the "thirty glorious years" (the years of reconstruction following the Second World War), Keynesianism seems to have reached its limits in the face of the crisis. The stagflation of the 1970s brought the thinking of Friedman to the forefront. The repetitive crises marked by the liquidity crises of the 1960s, the currency crises of the 1970s and the financial crises of the 1990s threw the world economic environment into heightened competition. In 1987, the United States experienced a stock market crash that led to the bankruptcy of American savings banks. From 2007, the sub-prime crisis and its manifestations led to the United States implementing monetary policies described as "unconventional" (*Quantitative Easing*), bringing renewed interest in the Keynesian and neo-Keynesian approaches.

The eurozone, for its part, was slow to follow the movement initiated by the United States Federal Reserve Bank (FED). In fact, the succession of debt crises in the eurozone led the European Central Bank (ECB) to accept the principle of monetary financing of budgetary deficits, despite institutional innovations (creation of the European Stability Mechanism or ESM) resulting in increased respect for the principles of German ordoliberalism so dear to Mrs. Merkel, the German chancellor.

The central banks are applying unconventional policies with a view to restoring the economy to normality from a situation of crisis. Three levers could be employed here: the first acting on agents' expectations, the second on holding agents' liquidity and the third on credit conditions. The two instruments of easing monetary policy are "Quantitative Easing" and qualitative easing or "Credit Easing" credit conditions. Effectively, quantitative easing policy consists in the central banks explicitly abandoning the interest rate policy that favoured a high quantitative availability target in the accounts of second-tier banks. This policy of increasing the monetary base essentially means the central bank acquiring government securities.[4] Credit Easing policy consists in the central bank refinancing or repurchasing securities representing lending to the economy.[5] Quantitative easing policy is oriented towards the liabilities[6] on the central bank's

[4] The money supply is therefore channeled towards the economic agent, the state, which assures spending with a certain effect on activity.

[5] commercial bills, corporate bonds or mortgage bonds.

[6] The objective is set in terms of increasing the monetary base.

balance sheet, while credit easing is oriented more towards the assets side of the balance sheet.

3.1.1.1 Monetary Policy of the Bank of Japan

Objectives

The current objective of the Bank of Japan is to completely eliminate deflation and support economic activity in Japan. To achieve this objective, its main missions are to establish the country's monetary policy, manage the issuing of banknotes, ensure the financial stability of Japan, publish economic reports and participate in the balance of international trade.

The Response of the Bank of Japan to the Crisis: From the Financial Bubble to Abenomics

The bursting of the financial bubble in Japan in the early1990s led to a deterioration in the situation of a number of Japanese commercial banks. This situation led to a contraction in economic activity with annual average growth fluctuating around the 1% mark between 1991 and 2002. Economic growth stood at −0.3% in 1999 and −0.7% in 2000.[7] The Japanese economy was thus sliding into deflation.

Between 1991 and 1998, to reboot economic activity, the Bank of Japan lowered its key interest rate, leaving it to fluctuate around the 0.5% mark. This decision made it possible to reduce the cost of access to liquidity and to contain the tensions of the financial system caused by the bankruptcy of successive financial institutions.

In March 2001, the Bank of Japan implemented the first Quantitative Easing, applied by targeting a significant quantity of liquidity to be distributed through the direct purchase of treasury bills from the banks.

In 2009, the Central bank of Japan performed a "liquidity injection operation", the purpose of which was to loan money to the commercial banks for a duration of three months. In order to encourage the banks to support growth by granting loans to business, in June 2010 the central bank adopted the "financing mechanism in support of growth". This mechanism, which was an integral part of the unconventional measures in place since 2001, made it possible to grant one-year loans to financial institutions that could be renewed three times. The downside of this was

[7] UNCTAD data.

that it made it possible to give loans to non-viable businesses. In October 2010, the Bank of Japan took a certain number of measures to stabilize prices. An asset purchase programme was implemented, mainly based on the repurchase of state securities and also private denominated assets in the form of bonds issued by undertakings.

The rise of Shinzo Abe to the position of prime minister and the nomination of Haruhiko Kuroda to the head of the Bank of Japan would change the monetary policy of the country. In April 2013, in order to improve the effectiveness of the easing, the Bank of Japan announced a change to its monetary policy, the aim of which was to achieve 2% inflation by 2015. One thousand one hundred (1,100) billion euros was to be injected into the Japanese economy within two years. The aim of increasing the monetary base was advocated at the expense of a key interest rate of between 0% and 0.1%. The banknote rule limiting the amount of repurchases was frozen. Repurchases of treasury bonds were raised to fifty thousand (50,000) billion yen annually, with an extension to their average maturity from three years to seven years and repurchases of 40-year bonds.

On 31 October 2014, the Bank of Japan increased its asset acquisition programme through easing monetary policies (Quantitative & Credit Easing). The Central bank of Japan increased its repurchases of securities, particularly the share of state bonds in these purchases. Assessed on an annual basis, its purchases were raised from 70,000 billion yen to around 80,000 billion yen, or the equivalent of 17% of GDP. In the absence of such a measure, in fact, the authorities feared that the country would regain its "deflationist trend". The purpose of this measure was to increase the level of inflation. This measure came on top of the increase in Value Added Tax (VAT), which came into effect in April 2014. The impact of the VAT rise on the economy was initially far more serious than anyone could have imagined. In the third quarter of 2014, GDP contracted by 0.4%, after having already fallen by 1.9% in the second quarter.

3.1.1.2 Monetary Policy of the United States Federal Reserve (FED)

Objectives

The United States Federal Reserve Bank, the FED pursues three objectives that are defined by the United States in the Federal Reserve Act (1913), amended by the Full Employment and Balanced Growth Act of

1978: full employment, price stability and moderate long-term interest rates.

The Federal Reserve does not use clearly determined intermediate objectives to guide its monetary policy; it has abandoned the policy of strict monitoring of monetary aggregates, notably M3. It practises a policy of fine tuning, adjusting its rates more frequently than its counterparts, making it more reactive.

3.1.1.3 FED Response to the Crisis: A Duality of Quantitative Easing and Credit Easing

In response to the sub-prime crisis, a number of modifications were made to the management of various monetary policies. Following the bankruptcy of Lehman Brothers, FED implemented policy instruments (Term Repurchase Transaction [TRT], Term Securities Lending Facility [TSLF] and the Term Auction Credit Facility [TAF]) to avoid financial systemic risks. Between 2007 and 2009, it implemented the easing policy by reducing its key interest rate, which was fluctuating around 0.25%. It being impossible to further reduce the key interest rates in the face of the continuing crisis, the United States Federal Reserve launched the first qualitative easing policy (Credit Easing), a worldwide programme of securities purchases (QE 1) followed by (QE 2) and (QE 3), which enabled FED to stimulate economic activity and re-establish confidence in investments in certain markets. Through the purchase of relatively risky assets, this policy enabled FED to spread liquidity mainly in the markets that had need of it and those in which the risk premiums measured by the gap between the Libor rate and the rate applied to risk-free assets had become much too high. Since 2008, the three above-mentioned operations made a variety of outcomes possible. The purpose of QE1 (2008–2010) was to repurchase toxic debts. Thus, the Paulson plan, valued at 700 billion United States dollars of purchasing, made it possible to redress the value of both financial and real estate assets. Launched in November 2010, QE2 was an opportunity for FED to regain the trust of speculators. FED thus turned away from real estate. It went on to purchase treasury bonds by self-financing the American debt.

In September 2012, FED also implemented spectacular easing measures (QE3). These operations, which took the form of massive repurchases of American sovereign securities and mortgage-backed security (MBS) products, were presented as a response to the fragility of the economic recovery. In response to the economic upturn in 2014, FED ceased its purchases of assets at the end of October 2014.

3.1.1.4 *Monetary Policy of the European Central Bank (ECB)*

Objectives

By virtue of Article 105 of the Treaty, the main objective of the Eurosystem is to maintain price stability. Without prejudice to this objective of price stability, it lends its support to the general economic policies of the European Community. In pursuing its objectives, the Eurosystem must respect the principle of an open-market economy in a context of free competition favouring the efficient allocation of resources.

In order to achieve its objectives, the Eurosystem has a series of monetary policy instruments: it performs open-market operations, offers permanent facilities and requires credit establishments to maintain compulsory reserves.

3.1.1.5 *ECB Response to the Crises: Sub-Prime Crisis and Greek Crisis*

In order to curb the crisis that resulted from the sub-prime crisis and the crisis that originated in the sustainability of the Greek debt and which impacted on the eurozone, ECB implemented conventional measures by reducing the key interest rates. On 8 December 2011, the ECB Governing Council reduced the key interest rates by 25 base points after an initial reduction of 25 base points already implemented on 3 December 2011, thus bringing the rate to 1%. In accordance with the Treaty of Maastricht, the direct acquisition of debt instruments of the central administrations of Member States by ECB or by the national central banks is forbidden. Consequently, ECB is unable to intervene in the primary market[8] for the purchase of public debt securities.

There are three reasons for this measure: (i) the discipline established by the Maastricht criteria and then confirmed by the Stability and Growth Pact would be rendered inoperative and free-rider behaviour facilitated, (ii) acquisition of the debts of the central administrations of Member States would compromise the independence of ECB and (iii) since the main objective of the European System of Central Banks (ESCB) is to

[8] Bond issue market.

maintain price stability, the monetization of debt securities could lead to inflationary spirals.

During the course of 2011, ECB applied its quantitative easing measure through its Long-Term Refinancing Operations programme (LTRO). This measure inflated its liabilities by increasing banking reserves with the aim of maintaining abundant liquidity on the money market (Fawley 2013). It should be remembered that, in response to the crisis, ECB monetary policy was characterized by its rigour.

On 22 January 2015, considering there to be threats of deflation within the eurozone, the European Central Bank decided to implement a policy of quantitative easing. It therefore planned for the purchase of 60 billion euros in assets, corresponding to 40 billion euros in public debts and 20 billion euros in private debts, each month until at least September 2016.

3.1.1.6 The Triad of the Bank of Japan, FED and ECB: A Comparative Approach

Analysis of the unconventional monetary policy implemented by the various central banks reveals varied results. All of the central banks of developed countries first lowered their key interest rates before implementing unconventional measures in response to the persistence of the crisis. Monetary policy became unconventional in Japan in 1998 and in the United States in 2008. It seems to have been less effective in Japan than in the United States.

The unconventional monetary policy thus implemented in Japan since 1998 did not boost the flagging growth of Japan, its continuing indebtedness, its declining productive investment rate, or the absence of accumulation of productive capital in the industry. In the United States, the unconventional monetary policy implemented from 2008 went some way to redistributing credit, but above all rebooted the economy, the accumulation of capital and employment (Patrick Artus 2012). The unconventional monetary policy implemented by FED, Credit Easing, was qualified by Ben Bernanke (2009) as a measure expressing the willingness to respond in an appropriate manner to the exceptional increase in credit spreads, and more generally to the dysfunctional debt securities markets. These measures have the advantage of directly reducing the cost of financing for households and undertakings, without calling upon a reticent banking sector. FED intervened directly in the economic activity with or without the intermediary of commercial banks. This was not the case with ECB or the Bank of Japan prior to the implementation of Abenomics. Consequently, among the easing measures used, that of FED was a success.

3.1.2 Exchange Rate Policy in Developed Market Economies

The monetary system decided on at the Bretton Woods conference in July 1944 functioned until almost the end of the 1960s. Since the collapse of the Bretton Woods system in the early 1970s, countries have been free to choose the exchange regime of their choice. A certain number of developed countries successfully maintained a floating exchange regime in force for long periods, having accepted the regular and sometimes very marked fluctuations in the exchange rate under the action of market forces. This was the case in the United States, the eurozone and Japan.

In the case of the United States, in contrast to the other countries, exchange rate policy was not part of the FED mission. Two reasons justify this choice: the economy of the United States is relatively closed and therefore less sensitive to the effects of variations in the exchange rate and the status of the dollar.[9] Should intervention in the exchange market become necessary, the decision would be taken in consultation between the Treasury[10] and FED.

In general, the exchange rate instruments theoretically available to the monetary authorities for intervention are, besides physical interventions on the exchange market: the short-term interest rate and verbal interventions, also known as "open mouth operations".[11] These three instruments are used by the central banks.

Consisting in verbal interventions, these are virtually non-existent in the eurozone. For Fratzscher (2004), verbal interventions effectively influence the exchange rates of the major currencies (euro-dollar, yen-dollar, etc.), and reduce their volatility.

It may therefore be concluded that there is no exchange rate policy in the eurozone and that ECB has chosen to favour price stability over exchange rate stability. ECB only takes decisions regarding the evolution of the exchange rate in the event of an inflationary threat.

[9] Reserve currency.

[10] The financial wing of the government.

[11] In reference to open-market operations, Guthrie and Wright 2000

The exchange rate regime applicable to the euro is an independently floating regime, as is the case with the currencies of the majority of industrialized countries. ECB is responsible for leading exchange rate policy, but this is ordered by the Council of the European Union, bringing together the Ministers of Economy and Finance of the Union. Exchange rate policy is therefore defined by the political authorities of the zone, but the directions adopted must not conflict with the objective of price stability.

For Marc Touati (2012), activity should ultimately be given the chance to rebound. Priority should be given to restoring stronger growth within the Economic and Monetary Union (EMU), mainly due to a weaker euro and an effective budget policy.

In contrast, the United States applies an exchange rate policy that is either neutral or countercyclical. One might conversely underline the fact that the United States has since 1992 enjoyed a stabilizing effect on its currency, with the exception of the 2001 shock. Until 2000, the dollar was appreciating in a phase of strong growth; from 2002, it depreciated as the economy recovered. With the exception of Germany, the strong euro made for a loss of competitiveness in European undertakings. For the future, the question of exchange rate policy in the eurozone becomes increasingly meaningful.

In the light of this analysis in developed market economies, what is the situation in emerging countries?

3.2 Emerging Countries

The economic growth of emerging countries was particularly strong between 2000 and 2012. It reached around 3.25% in the 1990s, then rose to 4.25% between 2000 and 2012. This acceleration may notably be explained by the rising prices of raw materials, accommodative financial conditions worldwide, the adoption of countercyclical macroeconomic policies or indeed booming international trade. In the event, the rising prices of raw materials booming international trade were both the cause and the result of the strong growth of the majority of developing countries. In response to the sub-prime crisis, emerging countries experienced a reduction in their rate of growth.

The emerging Asian countries are experiencing contrasting developments. In contrast to Hong Kong, Singapore and China, these countries are significantly behind in terms of development. Most of these countries are committed to a dynamic of convergence of their level of income with that of the more advanced countries. Laos, Vietnam, Malaysia, India and Thailand are making considerable efforts. According to IMF forecasts, the contribution of Asian growth to worldwide growth will be 50% by 2050.

The various simulations byCEPII confirm that the contribution of Asia to world GDP will grow significantly from 23% in 2008 to 33% in 2025 and to over 50% in 2050. With an average growth rate of 10.7% between 2006 and 2008 and a cumulative GDP of around 8,860 billion dollars in 2008, the BRICS economies are today the best performing and most competitive on the planet. Of the five countries comprising the BRICS, four are considered today's great emerging powers. In 2014, they were, respectively, the seventh, eighth, tenth, second and twenty-ninth world powers,[12] holding seventh, sixth, third, second and twenty-fifth place in terms of purchasing power parity.

The foreign exchange and cash reserves of China enable it to finance its projects and those of other countries, while the cost of the worldwide competition is constantly rising and the public debts of industrialized countries relegate research investments to the private sector. Consequently, China, which became the world's second economic power and first exporter in 2009 as well as the world's banker, India, and Brazil have been assessed to be the dominant powers in 2050 according to the World Bank.

In 2013, the contribution of emerging and developing economies to world GDP expressed as purchasing power parity exceeded that of the advanced countries for the first time; in 2000, these contributions were 37% and 63%, respectively (Destais and Piton 2013).

3.2.1 Monetary Policy in Emerging Countries

The monetary policy of the emerging countries is more oriented towards the aim of achieving strong and durable economic growth. Most of these countries practice an expansionist and discretionary monetary policy.

The last three quarters of 2013 and the 2014 year in emerging countries were characterized by a tightening of monetary policy marked by increases in key interest rates and fears of flights of capital in a context of a progressive exit from US Federal Reserve quantitative easing.

[12] Nominal GDP.

With a view to having more of a margin for manoeuvre in their monetary policy, in 2014 the BRICS created a development bank with 100 billion United States dollars shared equally between the five founding countries, the headquarters of which is in Shanghai. Concerning China, it played a major role in the creation of this new development bank and also created an Asian investment bank, the objective of which was to finance infrastructure projects without constrictive conditionality. These two new financial institutions should protect the member countries in the event of any new financial crises by implementing a reserve currency fund.

3.2.2 *Exchange Rate Policy in Emerging Countries*

The emerging countries re-examine their choice of exchange rate regime after every major monetary crisis. Thus, in the early 1970s, after the collapse of the Bretton Woods system, the governments had to adapt, for better or worse; some of them opting for flexibility in the exchange rate, while others preferring anchorage to the dollar zone. The explosion of inflation in the 1980s in numerous Latin American countries centred the debate on the virtues of policies of stabilization through nominal anchorage of the exchange rate.

By the 1990s, inflation was no longer a major problem in the majority of the countries, as the credibility benefits of fixed exchange rates had lost its significance. For numerous Asian countries committed to development strategies based on promoting exports, the major risk is becoming that of appreciation. Moreover, new dimensions have been added to the debate with the liberalization of movements of capital: moral risk, robustness of the financial system and fragility in the face of speculative attacks.

In the light of the Mexican (1994), Asian (1997), Russian (1998) and Brazilian (1999) crises, the theory propagated that all regimes other than totally independent floating or rigid institutional pegging were unstable. According to this theory of the unstable environment, financial globalization should cause the intermediate regimes to disappear in favour of the "corner solutions" of independent floating and rigid pegging (Gharbi 2005).

The Argentinian crisis (2002), which demonstrated the adverse effects of rigid pegging, led to most emerging countries abandoning management of their exchange rates in favour of a strategy of targeting inflation and floating their currency.

Therefore, the debate rebounded towards the importance of flexibility and the need to replace nominal anchorage of the exchange rate with a policy of targeting inflation. This recent trend leads us to question whether *de jure* flexibility is de facto verified.

The competitiveness strategy of the Asian countries was then transformed into a fear of appreciation that obliged them to accumulate enormous stocks of reserve currencies with a high cost. In Latin America, the raging inflation of the past makes for a real fear of depreciation.

It appears that the emerging countries barely have any alternative than to declare themselves floating and continue to manage their exchange rate de facto. Being very open to the international capital markets, these countries are condemned to accept the flexibility of their exchange rates; often, however, their tendency to inflation, dollarization of their debt or the fragility of their banking system condemns them to management.

3.2.2.1 Managed Exchange Rate Schemes: Credibility Versus Flexibility

The IMF identifies eight (8) categories of exchange rate regimes ranging from a rigidly fixed to a completely independently floating exchange rate.[13] The choice between fixing the exchange rate or leaving it to float comes down to the choice between credibility and flexibility. A fixed exchange rate imposes strong discipline on monetary and budgetary policy. The purpose of pegging the exchange rate to the currency of a country with low inflation is to import the credibility of that country.

Flexibility is the main advantage of floating. The absence of commitment to the exchange rate brings total independence to monetary policy, which theoretically guarantees the economy the necessary flexibility to accommodate a variety of shocks. The market automatically ensures equilibrium in the balance of payments and the authorities do not have to hold foreign exchange reserves. However, the system offers no nominal anchorage for inflationary expectations. If the monetary authorities lack credibility or if the country experiences significant supply shocks, economic agents will anticipate continuing and worsening inflationary

[13] Until 1998, the IMF classification only distinguished between four categories: pegged, flexibility limited, managed floating and independently floating. In 1998, the new IMF classification identified eight categories: (1) Regime with no separate legal tender, (2) Currency board, (3) Fixed peg, (4) Pegged within horizontal bands, (5) Crawling pegs, (6) Crawling bands, (7) Managed floating, (8) Independently floating.

developments. Furthermore, experience shows that even if the policies pursued are relatively virtuous, floating will result in high volatility in the nominal exchange rate that is liable to compromise external trade and macroeconomic stability.

Choosing an exchange rate strategy means choosing the optimum degree of flexibility to resolve these conflicting objectives. According to Rogoff et al. (2004), the fashion for intermediate regimes in emerging or developing countries may be explained by the fact that these regimes make it possible to combine the advantages of the two extremes (nominal anchorage and autonomy in the monetary policy), while at the same time reducing their disadvantages (risk of misalignment with the real exchange rate and excessive volatility).

The heart of the debate concerning the optimum exchange rate regime has always been this arbitrage: credibility versus flexibility. However, for a number of emerging countries, pegging the exchange rate is no longer a precondition for enjoying strong credibility and controlling inflation. Since the end of the 1990s, a growing number of emerging countries have been letting their exchange rates float. This trend is particularly noticeable among those that have succeeded in significantly reducing their rate of inflation, among them a number of Latin American countries. This explains the recent return of the objective of flexibility.

For Levy-Yeyati and Sturzenneger (2005), intermediate regimes are losing ground to floating or strongly pegged regimes in emerging and developed countries. But for underdeveloped and non-emerging countries, the trend towards corner solutions is not verified: the weakness of these countries' access to capital markets has enabled them to escape the obligation to adopt extreme regimes to avoid speculative attacks.

3.2.2.2 Intermediate Regimes: Source of Instability?

Since the mid-1990s, intermediate regimes have been at the heart of the crises that have affected emerging countries. These regimes have proven vulnerable to massive outflows of capital. All attempts to prevent this have resulted in losses of reserves and strong hikes in interest rates that weakened the banking systems and ended up provoking a recession. These exchange rate crises have often been accompanied by financial crises whose origin is attributed to domestic banks and businesses, confident in the official commitment of the monetary authorities not to devalue, taking excessive exchange risks. Intermediate regimes would therefore create a specific problem of moral hazard.

Therefore, a number of economists (Obstfeld and Rogoff 1995; Fischer 2001; Mussa et al. 2000), that Williamson qualifies as new orthodoxy, have condemned any form of the pegging of the exchange rate and incited developing countries to let their currencies float independently.

The idea that intermediate regimes favour the taking of exchange risks must be qualified. The Asian crisis appears to illustrate this, but the countries affected mostly opted for the most rigid form of intermediate regimes, namely a fixed exchange rate although one that is adjustable relative to the United States dollar.

In order to verify whether the extremes are less vulnerable to exchange crises than intermediate regimes, Bubula and Otker-Robe (2003) statistically analysed the frequency of crises, defined as periods of severe pressure on the exchange market,[14] for all IMF member countries under different exchange regimes between 1990 and 2001. They demonstrated that crises were more frequent under intermediate regimes than at either of the two extremes. However, they also showed that the extreme regimes are not invulnerable to speculative attacks (73% of crises concern intermediate regimes, 20% floating regimes and 7% strongly pegged regimes).

The fact that crises are more frequent under intermediate regimes does not mean that they are intrinsically unstable. These regimes have often coexisted with fragile fundamentals: high inflation (Columbia 1999), interest rates that are too high for the economic situation (SME 1992), chronic budget deficits and unsustainable external debt (Russia 1998, Brazil 1999), a banking system that is fragile in the absence of prudential capital regulation and control policies (Asian crisis 1997). The existence of these factors are conducive to the emergence of crises whatever the exchange regime in place.

According to Willett (2002), it is not the limited flexibility of the exchange rate that is the issue but rather the mismatch between exchange rate policy and monetary policy that often appears in intermediate regimes. Effectively, in a managed exchange regime, monetary authorities address conflicting objectives: their commitment to the currency on the one hand and their domestic objectives on the other. Investors doubt the credibility of the commitment to the currency when the authorities

[14] The "exchange market" pressure index is measured using a weighted average of the movements of the exchange rate and the interest rate. The regime is in crisis when this index is higher than its average by more than three times the standard deviation.

pursue budgetary or monetary policies that are incompatible in the long term with maintaining the exchange rate at its current level.

The theory that intermediate regimes are unstable is further challenged by the experiences of those countries (Chile, Poland, Hungary) that have succeeded in maintaining crawling band regimes for relatively long periods without crises.

Since the mid-1990s, more and more emerging countries have abandoned managed exchange regimes in favour of discretionary management in the form of managed or independent floating.

3.2.2.3 The Dangers of Rigid Management

A number of countries have been forced to abandon management of their exchange rate following a speculative attack resulting in a crisis (the severity of which has varied according to the situation in each country). The common factor in these crises is a rigid exchange rate management policy.

Managing the exchange rate means arbitrating between the objectives of inflation and competitiveness. Rigid management systematically favouring one objective at the expense of the other can prove costly in the long term. Favouring the inflation objective by maintaining a steady slight reduction or a tight fluctuation margin will result in appreciation in real terms if the inflation reduction rate is too slow. The outcome will be a large current account deficit financed by massive capital inflows.

The Mexican crisis of 1994 is one example of the cost of a policy favouring the inflation objective at the expense of overvaluation of parity. This experience shows that the overvaluation may be maintained for a long period without crisis thanks to the availability of capital flows and reserves but that correction is brutal.

In contrast, the experience of Columbia illustrates the dangers of management favouring the competitiveness objective despite high inflation. Management of the real exchange rate through passive reduction can lead to high inflation. However, this can be avoided if this management is accompanied by adequate macroeconomic policies. Thus, with the aid of prudent budgetary and monetary policies, Chile has succeeded in reducing inflation to levels comparable to those of developed countries despite a policy of passive reduction.

Flexible management, alternating the two objectives of inflation and competitiveness according to circumstance, makes it possible to resolve this conflict without risking overvaluation or chronic inflation. The countries that have succeeded in maintaining these regimes without crisis are those that have pursued flexible management by playing on the reduction rate by modifying the central parity when necessary.

Exchange rate volatility is a major preoccupation for the central banks of emerging countries whose monetary policy targets inflation.

According to Calvo (2000), the ideal remedy would be to opt for an exchange regime that makes it possible to introduce high levels of both transparency and credibility. He adds that only two types of regime can fulfil these conditions, namely the regimes of rigid fixity (dollarization in particular) and (very) independent float.

3.2.3 The Four Fears of Emerging Countries

3.2.3.1 Fear of Floating

Fear of floating constitutes a reticence to let the exchange rate float independently despite official announcement of the float. This aversion especially affects emerging countries. The combination of narrower exchange markets, significant shocks and large flows of capital means a risk that flexibility in these countries may turn into excessive volatility. Thus, contrary to what the theory predicts, for emerging countries, a flexible exchange rate is a potential source of instability rather than a means of absorbing external shocks. Fear of floating is justified by the fact that fluctuations in the exchange rate are more costly for emerging countries than for developed countries.

3.2.3.2 Fear of Management

If floating is costly for emerging countries, then exchange rate management is justified. However, more and more countries are declaring themselves floating while implicitly pursuing a management policy. This reticence to openly admit to a widespread practice leads us to conclude that the issue at stake is a fear of management rather than the fear of floating concluded by Calvo and Reinhart.

Announcing a precisely defined management rule exposes monetary authorities to judgement and potential market sanctions in the event of inconsistent economic policies. Any mismatch between the economic policies adopted and the value of the exchange rate will compromise the credibility of the exchange rate policy. Therefore, the authorities are obliged to pursue policies appropriate to the exchange rate regime.

3.2.3.3 Fear of Appreciation

Competitiveness is a primary objective for emerging countries. Movements in the real exchange rate are therefore a major preoccupation for the monetary authorities. The main lesson of the crises of the 1990s, both in Europe and in Asia, is that they are often the conclusion of a prolonged period of overvaluation, which in time results in large current account deficits that the market ultimately deems unsustainable.

The risk of appreciation in the exchange rate and a loss of competitiveness often lead monetary authorities to intervene. Thus, even in a flexible regime, the central banks of emerging countries are often led to intervene in order to prevent appreciation of the exchange rate. Some, like China, have even developed a fear of appreciation.

This fear of appreciation notably manifests itself in Asian countries. The exchange rates of these countries have certainly become more flexible since the 1997 crisis. These countries make massive efforts to resist the real appreciation of their currencies (Hernandez and Montiel 2001; McKinnon and Schnabl 2004). This fear is accentuated by the high competitiveness of China resulting from low wage costs and clear undervaluation of the Chinese yuan. It is therefore crucial for Asian central banks to oppose appreciation of their currencies.

For Mishkin and Savastano (2000), monetary policy should not be preoccupied with the objective of competitiveness. This objective is incompatible with that of price stability. However, in contrast to the Latin American countries, the Asian countries have no problems with inflation, which means that they can preoccupy themselves with the objective of competitiveness. Thus, they combine a policy of targeting inflation and combating appreciation.

3.2.3.4 Fear of Depreciation

Certain emerging central banks are particularly reticent regarding depreciation of their exchange rate, essentially for two reasons: the effects of exchange rate pass-through on prices and financial fragility due to partial dollarization.

3.3 Developing Countries

Since the 1980s, external demand has constituted an increasingly important driver for growth in developing countries, notably due to commercial liberalization and the rapid growth of value chains. As things stand, although their domestic activity may have become increasingly sensitive to demand from other developing countries, it will nonetheless remain essentially dependent on demand from the advanced countries, the ultimate links in the value chains.

However, the rise in the price of raw materials, itself partly explained by demand from emerging countries, has played an ambivalent role: on the one hand, it stimulated investment and activity more generally in the exporting countries by offering them generous incomes; on the other, it harmed the importing countries, although they knew how to compensate for the recessive effects by relying on other drivers of growth. Finally, due to the low interest rates in the advanced countries and the reduction in risk premiums, developing countries benefited from accommodative financing conditions. This also stimulated investment and growth more generally, especially in the most financially open countries.

What analyses can one make at the level of the economic growth of the countries in the West African zone? Do countries with flexible exchange regimes and those with fixed exchange regimes have the same levels of growth? What are the monetary and exchange policies in the countries in the ECOWAS zone?

3.3.1 ECOWAS-WAEMU: What Inflation for What Growth?

Analysis of the growth rate in the WAEMU zone shows that, compared to the other countries in the sub-region, the countries in the WAEMU zone have low economic growth rates and also low inflation rates. In 2010, the countries in the WAEMU zone recorded very low inflation rates. The seven (7) other ECOWAS countries beat the inflationary record with an annual variation ranging from 7.52% for Nigeria to 19.7% for Guinea (Tables 3.1, 3.2 and 3.3).

The 2013 year was marked by an alleviation of inflationary tensions in the WAEMU zone in the wake of the general tendency observed worldwide. The progression of the general price level as an annual average was thus established at 1.5% in 2013, down from 2.4% in 2012. A large part of this deceleration of inflation reflected the fall in local cereal prices, induced by the increase in cereal production during the course of the 2012–2013 agricultural campaign (Report on the franc zone 2013).

Within WAEMU, according to the BCEAO sub-regional note, in December 2010 the rate of inflation was estimated at 1.6% year-on-year. BCEAO adopted a target of 2%. The adoption of an inflation target of 2%

Table 3.1 Level of Inflation in the ECOWAS Zone in 2010

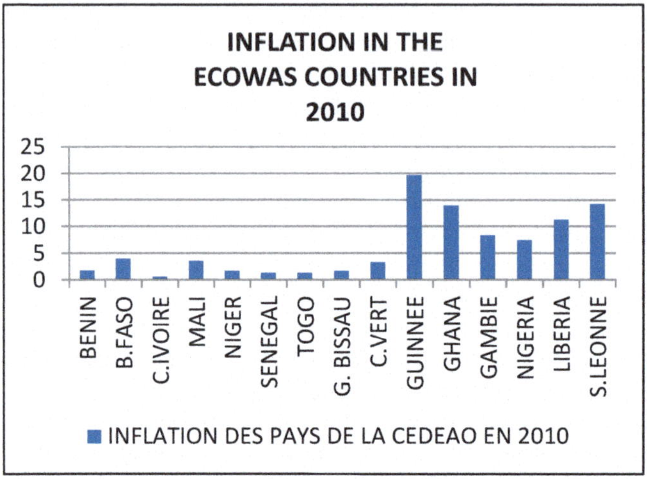

Source Authors, based on World Development indicator data

Table 3.2 Level of Inflation in the ECOWAS Zone in 2012 and 2013

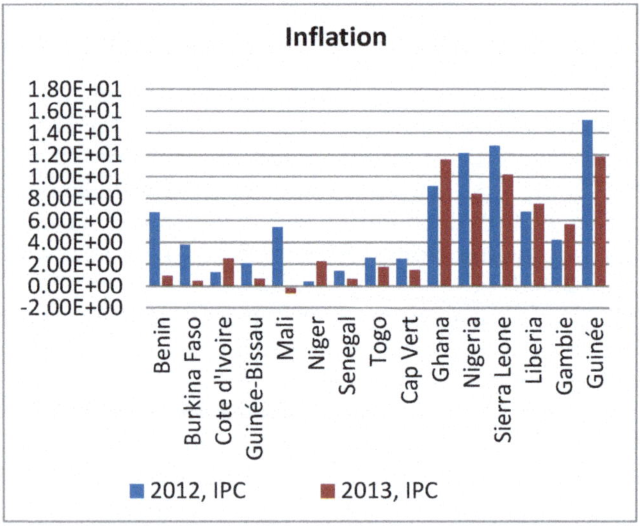

Source Authors, based on WDI data

Table 3.3 Real GDP Growth in the ECOWAS Countries

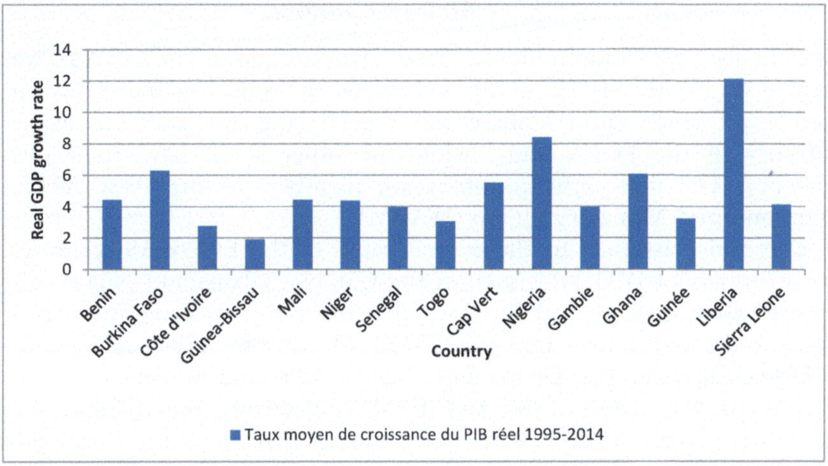

Source Authors, based on IMF data

could effectively seem exaggeratedly restrictive for economies that need a 7% annual growth in GDP to achieve their millennium development goals (MDGs), notably that of halving poverty by 2015, as well as the sustainable development goals (SDGs) under creation. It is astonishing to see the WAEMU central bank content to manage inflation without preoccupying itself with either growth or economic development. Empirical literature on the subject, however, is long-winded. We are familiar, for example, with the debate on the Phillips curve, which establishes that arbitrage must be performed between inflation and growth.

Analysis of the growth rates of countries in the ECOWAS zone over the period 1980–2014 shows that the countries with flexible exchange rate regimes averaged higher rates of GDP growth (4%) than those with fixed exchange rate regimes (3%). All of the countries in the ECOWAS zone experienced an average real growth rate of 3.5% over this period. over the post-devaluation period after 1994 (1995–2014), the average growth of countries in the WAEMU zone was 3.93% as compared to 6.22% for the other six countries with flexible exchange rate regimes. This difference in performance demonstrates the relevance of an analysis of the optimum exchange rate regime for the countries of West Africa.

3.3.2 Monetary Policy in Developing Countries: The Case of West African Countries

The Economic Community of West African States (ECOWAS) was created on 28 May 1975 in Lagos, Nigeria. It brings together 15 countries,[15] of which eight[16] share the French language and a common currency in the FCFA franc, while the other seven have their own currency. The first eight countries are members of the West African Economic and Monetary Union (WAEMU).

The duties assigned to the central banks of the ECOWAS countries, not members of WAEMU, such as the Gambia, Ghana and Nigeria ally the objective of price stability with the imperative of economic development through active exchange rate and currency policies. Just like WAEMU, the Gambia, Ghana and Nigeria, following monetary reforms implemented in 1980, 1987 and 1990, respectively, opted for monetary management mainly based on indirect bank liquidity regulation instruments.

3.3.3 Exchange Rate Policy in the ECOWAS Countries

The developing countries apply a wide range of exchange rate regimes, ranging from very rigid fixed parity to independently floating, via a number of variations. Among these developing countries, in the ECOWAS zone, the WAEMU countries and Cape Verde are in a fixed parity exchange while the other six countries are in a flexible exchange regime (Table 3.4).

Ferrari and Paula (2006) show that fixed exchange regimes have advantages and disadvantages regarding the economic performance of a country. According to these authors, the costs of adjusting exchange rates in fixed exchange regimes are very high.

One of the most ardent defenders of flexible exchange rates is Milton Friedman. Friedman (1953) spoke out against this system, inferring that fixed exchange rates generated speculative crises and instability.

Ripoll (2001) performed a comparative analysis of the macroeconomic performances of several dozen African countries including the countries

[15] Benin, Burkina Faso, Côte-d'Ivoire, Mali, Niger, Senegal, Togo, Guinea-Bissau, Nigeria, Ghana, Guinea, the Gambia, Liberia, Cape Verde, Sierra Leone.

[16] Benin, Burkina Faso, Côte-d'Ivoire, Mali, Niger, Senegal, Togo, Guinea-Bissau.

Table 3.4 The various ECOWAS countries and their currencies

Country	*Union*	*Money*
Benin	WAEMU	CFA
Burkina Faso	WAEMU	CFA
Mali	WAEMU	CFA
Niger	WAEMU	CFA
Senegal	WAEMU	CFA
Togo	WAEMU	CFA
G. Bissau	WAEMU	CFA
Cape Verde	-	Escudo
Ghana	-	Cedis
The Gambia	-	Dalasi
Guinea	-	Guinea franc
Liberia	-	Liberian dollar
Nigeria	-	Naira
Sierra Leone	-	Leone

Source Authors

in the franc zone. The analyses covered economic growth and inflation in the various countries according to their exchange rate regimes. The results of the study showed that the economic performance of fixed and flexible exchange rate regimes was largely identical. For Ripoll, inflation was significantly lower in the case of fixed exchange rates. The intermediate exchange rate regimes perform better in terms of inflation than in terms of growth.

In the case of countries in the West African sub-region, a number of studies have highlighted the appropriate exchange rate regime for the ECOWAS countries. Thus Kisu (2010) considers that fixed exchange regimes should be favoured for all of the countries in the ECOWAS zone, while for Dupasquier et al. (2005) flexible exchange rate regimes constitute appropriate regimes for countries in the West African sub-region.

Diop and Fall (2011) consider the fixed and intermediate exchanges to be appropriate. The fixed exchange rate regime offers advantages, as it makes it possible to stabilize the economy without reducing growth performance. They arrived at the conclusion that the intermediate exchange rate regime seemed to be more appropriate for all of the countries in the ECOWAS zone.

Table 3.5, below, shows us the development of the various exchange regimes of the ECOWAS countries over the period 1975–2014.

Table 3.5 Exchange regime in the ECOWAS countries from 1975 to 2014

Year	*Waemu*	*The Gambia*	*Ghana*	*Guinea*	*Liberia*	*Nigeria*	*Sierra Leone*	*Cape Verdi*
1975	Fixed	Fixed	Fixed	Fixed	Fixed	Fixed	Fixed	Fixed
1976	Fixed	Fixed	Fixed	Fixed	Fixed	Fixed	Fixed	Fixed
1977	Fixed	Fixed	Fixed	Fixed	Fixed	Fixed	Fixed	Fixed
1978	Fixed	Fixed	Fixed	Fixed	Fixed	Fixed	Fixed	Fixed
1979	Fixed	Fixed	Fixed	Fixed	Fixed	Intermediate	Flexible	Fixed
1980	Fixed	Fixed	Fixed	Fixed	Fixed	Intermediate	Flexible	Fixed
1981	Fixed	Fixed	Fixed	Fixed	Fixed	Intermediate	Flexible	Fixed
1982	Fixed	Fixed	Fixed	Fixed	Fixed	Intermediate	Flexible	Fixed
1983	Fixed	Fixed	Intermediate	Fixed	Fixed	Intermediate	Flexible	Fixed
1984	Fixed	Fixed	Intermediate	Fixed	Fixed	Intermediate	Flexible	Fixed
1985	Fixed	Fixed	Intermediate	Fixed	Fixed	Intermediate	Flexible	Fixed
1986	Fixed	Fixed	Intermediate	Flexible	Fixed	Flexible	Flexible	Fixed
1987	Fixed	Flexible	Intermediate	Flexible	Fixed	Flexible	Flexible	Fixed
1988	Fixed	Flexible	Flexible	Flexible	Fixed	Flexible	Flexible	Fixed
1989	Fixed	Flexible	Flexible	Flexible	Fixed	Flexible	Flexible	Fixed
1990	Fixed	Flexible	Flexible	Flexible	Fixed	Flexible	Flexible	Fixed
1991	Fixed	Flexible	Flexible	Flexible	Fixed	Flexible	Flexible	Fixed
1992	Fixed	Flexible	Flexible	Flexible	Fixed	Flexible	Flexible	Fixed
1993	Fixed	Flexible	Flexible	Flexible	Fixed	Flexible	Flexible	Fixed
1994	Fixed	Flexible	Flexible	Flexible	Fixed	Flexible	Flexible	Fixed
1995	Fixed	Flexible	Flexible	Flexible	Fixed	Flexible	Flexible	Fixed
1996	Fixed	Flexible	Flexible	Flexible	Fixed	Flexible	Flexible	Fixed
1997	Fixed	Flexible	Flexible	Flexible	Fixed	Flexible	Flexible	Fixed
1998	Fixed	Flexible	Flexible	Flexible	Flexible	Flexible	Flexible	Fixed
1999	Fixed	Flexible	Flexible	Flexible	Flexible	Flexible	Flexible	Fixed
2000	Fixed	Flexible	Flexible	Flexible	Flexible	Flexible	Flexible	Fixed
2001	Fixed	Flexible	Flexible	Flexible	Flexible	Flexible	Flexible	Fixed
2002	Fixed	Flexible	Flexible	Flexible	Flexible	Flexible	Flexible	Fixed
2003	Fixed	Flexible	Flexible	Flexible	Flexible	Flexible	Flexible	Fixed
2004	Fixed	Flexible	Flexible	Flexible	Flexible	Flexible	Flexible	Fixed
2005	Fixed	Flexible	Flexible	Flexible	Flexible	Flexible	Flexible	Fixed
2006	Fixed	Flexible	Flexible	Flexible	Flexible	Flexible	Flexible	Fixed
2007	Fixed	Flexible	Flexible	Flexible	Flexible	Flexible	Flexible	Fixed
2008	Fixed	Flexible	Flexible	Flexible	Flexible	Flexible	Flexible	Fixed
2009	Fixed	Flexible	Flexible	Flexible	Flexible	Flexible	Flexible	Fixed
2010	Fixed	Flexible	Flexible	Flexible	Flexible	Flexible	Flexible	Fixed
2011	Fixed	Flexible	Flexible	Flexible	Flexible	Flexible	Flexible	Fixed

(continued)

Table 3.5 (continued)

Year	*Waemu*	*The Gambia*	*Ghana*	*Guinea*	*Liberia*	*Nigeria*	*Sierra Leone*	*Cape Verdi*
2012	Fixed	Flexible	Flexible	Flexible	Flexible	Flexible	Flexible	Fixed
2013	Fixed	Flexible	Flexible	Flexible	Flexible	Flexible	Flexible	Fixed
2014	Fixed	Flexible	Flexible	Flexible	Flexible	Flexible	Flexible	Fixed

Source Authors

3.3.4 Monetary Policy in the WAEMU Zone

3.3.4.1 Institutional Framework of Monetary Policy

The institutional framework of the West African Economic and Monetary Union (UMOA) is governed by four (4) fundamental texts: the UMOA treaty of 14 November 1973, the agreement between France and the UMOA member states of 4 December 1973, the treaty of the West African Economic, and Monetary Union (WAEMU) of 10 January 1994 and the BCEAO statutes. The UMOA treaty in particular instituted a single currency and mint. Article 4 of the UMOA treaty stipulates that the States of the union must centralize their monetary assets in BCEAO. The conduct of monetary policy is defined by the UMOA treaty and the BCEAO statutes. Institutional reforms were made by the heads of state in 2007, thus leading to a revision of the texts that entered into force on 1 April 2010.

In accordance with Article 9 of the BCEAO statutes, the institution has the following fundamental duties: to define and implement monetary policy within UMOA, to ensure the stability of the UMOA banking and financial system, to promote the correct operation and provide supervision and security for payment systems in UMOA, to implement the UMOA exchange rate policy under the conditions ordered by the Council of Ministers and to manage the official foreign reserves of the member states.

> Article 8 of the BCEAO statutes stipulates that the main objective of the central bank's monetary policy is to ensure price stability; the objective of inflation is defined by the Monetary Policy Committee. BCEAO has two types of instruments for implementing its monetary policy: key interest rates and compulsory reserves.

3.3.4.2 The BCEAO Key Interest Rates

Since 1973, BCEAO has been using two bank rates, the preferential bank rate and the normal bank rate. From 1980 onwards, given the development of an unfavourable environment in the wake of the second oil shock, the deterioration of the union terms of trade, and other shocks, management of the money market with preferential and normal bank rates was no longer appropriate. Thus in 1989, the two bank rates were replaced by a single bank rate. This bank rate was also removed from 2 December 2010, by decision of the monetary policy committee. Two key interest rates were thus set by the BCEAO monetary policy committee: the repurchase tender rate and the marginal lending window rate, which followed the pension rate. In December 2014, these rates were 2.50% and 3.50%.

3.3.4.3 Compulsory Reserves

Compulsory reserves are compulsory deposits made by financial establishments with the central bank. Whether or not remunerated, according to the country, their amount generally constitutes a percentage comprising a reserve coefficient of their outstanding deposits, typically short-term deposits.

The compulsory reserve coefficient applicable to commercial banks at the end of the third quarter of 2014 was 5%, a coefficient reduced from 7% to 5% on 16 March 2012 (Report on monetary policy in WAEMU 2014).

The total reserves maintained by the banks in the third quarter of 2014 increased by an average of 109.1 billion relative to the second quarter and rose to 1,456.4 billion during the period for establishment of the compulsory reserve expiring on 15 September 2014.

This increase resulted from the 60.1 billion boost in support to banks from the Central Bank and the positive impact of 49.0 billion in autonomous liquidity factors. BCEAO refinancing, on average, stood at 2,019.1 billion during the establishment period, reaching maturity on 15 September 2014, as against 1,959.0 billion in the second quarter. The boost in support to banks from the Central Bank made it possible to compensate for the banks' own liquidity deficit. Exclusive of Central Bank refinancing, the structural liquidity position of the banks has remained in deficit to the tune of 562.7 billion. The positive impact of the autonomous factors may essentially be attributed to the return of banknotes to bank service windows, the effect of which has been attenuated by the negative balance of outward bank transfers.

The excess reserves for the whole banking sector totaled 746.9 billion on 15 September 2014 as against 681.5 billion the previous quarter. An analysis of the data as of 15 October 2014 indicated a rise of 33.1 billion in free reserves relative to 15 September 2014. The deficits observed at the level of the compulsory reserves stood at 8.3 billion and concerned seven (7) banks at the end of the period expiring on 15 October 2014.

3.3.5 *The Lessons of Monetary Policy for the WAEMU Zone*

The monetary policy of the West African Economic and Monetary Union (WAEMU) shows that in fact no economic and monetary union has ever before followed policies described as "monetarist competitive disinflation" so rigorously. Since 1989, monetary policy has been based on increased recourse to market mechanisms, enshrining the option of indirect regulation of banking liquidity, breaking with the administrative regulation system for credit that had hitherto prevailed (Nubukpo 2007). In a rapidly changing environment in which the majority of countries in the WAEMU zone have put the wheels in motion to lay the foundations of emergence, it is a matter of urgency that the zone's monetary policy undergo therapy. The various lessons of monetary policy relate as much to the objective and mission of the central bank as to operationalization of the policy. Five (5) avenues should be explored.

3.3.5.1 *BCEAO, an Imperative Objective of Growth*

Monetary management of the WAEMU zone must be correlated with achieving economic growth for the countries in the zone. Emergence requires countries to implement audacious policies necessitating a clear choice of strategies to achieve strong and sustainable economic growth. These strategies to achieve strong growth must be integral to the main objectives of the zone's central bank. In fact, a number of authoritative voices are increasingly calling for the objective of economic growth to be explicitly integrated into the duties of central banks. Such is the case, for example, with the United States central bank, FED.

3.3.5.2 *Revision of the Inflation Target, a Necessity*

The decision of BCEAO to maintain a target inflation rate of 2% originated in the pegging of the CFA franc to the Euro, as this target is the one adopted by ECB. However, in a fixed exchange rate regime with free movement of capital, it is impossible for BCEAO to have a monetary policy sustainably different from that of the anchor zone, namely the eurozone, as Mundell's impossible trinity shows. This institutional pegging therefore constrains BCEAO in its capacity to choose its monetary policy objective.

Effectively, in a fixed exchange rate regime, inflation contributes, due to the loss of competitiveness that it entails, to the progressive deterioration of external accounts and overvaluation of the exchange rate, thus weakening the parity between the currencies. Therefore, the inflation rate of 2% adopted byBCEAO, identical to that of the European Central Bank, seems imperative in view of the constraints resulting from the existence of a fixed exchange rate between the two zones. The question of the relevance of this inflation target for the zone arose the moment that, on the one hand, studies revealed that inflation in the zone was not of monetary origin[17] and on the other, the eurozone itself found itself in a credibility crisis in the face of the current financial and monetary crisis, the remedy for which is the return of Keynesian policies with the various easing measures: QE[18] and CE.[19] Furthermore, the challenges faced by the WAEMU countries including Togo are rather more complex and the potential contribution of the currency to achieving economic growth should be able to provoke broad reflection.

The Phillips curve takes into account the arbitrage between unemployment and inflation. The rise in the inflation rate, a consequence of the expansionist monetary policy, would be the price to pay to obtain strong growth. The inflation target of 2% seemed fairly restrictive for developing economies seeking emergence.

Although there is a consensus regarding the harmful effect of inflation on growth, there is some debate concerning the optimal threshold at which inflation becomes damaging to growth. Studying the link between inflation and growth in the WAEMU zone, Combey and Nubukpo (2010) determined an optimal inflation threshold for the zone of 7.9%. Similarly, Abu Bakkar Tarawali et al. (2012) determined an optimal inflation threshold for *Zone monétaire de l'ouest* (ZMAO)[20] that was

[17] Inflation in the country owes more to climatic variables than to an excessive money supply (Doe and Diallo 1997).

[18] Quantitative Easing.

[19] Credit Easing.

[20] Ghana, Nigeria, Sierra Leone, the Gambia and Guinea.

established to be 9%. Moreover, other studies have compared the relationship between inflation and growth in developed and developing countries. The results of these studies showed that developed countries should aim for an inflation target of 2 to 3%, while the inflation threshold for developing countries was in the order of 10 to 12%. These analyses therefore suggest that BCEAO should revise its inflation target upwards.

3.3.5.3 BCEAO, a Dynamic, Active and Proactive Monetary Policy

BCEAO monetary policy suffers from two main weaknesses that compromise its effectiveness. Firstly, there is unquestionably insufficient inward reflection on the role and duties of a central bank in the context of some of the poorest developing economies in the world, and which are poorly monetized and relatively unbanked. It seems desirable that BCEAO should follow the example of the debates in progress within the central banks of industrialized countries, particularly in the context of the current international economic crisis.

An in-depth analysis of strategies to achieve strong economic growth should permit BCEAO to implement expansionist monetary policies. The Phillips curve suggests that it is possible to obtain additional economic growth resulting in a fall in unemployment, through the application of expansionist monetary policy.

One of the important lessons learned from the unconventional measures implemented by the central banks of developed market economies is that BCEAO should be more dynamic and more active to support the economic growth of the WAEMU states.

In light of the corrective measures used by the various central banks to address the 2007 crisis, BCEAO should prioritize the implementation of such proactive measures as:

- strengthening the policy mix for the strong and sustainable economic growth of the economies of the WAEMU zone;
- taking into account studies on the transmission channels of monetary policy.

3.3.5.4 *For the Future: Fixed or Flexible Exchange Rate Regimes for WAEMU?*

At a technical level, the pivotal role of the centralization of foreign exchange reserves is more necessary than ever. However, serious thought should be given to proposals to improve the system to make it more supple and flexible.

Drawing lessons from the experiences of emerging countries and based on the structural development of our economies, a certain measure of flexibility has proven indispensable for the strong and sustainable economic growth of the WAEMU countries, a guarantee of emergence. The optimum exchange rate regime for the WAEMU zone should be an exchange regime with limited flexibility, with a currency tethered to a basket of currencies in varying proportions. The currencies to be included in this basket should be chosen according to the strategic direction of external trade and our main partners. One might therefore imagine a combination made up of the United States dollar, the euro, the yuan, the pound sterling and the yen. In this basket of currency, the dollar and the euro might be found in the largest proportions. Reflection could be given to making the plan to form a single ECOWAS monetary zone a reality.

3.3.5.5 *Towards Credit Easing in the WAEMU Zone*

The emergence of the WAEMU states requires a shift in development paradigms to be taken into account. Thus, the WAEMU zone countries should implement developmentalist strategies. These strategies for the WAEMU zone should be based on:

- *An expansionist monetary policywith two priorities: consideration of price stability and economic growth.*
    - o Given the weakness of economic growth in the WAEMU zone countries relative to the other countries in the ECOWAS zone, it is of primary importance that the monetary policy implemented by BCEAO take into account economic activity. The objective of direct financing of the economic activity could be among the objectives of the central bank of the Union.
- *A strong public–private partnership (PPP)*

- o Considered a method of financing whereby a public authority calls upon private services to finance and manage a project providing or contributing to a public service, the findings demonstrate that, in the WAEMU zone, public–private partnerships are more important in the fields of telecommunications and infrastructure. In order to fight poverty effectively, multi-level partnerships should be developed. Mechanisms should be implemented to build countries' capacities and those of the various PPP players, and to ensure the promotion and integration of the culture of PPP in countries' political programmes. The prerogatives of the West African Development Bank (BOAD) Public Private Partnership Development Unit should be strengthened.

- *An audacious private sector*
  - o The private sector of the zone must leave the beaten track. Strong intervention from the private sector in the fields of agriculture and health is desirable. Entrepreneurial knowledge must be channeled by decision-makers thorough the implementation of capacity building programmes in the entrepreneurial field.
- *A less risk-avoidant financial sector to support economic activity*
  - o The level of credit in the economy is very low in the WAEMU zone countries. Inward reflection should be given to raising this level with a view to permitting adequate financing of the zone's economic activity. In order to support the economic activity, the WAEMU banking institutions should increase the financing that they grant to Non-Financial Corporations and Quasi-Corporations (SQS/NF), and more specifically to SMIs/SMEs. The financial sector is more concentrated in urban environments. It is desirable that the banks draw closer to rural environments by financing agricultural activities. Entrepreneurship should be guided by the commercial banks.
- *The primacy of growth and investment in reducing poverty*
  - o Sectors that sustain growth should be developed, notably agriculture, energy, economic infrastructure, human capital, etc. (not an exhaustive list). Investment in these sectors could

contribute to the emergence of the economies of the WAEMU zone.

- *Strengthening the statistical institutes*
    - o It is important to strengthen statistical institutes to ensure the production and use of quality data for better development planning and to improve the well-being of the population, as defining appropriate policies and strategies requires reliable data to be available.
- *Structural reforms*
    - o Structural reforms should be pursued in the WAEMU zone to further improve the business climate and increase the attractiveness of the business environment in the zone. The financial markets are underdeveloped. Strong growth in the financial sector would facilitate the financing of growth, improve financial inclusion and the capacity of the private sector to overcome a volatile environment, and increase the effectiveness of macroeconomic policies (IMF, 2013). Fiscal reforms could be envisaged to ensure fairness in the tax system, rationalize the tax base, promote voluntary consent to taxation and combat corruption, tax evasion and fraud.

3.4 Conclusion

With the beginnings of economic emergence, this study has made it possible to revisit monetary policies in developed countries, emerging countries and developing countries, more specifically the countries of the West African sub-region, in order to learn the appropriate lessons. The lessons resulting from this work, centred on five (5) points, which relaunch the debate on the relevance of taking economic growth into account in the remit of BCEAO, since the monetary angle constitutes a powerful lever for development in emerging countries.

References

ALIPUI V. (1973) *Le rôle de la monnaie dans le développement économique et social de l'Ouest Africain* Thesis, University of Rennes, p. 123.

Arellano and Bond (1991) Some tests of specification for panel data: Monte Carlo Evidence and application to employment evidence, Review of economic studies, 55, pp. 277–297. Artus P. , 2012.Arellano and Bond (1991) Some tests of specification for panel data: Monte Carlo Evidence and application to employment evidence, *Review of economic studies*, 55, pp. 277–297.

Artus P. (2012) Pourquoi les politiques monétaires non conventionnelles ont-elles marché aux Etats-Unis et pas au Japon? *Natixis, Flash Economie, Recherche économique.*

Baffes Elbadawi and O'Connel (1999) Single Equation Estimation of the Equilibrium Real Exchange Rate in Exchange Rate Misalignment, in: Hinkle and Montiel (Eds), *Concepts and Measurement for developing countries,* World Bank: Policy Research Department Washington, DC.

Bank of France (2013) Rapport de surveillance multilatérale de la zone franc.

Bank of France (2014) Rapport de surveillance multilatérale de la zone franc.

Barro (1991) Economic Growth in a Cross Section of Countries. *The Quarterly Journal of Economics.*

BCEAO (2010) *Annuaires des banques et établissements financiers de l'UMOA en 2010.*

BCEAO (2010)*Evolution de la situation économique et financière de la zone UEMOA .*

BCEAO (2010) *Evolution du financement des économies de l'UEMOA depuis 2000 et Evolution économique et monétaire dans l'UEMOA.*

Benahji (2008) *Choix des politiques de change dans les pays en développements: Etude de la compétitivité de la Tunisie* Original Scientific Paper.

Benassy-Quéré et al (2008) *Politique de change de l'euro.*

Bernanke B. S. (2009)*The Crisis and the Policy Response*, Stamp Lecture at the London School of Economics, London, United Kingdom.

Christophe Destais and Sophie Piton (2013) *L'économe Mondiale en mutation*, L'économie mondiale en 2014, CEPII.

Creel, Laurent and Le Cacheux (2007) La politique de change de la zone euro ou le hold-up tranquille de la BCE. OFCE Review, Presses de Sciences Po, pp. 7–30.

Diop and Fall (2011) La problématique du choix de régime de change dans les pays de la CEDEAO, *Document d'Etude No 20*, Direction des Prévision et des Etudes Economiques (DPEE), Ministry of Economy and Finance, Senegal.

Dupasquier, Osakwe and Thangavelu (2005) Choice of Monetary and Exchange Rate Regime in ECOWAS: An Optimum Currency Area Analysis, *SCAPE, Policy Research Working Papers series 0510,* National University of Singapore, Department of Economy.

Gali et al (2005) Robustness of the Estimates of the Hybrid New Keynesian Phillips Curve, Mimeo, New York University.

Galí G. (1999) Inflation Dynamics: A Structural Econometric Analysis *Journal of Monetary Economics 44*, pp. 195–222.

Gharbi Hanan (2005) La gestion des taux de changes dans les pays émergents, la leçon des expériences récentes, *OFCE Review* No 95, pp. 279–326.

Guthrie, J. (2001) High-Involvement Work Practices, Turnover and Productivity: Evidence From New Zealand. Academy of Management Journal, 44, pp. 180–192.

Guthrie G. and J. Wright (2000) Open Mouth Operation, *Journal of Monetary Economies*.

Hausmann, Ricardo, Lant Pritchett & Dani Rodrik (2005), Growth Accelerations. *Journal of Economic Growth*, vol. 10, No 4.

IMF (2000) *Exchange Rate Regimes in an Increasingly Integrated World Economy*

IMF (2013) *Staff Report on Common Policies for Member Countries*

Jourdon J. (2010) *La monnaie unique européenne et sa relation au développement économique et social coordonné: une analyse cliométrique*, Tome II, données empiriques sur la période 1800–2000: histoires économique & monétaire de l'Europe.

Kisu (2010) Choice of Exchange Rate Regimes for African Countries: Fixed or Flexible Exchange Rate Regimes? Perspective on Modern African Currencies.

Kose, M. A., Christopher Otrok et Eswar Prasad (2008) Cycles économiques: découplage ou convergence? *Finances & Développement*. p. 36–40.

Marc Touati (2012) *Quand la zone euro explosera* Editions du moment.

Mbaloula Marcel, La problématique de l'émergence économique des pays en voie de développement, *Revue Congolaise de Gestion* 2/ 2011 (Number 14), pp. 107–118.

Nubukpo K. (2003) *L'efficacité de la politique monétaire de la banque centrale des Etats de l'Afrique de l'Ouest*. Mimeo, Matisse, Université Paris 1 Panthéon Sorbonne.

Nubukpo K. (2007) L'efficacité de la politique monétaire en situation d'incertitude et d'extraversion: le cas de l'union économique et monétaire ouest-africain (UEMOA), *The European Journal of Development Research*, Vol. 19, No 3, September 2007, pp. 480–495.

Nubukpo K. and Combey A. (2010): Effet non linéaire de l'inflation sur la croissance dans l'UEMOA *MPRA*

Nubukpo K. (2012) *L'improvisation économique en Afrique de l'Ouest. Du coton au franc CFA*. Editions KARTALA.

OUEDRAOGO O. (1985) *Autonomie monétaire, préalable à une politique monétaire de développement. Le cas des Etats de l'UMOA*; Thesis in Economic Sciences, Paris IX Dauphine.

Rogoff, K. S. et al (2004) Evolution and Performance of Exchange Rate Regimes, *IMF Occasional Paper*, No 229.

Rotemberg and Woodford (1997) *An Optimisation Based Econometric Framework for the Evaluation of Monetary Policy* NBER Macroeconomics Annual, vol. 12.
Schumpeter (1911) *The Theory of Economic Development*, Cambridge, Mass.
Sfia Mohamed Daly (2007) Le choix de régime de change pour les économies émergentes, MPRA.

CHAPTER 4

The Euro Experience: Lessons for Africa

Joerg Bibow

4.1 Introduction

This chapter identifies and highlights the key shortcomings and failures of Europe's Economic and Monetary Union (EMU) to then apply the insights and warnings gained from that experience to the African context.

Europe's Economic and Monetary Union (EMU) represents the most advanced case of regional integration in the world. As a model, it has inspired numerous other such initiatives for regional cooperation and integration around the globe, including among developing countries. For historical reasons, certain groups of West and Central African countries (the former "CFA franc zone") have been closely tied to the euro from the beginning, namely: the West African Economic and Monetary Union (WAEMU) and the Central African Economic and Monetary Community (CEMAC). Policies and institutions prevailing under current arrangements in these two currency zones (and similarly as envisioned for certain future arrangements that also include other English-speaking countries in

J. Bibow (✉)
Skidmore College, New York, USA
e-mail: jbibow@skidmore.edu

D. Barrowclough et al. (eds.), *South–South Regional Financial Arrangements*, International Political Economy Series,
https://doi.org/10.1007/978-3-030-64576-2_4

the region) show a strong resemblance to the (Maastricht) policy regime underlying Europe's EMU.

There have always been questions concerning the suitability of the "Maastricht regime" of EMU for developing countries in Africa (and more generally). In the light of the euro experience since 1999, and especially in view of the euro area's protracted and still unresolved crisis since 2008, a thorough assessment of this issue seems timely.

Section 2 provides an overview of the current state and future prospects of regional cooperation and integration in West and Central Africa. Section 3 reviews the relevant theory and actual experiences made in Europe's EMU while section 4 distils and applies some key lessons of the euro experiment to the future of regional cooperation and integration in West and Central Africa. Section 5 summarizes the main findings and offers policy recommendations.

4.2 Regional Cooperation in West and Central Africa: History, Status Quo, and Vision for the Future

French Africa's colonial past has left its monetary mark on the continent. First created as the "Colonies françaises d'Afrique franc" in 1945, today's common meaning of "CFA franc" is: Communauté financière africaine (African Financial Community). More precisely, there exist two monetary unions in West and Central Africa that each uses a modern version of the CFA franc as their respective legal tender and both of which are tied today to the euro at a fixed parity through a long-standing convertibility guarantee by the French Treasury.[1] Sharing common colonial roots, both CFA franc monetary unions are but facets of broader agendas for regional cooperation and integration among these groups of African countries.

The West African *Franc CFA*, where CFA stands for Communauté financière africaine (African Financial Community), is issued by the Banque Centrale des États de l'Afrique de l'Ouest (Central Bank of the

[1] A similar arrangement is in place for the Comorian franc, currency of the Comores, another former French African colony. The Comores will not be part of this study. The Banque de France (2002, p. 1) refers to the "franc zone" as an "economic, monetary, and cultural area" and observes that "after attaining their independence, most of the newly-created African states decided to remain within a homogenous group characterized by a new institutional framework and a common exchange rate mechanism."

West African States; BCEAO), which is located in Dakar, Senegal. The BCEAO is a supra-national monetary authority issuing and managing the common—Franc CFA—currency shared by the eight member states of the Union Économique et Monétaire Ouest Africaine (UEMOA; West African Economic and Monetary Union, WAEMU) that was established in 1994[2], by Benin, Burkina Faso, Côte d'Ivore, Guinea-Bissau, Mali, Niger, Senegal, and Togo. Two other former French colonies in the region that were initially part of the CFA franc zone after World War Two, Guinea-Conakry and Mauritania, left the CFA franc currency zone in 1960 and 1973, respectively. Mali had also left in the 1960s but rejoined in 1984. On the other hand, the former Portuguese colony Guinea-Bissau only joined WAEMU in 1997.

The Central African *FrancCFA*, where CFA also stands for Coopération financière en Afrique centrale (Financial Cooperation in Central Africa) is issued by the Banque des États de l'Afrique Centralee (Bank of the Central African States; BEAC), located in Yaoundé, Cameroon. The BEAC is a supra-national monetary authority issuing and managing the common—Franc CFA—currency shared by six member states of the Communauté Économique et Monétaire de l'Afrique Centrale (CEMAC; Economic and Monetary Community of Central Africa, CAEMC) that was also established in 1994, namely: Cameroon, Central African Republic, Chad, Republic of Congo (Brazzaville), Equatorial Guinea, and Gabon.[3]

Indirectly, through their euro pegs, the two Franc CFA monetary unions' exchange rate currently corresponds to a 1:1 parity. Cooperation between the two monetary unions and their central banks exists in certain areas such as training and research. There is also an ongoing initiative between the BCEAO and BEAC to connect their payment systems and broader ideas for advancing financial integration exist as well. Nonetheless the two monetary unions remain separate entities, the two currencies have only legal tender status in their respective domain, and no

[2] The WAEMU Treaty of 1994 currently coexists with the earlier "West African Monetary Union" (WAMU) Treaty of 1960 (reformed a number of times, most recently in January 2007). It is planned that the two treaties will be merged eventually.

[3] Of these Equatorial Guinea is a former Spanish colony while Cameroon was a German colony until World War I, after which its territory was at first divided between France and Great Britain under League of Nations mandates.

direct convertibility guarantee exists either. In principle, the two monetary unions could part ways and chose different monetary paths in future; particularly as economic structures and developments in the two unions are diverging rather than converging (Gulde 2008). In general, it would appear that WAEMU and the BCEAO are somewhat more advanced in terms of fostering regional cooperation and integration among West African members as compared to their Central African Francophone peers.

There are also long-standing ambitions to somehow merge the predominantly Francophone WAEMU with another—predominantly Anglophone—West African monetary union (to-be!), and establish a common currency for all members of the "Economic Community of West African States" (ECOWAS/CEDEAO; see Oshikoya 2010). This vision for a possible joint West African monetary future will be briefly considered further below. In early 2015 ECOWAS undertook another step toward realizing its planned customs union by establishing a common external tariff.

As to their monetary status quo, both CFA Franc monetary unions can best be characterized as "hard pegs," though not currency boards.[4] Parities to their exchange rate anchor are fixed without any margin of variation. The most recent adjustment in the exchange rate peg(s) occurred in January 1994, when the CFA franc was devalued by 50%, from 50:1 to 100:1 vis-à-vis its French franc anchor (following over 30 years of stability). With the French franc's conversion and launch of the euro in 1999 the peg became: Franc CFA 656 for one euro. While maintaining exchange rate stability vis-à-vis their anchor, the BCEAO and BEAC do not strictly operate as currency boards by completely tying their domestic currency issuance to their foreign exchange reserve holdings with 100% backing. Instead, they enjoy some degree of freedom in fulfilling their respective central banking functions.

The BCEAO and BEAC each have a "compte d'operations" (operational account) at the French Treasury, featuring an unlimited overdraft facility, which is the external backing behind the convertibility promise. The French Treasury, in turn, lays down certain conditions for providing

[4] The IMF used to do so until it redefined "hard pegs" in 2010, restricting them to "dollarized" economies and currency boards. Under the IMF's current classification of "De Facto Exchange Rate Arrangements and Monetary Policy Frameworks" both CFA franc monetary unions are classified as "conventional pegs" that use the euro as their exchange rate anchor in monetary policy. See IMF 2014.

this external backstop for the CFA franc(s). In particular, the French Treasury requires that member states' reserves are pooled at the BCEAO and BEAC, respectively, which in turn are obliged to deposit at least 50% (65% in the case of the BEAC) of their respective net external assets with the French Treasury. Further safeguards are designed to forestall the actual use of the overdraft facility.[5]

Although the euro functions as exchange rate anchor in the monetary policy framework of the BCEAO (and similarly the BEAC[6]), the BCEAO officially pursues price stability as its primary objective. Resembling the European Central Bank's (ECB) hierarchic mandate, it is only without prejudice to price stability that the BCEAO is required to support WAEMU general economic policy. Since April 2010 the BCEAO's operational price stability target "has been defined as an annual inflation rate in the Union within a range of one percentage point (1%) above or below the central value of 2% over the next 24 months" (BCEAO, Annual Report 2013). The BCEAO announces two monetary policy interest rates, the key policy rate applying to its regular repurchase operations (repos), and the (higher) interest rate on its (discount window type) marginal lending facility. In recent years the BCEAO has operated in an environment of a structural liquidity shortfall, despite reducing its reserve requirement ratio to a uniform five-percent rate across WAEMU in 2012.[7] Similar to standard central banking practices in continental Europe, the BCEAO implements its liquidity operations mainly through regular (weekly and monthly) repos in which the liquidity-seeking banks rely primarily on government debt securities as collateral. The issuance

[5] There is a 20% minimum coverage of sight liabilities at the central bank by foreign exchange reserves and, in the case of the BEAC, a ceiling of 20% of last year's tax revenues of any central bank lending to governments; while the BCEAO has been prohibited from any such lending to governments since 2001. The operational account last went heavily into deficit in 1992 when it was suspended at some point, leading up to the 1994 CFA franc devaluation. It appears that the operational account has not been in deficit again ever since. See Banque de France 2002, Veyrune 2007, Hallet 2008).

[6] In the following we will mainly focus on the WAEMU and BCEAO as the BEAC is lagging behind in its official publications. The BCEAO's most recent published annual report is for the year 2014, the BEAC's for the year 2009.

[7] Prior to December 2010, when the reserve requirement ratio was set at a uniform 7% rate, reserve requirements varied across WAEMU (Sy 2006, IMF 2013).

of *national* public debt securities (mostly T-bills) has been instrumental to the development of local money markets and banks' liquidity management (Sy 2006, 2007).

In a world of unhindered, costless arbitrage one would expect WAEMU money market rates to closely follow money market rates in Europe's EMU as determined by the ECB. In practice, while money market interest rates in both areas do generally follow common trends, sizeable interest rate differentials are observed. In fact, differentials vis-à-vis euro interest rates have varied over time and money market interest rates (and financial conditions more broadly) also vary significantly within WAEMU, reflecting the fact that WAEMU's (extra-regional) capital mobility and (intra-regional) financial integration remain low today. Capital controls hinder the former. The state of financial system development hinders both. In principle, these two factors create some policy space for the BCEAO despite the existing external constraint posed by the hard euro peg (Veyrune 2007, Dufrénot 2011). At the same time, financial underdevelopment may limit or undermine the effectiveness and uniformity of conventional interest rate policies while, ultimately, policy constraints on both monetary and fiscal policies can arise through WAEMU's external position—highlighting the dangers of currency overvaluation.

Manifold initiatives are planned and/or in the process of implementation that are designed to foster the development and integration of the WAEMU financial system. The BCEAO has authority in payment system policy and also plays a role in financial stability policy. In particular, the BCEAO supports the WAEMU Banking Commission in the sphere of bank regulation and supervision, and it can (and does) act as "lender of last resort" in crisis situations (even if it has no formal authority to do so). In this regard, too, the BCEAO's policy space is enlarged by the lack of global financial integration on the one hand and the fact that it is not operating like a strict currency board regime on the other.

The tight constraints that hard peg regimes generally pose on domestic macro policymaking are therefore somewhat alleviated by the element of flexibility that the French Treasury's external backstop of the CFA franc(s) allows for (compared to strict currency board regimes). Apart from permitting some policy flexibility, the arrangement with the French Treasury also features a kind of seigniorage sharing scheme as the BCEAO's reserves held with the French Treasury are remunerated at 100 basis points above the ECB's key policy rate, while the BCEAO also gets compensated for valuation losses on its reserves resulting from euro depreciation.[8] Overall, the French Treasury's backstop of the peg should also facilitate some economy in foreign exchange reserve holdings. The arrangement thereby enables some cost savings with regard to WAEMU's foreign exchange reserve holdings.

These favorable aspects of the—French Treasury-anchored—link to the euro need to be weighed against the external influence on the WAEMU macro regime design and institution-building as well as macro policy-making arising, at least partly, through the conditionality of the French Treasury's external backstop provision. In many ways, the euro and Europe's EMU have also served as a model for regional integration in the former CFA franc zone. For long this external influence on shaping WAEMU's presence and future was widely perceived as altogether benign and favorable, as fostering stability and growth. Especially in light of the euro crisis experience this presumption may need to be reconsidered.

Another relevant question is whether currency stability vis-à-vis the euro is really the best policy option for WAEMU compared to either some alternative external currency anchor or greater exchange rate flexibility.[9] The WAEMU inflation record over the past few decades shows relatively low inflation and inflation variability compared to other countries in the region and sub-Saharan Africa in general. But favorable inflation performance by itself does not necessarily favor growth and development. In fact, WAEMU's growth performance and broader development in terms of structural transformation compares rather unfavorably to its Sub-Saharan peers (IMF 2010, Kinda and Mlachila 2011). WAEMU even appears to have experienced some degree of reverse-industrialization (from an already very low level). Based on WAEMU's "low inflation, low growth" record under its euro hard peg there would appear to be some prima facie scope for more growth-friendly macro policies in the region.

[8] Historically, France's role as external anchor and stabilizer in the region has gone beyond the currency sphere and also featured fiscal transfers and even military engagements (most recently in support of the fight against Boko Haram and al Qaeda linked militants). While France has lost much of its role as WAEMU's foremost trade partner it remains important both in terms of official aid and private remittances. Yehoue (2005, 2007) argues that France has acted as a shock absorber by varying its official aid anti-cyclically.

[9] Qureshi and Tsangarides 2012 find evidence for trade-generating effects of pegs over more flexible exchange arrangements that are especially strong in Africa.

While the WAEMU macro policy regime and its peg to the euro are up for reconsideration, this study will not principally challenge or question the ambition for deeper regional cooperation and integration in the region. Both the literature and the experience gained on a mission to the BCEAO for this project in August 2012 have confirmed to us that a strong sense of commitment to a shared future exists in the region. The rationale for these regional ambitions goes well beyond the realm of economics—which will however be the sole basis and source of assessment in this study.

Furthermore, we need to acknowledge right away that the idea of a common ECOWAS currency would create new challenges of its own. To begin with, this option raises the question whether the French Treasury would stand ready to extend its current external backstop to a broader and more heterogeneous grouping of countries; assuming this would be both desirable and desired. The analysis in the following will therefore mainly focus on WAEMU as arguably the most advanced case of regional cooperation in Africa today. A key question is whether and to what extent Europe's EMU should continue to serve as model and inspiration for deeper WAEMU cooperation and integration.

Today, the far-reaching influence of Europe's EMU on developments in West Africa is not only visible in terms of the peculiar design of the WAEMU policy regime, but also as far as the focussation on "convergence," *as defined by peculiar criteria*, is concerned. Policy prescriptions for WAEMU policymakers (and quite similarly for policymakers of other ECOWAS countries that in 2001 established the "West African Monetary Zone" (WAMZ; including: Gambia, Ghana, Guinea, Liberia, Nigeria, and Sierra Leone) which they aspire to turn into a "West African Monetary Union (WAMU), later to be merged with WAEMU) clearly take their cue from the "stability-oriented" Maastricht wisdom of the European EMU model.

In particular, in 1999, in time with the euro's launch, a set of "convergence criteria" and a process of "multilateral surveillance" over macroeconomic policies and performances of member states were put in place (under the union's "Convergence, Stability, Growth, and Solidarity Pact") to assure convergence and cohesion within WAEMU.[10] The

[10] "The Maastricht criteria have become something of a model for African countries. Thus, for instance, when in April 2000, in Accra, Ghana, the leaders of five West African countries declared their intention to establish a monetary union by January 2003, the

convergence criteria have been revised more recently, as will be discussed further below. We will argue that the euro experiment has provided some important lessons for WAEMU that may warrant a more fundamental rethink rather than mere tinkering.

The next section highlights some crucial experiences gained in Europe under the euro, especially in recent crisis years. The subsequent section will discuss what lessons—and warnings—the euro experience holds in store for regional cooperation and integration in the WAEMU region (and beyond).

4.3 Europe's Economic and Monetary Union: Theory and Actual Experiences

The euro experience has been rather sobering. Even prior to the still unresolved crisis that started as a global financial crisis in 2008 but then turned into a more regional affair in 2010, the euro area's economic performance had been less than stellar. In the mid-2000s, in the context of the record global boom, Martin Wolf (Financial Times, 27 March 2007) observed that the euro area "was the sick giant of the world economy." The euro area really only started to participate in the global boom when that was on its final leg; a brief encounter that was followed by severe crisis and protracted stagnation. The euro area was a laggard during the global boom and a massive drag during the recovery from the global crisis. Essentially the euro area has trouble generating home-made growth and seems peculiarly ill-equipped at countering recessions and crises. As a result, it is conspicuously reliant on global growth.

The rationale for European integration in general and for Economic and Monetary Union in particular has always spanned beyond economics. Some political actors saw the euro as a means for deeper political integration. Some even considered the euro as a means to secure lasting peace in Europe. As far as the expected economic benefits of the euro

extent to which the criteria were influence by the Maastricht plan was self-evident" (UNECA 2008, p. 88). Hallet (2008, p. 16) refers to "the EU as a blueprint for macroeconomic surveillance in the CFA franc zone." See also Hitaj and Onder 2013. UNCTAD 2007 and UNECA 2008 offer a more balanced view. An important difference is that in Europe's EMU the convergence criteria provided entry conditions for participation in a new monetary union, while in WAEMU's case the agreed criteria aim at fostering deeper regional economic integration and convergence (rather than divergence) in order to sustain a preexisting monetary union.

were concerned, the European Commission emphasized microeconomic efficiency gains through transaction cost savings on the one hand and macroeconomic stability and growth gains stemming from the peculiar "stability-oriented" design of the Maastricht policy regime of EMU on the other. A related view held that by pooling sovereignty and joining regional forces the union would become less dependent on, and less vulnerable to, international shocks—and more of a global force to reckon with, too. As far as the perceived risks of the common currency project were concerned, "optimum currency area" (OCA) theory provided the general point of reference.

OCA theory has gone through a number of reincarnations. The original contributions by Mundell (1961), McKinnon (1963), and Kenen (1969) emphasized the risk of "asymmetric shocks" as destabilizing the considered currency union and went on to identify factors that would either affect the probability and severity of such shocks or ways to counter them; either through market adjustment or by the use of specific policies. The factors identified as vital by OCA include: international factor mobility and wage-price flexibility, openness and inter-industry factor mobility, trade specialization/diversification, and fiscal arrangements.

While the original OCA contributions still had the distinctive Keynesian flavor of the 1960s, the focus of attention shifted toward issues of policy discipline and credibility in the 1980s. More generally, as the "time inconsistency" idea took hold, "discretion" in policymaking became widely seen as costly, while "rule-based" policymaking rose in esteem accordingly (Tavlas 1993). Macro stabilization policies were downgraded, market adjustment and flexibility promoted in prominence. Finally, the 1990s then added the idea that countries' degree of fitness for sharing a common currency was partly "endogenous" in the sense that the very act of sharing a common currency would itself tend to foster both deeper integration and business cycle synchronicity among currency union members (Frankel and Rose 1997; Rose 2000, Mongelli 2002). If anything, these ideas encouraged neglecting the need for macroeconomic stabilization even more.

In accordance with the German narrative of the country's economic success under the deutschmark and the Bundesbank as its independent monetary guardian of stability, price stability and fiscal discipline became the corner stone of the Maastricht regime of EMU. From this perspective, it is economic policy rather than the economy that needs to be stabilized. The state should establish the market order but not interfere in market processes, the German ordoliberal mantra goes. The 1980s reincarnation of OCA theory with its fascination for discipline and credibility, rather timely within the context of Europe's push toward the euro, seemed well aligned with these German views (and the neoliberal Zeitgeist more generally too). From a German perspective it did not seem problematic that euro area member states would at the same time lose national control over monetary and exchange rate policies and also see their national fiscal policy "disciplined," i.e., severely constrained. If anything, this was seen as a welcome guarantor of stability—while, on the German view, price stability is believed to somehow also cause growth (Bibow 2009, 2013a).

On this view, then, the absence of any deliberate aggregate demand management, featuring a suitable mix of monetary and fiscal policies, does not constitute an alarming regime deficiency, but appears to provide a growth-enhancing safeguard of monetary dominance. A neoliberal rationalization along 1980s OCA lines might then suggest "structural reforms" directed at perfecting market flexibility as a *substitute* for macroeconomic demand management—suggesting that Europe's EMU could survive and prosper without proper macro management if only its markets, especially its labor markets, were made sufficiently flexible. As it turned out, building Europe's EMU on the German model amounted to little else but institutionalized mercantilism.

Even before the launch of the euro OCA theory was subjected to a fundamental chartalist critique (Goodhart 1998; Godley 1992, for instance). From a chartalist perspective the focus of OCA theory on money as a means of exchange and on currency union as an advisable means to reduce transaction costs (unless deep-seated rigidities hinder market adjustment) is much beside the point. Against the European Commission's marketing slogan "One Market, One Money," chartalists, viewing "money as a creature of the state," see the vital connection instead as: "One State, One Money." Therefore, from a chartalist perspective, Europe's unique adventure of combining a common currency and monetary policy with national fiscal policies seemed to stand on rather shaky grounds from the beginning.

The euro regime's essential flaw and ultimate source of vulnerability is the decoupling of central bank and treasury institutions in the euro currency union. The divorce of monetary and fiscal policies is leaving all players vulnerable. Lacking a central bank partner, the national treasuries issue debt that is subject to default and hence runs. Equally, lacking a Euro Treasury partner and common euro treasury debt, the ECB became subject to legal challenges of its quasi-fiscal policies as applied to national debts.

German ordoliberals may see the "denationalized" euro currency as a dream come true. By contrast, from a chartalist perspective, a currency union in which the vital treasury-central bank axis of power is absent looks more like a nightmare—an inherently vulnerable and ultimately nonviable construct. Members of such a currency union do not only lose national control over monetary and exchange rate policies, they lose their fiscal sovereignty as well; since, under a common currency, they effectively issue their national debts in a foreign currency (a source of vulnerability also known as "original sin" in the developing country context). The strength of a sovereign currency issuer derives from the pairing of two institutions, a debt-issuing treasury and a money-issuing central bank.

The euro authorities have yet to come to grips with this most vital defect of the euro currency union. Series of misdiagnosis and misguided policies based on them have left the euro area stuck in depression: eight years after the start of the crisis domestic demand is still below its pre-crisis level and unemployment remains extremely high. The euro currency union represents a first-order economic policy calamity in the world economy today. In light of this dismal experience considering the euro currency union as a blueprint for prosperity in Africa is inhumanly optimistic.

The euro authorities first blamed their fate on Wall Street's reckless financial engineers, completely ignoring that euro area banks and the City of London stood at the very center of the very activities that led to the global financial crisis of 2007–09. The "innocent bystander" myth then turned into the "fiscal profligacy" myth when events in Greece gave birth to the convenient narrative of a "sovereign debt crisis" (Pisani-Ferry 2014). Finally, as member states in the euro area "periphery" were falling over like dominos, the blame zoomed in on their supposedly irresponsible "loss of competitiveness" under the euro. Policy prescriptions thus suited the German preoccupation with competitiveness: wage deflation paired with area-wide fiscal austerity, joined by a central bank that is always scared of inflation, were held to boost confidence and growth.

Unsurprisingly the chosen macro policy mix suffocated euro area domestic demand instead—declining for straight eight quarters in 2011–2013! As witnessed by its soaring current account surplus, external demand provided the euro area's sole lifeline; partly exporting the deflationary consequences of its dysfunctional policy regime and ill-guided policies.

In preparing the ground for distilling some crucial lessons from this experience for WAEMU (and related or similar initiatives in Africa), the following five critical blunders may be singled out as the root causes behind the failure of the euro currency union and the gigantic economic and social costs that the failed euro experiment has entailed.

The first blunder actually started long before the euro with the "Single Market Programme" of the late 1980s that was meant to complete the "common [European] market" by 1992. Full financial integration through all-round liberalization was an important part of the endeavor, with the promise that this would lead to a more efficient allocation of resources and deeper risk sharing. In essence, Europe embarked on market integration without parallel policy integration.

All-round market liberalization meant undermining the national authorities' control over national markets—but without simultaneously establishing proper supra-national control over the common financial market. The European Commission already had authority in the domain of competition and state-aid policies. But regarding financial regulation and supervision the approach was: minimum harmonization cum mutual recognition. Essentially, the national authorities, including the national central banks that are part of the Eurosystem, stayed in charge—albeit lacking the necessary powers, especially once the euro also divorced the national fiscal and monetary authorities.

And this once again highlights the second crucial blunder, which was already identified above as the ultimate flaw of the euro regime: the fiscal-monetary divorce. This issue came to the forefront under crisis conditions when it was dubbed the "bank-sovereign doom-loop." As the chartalist critique of OCA theory had stressed, banks and their sovereign are deeply interconnected in terms of their liquidity and solvency status. Governments rely on banks as lenders and investors. Banks rely on both the central bank as lender of last resort for liquidity support and their sovereign for potential solvency support. If either systemic banks' or the sovereign's own credit rating drops sharply, this will drag the other party down as well. Runs on banks and/or the sovereign will loom large, and for a national treasury lacking a national central bank as liquidity backstop, illiquidity can quickly turn into insolvency. The euro "doom-loop" got further amplified as the real economy was hit by a credit crunch and untimely austerity.

Europe's ongoing "banking union" project is meant to overcome the "doom loop." A Single Supervisory Mechanism and a Single Resolution Mechanism were put in place recently, each featuring lead roles for the ECB. In future "bail-in" of creditors is supposed to forestall treasury "bail-outs" on taxpayers' behalf. Alas, while this may work for individual banks, it will most likely fail to halt and contain systemic events. The European Stability Mechanism is only a lightweight fiscal firewall. And banking union is still lacking a common fiscal backstop for its deposit insurance and bank resolution funds; remaining national for now. In short, the banking union that was meant to complement Europe's currency union remains incomplete without fiscal union. Europe's "doom-loop" may seem dormant for now, but it lives on.

Two further blunders were already apparent in pre-crisis times. For one thing, the absence of proper aggregate demand management left the euro area incapable of generating sufficient home-grown demand and thus overly reliant on the external environment. For another, in their blind adoration of competitiveness strive, the authorities failed to prevent the occurrence of persistent divergences in competitiveness positions inside the currency union and the corresponding buildup of imbalances. In other words, the euro area proved both incapable of dealing with symmetric shocks and preventing—wholly preventable—(endogenous) asymmetric shocks (Bibow 2006, 2012).

These two blunders actually reinforced each other as stagnation befell the core of the euro area following the 2001 global slowdown. Facing the "excessive deficit procedure" under the SGP, Germany added fresh rounds of fiscal austerity to its notorious wage repression policy that had begun in the second half of the 1990s. As a result, domestic demand shrunk for years while Germany ramped up cumulative competitive gains vis-à-vis its euro partners and became wholly reliant on exports for its meager growth. The EMU policy regime further amplified intra-area divergences while euphoric capital flows enabled the buildup of imbalances: Germany's current account surplus soared to over 7% of GDP, euro crisis countries (to-be) ran up deficits of around 10% of GDP; as their net international investment positions deteriorated to around negative 100% of GDP. These divergent internal developments turned Europe's currency union into an accident waiting to happen.

The final blunder featured the before-mentioned series of misdiagnoses and the pursuit of counterproductive policies and institutional reforms once the inevitable implosion of imbalances occurred and full-blown crisis erupted. Following a small initial fiscal stimulus in 2009–10, the euro authorities embraced area-wide austerity in the course of 2010. Adjustment was lacking symmetry and supportive macro policies. Crisis countries were forced into "internal devaluation" while Germany kept fighting "internal revaluation." The ECB proved fairly creative in meeting the banks' surging liquidity needs that was concentrated in euro crisis countries hit by a "sudden reversal" type of event. But that alone did not prevent stark financial fragmentation inside the currency union as contagion spread among vulnerable sovereigns and the "doom-loop" played out. Overall, the ECB's monetary policy stance was grossly inadequate. In 2011 the ECB even prematurely hiked its policy rates twice. All along regime reforms focused on further tightening the fiscal screws as fiscal profligacy and moral hazard were wrongly seen as the root cause of all troubles.

It is very clear today that the euro has neither fostered joint prosperity nor cohesion among its members. Economically, the euro is a first-order policy failure. Politically, the euro has not served as a means toward political union and regional unity but quite the opposite. Today, Europe is not moving toward but further away from its declared ideal of "an ever-closer union of the peoples of Europe." No doubt the euro experience offers important lessons—and vital warnings—for WAEMU (and beyond).

4.4 What Lessons Does the Euro Experience Have in Store for Africa?

There have always been questions concerning the suitability of the "Maastricht regime" of EMU for developing countries in general and the African member countries of the CFA Franc zone(s) in particular. In the light of the euro experience since 1999, and especially in view of the euro area's protracted depression since 2008, a reassessment of this issue is timely. That said, in view of vast existing economic differences between the currency unions, a 1:1 translation of the euro experience into lessons for WAEMU seems hardly possible. Similarly, any reforms of WAEMU institutions and policies—the design and formulation of which is currently highly influenced by the same ideas that originally informed the euro regime—are unlikely to happen overnight either.

What we are aiming at in the following, then, is an analysis of the most pertinent risks and challenges that WAEMU will likely be facing under its current policy regime and how the region's future challenges may be best met by cautiously reorienting the path of institution-building and policy-formulation going forward.

No doubt the (price-) stability-(only-) oriented euro regime has a poor growth record—by far the worst in the developed world. There is a clear risk of "spilling over" to WAEMU. The euro regime's "presence" in WAEMU goes well beyond the euro peg as such, but also includes the "strings attached" to the peg, both in terms of institutions and policies as well as an intellectual force more generally. The euro crisis presents WAEMU with the double-task of emancipating itself from the wisdom of Maastricht while exploring the available options for regulating and managing the region's development and transformation within a more growth-friendly policy regime.

Currently the WAEMU region is very poor by any standard, whether measured in U.S. dollars, in purchasing power parity terms, or based on broader measures such as the United Nation's (UN) Human Development Index, for instance. Severe poverty is pervasive in the region. The WAEMU economy and its (intra and extra-regional) trade currently represent very small shares of the world economy; small also relative to France and the euro area. At roughly 25% of GDP agriculture is the largest sector of the economy in terms of employment and its export structures are highly specialized; coffee, cacao, seed cotton, cashews, and groundnuts are the most important agricultural commodities. Mining too focuses on a narrow range of minerals (gold, uranium, and phosphate, for instance) as well as oil (the production of which started in Niger a few years ago). In general, the transformation of the economy away from agriculture (including widespread subsistence farming) toward industry and services appears to have largely stalled for some time.

Meanwhile some large foreign financial institutions (mainly of French origin) as well as Pan-African institutions (mainly of Moroccan and Nigerian origin) have established subsidiaries in the region (see Sy 2006, 2007, IMF 2015). But the banking and financial system in general remains underdeveloped both in terms of the provision of basic financial services to households and channels of credit to businesses (Kpodar and Gbenyo 2010, IMF 2013). Despite long-standing initiatives for regional cooperation and integration both intra-regional trade in products as well as financial integration remain fairly low. Political instability is a recurrent theme in the region too.

Currently home to a population of 113, UN (medium variant) population projections for the WAEMU region show an increase to 287 million by 2050. (The current ECOWAS population of 349 million is projected to reach 789 million by that time, CEMAC's current 49 million is projected to grow to 108 million). Apart from fast population growth, if any significant degree of development and catching up in incomes were to continue, which is an urgent requirement, the implied shift in the balance in economic weight between WAEMU and France would raise questions concerning the French Treasury's backstopping of the current regime, specifically the euro peg through its unlimited overdraft facility. This would be even more so the case if the envisioned ECOWAS monetary union became reality. Clearly the euro peg is not an optimal long-term solution for the region.

But even today the suitability of the euro peg may be questioned. Traditionally trade of the former French colonies that constitute WAEMU was predominantly with France. Today, however, WAEMU's trade share with the euro area as a whole has shrunk to only roughly one third.[11] The U.S., China, India, and other emerging and developing countries have gained much in importance. Accordingly, the U.S. dollar is at least as important as the euro to WAEMU's external trade, especially when the dollar's predominant role in commodity pricing and China's de facto peg to the U.S. dollar are also taken into account. This factor would speak in favor of pegging the CFA franc to a currency basket (consisting largely of the U.S. dollar and the euro) rather than the euro alone in order to avoid unwarranted sharp swings and protracted misalignments in external competitiveness as have occurred in the past (affecting WAEMU more than the euro area itself; Longkeng Ngouana 2012).

One such episode happened in the late 1980s when WAEMU suffered an external double-blow owing to a negative terms-of-trade shock and U.S. dollar weakness. It is easy to blame the ensuing crisis of the early 1990s that led to the CFA franc devaluation in 1994 on fiscal profligacy. On this view WAEMU member governments simply failed to keep their fiscal houses in order, partly relying on banks as temporary cover-up that later needed to be bailed out. A more comprehensive assessment may

[11] In February 2014 WAEMU as well as CEMAC each adopted an Economic Partnership Agreement with the European Union.

need to acknowledge though that the French franc peg left WAEMU in a tight spot at the time, with external competitiveness and export revenues getting squeezed and public finances deteriorating largely as a consequence. The 1994 devaluation then restored competitiveness and set the stage for recovery in the region (IMF 1996, 1998, Klau 1998, Boogaerde and Tsangarides 2005, Metzger 2008).

Another such episode occurred in the 2000s (see Abdih and Tsangarides 2010; Hallet 2008; Gnimassoun 2012, Couharde et al. 2012, for instance) when the euro appreciated sharply after 2001. The euro area's sluggish growth together with the appreciation of WAEMU's real effective exchange rate kept WAEMU lagging behind the global boom. Political instability and protracted recession in Côte d'Ivore provided an additional brake on the region's growth at the time (Egoume and Nayo 2011). The subsequent global and euro crises then hardly helped either, at least initially. More recently, however, euro weakness together with a sharp easing in global and regional financial conditions may have handed a welcome window of opportunity to WAEMU where growth has accelerated since 2011. This also owed to a return of political stability and growth in Côte d'Ivore.

In reconsidering the hard peg to the euro another downside is that the peg requires WAEMU to keep inflation at two percent (or even lower) in order to prevent competitiveness losses vis-à-vis the euro area. This is an extremely low inflation target level for a group of poor developing countries (UNCTAD 2014). In fact, in view of the global crisis (and "liquidity trap") experiences of recent years, it is once again controversial whether 2% inflation may not be even too low a target level in advanced economies (Blanchard et al. 2010). Unless political economy is such that a very tight rein can be kept on wage developments at all times an economy experiencing vast transformations of its structures and rise of its non-tradable sector is likely to generate faster inflation than 2% simply as a concomitant phenomenon of growth and structural transformation *in equilibrium*—so that keeping inflation lower risks acting as a monetary restraint on growth.[12]

[12] That said, China provides an example of fast-track growth and development at low inflation (or even temporary deflation); similar to West Germany's post-war reconstruction at low inflation (Bibow 2013a). Arguably, in both cases low inflation was part of a mercantilist development strategy.

Of course, the single-minded focus on price stability in the euro area with its "spill-over effects" on WAEMU through the euro peg also provides the rationale for the utmost emphasis on fiscal discipline. This is certainly not a call for limitless wasteful public spending, which would be bound to cause inflation rather than development. Instead, we merely wish to emphasize that the public sector and specifically public infrastructure investment have a vital role to play in development in general, and that their creative financing, involving the central bank, banks, and public debt markets, is also a crucial factor in the development of the financial system in particular. In the monetary union of developing countries at hand here an additional challenge is to determine whether coordination of national fiscal policies, featuring some scope for national flexibility in response to country-specific shocks, may be sufficient to support macroeconomic stability and development, or whether some central fiscal capacity may have to be established, and, if yes, of what scope.

Recall here that this issue is also at the very heart of the failure of the euro experiment. Europe's EMU failed—by design—to assure an appropriate fiscal stance and macro policy mix for the union as a whole. Preoccupied with disciplining member countries' fiscal policies, this critical imbalance left the union's economy rudderless and vulnerable. The monetary-fiscal divorce and absence of a central fiscal capacity then also left the euro authorities impotent in countering the fallout of the unfolding financial and economic crisis (Bibow 2013b,2015b).

The chartalist critique of OCA theory calls for a central fiscal capacity rather than mere coordination of national fiscal policies. This is vital both for macro policy reasons and as a fiscal backstop of any "banking union" deserving that name. Currency unions, like national economies, are subject to symmetric and asymmetric shocks, including financial crises.

To begin with, as WAEMU develops, it will likely remain subject to *common/symmetric shocks* (of external or internal origin). Potentially these may be addressed to some extent by the common monetary policy—unless the exchange rate and financial account regimes leave no such policy space at all. Ideally, however, WAEMU should move toward properly pairing monetary and fiscal policies in defense against common shocks. Even if any meaningful capacity for proper countercyclical demand management by fiscal means may remain elusive in the foreseeable future, the capability to at least maintain steady public spending, especially public infrastructure investment, would itself go a long way toward maintaining growth momentum. And the smaller the monetary policy space, the greater the need to develop the capacity to at least maintain steady public spending under adverse conditions.

In addition, WAEMU will also likely remain subject to *asymmetric shocks* including sizeable terms-of-trade shocks). In this regard, the issue is whether some fiscal transfer mechanism should be established, designed to stabilize, but not level, incomes inside the currency union, thereby preventing internal divergences and regional destabilization.[13]

Asymmetric shocks do not need to be exogenous or external in character, they may also arise endogenously or purely from the internal workings of the currency union itself. In fact, in the case of Europe's EMU, the real matter was not that the currency union was actually hit by any proper asymmetric shock as analyzed in the OCA literature. Instead, it was the failure to forestall persistent internal trends that would endogenously degenerate into (preventable) asymmetric shocks over time.

In case of WAEMU the risk of proper (exogenous) asymmetric shocks seems significantly higher currently, while the endogenous variety that proved calamitous in the euro area may be less likely to arise and develop into any major force given that both trade and financial integration are so much lower in WAEMU at this point. Market integration and policy integration need to advance in parallel. Specifically, the need to develop safeguards against internal divergences in competitiveness positions, driven by national wage and unit-labor cost trends in particular, will become an urgent matter as regional trade and financial integration progress. "Negative" policy coordination, designed to prevent divergences, may not be sufficient. "Positive" policy coordination, designed to actively promote convergence through common policies and instruments, may be required to secure long-term cohesion.

At least in one regard WAEMU appears to enjoy a head start over Europe's EMU. Already in 1994, the union established a common (WAMU) "Banking Commission" that is in charge of area-wide banking regulation and supervision. Europe's failure to complement market integration with parallel policy integration, particularly in the financial

[13] A vast empirical literature exists on the prevalence of asymmetric shocks in the region. See, for instance, Bayoumi and Ostry 1997, Tabsoba 2009, IMF 2013b. Empirical research in the European context suggests that a small fiscal transfer budget specifically designed for stabilization can make a big difference (see Pisani-Ferry, et al. 1993). The IMF (2014, p. 62) makes a similar case for WAEMU specifying fiscal transfers of around 1% of GDP as quite sufficient. See also Adedeji and Williams 2007.

domain, proved a major mistake. Following the principle of mutual recognition, the national supervisory authorities were effectively issuing their supervisees "European passports." Nationally-supervised banks then embarked on adventurous regional (and global) business expansion and wholesale banking markets integrated deeply—at least until crisis struck. As bank losses mounted contagion spread fast—but saw the national authorities struggling to stem the plight. Worse, for lack of policy tools and/or firepower, supervisory initiatives to "ring-fence" their own national banks amplified pressures elsewhere in the system, causing financial fragmentation in its trail. System-wide lending of last resort on the part of the ECB relieved liquidity shortages of banks but cannot resolve solvency issues affecting banks and/or their sovereigns.

It is therefore noteworthy that in WAEMU financial policy integration has preceded the process of financial market integration and may also partly foster progress of financial market development in the first place. With the common Banking Commission in charge of area-wide banking regulation and supervision, other related common initiatives include deposit insurance and bank resolution. In this regard, the union has recently established a common deposit insurance fund and a common financial stability fund, which have yet to become fully operational, while the BCEAO appears to ready itself to play the lead role with respect to macro-prudential supervision and overall financial stability.

This is not to suggest that these important financial system matters have really been solved satisfactorily at this point. Just as the financial system remains underdeveloped and financial integration low at this time, the above aspects of financial system policy only exist in rudimentary forms. Moreover, prudential standards appear to be low in WAEMU and non-performing loans high at this point (IMF 2016). But at least conceptually the authorities are pursuing market integration and policy integration in parallel, which would avoid the precarious mismatch that arose as one of the key blunders of Europe's EMU; playing catch-up today with its belated "banking union" project.

That said, even if WAEMU succeeded in establishing the above components of its banking union—complementing monetary union—more in line with the ongoing process of financial development and integration, the WAEMU banking union would still remain incomplete without some form of common fiscal backstop empowered to deal with systemic solvency threats. From a chartalist perspective this gap leads us to the most fundamental issue with regard to the long-run viability of WAEMU:

the need to establish a central fiscal capacity as a partner of the BCEAO. To repeat: the lack of a central fiscal authority—the monetary-fiscal divorce—is the key flaw of Europe's EMU. As the process of regional economic and financial integration progresses, and especially as the option of severing the CFA Franc's tight peg to the euro is being considered, WAEMU will need to complement its monetary union with fiscal union by establishing some form of central fiscal authority. To function as backstop for WAEMU's banking union is only one of the reasons behind this vital requirement.

Other important reasons are both macroeconomic and microeconomic in nature. The foremost macro policy reason is to enable the setting of an appropriate fiscal stance (and macro policy mix) for WAEMU as a whole, while alleviating the risk of national fiscal policies as either causing or amplifying intra-regional divergences.

The foremost microeconomic reason is that establishing a truly common financial market while fostering financial development critically depends on the existence of a common safe asset. A common safe asset serves as the foundation of a common term structure of risk-free interest rates. It can be provided in the most straight-forward way through issuance by a common fiscal authority. In addition, both in light of the euro experience and also in view of the development challenges facing WAEMU, it appears to me that it would be best to focus the responsibility of the common fiscal authority on safeguarding adequate and steady public infrastructure investment throughout WAEMU. Securing steady infrastructure investment is key to promoting balanced development throughout the region.

Currently the WAEMU authorities do not seem to envision any such move toward fiscal union. Instead, the sole attention of the current fiscal regime is on disciplining national fiscal policies. Similar to the euro experience WAEMU therefore risks that the fiscal regime currently in place will (continue to) restrain growth and development.

For example, the new "convergence criteria" agreed in early 2015 and supposed to be met by 2019 as part of the revised surveillance framework remain wholly inadequate for securing steady growth and development; nor WAEMU's long-term viability for that sake. The new "first-order" convergence criteria[14] require a public debt ratio that does not exceed

[14] There are also two "second-order" convergence criteria, namely to raise tax revenues of at least 20% of GDP and to respect a ceiling of 35% for wages and salaries as a share

70% of GDP, budget deficits that are not greater than 3% of GDP, and inflation that does not exceed 3%. Note the conspicuous *asymmetry* of all these definitions, only ceilings but no floors are stated, and also consider the provision in the BCEAO's statutes (in place since 2001) that prohibits *any* central bank lending to the state (so-called "monetary financing").[15]

The odd asymmetry of these provisions reflects Maastricht wisdom as inspired by the "ghost of Weimar": an all-pervasive fear of fiscal dominance and hyperinflation. Asymmetry in the design of fiscal institutions and policies is seriously misplaced, in fact dangerous. The same holds for the inflation ceiling. Asymmetry yields neither stability nor growth. It is symmetry in macroeconomic policy design and approach which is key for both growth and stability.

Starting with the inflation ceiling, members of a currency union need to align their national inflation rates with the common inflation target, as currently defined by the BCEAO as 2% (with a one-percentage point band). No persistent divergences *in either direction* by individual member countries from the 2% target can be tolerated; unless any real need for restoring intra-union competitiveness positions exists. It took less than a decade of persistent 2–3 percentage point differentials in unit-labor cost trends (between Germany and euro crisis countries) to yield bloated imbalances that have lastingly undermined Europe's EMU.

In Europe, deep trade and financial integration created huge *direct* exposures between creditor and debtor countries. In WAEMU fragilities are currently more likely to arise *indirectly* with divergences in competitiveness positions largely showing up as diverging extra-regional external positions; without necessarily involving extensive direct exposures among WAEMU members. Yet the underlying problem is quite the same: as individual member countries' inflation rates persistently diverge from the common 2% norm, in either direction, both the common CFA franc exchange rate and common monetary policy stance as set by the BCEAO deviate more and more from the "one-size-fits-all" requirement

of tax revenue. WAEMU's public sector is as underdeveloped as the rest of the economy. Seen as guidelines for raising the government's fiscal capacity while protecting its policy space beyond public sector employment the "second-order" criteria would seem to make more economic sense than the "first-order" ones.

[15] Masson and Pattillo 2001b, Debrun, Masson, and Pattillo 2002, Debrun and Kumar 2007 discuss the supposed mainstream rationale for this kind of constraint.

for convergence and cohesion—preparing the ground for endogenous asymmetric shocks.

If any individual WAEMU member's external vulnerability finally yields to crisis, the impact on its banking system and economy are unlikely to stay local; even given the currently low levels of WAEMU integration. In any event, in case of a severe enough crisis, the fiscal consequences of such developments will likely trigger the sovereign-bank doom-loop that caused so much havoc in Europe's EMU, risking further destabilization through counterproductive fiscal austerity in its trail. At least this will be the case as soon as financial development and integration in WAEMU reach levels that are sufficient for bond market speculation and regional financial contagion. Currency union members might have wished to avoid fiscal transfers (of one form or another) and keeping the common central bank's balance sheet "clean" from such accidents by prohibiting monetary financing, but that can quickly prove practically impossible, as the euro experiment has all too clearly shown.[16]

In other words, a sound fiscal policy framework for WAEMU must go beyond simply imposing discipline through ceilings on national budget deficits. A more constructive approach toward securing an appropriate fiscal stance and a high level of public infrastructure investment is needed. In particular, WAEMU's fiscal regime should include a central fiscal authority that issues a common debt instrument as the union's common safe asset. The primary focus of WAEMU's fiscal regime should be on growth and development: with securing an appropriately high and steady level of public infrastructure investment as the policy priority. Beware that public infrastructure investment has plunged to historic lows in Europe's currency union based on Maastricht wisdom. Europe's obsession with fiscal discipline has backfired dismally. WAEMU cannot afford repeating Europe's folly. WAEMU's fiscal regime needs to be more balanced and growth-oriented, it needs to actively foster balanced development and convergence throughout the region rather than divergence.

[16] The BCEAO appears to have played a role in the Ivorian sovereign debt crisis, enabling the rollover and restructuring of Ivorian debt held in the region in 2010–2011 (see IMF 2011, 2012). The issue of implicit fiscal transfers facilitated through the central bank's balance sheet can also arise in the case of emergency lending to banks that turn out to be insolvent. In Europe's EMU these matters have prompted legal challenges of the ECB (Bibow 2012, 2015a). The lack of a common fiscal backstop and rules on seignorage use represents a political risk.

This is not to deny that limiting *national* budget deficits, so as to keep *national* public debts at low levels, is a well-justified concern. For instance, U.S. states generally have debt levels of around 10% of GDP and rarely higher than 20%. High levels of public debt at the (U.S.) state or (EMU/WAEMU) national level are indeed very risky, precisely because of the fiscal-monetary divorce. State/national treasuries are lacking a central bank partner. Runs on national debt—for fear of default or mere panic—can therefore arise, with illiquidity causing insolvency.

But this systemic fragility stemming from the fiscal-monetary divorce is no excuse for believing that forcing national public debt levels to low levels union-wide would be sufficient and *by itself* somehow conducive to growth; or even be feasible for that matter. Quite the opposite is true. The point is that the (majority of the) public debt should instead be issued at the union level—as a common debt that is ultimately supported by the common central bank. This would create the very axis of macroeconomic policy powers that usually exists at the center of sovereign states. WAEMU itself is not a sovereign state but a union of sovereign states. The (limits of) power and authority of the proposed central fiscal authority therefore need to be clearly pre-defined. Its limited powers should be focused on securing balanced infrastructure investment throughout the region.

Standard mainstream policy advice offered to the WAEMU authorities completely misses the true source of WAEMU's fiscal vulnerability. country reports (IMF 2015, 2016; see also the Banque de France's annual reports on the Franc Zone) observed that the growth acceleration in WAEMU since 2012 was largely driven by a boost to public infrastructure investment; a boost of about three percentage points (from roughly 7 to 10% of GDP for WAEMU as a whole, albeit with large disparities among its members). And the IMF does not deny that in view of the stark infrastructure gap existing in WAEMU such a boost in public infrastructure investment—that, incidentally, has also seen a concomitant rise in private investment, i.e., *crowding in*!—is indeed highly warranted. Nonetheless, the IMF criticized the rise in (the aggregate) budget deficit to just over 4% of GDP and advised that the authorities focus on the new convergence criteria and their agreed "consolidation plans" limiting national budget deficits to 3% by 2019.

Granted, the IMF recommends that public investment should be maintained and austerity measures instead focus on tax revenues and public consumption (which would also be in line with the second-order criteria).

Yet the real issue is that despite the recent boost to public infrastructure investment that has proved to be a much-needed growth engine in WAEMU, public and private investment remain vastly insufficient in WAEMU. WAEMU's asymmetric macro policy regime risks acting as the same kind of straight jacket hindering growth and stability that has impoverished Europe.

Warning that the 70% ceiling for the public debt ratio should be seen as a limit rather than some optimal or target level, the IMF seems to consider a public debt ratio of 30–40% as more appropriate, and advises fiscal restraint to attain it. This would be twice wrong though: at the national level, even that lower number may actually be too high and risky, while, at the aggregate WAEMU level, directly targeting a public debt level in that ballpark might act as a growth restraint. We do not suggest here that the WAEMU authorities should deliberately target a rise in the debt ratio to a level of, say, 70%. Rather, the point is to stop permanently prioritizing deficit reduction, but to focus policy on sustaining, if not even raising, public infrastructure investment and securing its proper funding instead.

Establishing a central fiscal authority would bring many benefits. WAEMU must marshal any potential financial resources to boost its infrastructure investment further since currently total investment barely exceeds 20% of GDP (UNCTAD 2014). Creating a common WAEMU public debt would greatly support fostering financial development and integration in the region. The common debt instrument would quite naturally serve as the banks' (and other financial institutions') safe asset.[17] Potentially it would also help to attract portfolio investments from international investors (if that were desired as part of financial account management[18]). Instead of betting on the fate of any individual WAEMU member country the common debt instrument would diversify regional risk for international investors—while putting WAEMU's policy regime on a much sounder footing.

[17] Diouf and Boutin-Dufresne 2012 discuss recent developments in the regional securities market, particularly the role of national public debt markets. See also Sy 2006, 2007 and IMF 2013.

[18] Currently only Côte d'Ivoire and Senegal issue national debt instruments to international investors at all (though only small amounts compared to neighboring country "frontier markets" Ghana and Nigeria; see UNECA 2014). Significant amounts of their public debt issues (especially Senegal's) are held by WAEMU partner countries.

As a related matter the IMF (2015) also raises more specific concerns about the mode of financing of the recent rise in public infrastructure investment. Concomitant to the rise in public investment the banking system's credit creation has accelerated in recent years, both to the economy at large and to the public sector in particular. Accelerated credit growth has come along with a rise in the banks' recourse to refinancing at the BCEAO; and since 2013 the WAEMU banks' aggregate liquidity position has turned from a surplus into a deficit while "excess reserves" have increased at the same time. The IMF attributes this phenomenon to a kind of "carry-trade" activity on the part of some banks taking advantage of government bond yields that exceed their refinancing costs (i.e., the BECAO's policy rate).

It must be noted that this kind of business conduct constitutes standard practice of banks in advanced economies. It is also an integral part of how an easier monetary stance gets transmitted to financial conditions and the economy. Perhaps the real fear is that credit to the public sector has expanded at a faster rate than to the private sector and that the tripartite funding modus may be seen as "monetary financing at one remove": instead of the BCEAO buying the public debt directly, whether in the primary or secondary market, it refinances the banks' "carry-trade" purchases of such. Notorious inflation hawks seem to get alarmed about any expansion in public debt involving the banking system's balance sheet.[19]

This concern would be much beside the point though, and not only in light of the fact that WAEMU inflation has been between zero and one percent in recent times. Whenever the banks expand credit, and no matter in what direction, the banks' refinancing demand at the central bank will tend to grow too. More relevant questions concern, first, the rise in excess reserves and, second, whether the banks may be taking on excessive risks in the process. The former issue may reflect both inefficiencies in WAEMU's nascent interbank market and the fact that the credit expansion and boost in public infrastructure investment is undertaken

[19] In this context it must be emphasized that the prohibition of any direct central bank lending to the government is extreme and exceptional in the developing world (see Dullien 2009 and Jácome et al. 2012). Prior to Europe's EMU even the German Bundesbank was permitted to provide a limited amount of bridging loans ("Kassenkredite") to the government. Apart from the prohibition of any direct lending to the government the BCEAO's refinancing exposure to government securities is limited to a maximum of 35% of previous year's fiscal revenues.

very unevenly throughout WAEMU. The latter issue highlights potential vulnerabilities stemming from risk concentrations that can arise when banks invest too heavily in ***sub-federal*** public debt that is subject to default risk and hence runs (the "doom-loop").

Establishing a central fiscal authority as a vehicle that pools public investment spending throughout WAEMU, funded through common debt, would avoid these issues.[20] The central fiscal authority—call it the "WAEMU Treasury"—would be set up to provide a steady (more precisely, steadily growing) stream of investment grants to member states while borrowing on behalf of the union to fund public infrastructure investment throughout the union. If no fiscal "transfer union" is desired for the time being, both investment grants and the taxes raised from members[21] for servicing the interest on the common debt could be apportioned according to member countries' GDP shares. The WAEMU Treasury would not only ***safeguard*** WAEMU's infrastructure investment as such, but also contribute toward a ***steady and more even development*** throughout WAEMU; thereby acting as an anchor of regional convergence and cohesion. Created as the common safe asset, the interest burden on WAEMU Treasury debt gets lowered compared to national public debts; a benefit shared by all members.

With public infrastructure investment funded centrally through a common capital budget, national budget targets need to be lowered correspondingly, so that national debt ratios will converge to low and safe levels. But any national budget targets need to be defined in a symmetric and cyclically-adjusted way. Excessive national austerity has spillover effects just as national profligacy does too. Budget discipline is upheld by withholding WAEMU Treasury investment grants in case member countries deviate from their national budget targets.

The WAEMU Treasury's debt issuance does not need to be the only source of public investment funding in WAEMU. Official grants provide close to three percent of GDP annually. These external funds may also be pooled and—as a benchmark—shared by WAEMU members in proportion to their GDP. Alternatively, some mechanism may be designed that

[20] The recently created regional debt management agency ("Agence UMOA Titres") is helpful as such but the current focus (and reliance) on national as opposed to common public debt is misplaced.

[21] Any central bank monetary income (seigniorage) should serve as common income for this purpose.

temporarily favors member countries that are either lagging behind in terms of their income levels and/or are currently suffering from some idiosyncratic shock/crisis. In addition, member countries can continue to also fund public investment from their national budgets (while abiding by their symmetric budget rules).[22]

The overall aim is to maintain the increased level of public investment (or raise it even further), funded in a sustainable way, and spent in a steady and balanced way throughout WAEMU. For it is safer and comes with numerous other benefits to provide for common funding at the union rather than the national level. Europe's EMU is the only (advanced country) monetary union that does not include any fiscal union. Europe's EMU is clearly dysfunctional and should not serve as WAEMU's model any longer.

Needless to say, the efficiency of public investment matters greatly too. The WAEMU policy focus on public infrastructure investment should be coordinated closely with the WAEMU Commission and the West African Development Bank (Bank Quest Africaine de Devéloppement, BEOA). The authorities should aim at efficiency in their own undertakings and "crowding in" of private investment, with a view of mobilizing domestic resources to their fullest potential.

As previously mentioned, the public investment boost and growth acceleration in WAEMU in recent years occurred at declining rates of inflation. Inflationary pressures best indicate domestic supply constraints. Apart from domestic supply constraints WAEMU's external position needs to be considered too. The IMF's concerns are also based on the fact that WAEMU's current account deficit has increased in tandem with its budget deficit, with both reaching levels that exceed their historical averages of the past two decades. To some extent this was inevitable as the boost to public infrastructure investment has come along with a surge in capital goods imports. Perhaps part of the current account deterioration

[22] All WAEMU member countries have benefited from substantial relief on their external debt. As beneficiaries of the 1996 (joint IMF-World Bank) HIPC initiative WAEMU member countries have received budget relief of up to 3% of GDP annually (WAEMU aggregate). The budget relief comes in the form of reduced debt service on legacy debts and is earmarked for boosting social spending and poverty reduction. As beneficiaries of the 2005 MDRI initiative WAEMU member countries have received full debt relief on debts owed to the IMF, the International Development Association of the World Bank, and the African Development Fund.

will prove temporary depending on terms-of-trade developments going forward.

WAEMU's trade and current account deficits have recently been in the order of 10% of GDP; including official current transfers reduces the latter deficit to around 7% of GDP. The primary income balance shows a deficit of around 2.5% of GDP, but WAEMU also receives private current transfers (remittances) of about 3% of GDP. Furthermore, the capital account features capital transfers of about 2% of GDP annually. The remaining gap is largely covered by foreign direct investment inflows of 3–4% of GDP annually while both portfolio and other investments play only a smaller role. There is fairly little variability in official reserves (as a percent of GDP) from year to year.

Nevertheless, the current picture suggests that the external funding constraint may be (close to) binding. Liberalizing the financial account must be handled with much care and precaution (UNCTAD 2014; Mougani 2012). Attracting more foreign direct investment to the region would be the safest option. Gradually opening up to portfolio investment in the common public debt might be seen as a way to enlarge external funding space. But this consideration also leads us back to the exchange rate issue: the hard peg to the euro currently in place.

In the past few years WAEMU has enjoyed easy monetary conditions and, more recently, also a decline in its real effective exchange rate. Yet, if anything, the CFA franc still seems to be somewhat overvalued, including vis-à-vis its euro anchor itself. Currency overvaluation can act as a hindrance to growth and development. The opposite would be desirable (Levy-Yeyati and Sturzenegger 2007; Rodrik 2008). The WAEMU authorities should investigate the optimal timing of letting go of the union's current currency anchor. For one thing, euro break-up is still a significant latent risk. For another, decoupling from the euro is really only a matter of optimal timing anyway.

Our assessment has focused on WAEMU. In principle, much the same also applies to CEMAC. In at least one respect CEMAC is more homogenous than WAEMU since all but one member-country are oil producers (with vast differences in income levels though). Extending the analysis to WAMZ and ECOWAS would need to take a number of additional considerations into account. Regarding the envisioned merger of WAEMU and WAMU I am not convinced that creating WAMU first to then merge it with WAEMU is preferable to a strategy that has non-WAEMU ECOWAS members joining WAEMU individually when they are ready. Including

Nigeria would be a special challenge considering both the country's size and its extreme dependence on oil.[23]

4.5 Summary and Policy Recommendations

Regional cooperation and integration is a laudable endeavor that may also be motivated by considerations other than fostering economic well-being alone. But both with regard to actually fostering economic well-being per se and as a means toward higher political ends regional economic cooperation and integration can only deliver if economic institutions and policies are well designed and fit for purpose. Otherwise the endeavor can also backfire as economic failure may give rise to political disunion and undermine regional trust among nations.

As an ill-designed currency union, the euro experiment has failed, handing its members poor economic performance if not severe distress. As a result, the process of European integration has stalled and is at risk of reversing. Mistrust is on the rise, political instabilities rife. Yet the ideas underlying the euro regime continue to inspire its African cousins and pegging dependents, WAEMU and CEMAC. The authorities would be well advised to take the lessons from the failed euro experiment serious.

Three key lessons are: first, market integration must be paralleled by policy integration, especially in the domain of financial integration, second, persistent divergences in intra-union competitiveness positions must be prevented, and third, monetary union without fiscal union is ultimately nonviable. While WAEMU has been pursuing its own banking union project alongside the creation of its common financial market, the latter two lessons remain as open challenges today.

Clearly the current set of asymmetrically specified "convergence criteria" is ill-suited and represents a risk to growth and development in WAEMU. National wage-price inflation trends need to be well aligned with the BCEAO's inflation target, persistent deviations *in either direction* must be prevented. Fiscal policies too need to be set in a symmetric

[23] The empirical literature emphasizes the prevalence of asymmetric shocks in WAMZ and ECOWAS. See: Masson and Pattillo 2001a, Houssa 2008, Tsangarides and Qureshi 2008, Debrun, Pattillo and Masson 2010, Carton et al. 2010, Asenso 2011, Alagidede at al. 2011, Omotor and Niringiye 2011, Chuku 2012, Atanda and Akanni 2013, Coulibaly and Gnimassoun 2013, Sireh-Jallow 2013, Asongu 2014, Kemegue and Seck 2014, for instance.

fashion. A sound fiscal regime must go beyond disciplining "excessive (national) deficits" to ensure a growth-oriented aggregate fiscal stance and macro policy mix.

To complement and safeguard WAEMU's monetary union it is advisable to establish a common fiscal authority as soon as possible. As an embryonic fiscal union the "WAEMU Treasury" proposed here would pool the union's public infrastructure investment and fund it through the issuance of common debt instruments. To preclude a transfer union by design both investment grants and the taxes raised to pay the interest on the common debt could be shared proportionately based on WAEMU members' GDP shares. Other mechanisms may be added that are designed to counter intra-union instabilities and foster convergence and cohesion.

In the first instance the WAEMU Treasury would ensure steady and balanced infrastructure public investment throughout the union, acting as an anchor to balanced economic development in the region. Investment spending and common debt issuance at the center would enable the convergence of national public debt ratios to low and safe levels. The issuance of common debt instruments would also contribute toward financial system development and integration. At times of crisis the WAEMU Treasury would be the natural fiscal backstop to the WAEMU banking union. Partnering up the BCEAO with a WAEMU Treasury would re-couple fiscal and monetary policies at the union level. Debt issuance by the WAEMU Treasury is strictly constrained to meet its public investment program. The BCEAO can intervene in the secondary market of the common debt instrument for monetary policy purposes.

Driven by a marked rise in public infrastructure investment, the somewhat unbalanced growth acceleration in WAEMU in recent years has occurred at (too) low inflation rates. While maintaining, or preferably further boosting, the ongoing momentum in the mobilization of domestic resources must be the policy priority, WAEMU's external position risks becoming a binding constraint and potential source of vulnerability. Persistent overvaluation must be avoided. A mild degree of undervaluation is both safer and can also help to alleviate the external constraint and better support growth and development.

The ongoing weakness of the euro anchor is lending some welcome support in this regard at the current juncture. At least in some respects the euro peg has provided certain benefits and may have also bolstered regional stability and cohesion in the past. Yet unpegging from the euro is really a matter of optimal timing. The authorities should focus their planning in this regard on designing an external regime that provides some measure of stability but avoids persistent overvaluation, and without unduly constraining any potential macro policy space. A somewhat softer peg to a basket of currencies combined with cautious financial account management appears advisable.

References

Abdih, Y. and Tsangarides, C. (2010). REER for the CFA franc, *Applied Economics* 24: 2009-29.

Adedeji, O.S. and Williams, O. (2007). Fiscal Reaction Functions in the CFA Zone: An Analytical Perspective, IMF, WP 07/232.

African Development Bank (AfDB) (2011). Building Capacity for Bank Regulation in the Era of Basel III: Challenges and Opportunities for Africa, Africa Capacity Development Brief vol. 2(3).

AfDB (2011). Institutions for Credit Markets in Africa, Africa Capacity Development Brief, vol. 2(5).

Alagidede, P., Coleman, S. and Cuestas, J.C. (2011). Inflationary shocks and common economic trends: implications for West African Monetary Union membership, *Journal of Policy Modeling*, 34 (3), 460-475.

Asenso, J. (2011). The West African Monetary Zone: Eligibility for Monetary Unification

Asongu, S.A. (2014). Are proposed African monetary unions optimal currency areas? Real, monetary and fiscal policy convergence analysis, Research Gate, Working Paper, April.

Atanda, M.S. and Akanni, Y.I. (2013). Application of the augmented gravity model on currency unification and trade drifts in ECOWAS, *International Economics and Finance Journal* 8(2): 117-33.

Bayoumi, T. and Ostry, J.D. (1997). Macroeconomic shocks and trade flows within sub-Saharan Africa: implications for optimum currency arrangements, *Journal of African Economies*, 6(3): 412-44.

BCEAO (various years). Annual Report: Summarised Version.

Banque de France (2002). The Franc Zone, Fact Sheet no. 127, updated 2010.

Banque de France (various years). Franc Zone, Annual Report.

Bibow, J. (2006). The Euro Area Drifting Apart: Does Reform of Labor Markets Deliver Competitive Stability or Competitive Divergence? In: *Structural Reforms and Macro-Economic Policy*, ETUC, 76-86.

Bibow, J. (2009). On the origin and rise of central bank independence in West Germany, *European Journal of the History of Economic Thought* 16(1): 155-90.

Bibow, J. (2012). The Euroland crisis and Germany's euro trilemma, International Review of Applied Economics 27(3): 360-85.

Bibow, J. (2013a). On the Franco-German euro contradiction and ultimate euro battleground, *Contributions to Political Economy* 32: 127-49.

Bibow, J. (2013b). Lost at Sea: The Euro Needs a Euro Treasury, Macroeconomic Policy Institute, IMK Study no. 35, November.

Bibow, J. (2015a). The Euro's Savior? Assessing the ECB's Crisis Management Performance and Potential for Crisis Resolution, Macroeconomic Policy Institute, IMK Study 42, June.

Bibow, J. (2015b). Making the euro viable: the Euro Treasury Plan, Levy Economics Institute, Working Paper no. 842, July.

Blanchard, O., Dell'Ariccia, G. and Mauro, P. (2010). Rethinking Macroeconomic Policy, IMF Staff Position Note 10-03, February.

Boogaerde, P. and Tsangarides, C. (2005). Ten Years After the CFA Franc Devaluation: Progress Toward Regional Integration in the WAEMU, IMF, Working Paper 05/145.

Carton, B., Benassy-Quere, A., Dufrenot, G. and Batte, L. (2010). Asymmetric term-of-trade shocks in a monetary union: an application to West Africa, *Journal of African Economies* 19(5): 657-90.

Chuku, C. (2012). The Proposed Eco: Should West Africa Proceed with a Common Currency?, MPRA 43739.

Couharde, C., Coulibaly, I., Guerreiro, D. and Mignon, V. (2012). Revisiting the theory of optimum currency areas: Is the CFA franc zone sustainable?, CEPII, WP 13.

Coulibaly, I. and Gnimassoun, B. (2013). Optimality of a monetary union: new evidence from exchange rate misalignments in West Africa, *Economic Modelling* 32: 463-82.

Debrun, X., Masson, P. and Pattillo, C. (2002). Monetary Union in West Africa: Who Might Gain, Who Might Lose, and Why?, IMF, WP 02/226.

Debrun, X. and Kumar, M.S. (2007). The Discipline-Enhancing Role of Fiscal Institutions: Theory and Empirical Evidence, IMF

Debrun, X., Pattillo, C.A. and Masson, P.R. (2010). Should African Monetary Unions be Expanded? An Empirical Investigation of the Scope for Monetary Integration in Sub-Saharan Africa, IMF.

Diouf, M.A. and Boutin-Dufresne, F. (2012). Financing Growth in the WAEMU Through the Regional Securities Market: Past Successes and Current Challenges, IMF, Working Paper 12/249.

Dufrénot, G. (2011). Monetary autonomy in the West African countries: What do the policy rules tell us? *Journal of International Development* 23(1): 63–81.

Dullien, S. (2009). Central banking, financial institutions and credit creation in developing countries, UNCTAD, Discussion Paper no. 193.

Egoume, P. and Nayo, A. (2011). Feeling the Elephant's Weight: The Impact of Cote d'Ivoire's Crisis on WAEMU trade, IMF, WP 11/80.

Frankel, J.A. and Rose, A.K. (1997). Is EMU more justifiable ex post than ex ante? *European Economic Review* 41(3) : 753-60.

Gnimassoun, B. (2012). Taux de change et mesalignements du franc CFA avant et après l'introduction de l'euro, Universite Paris Ouest Nanterre La Defense, Working Paper no. 03.

Godley, W. (1992). Maastricht and All That, *London Review of Books*, vol. 14, no. 19, October 8.

Goodhart, C.A.E. (1998). The two concepts of money: implications for the analysis of optimal currency areas, *European Journal of Political Economy* 14: 407-32.

Gulde, A.-M. and Tsangarides, C.G. (eds.) (2008). The CFA Franc Zone: Common Currency, Uncommon Challenges. IMF.

Hallet, M. (2008). The Role of the Euro in Sub-Saharan Africa and in the CFA Franc Zone, European Economy, Economic Papers 347, European Commission, November.

Hitaj, E. and Onder, Y.K. (2013). Fiscal Discipline in WAEMU: Rules, Institutions, and Markets, IMF, WP 13/216, October.

Houssa, R. (2008). Monetary union in West Africa and asymmetric shocks: a dynamic structural factor model approach, *Journal of Development Economics* 85(1-2); 319-47.

IMF (1996). Aftermath of the CFA Franc Devaluation, Occasional Paper no. 138, by Jean A.P. Clement el al.

IMF (1998). The WAEMU: Recent Developments and Policy Issues, Occasional Paper no. 170, by Staff Team led by Ernesto Hernandez-Cata.

IMF (2010). Regional Economic Outlook. Sub-Saharan Africa: Resilience and Risks, October.

IMF (2013a). West African Economic and Monetary Union: Financial Depth and Macro Stability.

IMF (2013b). Responding to Shocks and Maintaining Stability in the West African Economic and Monetary Union.

IMF (2014). Annual Report on Exchange Arrangements and Exchange Restrictions.

IMF (2015). Pan-African Banks: Opportunities and Challenges for Cross-Border Oversight.

IMF (various years). CEMAC. Country Report

IMF (various years). WAEMU. Country Report.

Jácome, L.I., Matamoros-Indorf, M., Sharma, M. and Townshend, S. (2012). Central Bank Credit to the Government: What Can We Learn From International Practices?, IMF, Working Paper 2012–2016.

Kemegue, F.M. and Seck, O. (2014). Do African Monetary Arrangements Make Sense? Evidence Based on Sructural Symmetry, *Regional Economic Integration in West Africa*, Springer, pp. 79–100.

Kenen, P. (1969). The Theory of Optimum Currency Areas: An Eclectic View, in Mundell and Swoboda (eds.) *Monetary Problems in the International Economy*, University of Chicago Press, Chicago.

Kinda, T. and Mlachila, M. (2011). The Quest for Higher Growth in the WAEMU Region: The Role of Accelerations and Decelerations, IMF, WP 11/174.

Klau, M. (1998). Exchange Rate Regimes and Inflation and Output in Sub-Saharan Countries, BIS, Working Paper no. 53, March.

Kpodar, K. and Gbenyo, K. (2010). Short- Versus Long-Term Credit and Economic Performance: Evidence from the WAEMU, IMF, WP 10/115.

Levy-Yeyati, E. and Sturzenegger, F. (2007). Fear of Appreciation, Policy Research Working Paper Series 4387, World Bank.

Longkeng Ngouana, C. (2012). Exchange Rate Volatility Under Peg: Do Trade Patterns Matter?, IMF, WP 12/73.

Masson, P. and Pattillo, C. (2001a). Monetary Union in West Africa (ECOWAS): Is it Desirable and How Could it be Achieved?, IMF, Occasional Paper no. 204, March.

Masson, P. and Pattillo, C. (2001b). Monetary Union in West Africa: An Agency of Restraint for Fiscal Policies?, IMF, WP 01/34.

McKinnon, R.I. (1963). Optimum currency areas, *American Economic Review* 53(4): 717-25.

Metzger, M. (2008). Regional Cooperation and Integration in Sub-Saharan Africa, UNCTAD Discussion Paper no. 189.

Mongelli, F. (2002) 'New' Views on the Optimum Currency Area Theory: What is EMU Telling Us, European Central Bank, Working Paper, No. 138.

Mougani, G. (2012). An Analysis of the Impact of Financial Integration on Economic Activity and Macroeconomic Volatility in Africa Within the Financial Globalization Context, African Development Bank Group, Working Paper no. 144.

Mundell, R.A. (1961). A theory of optimum currency areas, *American Economic Review* 51(4): 657-65.

Omotor, D.G. and Niringiye, A. (2011). Optimum currency area and shock asymmetry: a dynamic analysis of the West African Monetary Zone (WAMZ), *Journal for Economic Forecasting* 3: 71-82.

Oshikoya, T.W. (ed.) (2010). *Monetary and Financial Integration in West Africa*, Routledge.

Pisani-Ferry, J., Italianer, A., and Lescure, R. (1993). Stabilization Properties of Budgetary Systems: A Simulation Analysis, *European Economy*, no. 5, section V, pp. 511–538.

Pisani-Ferry, J. (2014). *The Euro Crisis and its Aftermath*, Oxford, Oxford University Press.

Qureshi, M.S. and Tsangarides, C.G. (2012). Hard or soft pegs? Choice of exchange rate regime and trade in Africa, World Development, vol 40(4), 667-680.

Rodrik, D. (2008). The real exchange rate and economic growth, Brookings Papers on Economic Activity, 2, 365-412.

Rose, A.K. (2000). One money, one market: the effect of common currencies on trade, *Economic Policy: A European Forum* 30: 7-33.

Sireh-Jallow, A. (2013). The empirics of an optimal currency area in West Africa, *International Journal of Economics and Finance* 5(4): 100-108.

Sy, A.N.R. (2006). Financial Integration in the WAEMU, IMF, WP 06/214.

Sy, A.N.R. (2007). Local Currency Debt Markets in the WAEMU, IMF, WP 07/256.

Tapsoba, S.J. (2009). Trade intensity and business cycle synchronicity in Africa, *Journal of African Economies* 18(2): 287-318.

Tavlas, George S. (1993). The 'New' Theory of Optimum Currency Areas, *The World Economy*, 16, pp. 663-685.

Tsangarides, C.G. and Qureeshi, M.S. (2008). Monetary union membership in West Africa: a cluster analysis, *World Development* 36(7): 1261-79.

UNCTAD (2007). Trade and Development Report 2007: Regional Cooperation for Development.

UNCTAD (2014). Economic Development in Africa Report 2014: Catalysing Investment for Transformative Growth in Africa.

UNECA (2008). Assessing Regional Integration in Africa III. Towards monetary and financial integration in Africa. Especially ch. 8: Movement of investment and capital in Africa, pp. 123–144.

UNECA (2014). Frontier Markets in Africa—Misperceptions in a Sea of Opportunities, July.

Veyrune, R. (2007). Fixed Exchange Rate and the Autonomy of Monetary Policy: The Franc Zone Case, IMF, WP 07/34, February.

Wolf, M. (2007). The Pain in Spain will Follow Years of Rapid Economic Gain, Financial Times, 27 March, https://www.ft.com/intl/cms/s/1/16e554ac-dc80-11db-a21d-000b5df10621.html#axzz3wDPvYfyU.

Yehoue, E.B. (2005). International Risk Sharing and Currency Unions: The CFA Zones, IMF, WP 05/95.

Yehoue, E.B. (2007). The CFA Arrangements—More Than Just an Aid Substitute?, IMF, WP 07/19, January.

PART II

Short-Term Liquidity

CHAPTER 5

Regional Monetary Cooperation in the Developing World Taking Stock

Laurissa Mühlich and Barbara Fritz

5.1 Introduction

Regional cooperation has significantly increased during recent decades, not only economically via increasing South-South trade, but also in monetary and financial terms. Varieties of active efforts for monetary and financial cooperation can be observed in different parts of the world, which range from informal policy dialog to informal or formal regional policy coordination, regional payment systems, regional liquidity sharing mechanisms, regional exchange rate arrangements, and a formal currency union. In view of the instable global monetary and financial system that does not sufficiently contain economic volatility (Cohen, 2000), forming regional economic and monetary blocs can be understood as a possible

L. Mühlich · B. Fritz (✉)
Freie University of Berlin, Berlin, Germany
e-mail: barbara.fritz@fu-berlin.de

L. Mühlich
e-mail: laurissa.muehlich@fu-berlin.de

D. Barrowclough et al. (eds.), *South–South Regional Financial Arrangements*, International Political Economy Series,
https://doi.org/10.1007/978-3-030-64576-2_5

response. Against this background, the vivid interest of developing countries and emerging markets in regional monetary policy strategies is largely motivated by three factors.

First, under the current conditions of liberalized capital flows and flexible exchange rates, developing countries and emerging markets find it particularly difficult to achieve macroeconomic stability and favorable conditions for economic growth and development. With the breakup of the Bretton Woods system in 1973, and especially since the increased financial liberalization at the global level from the 1990s on, the volatility of international capital flows and exchange rates between international key currencies has increased the risk and magnitude of economic and monetary shocks.

Second, the introduction of the Euro in the European Union (EU) in 1999 attracted particular attention in developing countries. The introduction of the Euro represented the most advanced form of regional economic and monetary bloc-building around an international key currency, the former Deutsche Mark. Hence, the question of whether South-South regional monetary bloc-building could be a viable monetary policy strategy—considering the limited possibility of integrating with key currency areas—became even stronger with the Euro crisis since 2010. This crisis seriously called into question the feasibility of regional monetary integration without full political integration of the member countries, and without jeopardizing sustainable growth for all member countries.

Third, both the series of emerging market crises of the 1990s and the global financial crisis a decade later had regional contagious elements in terms of crisis diffusion. The unfolding of the Asian financial crisis from its origins in South-East Asia in 1997 to the Russian, Argentinean and Brazilian financial crisis and regional economic downturn in South America and South Africa is telling in this regard. Being tied together through the regional contagion of financial crises that provoked the formation also triggered the emergence and expansion of regional monetary arrangements.

As economic literature lacks a clear definition of regional monetary cooperation, regional monetary cooperation is understood here in a broad sense, following Schelkle (2001). Regional monetary cooperation may range from informal policy dialog to formal or informal policy coordination to various formal forms of regional monetary cooperation as analyzed here (see also Frankel 1988, Bénassy-Quéré/Coeuré, 2005).

It is important to note that the different forms of regional monetary cooperation have no pre-determined sequencing and are not mutually exclusive. More shallow forms of regional monetary cooperation—such as regional payment systems—may serve as learning grounds for deeper forms of regional monetary cooperation, such as regional exchange rate coordination, but do not necessarily automatically transform themselves into such deeper and more binding forms of cooperation (Grabel 2018). While macroeconomic cooperation creates the grounds for increasing regional shock buffering capacity in general, each form provides a specific buffering potential against negative effects of financial volatility. In general, harmonized regional macroeconomic policy stances contribute to regional macroeconomic stability. More importantly—from our perspective—is the crucial precondition for reducing macroeconomic vulnerability in peripheral developing countries: to achieve and sustain a stable and competitive real exchange rate level that contributes to reducing external vulnerability. It is under such conditions that the economy is able to build up macroeconomic capabilities to buffer external shocks and enhance economic growth. We map out existing mechanisms of two forms of regional monetary cooperation regarding their respective contribution to establishing macroeconomic conditions that enable the region to buffer external shocks and reduce its vulnerability to financial volatility (for an extended discussion, see UNCTAD, 2011).

5.2 Development Goals and Objectives of South-South Regional Monetary Cooperation

In the following, we first present a systematization of regional monetary cooperation mechanisms alongside their respective development goals (part II). In part III, we present case studies of two specific types that have gained momentum in all parts of the developing world, namely, regional liquidity pools, and of regional payments systems. The overview only includes those mechanisms that involve developing countries and emerging markets that are not linked in any form to an international key currency, such as the Euro or the US dollar (see Fritz/Metzger, 2006; Mühlich, 2014). In section IV, we conduct a general evaluation based on exemplified observations of the major characteristics of the mechanisms presented in section III.

In face of the repeatedly volatile global economic and monetary conditions, it is important to systematically address the question of how each form of regional monetary cooperation may contribute to reduce macroeconomic volatility and buffer exogenous shocks for developing countries and emerging markets. The small body of more systematic literature offers various alternative ways to classify arrangements of regional monetary and financial cooperation (Edwards 1985; Ocampo, 2006; UNCTAD, 2007). Here, we follow the approach developed in UNCTAD (2011) and further developed in Fritz/Mühlich (2014).

5.2.1 *Facing Short-Term Balance-of-Payments Imbalances: Regional Liquidity Pooling*

Preventing short-term balance-of-payments problems is a necessary condition for buffering volatility. Developing countries have recently exerted considerable efforts to accumulate foreign exchange reserves, partly as a means of self-insurance against external shocks. Pooling foreign exchange reserves with neighboring countries in either a jointly-managed fund or through currency swap arrangements is a more efficient way of self-insurance (Ocampo 2006). Further, a regional liquidity pool can be more easily and rapidly accessed than international mechanisms of liquidity provision.

However, regional self-insurance mechanisms only work as insurance mechanisms if the pooled resources—are not drawn on by all member countries at the same time (Eichengreen, 2006). Further to this, regional liquidity sharing is more effective the smaller that the member country is, as it may benefit relatively more in relation to the size of the regional liquidity fund (ibid.). Beyond size, regionally-adapted surveillance and enforcement rules within regional mechanisms are highly relevant not only to ensure the financial sustainability of the fund, but also ownership of the member countries. The non-use of the Chiang Mai Initiative Multilateralization (CMIM) is highlighted by some scholars as a telling example of missing regionalization of surveillance and enforcement (Grimes, 2011; Kawai/Houser 2007).

When adequately designed, regional liquidity sharing may play a complementary role to established international forms of liquidity provision through the IMF (Henning/Khan, 2011). Some cases exist in which small member countries even substitute the IMF, such as in the case of the Latin American Reserve Fund (FLAR, according to its Spanish acronym; Mühlich/Fritz, 2018).

In contrast to most other forms of regional cooperation arrangements, regional asymmetries are beneficial to regional reserve pooling since the participating countries' demand for liquidity should differ in time and volume to avoid simultaneous drawings that would exceed the volume of available pooled reserves (Imbs/Mauro, 2007). As such, regional liquidity sharing may be adopted even at a low level of regional macroeconomic coordination.

5.2.2 *Reducing Exposure to Exchange Rate Volatility and Promoting Inter-Regional Trade: Regional Payment Systems*

Besides trade integration schemes such as customs unions, the mechanism that directly addresses intra-regional trade is a regional payment system. The objective of such a system is to foster trade between member countries by reducing the transaction costs of foreign exchange market operations through the use of domestic currencies.

According to Chang (2000: 3), a reduction of foreign currency flows and associated transaction costs is realized in two ways. First, the number of transactions is reduced to net final settlement at the end of the period, while transactions of equal value cancel out. Second, temporary liquidity is provided to the member countries' central banks, as they allow each other to cancel mutual obligations at the end of the clearing period, as opposed to immediately. In effect, an efficiently run regional payment system in its simple version may slightly improve the terms of trade for intra-regional trade transactions (see Fritz et al. 2014 for a detailed analysis).

While such small-scale regional cooperation arrangements provide important learning ground for regional policy coordination beyond intra-regional trade (Birdsall/Rojas-Suarez, 2004; Grabel, 2018), they generally represent a small instrument to enhance intra-regional trade and thus contribute in a—modest—way to reducing the participating countries' macroeconomic vulnerability. At the same time, regional payment systems can only effectively contribute to reducing a region's macroeconomic volatility if the participating countries are able to design the system's clearing mechanism in a way that adequately reflects macroeconomic shifts of the participating countries. For such purposes, regional payment systems may provide an initial step toward further forms of regional monetary cooperation.

5.2.3 *Promoting Structural Transformation, and Increasing Policy Space for Sustainable Growth and Development: Macroeconomic Cooperation and Integration*

Regional bilateral monetary cooperation can range from policy consultation to the explicit coordination of exchange rates and other monetary policy fields. Regional cooperation needs to devote particular attention to preventing regional contagion and internalizing the external effects of domestic macroeconomic policies on regional partners (Ocampo, 2006; Akyüz, 2009; UNCTAD, 2009).

Unilateral currency devaluation and deflationist policies trigger contagious effects to regional neighbor countries. First, due to hoarding behavior based on insufficient information of investors, the devaluation of one currency within a region increases expectations regarding the devaluation of other currencies in the region, thus triggering sudden stops of capital flows and the spreading of a financial crisis in the region. Second, restrictive domestic policies following currency devaluation produce restrictive effects on regional partners through direct trade and financial links in the region: falling demand and changes in the direction of financial flows due to higher yields in the adjusting economy create a deflationary effect on other countries within the region. Deleterious effects of "beggar-thy-neighbour" policies increase with the depth of regional market economic integration that has already been achieved if the monetary and overall macroeconomic cooperation are not sufficiently enforced to protect economic integration. Even in regional blocs that have rather low levels of economic integration but whose members have similar production structures, a currency devaluation in one country will give rise to competition for export earnings and foreign direct investment and hinder deeper economic integration. Hence, the crucial role of regional monetary cooperation in the form of a coordinated exchange rate policy is to mutually enforce regional trade and financial integration.

However, despite a series of initiatives—especially in Africa—we are not aware of a single case of realized bilateral monetary coordination, formally agreed, or even bilateral currency integration. While we therefore cannot examine case studies on these mechanisms here, we nevertheless address the achievements made in the only hitherto existing case of regional monetary cooperation in the Common Monetary Area (CMA) and develop some explanations why others have not yet been realized.

5.3 Taking Stock of Existing and Planned Regional Monetary Cooperation Mechanisms

5.3.1 Liquidity Sharing Mechanisms

a. Latin American Reserve Fund/Fondo Latinoamericano de Reservas (FLAR)

FLAR
Date of Foundation: 1978 as Andean Reserve Fund (FAR), 1991 transformed into FLAR **Website**: https://flar.net/ **Legal form**: legal entity of public international law (FLAR Agreement, Art.1) **Headquarters**: Bogotá, Colombia **Member States (year of access)**: Bolivia (1988), Colombia (1988), Costa Rica (1999), Ecuador (1988), Paraguay (2015), Peru (1988), Uruguay (2008), Venezuela (1988)

The regional liquidity fund FLAR has a comparatively long history. It was first founded in 1978 as a regional reserve fund based on the Pacto Andino (today's Andean Community). In 1988, after the experience of severe debt cries in Latin America during the 1980s, FAR was expanded to FLAR to invite new member countries from all over Latin America. However, to date only Costa Rica, Uruguay, and Paraguay have joined.

The fund's overall size in terms of credit disbursement and member countries is comparatively small, and its current size the fund has not been able to respond to liquidity demands of the larger member countries (Mühlich/Fritz 2018). In 2019, the FLAR had a volume of about USD 3.9 billion, of which about USD 3 billion was paid-in capital. Despite its small size and little diversification in membership, FLAR holds an AA rating, the highest of all Latin American institutions and/or countries, as FLAR (n.d.a) states. Such favorable borrowing conditions enable the fund to play a complementary role when it comes to leveraging the international borrowing of its member countries (Rosero, 2014: 80). FLAR provides its facilities with a very rapid response to loan requests of 28 days on average. Such a quick response has facilitated leveraging other sources of emergency finance and "contributed to overcoming coordination failures associated with the first-mover disadvantage in lending" (Rosero, 2014: 83).

Just like the AMF (see below), FLAR provides very flexible emergency credit lines to its members and is frequently used at small drawings, which are sometimes complemented by IMF programs. FLAR understands itself as a complement to the IMF. For smaller member countries, FLAR may even substitute IMF; for example, to date Ecuador has borrowed more than twice as much from FLAR than from the IMF (Mühlich/Fritz, 2018). The larger member countries Colombia, Peru, and Venezuela turn to larger sources of funds, such as the IMF or bilateral currency swap agreements with extra-regional countries (ibid.).

Any expansion of the fund's volume and membership would need to take into consideration a change in the current voting mechanism of one vote per member country, especially if larger Latin American economics—such as Brazil—are about to join. At the same time, it is precisely the egalitarian governance structure that fuels the strong ownership of its membership and may explain the absence of any arrears in repayment ever since (Titelman et al., 2014: 23).

FLAR Capital Structure

	Subscribed capital (millions USD)	*Paid-in capital (millions USD)*	*"Fire power" Accessible capital one-year maturity (millions USD)*	*Share of total capital (%)*
Bolivia	328	256	361	8.3
Colombia	656	513	656	16.7
Costa Rica	656	513	484*	16.7
Ecuador	328	256	361	8.3
Paraguay	328	256	328	8.3
Peru	656	513	656	16.7
Uruguay	328	257	328	8.3
Venezuela, R.B.	656	498	656	16.7
Total paid-in capital	3,983	3,062		

Source FLAR n.d.b
Note *Own calculation based on since data for Costa Rica is not provided by FLAR

FLAR Loan Categories & Conditions

Conditions	*Balance of Payments*	*Liquidity*	*Contingency*
Maturity	3 years; 1-year grace period	Up to 1 year	6 months renewable
Access Limits	2.5 times paid-in capital	Paid-in capital	2 times paid-in capital
Attribution for approval	Board	Executive President	Executive President

Source FLAR 2018
Note In the case of balance of payment credits, debt restructuring, liquidity, and contingency, central banks from Bolivia and Ecuador have 0.1 additional access relative to paid-in capital compared to the other members

b. Chiang Mai Initiative Multilateralization (CMIM)

CMIM

Date of Foundation: The CMIM was signed on 24 December 2009 as a successor of the Chiang Mai Initiative (CMI).
Website: http://www.asean.org; https://amro-asia.org/
Legal form: Multilateral swap arrangement (Bank of Japan, 2009).
Headquarters: Not defined, ASEAN Headquarters in Jakarta, Indonesia
Member States (year of access): plus-three partner countries (2000/2009): China (incl. Hong Kong), Japan, Korea, ASEAN member countries (2000/2009): Indonesia, Thailand, Malaysia, Singapore, Philippines, Vietnam, Cambodia, Myanmar, Brunei, Lao PDR

At present, probably the most popular liquidity sharing mechanism is the Chiang Mai Initiative Multilateralization (CMIM). It was initially set up as a network of bilateral swap arrangements in 2001 among the member states of the Association of Southeast Asian Nations (ASEAN) and its plus-three partner countries of China (incl. Hong Kong) and South Korea, as well as the northern partner country Japan (Chiang Mai Initiative, CMI) in reaction to the Asian financial crisis. In reaction to the 2007/08 global financial crisis, CMIM was established in 2010 as a multilateral arrangement that comprises about USD 240 billion of paid-in capital in 2019 (AMRO, n.d.; Henning, 2009; Eichengreen, 2012). CMIM represents a swap fund in the sense that each country's foreign exchange contributions are made on demand rather than in advance.

However, to date the mechanism has never been utilized by its member states. On the one hand, "the accumulation of record levels of 'self-defence' in the form of large international reserves may have slowed the pace of action" (Ocampo 2006: 32). On the other hand, intra- and extra-regional bilateral swap arrangements besides CMIM represent an alternative means of short-term access to liquidity without the strong IMF link that drawing on CMIM still entails and that member countries associate with painful stigmatization (Denbee et al. 2016). Such bilateral swap arrangements partly exceed the countries' quota in CMIM (Mühlich 2014: 161). Initially, CMI countries could draw on up to 10 and from 2005 onwards up to 20 percent of the maximum amount of the entitled disbursement volume without the need to agree to an IMF program. In 2012, the limit was raised to 30 percent, with a perspective to further increase the ceiling of non-IMF-linked disbursements to 40 percent of the maximum amount of drawings for each country (Kawai/Houser, 2007).

The most essential task for CMIM at present is to develop a forceful regional monitoring and surveillance system to guarantee that the respective lending is adequately protected, and that the long-term sustainability of the mechanism is provided. To date, the reluctance of member states to use CMIM as it stands suggests a lack of certain constituting elements required to live up to the agreed objectives of the regional liquidity pool. CMIM member countries took on this task by creating an independent regional surveillance unit based in Singapore, the ASEAN + 3 Macroeconomic Research Office (AMRO) (Siregar/Chabchitrchaidol 2013). AMRO was officially founded in 2011 as a company and transformed into an international organization in 2016. AMRO's advisory role requires asserting its independence and distinction from IMF advice to build up a truly regional liquidity-providing mechanism. Nonetheless, CMIM is faced with the question of how to introduce adequate enforcement mechanisms while ensuring sufficient flexibility, as well as defining the role of the IMF in CMIM (cf. Dullien et al., 2013; Siregar/Chabchitrchaidol, 2013: 14).

CMIM Contributions, Purchasing Multiples, and Voting Shares

Country	*USD billion*	*(%)*	*Purchasing multiple*	*Voting share (%)*	*"Fire power" Accessible capital (USD billion)*
China (incl. Hong Kong)	68.4	32	0.5	25.43	34.2
Hong Kong	8.4	3.5	2.5	2.98	6.3
Japan	76.8	32	0.5	28.41	38.4
Korea	38.4	16	1	14.77	38.4
Plus-Three	192	80	–	71.59	117.3
Indonesia	9.104	4	2.5	4.369	22.76
Thailand	9.104	4	2.5	4.369	22.76
Malaysia	9.104	4	2.5	4.369	22.76
Singapore	9.104	4	2.5	4.369	22.76
Philippines	9.104	3.1	2.5	4.369	22.76
Vietnam	2	0.8	5	1.847	10
Cambodia	0.24	0.1	5	1.222	1.2
Myanmar	0.12	0.1	5	1.179	0.6
Brunei	0.06	0	5	1.158	0.3
Lao PDR	0.06	0	5	1.158	0.3
ASEAN	48	20	–	28.41	126.2
Total	120	100	–	100	243.5

Source AMRO n.d
Note *Hong Kong, China's purchasing is limited to IMF delinked portion because Hong Kong, China is not a member of the IMF

CMIM Instruments & Terms

Instrument	*Maturity*	*Grace/Rollover period*
Swap, Precautionary line (CMIM-PL)		
IMF—delinked	6 months	Renewable up to 2 years
IMF—linked	1 year	Renewable up to 3 years
0.15% commitment fee		
Swap, Stability Facility (CMIM-SF)		
IMF—delinked	6 months	Renewable up to 2 years
IMF—linked	1 year	Renewable up to 3 years
Conditions: Beyond 30% of a country's allotment, disbursements must be linked to IMF program.		

Source Kawai 2015: 17

c. Arab Monetary Fund (AMF)

AMF

Date of Foundation: 1976 by Economic Council of the League of Arab States
Website: http://www.amf.org.ae/
Legal form: Juridical person (AMF Agreement, 2010).
Headquarters: Abu Dhabi, United Arab Emirates
Member States: People's Democratic Republic of Algeria, Kingdom of Bahrain, Union of the Comoros, Republic of Djibouti, Arab Republic of Egypt, Republic of Iraq, Kingdom of Jordan, State of Kuwait, Republic of Lebanon, State of Libya, Islamic Republic of Mauritania, Kingdom of Morocco, Sultanate of Oman, State of Palestine, State of Qatar, United Arab Emirates of Saudi Arabia, Federal Republic of Somalia, Republic of the Sudan, Syrian Arab Republic, Republic of Tunisia, Republic of Yemen

Today's AMF has the objective of providing liquidity in times of balance-of-payments imbalances. It provides short- and medium-term financing with a maturity of up to seven years. With a total amount of subscribed capital of AAD 900,000 (Arab Accounting Dinars, equivalent to SDR 2.7 billion or USD 3.78 billion; AMF, 2018), the AMF provides very flexible emergency credit lines to its members and is frequently utilized at small drawings, sometimes as a complement to IMF lending.

The AMF came into being in 1977 with 22 West Asian and African countries within the framework of the League of Arab States, founded in 1945. The oil-price boom in the early 1970s provided the economic and political context of the AMF's foundation: "... [oil rich] Arab countries were encouraged to promote Arab regional financial agencies and to supply them with adequate resources [...]" (Corm, 2006: 294). While these conditions did not last long, the AMF "survived the sharp downturn in oil prices during the 1980s and 1990s, and operations continued, albeit at lower levels than in the 1970s" (Corm, 2006: 291).

In times of crises, IMF and AMF programs go hand in hand to provide short-term liquidity support. AMF loans are disbursed in a more timely manner but with a smaller volume: in reaction to the political upheaval during the Arab spring in 2011 and the devastating economic consequences, in 2014 the IMF provided short-term liquidity assistance to several AMF member countries, first and foremost to the newly-elected democratic governments in Tunisia (USD 500 million) and Yemen (USD 550 million). In 2012, the IMF included Morocco in the Precautionary Credit Line program with the offer to make use of a USD 6.2 billion loan in case the repercussions (swings in oil price, decline in exports) of the 2007/08 global financial crisis and the Eurozone crisis rapidly worsened the generally sound economic conditions of the country. Preceding the IMF engagement, in 2012 and 2013 the AMF disbursed a total number of four loans with the aim of reinforcing Tunisia's balance of payment and external position and foreign exchange market, as well as supporting fiscal and financial reforms. In 2012, Yemen also received support to the country's financial and economic reform program from the AMF. In the same year, Morocco and AMF started negotiating a USD 127 million loan to deal with rising food prices and protect political stability after political upheaval in the surrounding nations.

For a joint liquidity fund, the AMF member countries' macroeconomically diverse development provides excellent conditions since the likelihood that all member countries draw on the fund's resources at the same time is less than in a perfectly harmonized group of countries. At the same time, the largest and mostly lending member countries—such as the United Arab Emirates—rely on bilateral currency swaps rather than drawing from the AMF, as the latter's volume would not respond to their emergency finance needs.

AMF Capital Structure

	Subscribed capital (thousands AAD)	*Paid-in capital (thousands AAD)*	*"Fire power" Accessible capital 1-year maturity (USD million)**	*Voting share (%)*
Jordan	14,850	14,850	32.3	7.07[5]
United Arab Emirates	52,950	52,950	114.7	15.13[1]
Bahrain	13,800	13,800	30	6.77[4]
Tunisia	19,275	19,275	42	12.87[2]
Algeria	116,850	116,850	252.9	12.27
Saudi Arabia	133,425	133,425	289.1	13.96
Sudan	27,600	23,000	40.5	19.65[3]
Syria (suspended)	19,875	16,563	29.5	7.07[5]
Somalia	11,025	9,188	16.2	19.65[3]
Iraq	116,850	116,850	252.8	12.27
Oman	13,800	13,800	29.9	6.77[4]
Qatar	27,600	27,600	59.6	6.77[4]
Kuwait	88,200	88,200	191.1	15.13[1]

(continued)

(continued)

AMF Capital Structure

	Subscribed capital (thousands AAD)	*Paid-in capital (thousands AAD)*	*"Fire power" Accessible capital 1-year maturity (USD million)**	*Voting share (%)*
Lebanon	13,800	13,800	29.8	7.07[5]
Libya	37,035	37,035	80.4	12.87[2]
Egypt	88,200	88,200	191.1	19.65[3]
Morocco	41,325	41,325	89.7	12.87[2]
Mauritania	13,800	13,800	29.9	12.87[2]
Yemen	42,450	36,790	68.4	19.65[3]
Palestine	5,940	0	0	7.07[5]
Djibouti	675	563	1	19.65[3]
Comoros	675	563	1	19.65[3]
Total capital	900,000	878,425		

Source AMF 2018
Notes *Calculation by the authors. Notes: Group seats in the decision-making bodies include: [1]UAE, Kuwait; [2]Morocco, Libya, Tunisia, Mauritania; [3]Egypt, Yemen, Sudan, Somalia, Djibouti, Comoros; [4]Qatar, Bahrain, Oman; [5]Syria, Jordan, Lebanon, Palestine

AMF Loan Conditions

Instrument	*Duration*	*Grace/rollover period*	*Interest rate (as of September 2019, %)*
Automatic loan[1]	3 years	1.5 years	1.35
Ordinary loan[1]	5 years	3.5 years	1.36
Extended loan[3]	7 years	3.5 years	1.41
Compensatory loan[2]	3 years	1.5 years	1.35
Structural Adjustment Facility[3]	4 years	2 years	1.35
Short-term liquidity[2]	6 months	renewable two times	1.64

Source AMF, n.d.; AMF Agreement, 2010
Notes: [1]up to 75% of paid-up subscription; [2]up to 100% of paid-up subscription; [3]up to 175% of paid-up subscription; In 2007, the AMF introduced the Trade Reform and the Oil Facility and in 2016, the small and medium enterprises facility was set up. We do not include those facilities here, since they are not as closely related to the objective of balance of payment support as the aforementioned facilities

d. Eurasian Fund for Stabilization and Development (EFSD)

EFSD

Date of Foundation: June 2009 as EURASEC Anti Crisis Fund
Website: https://efsd.eabr.org/en/
Legal form: Trust fund (Treaty ACF 2009).
Headquarters: Operations Management Department of EurAsEC ACF, EDB Office in Moscow, Russia
Member States (year of access all 2009): Armenia, Belarus, Kazakhstan, Kyrgyz Republic, Russian Federation and Tajikistan.

In 2009, some of the member countries of the Commonwealth of Independent States (CIS)—namely, Armenia, Belarus, Kazakhstan, Kyrgyz Republic, Russia, and Tajikistan—established the Anti-Crisis Fund of the Eurasian Economic Community (ACF) with a funding volume of about USD 8.5 billion. It is set up as a trust fund and managed by the Eurasian Development Bank (EDB). In 2015, it was renamed the Eurasian Fund for Stabilisation and Development (EFSD) because the Eurasian Economic Union (EAEU) was established as a successor of the EurAsEC.

The fund aims to achieve its objectives by disbursing financial credits, investment loans, and grants. While it mentions emergency financing in times of balance-of-payments stress in its objectives, the EFSD is not oriented toward further regional monetary cooperation. The highest and only decision-making body is the Council, which is composed of member state Finance Ministers and chaired by the Finance Minister of the Russian Federation. Lending decisions are based on the perceived urgency of a country's financing needs, as well as its creditworthiness and long-term debt sustainability. The absorption capacity of the borrower also plays a role. Our evaluation of the available documentation of the five loan disbursements by the EFSD to date suggests a considerably lower speed than in other RFAs (Mühlich/Fritz 2018). The internal decision time is quicker the lower the loan amount.

The EFSD essentially provides only one line of emergency finance with very long-term credits for several years, which requires a reform program whose implementation is rigorously monitored for disbursement decisions.[1] The EFSD conditions its lending upon the debt history of the requesting country with the EFSD, its member countries, or other financial institutions. The borrower should not be in arrears with any of those. Financial credits are intended to finance budget deficits, providing support in case of balance-of-payments problems or to stabilize national currencies. Since 2018, the EFSD has announced competitive offers for grants from the fund's net profit to finance social programs of the member countries' governments.

Since its foundation, the EFSD has been drawn upon five times by Armenia, Belarus (twice), and Tajikistan (twice).[2] In some cases, emergency liquidity financing is approved in coordination with other financial institutions or partners, including co-financing arrangements. For example, in Armenia, the EFSD and the IMF co-financed a budget support to stabilize the economy in 2014 and 2015. The IMF set the program objectives and EFSD funded the necessary supporting activities. The borrowing member countries of the EFSD use their regional fund frequently but mostly in combination with the IMF and/or bilateral swaps, to which most of the member countries are a partner.

EFSD Capital Structure

Country	*Subscribed capital (million USD)*	*Share of total capital (%)*	*"Fire power" Access limits (million USD)*
Armenia	1	0.01	1,106.69
Belarus	10	0.12	1,787.73
Kazakhstan	1,000	11.75	2,043.12
Kyrgyz Republic	1	0.01	255.39
Russian Federation	7,500	88.11	3,149.81
Tajikistan	1	0.01	170.26
Total	8,513.0*		8,513.0

Source EFSD 2019
Note *10% paid-in capital

[1] The EFSD disburses financial credits and investment loans. Investment loans are intended to finance interstate investment projects. The EFSD is the only regional liquidity fund that provides long-term investment finance in parallel with emergency finance for balance-of-payments stress. As such, it pursues two mandates in parallel: short-term finance and long-term development finance, such as multilateral development banks.

[2] In addition, Armenia received a health care dedicated grant of USD 1 million in 2018.

EFSD Instruments & Conditions

Instrument	*Maturity/Program duration*	*Grace period*	*Interest rate*
Financial Credits (FC)			
Stabilization credit (low inc)	20 years/ 3 years	5 years	1–3% (fixed)
Sovereign loans (middl inc)	10 years/ 3 years	5 years	LIBOR/Floating Rate*
Investment Loans (IL)			
Contracted by member state	15 years	5 years	LIBOR/Floating Rate**
Contracted by project company	10 years	5 years	LIBOR/Floating Rate**

*Rate calculated for each six-month interest accrual and equal to the cost of borrowing for Kazakhstan and Russia on international markets
**For low income countries terms consistent with the requirements of IFIs sovereign loans
Requirement for co-financing by recipient: No less than 20% of the amount of the project
Source EFSD n.d

5.3.2 Regional Payment Systems

a. Latin American Agreement on Reciprocal Payments and Credits (CPCR- LAIA)

CPCR-LAIA

Date of Foundation: Agreement signed in September 1965, modified in 1982
Website: http://www.aladi.org/
Legal form: Central bank agreement (ALADI Agreement, 2014a)
Headquarters: Montevideo, Uruguay
Member States (year of access, all 1965): Argentina, the Bolivarian Republic of Venezuela, Bolivia, Brazil, Chile, Colombia, the Dominican Republic, Ecuador, Mexico, Paraguay, Peru, Uruguay

LAIA's CPCR[3]—as it stands today—was founded in 1982 (in continuance of the 1965-initiated Mexico Agreement), with the aim to encourage

[3] A more extensive analysis of regional payment systems can be found in Fritz et al. 2014.

the use of local currencies in intra-regional trade. The CPCR serves to reduce transaction costs through settlement in domestic currency at the firm level and provides temporary liquidity during a clearance period of four months. At the end of that period, the net amount of all credits is settled multilaterally in US dollars.

While this mechanism was intensively used during the 1980s, the transaction volume channeled through CPCR has significantly declined since the 1990s. The declining use of the CPCR relates to a series of rather specific problems within the system, which also are currently debated within the institution. First, the CPCR has not been able to keep up with the expansion of intra-regional trade since the mid-1990s. For example, intra-regional trade within the free trade agreement of MERCOSUR was conducted without making use of the CPCR. Second, there has been a significant increase in pre-payments (i.e., voluntary settlement of claims before the maturity date of four months). A claim is only settled in advance if there are no better alternatives available for one or both sides of the contract. The increase in pre-payments has caused a steady decline in the comparative advantage of the CPCR in the settlement of intra-regional trade transactions in terms of its providing temporary liquidity by central banks. Third, the incentives to use the CPCR have developed asymmetrically among the members, since increasingly diverging creditor and debtor positions have developed between the largest member countries.

CPCR Operations Summary 2004–2014 (Values in thousands USD)

Year	*Intra-regional Transfers*	*Channeled operations*	*% of intra-regional imports*
2004	2,233.40	2,402.00	3.8
2005	3,917.10	4,106.50	5.1
2006	6,013.70	6,233.80	6.5
2007	11,150.40	11,403.80	9.8
2008	12,316.60	12,657.40	8.8
2009	6,834.50	7,063.40	6.7
2010	4,946.80	5,169.30	4
2011	5,624.50	5,822.70	3.6
2012	5,756.10	22,735	3.9
2013	5,291.90	17,345	3.6
2014	3,818	12,285	2.8
2015	2,021	8,345	1.9

(continued)

(continued)

CPCR Operations Summary 2004–2014 (Values in thousands USD)			
Year	*Intra-regional Transfers*	*Channeled operations*	*% of intra-regional imports*
2016	1,413	4,174	1.5

Source ALADI, 2014b; 2017

b. Payments System in Local Currencies (Sistema de Pagos En Monedas Locales) between Argentina and Brazil (SML)

SML
Date of Foundation: Agreement signed in September 2008. **Website**: http://www.bcb.gov.br/?SML **Legal form**: Central bank bilateral agreement (Banco Central de Argentina, 2008). **Headquarters**: Buenos Aires, Argentina; Brasília, Brazil **Member States**: Argentina and Brazil (since 2008); Uruguay (since 2014); Paraguay (since 2018)

The SML between Argentina and Brazil started its operations in October 2008, and subsequently Uruguay and then Paraguay have joined the mechanism. It is a simple payment system that uses the national currency for trade factorizing and clearing of bilateral trade operations between an importer, an exporter and commercial banks. It is designed to overcome only the transactions costs associated with international trade operations. Use of the SML is voluntary.

Despite the modest ambition, an explicit goal of the mechanism is to develop the foreign exchange market between these two countries: the exchange rate between the Argentinean peso and the Brazilian real is determined on a daily basis and triangulated through the respective dollar exchange rates. Payments are made like in other international transactions, by local banks previously authorized to transfer the operations, which means that credits can be granted in local currencies. Each operation between the central banks via the SML is cleared through the international banking system in New York. The maximum period for this clearing is three days, but it usually takes only 24 h. Thus, there is no clearing period, which enables saving foreign exchange reserves by accumulating and final clearing of net positions between the monetary authorities.

The mechanism started operating with a limited number of operations and trade volume, but especially bilateral trade between Argentina and Brazil increased rather steadily. The trade volume operated via SML since 2012 is over two billion BRL. More impressive is the total number of operations channeled through the SML, which has grown from roughly 1,200 operations in 2008 to around 9,000 to 11,000 operations per year since 2012. Measured in terms of intra-regional trade share, since 2012 it has aggregated between five and six percent of Brazil's exports to neighboring Argentina. This is a small share of Brazilian overall exports, bearing in mind that Argentina accounts for roughly 7 to 8 percent of total trade. For Argentina, Brazil is a larger commercial partner, with relative shares of 20 to 25 percent of imports, and 15 to 20 percent of exports during this time. For bilateral trade between Brazil and Uruguay, a steady increase of operations via SML is also observed, albeit at an even lower relative level compared to trade between Argentina and Brazil.

The SML is designed to cater to the specific needs of small and medium-sized enterprises (SMEs), which have a costlier access to the foreign exchange market due to high transactions costs relative to their small size. Unlike the larger companies in both countries, for these smaller firms the option to pay and receive payments in local currency represents significant cost reductions.

The SML could gain importance by expanding regionally, especially to include other members of MERCOSUR. Uruguay and Brazil negotiated the mechanism from 2009 but took until 2014 to start operations, while Uruguay and Argentina agreed in 2012 and started effectively in 2015 (*INTAL* 2015). Operations with Paraguay are still awaiting regulation, as stated on the Brazilian central bank website.

SML, Summary of Operations (Brazil 2009–2018)

Year	*No. of Export Operations*	*Exports ($R million)*	*No. of Import Operations*	*Imports* (in Million $R)*
2008	31	9.88	10	1.32
2009	1,163	451.06	72	4.30
2010	3,353	1,252.70	40	9.00
2011	4,870	1,623.20	50	8.74
2012	7,431	2,277.90	83	17.25
2013	9,041	2,581.45	47	10.53
2014	9,190	2,313.26	38	5,033.62
2015	10,788	2,504.49	38	37,573.23

(continued)

(continued)

SML, Summary of Operations (Brazil 2009–2018)				
Year	*No. of Export Operations*	*Exports ($R million)*	*No. of Import Operations*	*Imports* (in Million $R)*
2016	8,264	2,469.90	34	21,772.79
2017	7,619	2,341.90	22	4,092.22

Source BCB n.d
Note *The value of imports is the sum of SML transactions which are set in Argentinean pesos and converted to Brazilian reais using the SML rate. This is the amount charged by the financial institutions

c. Unified System for Regional Compensation (Sistema Unitario de Compensación Regional de Pagos) (SUCRE)

SUCRE
Date of Foundation: Agreement signed in April 2009 **Website**: http://www.sucrealba.org **Legal form**: The SUCRE Regional Monetary Council is an international juridical person (SUCRE Agreement 2009). **Headquarters**: Caracas, Bolivarian Republic of Venezuela **Member States** (year of access): Bolivia (2009), Cuba (2009), Ecuador (2009), Nicaragua (2009, ratified in 2012) and Venezuela (2009), Honduras (2009, but not yet ratified), Uruguay (application in 2013)

In April 2009, the member countries of the Bolivarian Alliance for the Peoples of Our America (ALBA) initiated the so-called Unified System for Regional Compensation (Sistema Unitario de Compensación Regional, SUCRE). In its initial stages, the SUCRE initiative aims to reduce transaction costs in intra-regional trade through the use of domestic currencies and it is linked to the saving of foreign exchange by allowing delayed settlement of trade transactions. Its specific political aim is to eliminate the US dollar in intra-regional trade (Trucco, 2012: 116).

The mechanism offers the option of settling final net payments of net trade surpluses and deficits in a domestic or international currency. A key feature of the SUCRE proposal is that it involves the creation of a regional unit of account—the sucre—to replace the dollar for invoicing regional transactions. Its use does not involve the physical emission of sucre and is restricted to only invoicing operations relative to intra-regional trade payments at the central bank level. The sucre was designed to be a common unit with its value derived from a basket of currencies of the member countries weighted according to their relative economic size.

The sucre is a voluntary payment system. From its start in 2010, trade transactions in sucre amounted to 730 million sucre or USD 900 million in 2013. It has been used in an asymmetric manner since its beginning. For instance, until 2012 mainly Venezuela used the sucre for its imports (92.78 percent of all transactions), followed by Ecuador (7.1 percent) and Bolivia (0.12 percent) (SUCRE, 2012: 23).

Among others, the distortions created by the multiple exchange rate system in Venezuela, and the country's deep economic crisis probably explain the small increase in terms of volume transacted during the first years, and its subsequent rapid decline, even from this low level. Since 2016, the mechanism does not provide any data on its transactions. A flexible adaptation of the currency unit to de facto macroeconomic changes in the member countries has never been introduced. Such inflexibility may disincentivize the use of the mechanism.

Summary of Operations SUCRE, 2010–2013

Year	*Operations*	*Value (In millions XSU)*	*Value (In millions USD)*	*Average operation value (in thousands XSU)*	*Average operation value (in thousands USD)*
2010	6	10.00	12.51	1,666.67	2,084.83
2011	431	216.13	270.36	501.46	627.28
2012	2,647	852.07	1,065.85	321.90	402.67
2013	2,094	729.19	908.95	348	434.07

Source SUCRE, 2012, 2013

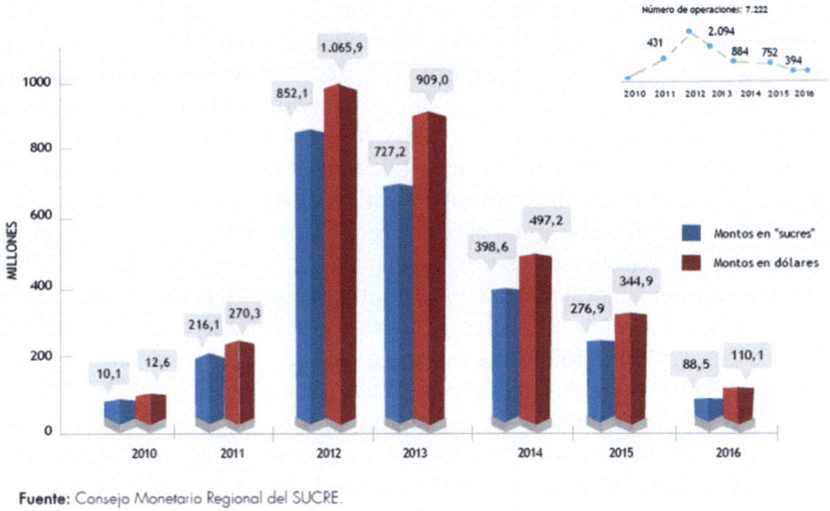

Source: SUCRE 2016.

5.3.3 Macroeconomic Coordination and Monetary Integration Arrangements

A multitude of initiatives to coordinate monetary policies and integrate currencies regionally coin the global South. Instead of proceeding into details about the state of plans in every one of those, we briefly present the challenges that the longest-standing regional monetary cooperation mechanism—the CMA—faces, and then briefly list the planned initiatives. While the CMA is a unique case of regional monetary integration as it roots in colonial initiatives to stabilize the Southern African region's currencies, it nevertheless shows the difficulties of sub-ordinating monetary sovereignty under a regional mechanism.

The Common Monetary Area (CMA) was founded in 1986 as a successor of the Rand Monetary Area (RMA) that had been in place since 1974 between Lesotho, South Africa, and Swaziland. Botswana participated in the negotiations but did not join the agreement, and it left the RMA in 1975 for monetary independence. When Namibia joined in 1992, the CMA was replaced by the Multilateral Monetary Agreement (MMA). The smaller member countries peg their exchange rates at par to the South African rand, which circulates as an additional legal tender in the three smaller member countries. Swaziland had ended the use of the South African rand as legal tender and introduced its own legal currency with the introduction of CMA, and it reintroduced the rand as a parallel legal tender to the national currency in 2003. The rand is the de facto common currency of the CMA Multilateral Agreement. Since the beginning, the SARB's monetary policy has stood at the heart of CMA, preceding and succeeding arrangements. CMA is an integrated financial market with common capital account regulation. The CMA members take joint monetary policy decisions, albeit which are strongly determined by SARB's monetary policy decisions. South Africa determines the reference values for intra-regional exchange rates for the CMA and—because the South African rand follows a managed floating exchange rate regime—extra-regional exchange rates. South Africa's role as a regional lender of last resort is facilitated by the region's pronounced economic heterogeneity. The small market size of the smaller member countries reduces the risk of destabilizing influences on the region; for example, through swings in capital flows (Metzger, 2008: 6). From a historical long-term perspective, Masson and Pattillo (2005: 26) find the role of South Africa as the benignly leading economic power of the region to be the decisive element that has allowed a mutually advantageous regional cooperation arrangement until today. At the same time, economic development in the smaller countries is highly dependent on the anchor role of South Africa.

In different parts of the global South, developing countries aim to achieve similar coordination levels in monetary terms. In Africa, such efforts are numerous, although their progress is limited. In many cases, trade and political disputes and disparate economic developments hinder further monetary coordination. Finding a common denominator for stabilizing intra-regional exchange rates is difficult since harmonization requires giving up perceived monetary policy independence. On the one hand, the trade-off between gaining policy space through a stabilized regionally coordinated monetary policy and giving up decision-making power to regional decisions hinders many countries from committing their policies to the regional initiatives. On the other hand, most of the planned monetary integration schemes have used the Euro as a blueprint, and lost interest in using the Euro zone as a role model since the outbreak of the Euro crisis. Furthermore, political disputes in either initiative are either military or territorial conflicts, as is mostly the case in the African or the Arab context, or—as is the case in MERCOSUR—macroeconomically different political approaches that led to beggar-thy-neighbor policies, which in turn hindered deeper macroeconomic coordination paths. Finally, many of the planned initiatives deal with overlapping membership, whereby countries and mechanisms need to solve contradicting commitments in their membership. In Africa, the African Economic Community (AEC) as laid out in the Abuja treaty is the overarching goal of most monetary coordination initiatives. Since 1992, member countries have aimed to harmonize exchanges rates in the Southern African Development Community (SADC), the Common Market for Eastern and Southern Africa (COMESA), and the East African Monetary Union (EAMU) of the East African Community (EAC). In COMESA, this process seems to be most dynamically advancing in the COMESA Monetary and Fiscal Policy Harmonization (MFHP) program. A monetary union in the Economic and Monetary Community of Central Africa/Communauté Economique et Monétaire d'Afrique Centrale (CEMAC) would have close ties to the former CFA Franc, today the Euro. Such shielding against international financial volatility by asymmetric cooperation with a northern key currency—such as the former Franc and now the Euro in the CFA Franc zone—has provoked the appearance of new regional monetary integration proposals in West and Central Africa as a southern response to delink and form an independent regional currency. The planned West African Monetary Zone (WAMZ) is composed of non-CFA member countries that aim to establish an equally stable monetary policy environment. While in the CFA Franc zone member countries economically suffered from the currency board arrangement due to exchange rate overvaluation and economic crisis, a successfully delinked initiative on regional monetary policy grounds could circumvent dependence on extra-regional monetary policy decisions.

5.4 Discussion of South-South Regional Monetary Cooperation Mechanisms in Comparative Perspective

5.4.1 Liquidity Sharing Arrangements

Emerging markets stock piling foreign exchange reserves in reaction to financial and currency crises as well as the euro and the global financial crisis have given new impetus to liquidity sharing mechanisms that are partly planned as a substitute but hitherto mostly complementary to IMF funding. Moreover, regional development banks such as the Development

Bank for Latin America (CAF) (not further explored in this paper) entered into the provision of very flexible short-term liquidity provision, not to mention the IMF and the World Bank's increasing provision of contingent lending facilities, and more flexible lending with ex-ante conditionality and access criteria.

We can identify three waves of regional liquidity sharing arrangements. They all share a perception of the imperfections of multilateral institutions such as the IMF regarding developing countries' needs in terms of governance structure and short-term liquidity provision in the case of balance-of-payments stress (Grabel 2018). First, in face of the evolving Latin American debt crises of the 1980s, the former Andean and now Latin American Reserve Fund (FLAR) was founded as a regional self-insurance mechanism. Within this first wave of regional liquidity sharing arrangements, but with excess liquidity due the oil-price boom in the early 1970s at least in the oil-rich member countries, the Arab Monetary Fund (AMF) was created with the aim of sharing liquidity reserves in the form of loans to less well-off countries. Second, the series of financial crises in emerging economies led to the perception that independent regional crisis prevention would be needed to avoid inadequate conditionality by IMF programs. It is in this context that the CMI was launched. In face of the volatility caused by the 2007/08 global financial crisis, the initiative was multilateralized and strengthened in terms of volume and institutional design to today's CMIM. Third, precisely the same experience of global financial volatility and a missing international multilateral framework for short-term liquidity provision also led to the development of new liquidity sharing initiatives, such as the Eurasian Fund for Stabilization and Development (EFSD).

As mentioned above, in each of these periods the countries were discontent with the ruling global monetary and financial order. Especially since financial liberalization has spread to emerging market economies, the IMF has been criticized for being too slow in disbursing emergency funds. Second, a heated debate remains about the appropriateness of the (ex-ante and ex-post) conditionality criteria attached to IMF lending (Grimes, 2011; Kentikelenis et al., 2016). Third, its governance structure—which links countries' voting rights to the shares that they hold in the fund—is considered to be outdated due to the dominance of industrialized countries. The 14th quota reform has shown some progress in this regard, although the topic has emerged again in the 15th quota reform. As a result, developing countries and emerging markets perceive a lack of adequate short-term liquidity provision at the international level. In this vein, Eichengreen (2006: 9) suggests that "in the absence of a global fund, the insurance in question could be provided by a regional pool of reserves."

An additional argument in favor of regional arrangements of liquidity sharing or even deeper forms of regional monetary cooperation is based on the fact that regional arrangements allow regionally adapted means of policy response rather than "one-size-fits-all" solutions. Rules for mutual financial support can be adapted during the course of the cooperation in terms of the participating parties, volume, maturity, and conditionality involved (Birdsall/Rojas-Suarez 2004; Ocampo/Titelman 2010; Grabel 2018).

A topical issue is the question of how such regionally-funded and -owned initiatives implement and enforce conditionality criteria for borrowing member countries. While AMF developed its own lines of credit with different lending terms, FLAR does not impose conditionality at all. To date, FLAR shows a redemption rate of 100 percent. By contrast, CMIM has linked its liquidity disbursement to the IMF for withdrawal of funds of more than 30 percent. Thus far, CMIM has not been used by its member countries, not even during the global financial crisis; rather, member countries turned to extra- and intra-regional bilateral currency swap arrangements to counter balance of payment stress and at the same time circumvent the stigma associated with IMF involvement.

Member countries need to be highly committed to jointly enforcing the agreed-upon conditionality criteria: "[R]isk sharing may be limited not because the gains it affords are too small to matter, but rather because contract enforcement may be difficult exactly where risk sharing gains would be largest" (Imbs/Mauro 2007: 40). In addition, a liquidity sharing arrangement needs to avoid problems of moral hazard occurring with regional reserves pooling through a strong surveillance mechanism and enforceable conditionality on emergency lending. For the case of the CMIM, the diversity in terms of contributions and borrowing capacities seems to play an important role in explaining the problems of finding institutional solutions for mutual surveillance and conditionality.

Associated with the question of regional asymmetries and conditionality criteria, a final open question is the appropriate size of liquidity sharing mechanisms: on the one hand, the involvement of larger and more financially developed member countries is needed to sufficiently finance the mechanism; while on the other hand, in most cases those larger member countries will not be able to draw on the fund since it would not provide sufficient financial volumes in a sustainable manner.

5.4.2 Regional Payment Systems

The overview shows that especially within regional payments systems, variation in terms of both development goals and mechanisms is diverse. The mechanisms range from rather simple versions with a focus on reducing transaction costs in regional trade to highly ambitious and complex regional arrangements, including temporary credit provision to intra-regional net importers, and even compensation mechanisms for intra-regional trade imbalances. Such complex mechanisms partly resemble the famous Keynes Plan of a global payment system as an alternative to the Bretton Woods order established in 1948 (Fritz et al., 2014).

On the one hand, one finds long-standing mechanisms between developing countries, such as the Latin American-wide Agreement on Reciprocal Payments (CPCR-LAIA), which was founded in the context of severe economic volatility and debt crises in the 1970s and 1980s. On the other hand, a new wave of mechanisms emerged especially in Latin America in the context of global financial instability and regional block building, such as the Southern American System of Payment in Local Currency (SML) between the core MERCOSUR member countries, and the Unified System for Regional Compensation (SUCRE) between some of the ALBA member countries. These mechanisms are regionally overlapping in part with the older CPCR-LAIA.

As an outcome of the diversity of Latin American regionalism, these mechanisms are associated with a high diversity of development aims, goals, and instruments. SML seeks to enable transnational transactions between MERCOSUR member countries, without having to resort to US dollars, which seems to be especially relevant for small and medium-sized firms in Brazil. However, since its foundation, it has not significantly moved beyond this small target group. While ambitiously starting with the long-term aim of substituting the US dollar in intra-regional transactions, the SUCRE has operated as a regional payment system that only resorts to the sucre as an accounting unit at a low level for some years, with mainly one member country—Venezuela—using it for imports from its neighboring countries, especially Ecuador. The mechanism has recently entered into crisis. Such asymmetries reflect not least different incentives to use the mechanism due to highly diverse macroeconomic stances in the member countries, especially regarding exchange rate policies and incentives for economic actors to hold the domestic currency. The economic and balance-of-payments crisis of Venezuela—together with political shifts in the region—has recently seemed to eliminate the incentives to use and further expand the mechanism. The effectiveness of the Latin American payment system CPC-LAIA is significantly dampened by the fact that deficits at the central bank level—caused by private trade operations—are covered by public guarantees. While this may have been appropriate in times of severe external debt crisis, it currently gives way to the socialization of private risks, making central banks unwilling to participate. Hence, hitherto existing regional payments systems show that proper adjustment to changing regional and global circumstances over time is crucial for the sustained use of the mechanism.

There are a series of regional efforts under way to harmonize national payment systems to facilitate financial transactions within the region. While in many cases the efforts are limited to facilitating market relations, in other cases these seem to be at least open to establishing regional clearing mechanisms to provide liquidity and enable the use of regional currencies in the future, linked to long-term plans of establishing a common regional currency, as is the case in the SADC, the West African Monetary Union (WAMZ), or the EAC.

5.4.3 Macroeconomic Coordination and Monetary Integration Arrangements

While macroeconomic coordination agreements and plans to implement currency unions have gained new momentum for some time in response to volatile global financial markets, most of the initiatives thus far have failed to implement binding coordination mechanisms. Of the numerous ambitious monetary integration plans, most implementation roadmaps have seemed to draw on the idea of the sequencing of the European integration process from trade to monetary integration, primarily including establishing rigorous convergence criteria that hardly any member country is able to meet in the self-imposed timeframes. Hence, such a route seems to be overly challenging, since problems of developing economies and emerging markets are essentially rooted in vulnerability toward external (trade and financial) shocks (see above).

Most vivid are the plans to implement fully-fledged currency unions in West and East Africa, while the longest-standing macroeconomic coordination arrangement in the form of exchange rate coordination exists in Southern Africa with the CMA. However, the CMA is different from all other regional integration initiatives, given that South Africa economically dominates the region and hence takes on an anchor role for the CMA arrangement, which would not be present in any other planned initiative.

The observed detrimental and ambivalent processes demonstrate the inadequateness of conventional concepts of a linear approach to regional monetary cooperation. A linear approach follows the European example and aims to sequence integration from trade toward financial and monetary integration. The idea behind this concept is to improve real sector allocation through market harmonization and bring this to perfection by abolishing intra-regional exchange rates through monetary integration. However, this seems to be even less adequate for developing countries than it is for advanced economies. The Euro crisis shows that regional integration of the real economy and a common currency cannot substitute region-wide financial regulation and surveillance mechanisms, and that intra-regional imbalances in real and financial terms may create fundamental instability that may disturb further steps toward regional monetary integration.

Apart from the inability to meet such initially set targets, in most regions a reluctance to further share policy sovereignty at a regional level can be observed, often linked to uncertainty about the potential gains of regional monetary integration. Hence, national economic, monetary and exchange rate policy stands in the way of a further and deeper cooperation in monetary terms. In fact, such challenges can be observed in the Euro zone until today and make part of the Euro crisis. Most trade-first integration initiatives get stuck along the way toward any form of monetary cooperation.

To sum up, the stocktaking exercise on regional monetary cooperation efforts in the developing world offers us several relevant insights into the understanding of "the regional" in today's multipolar globalized monetary (non)system.

First, we find a surprisingly rich variety of responses to the dissatisfaction with the global forms of crisis finance, currency dominance in the denomination of trade and financial transactions, and the volatility of global financial markets. Such variety surely provides learning grounds for each neighboring region in terms of gaining trust in cooperating and coordinating with other countries in the region, supporting them in finding regional solutions for the incoherence and dramatic shortcomings of current globalization. To varying extents, it helps emerging markets and developing countries to increase their policy space through regional coordination, increasing their productivity in terms of macroeconomic stabilization and development.

Second, those regional mechanisms that are able to most adequate find solutions for the specific problems and challenges of the region, and those that are most capable of adjusting to changed circumstances over time are more likely to satisfy member countries' needs in terms of liquidity provision, fostering regional trade, and intra-regional exchange rate stabilization. Their adaptability to the member countries' changing challenges due to changing global environments on the one hand and their macroeconomic development and achievements on the other is key to surviving as a vivid regional alternative to the missing global system.

Acknowledgements We thank Elia Braunert and Daniel Perico for valuable research assistance. Parts of this contribution were developed for the UNCTAD project "Strengthening pro-growth macroeconomic management capacities for enhanced regional financial and monetary co-operation among selected countries of Latin America and the Caribbean, and West and Central Africa."

References

Akyüz, Y. (2009) *Exchange rate management, growth, and stability: national and regional policy options in Asia*. Colombo, Sri Lanka: UNDP Regional Centre for Asia Pacific Colombo Office.

ALADI (2014a) *Convenio*. Retrieved from: http://www.aladi.org/nsfaladi/arquitec.nsf/VSITIOWEB/cooperacion_financiera_y_monetaria (19/09/01).

ALADI (2014b) *Evaluación del funcionamiento del Sistema de Pagos de la ALADI en el año 2013*. Retrieved from: http://www.aladi.org/nsfaladi/convenio.nsf/documentos/$file/Secdi%202582%20-%20evaluacion%20Convenio%202013.pdf (19/09/01).

ALADI (2017) Evaluación del funcionamiento del sistema de pagos de la ALADI en el año 2016. Retrieved from: http://www2.aladi.org/SitioAladi/documentos/ConvenioDePagos/Evaluacion2016.pdf (19/09/01).

AMF (2018) Annual Report 2018. Abu Dhabi: Arab Monetary Fund.

AMF (2010) *The Articles of Agreement of the Arab Monetary Fund Update 2010*. Abu Dhabi: Arab Monetary Fund.

AMF (n.d.) Types of lending. Retrieved from: https://www.amf.org.ae/en/page/types-lending (19/09/01).

AMRO (n.d.) Overview of the CMIM. Retrieved from: https://amro-asia.org/about-amro/amro-and-the-cmim/#overview (19/09/07).

Banco Central de la República Argentina (2008) *Convenio del Sistema de Pagos en Moneda Local Entre La República Argentina y La República Federativa Del Brasil (SML).* Retrieved from: http://www.bcra.gov.ar/pdfs/sml/convenio%20sml.pdf (19/09/01).

Banco Central do Brasil (BCB) (n.d.) SML trade volume and numbers of operation (19/09/01). https://www.bcb.gov.br/en/statistics.

Bénassy-Quéré, A. & Coeuré, B. (2005) Big and small currencies: The regional connection. In Artus, P., Cartapanis, A. & Legros, F. (Eds.). *Regional currency areas in globalization.* Cheltenham: Edward Elgar Publishing.

Birdsall, N. & Rojas-Suarez, L. (Eds.) (2004) *Financing Development: The power of regionalism.* Washington, DC: Center for Global Development.

Chang, R. (2000) *Regional monetary arrangements for developing countries.* New Brunswick, NJ: Ruttgers University. Retrieved from: https://www.g24.org/wp-content/uploads/2016/01/Regional-Monetary-Arrangements.pdf (19/09/01).

Cohen, B. J. (2000). *The Geography of Money.* Ithaca, NY: Cornell University Press.

Consejo Monetario Regional del Sistema Unitario de Compensación Regional de Pagos (SUCRE) (2009) *Tratado Constitutivo del SUCRE.* Retrieved from: http://www.sucrealba.org/imagenes/documentos/Tratado-Constitutivo-del-SUCRE.pdf (19/09/01).

Consejo Monetario Regional del Sistema Unitario de Compensación Regional de Pagos (SUCRE) (2012) *Informe de gestión 2012.*

Consejo Monetario Regional del Sistema Unitario de Compensación Regional de Pagos (SUCRE) (2013) *Informe de gestión 2013.*

Consejo Monetario Regional del Sistema Unitario de Compensación Regional de Pagos (SUCRE) (2016) *Informe de gestión 2016.*

Corm, G. (2006) The Arab experience. In J. A. Ocampo (Ed.), *Regional Financial Cooperation*, 291–328. Washington DC: Brookings Institution Press.

Denbee E., C. Jung and F. Games Paternò (2016) Stitching together the global financial safety net, Bank of England Financial Stability Paper 36.

Dullien, S., B. Fritz and L. Mühlich (2013) Regional Monetary cooperation in developing areas: lessons to be learnt from the Euro crisis? *World Economic Review*, 2, 1–23.

Edwards, R. (1985). *International monetary collaboration.* Transnational Publishers: New York.

EFSD (2019) The Eurasian Fund for Stabilization and Development. Retrieved from: https://efsd.eabr.org/upload/docs/en/EFSD_eng_2019.pdf (19/09/01).

EFSD (n.d.) Instruments. Retrieved from: https://efsd.eabr.org/en/about/instruments/ (19/09/01).

Eichengreen, B. (2006). *Insurance underwriter or financial development fund: what role for reserve pooling in Latin America?*, NBER Working Paper No. 12451. Cambridge, MA: National Bureau of Economic Research.

Eichengreen, B. (2012). *Regional financial arrangements and the International Monetary Fund*, Working Paper Series 394. Tokyo: Asian Development Bank Institute.

FLAR (n.d.a) Información financiera. Retrieved from: https://flar.net/informacion-financiera (19/09/01).

FLAR (n.d.b) Estructura de capital. Retrieved from: https://flar.net/estructura-de-capital/ (19/09/01).

FLAR (2018) Convenio Constitutivo 20, May 2018. Retrieved from: http://flar.net/wp-content/uploads/2018/12/Convenio-Constitutivo-FLAR.pdf (19/09/07).

Frankel, J. (1988) *Obstacles to international macroeconomic policy coordination*, NBER Working Paper No. 2505. Cambridge, MA: National Bureau of Economic Research.

Fritz, B. and M. Metzger (2006) *New issues in regional monetary coordination – understanding north-south and south-south arrangements*. London: Palgrave Macmillan.

Fritz, B. and A. Biancarelli, L. Mühlich (2014) Regional payment systems: A comparative perspective on europe and the Developing World. *El Trimestre Económico*, LXXXI (4), 324, 875–908.

Grabel, Ilene (2018) *When Things Don't Fall Apart. Global Governance and Developmental Finance in an Age of Productive Incoherence*. Cambridge: MIT Press.

Grimes, W. W. (2011) The future of regional liquidity arrangements in East Asia: Lessons from the global financial crisis. *Pacific Review*, 24(3), 291–310.

Henning, R. C. and M.S. Khan (2011) Asia and global financial governance, Working Paper Series WP 11–16. Washington, DC: Peterson Institute for International Economics.

Henning, R. C. (2009) The Future of the Chiang Mai Initiative: An Asian Monetary Fund?, Policy Brief PB09–5. Washington, DC: Peterson Institute for International Economics.

Imbs, J. and P. Mauro (2007) Pooling risk among countries, IMF Working Paper WP/07/132. Washington, DC: International Monetary Fund.

Institute for the Integration of Latin America and the Caribbean (INTAL) (2015) Sistema de Pagos en Moneda Local entre Argentina y Uruguay. Carta Mensual INTAL No. 226.

Kentikelenis, A, Stubbs, T, & King, L (2016) IMF conditionality and development policy space, 1985–2014. *Review of International Political Economy*, 23(4), 543–582.

Kawai, M. (2015) From the Chiang Mai Initiative to an Asian Monetary Fund. Tokyo: ADBI Working Paper No. 527. Tokyo: Asian Development Bank Institute.

Kawai, M and C Houser (2007) Evolving ASEAN + 3 ERPD: Towards Peer Reviews or Due Diligence? ADBI Discussion Paper 79. Tokyo: Asian Development Bank Institute.

Masson, P. and C. Pattillo (2005) *The monetary geography of Africa*. Washington, DC: Brookings Institution Press.

Metzger, M. (2008) *Regional cooperation and integration in Sub-Sahara Africa*, Discussion Paper 189. Geneva: United Nations Conference on Trade and Development (UNCTAD).

Mühlich, L. (2014) Advancing regional monetary cooperation - The case of fragile financial markets. In Tomann, H. & Hölscher, J. (Eds.), Studies in Economic Transition. Houndmills, Basingstoke: Palgrave.

Mühlich, L. and B. Fritz (2018) Safety for Whom? The Scattered Global Financial Safety Net and the Role of Regional Financial Arrangements, *Open Economies Review* 29(5), 981–1001.

Ocampo, J. A. and D. Titelman (2010) Subregional financial cooperation: The South American Experience, *Journal of Post Keynesian Economics*, 32(4), 249–268.

Ocampo, J.A. (2006) Regional financial cooperation: Experiences and challenges. In J.A. Ocampo (Ed.), *Regional financial cooperation*, 1–39. Washington, DC: Brookings Institution Press.

Rosero, L. D. (2014) Regional Pooling of International Reserves: The Latin American Reserve Fund in Perspective. *Latin American Policy*, 5, 62–86.

Schelkle, W. (2001) *Monetäre Integration*. Heidelberg: Physica.

Siregar, R. Y. and A. Chabchitrchaidol (2013) Enhancing the effectiveness of CMIM and AMRO: selected immediate challenges and tasks, Working Paper Series 403. Tokyo: Asian Development Bank Institute.

Titelman, D., and C. Vera, P. Carvallo, E. Pérez-Caldentey (2014) Un fondo de reservas regional para América Latina. *Revista De La CEPAL*, 112, 7–29.

Trucco, P. (2012) The rise of monetary agreements in South America. In Riggirozzi, P, and D. Tussie (Eds.), *The rise of post-hegemonic regionalism: The case of Latin America*, Vol. 4 (Ch. 6). Dordrecht: Springer.

UNCTAD (2007) *Regional Cooperation for Develop-ment.* Trade and Development Report. Geneva: United Nations Conference on Trade and Development.

UNCTAD (2009) *Responding to the global crisis – climate change mitigation and development*. Trade and Development Report. Geneva: United Nations Conference on Trade and Development.

UNCTAD (2011) *Regional monetary cooperation and growth-enhancing policies: The new challenges for Latin America and the Caribbean*, Geneva: United Nations Conference on Trade and Development.

CHAPTER 6

The Clearing Union Principle as the Basis for Regional Financial Arrangements in Developing Countries

Jan Kregel

6.1 Introduction

6.1.1 Developing Countries and the International Financial System

Ever since the creation of the Bretton Woods system, developing countries have argued that their interests were not adequately represented by the major multilateral financial institutions. This has led to repeated calls for reform of representation of developing countries within the IMF governance system and at the same time for the introduction of IMF policies that are more supportive of economic development in the world's less-industrialised countries.

Initially these proposals were limited to calls for an adjustment in IMF quotas to better reflect the modern disposition of economic power that

J. Kregel (✉)
Levy Economics Institute of Bard College, Annandale-on-Hudson, NY, USA
e-mail: kregel@levy.org

D. Barrowclough et al. (eds.), *South–South Regional Financial Arrangements*, International Political Economy Series,
https://doi.org/10.1007/978-3-030-64576-2_6

has been shifting in favour of the developing countries. More recently, there have been calls to replace the IMF and World Bank by regional organisations that would be more representative of the interests of developing countries. The appeal to regional solutions recalls the criticisms of the IMF made by Robert Triffin, and his proposals that the IMF would be more efficient if it were operated on a regional basis because such an arrangement could better represent the interests of developing countries of specific regions and provide policies designed on better recognition of the particular problems they face.

In addition to the calls for the creation of regional financial institutions, many developing countries have called for the replacement of the US dollar at the centre of the international financial system. This also echoes Triffin's early prediction that the Bretton Woods system as originally conceived was based on an internal contradiction caused by the use of a national currency, the dollar, as the basis of international settlement. Although originally designed to deal with the problem of deficient dollar liquidity in the 1970s reforms of the Bretton Woods system, many have suggested that the use of special drawing rights (SDRs) might better be used as a substitute to the US dollar as the major invoice and settlement currency in the international trading system.

These issues reflect the intrinsic differences between the national banking system and the international system of providing international stability, which are a source of instability. These differences were long-identified by Keynes in his assessment of the gold standard system and have nonetheless been preserved in the operation of the IMF. In today's system, the measures required to restore external equilibrium require adjustment in the form of a reversal of the country's deficit to achieve a surplus. But balance of payments accounting says that globally surpluses and deficits sum to zero, thus a deficit country can only repay its borrowing to the Fund if there are offsetting surpluses elsewhere in the system, but the Fund does not insure that this will happen. Thus, if there is no adjustment in the rest of the world to allow increasing deficits, the adjustment can only take place through reductions in the level of income in the borrowing country and thus for the world economy. The paradoxical result is that the mechanism to ensure financial stability imposes instability on the global economy in the absence of coordination of policies between deficit and surplus countries.

As a result, groups of developing countries at a similar level of development have implemented proposals to create arrangements for the regional or bilateral swap of reserves and even for the creation of regional currencies. Such arrangements have been proposed or are already in existence in the ASEAN Ching-Mai initiative, MERCOSUR, and the BRICS countries, and a number of financial institutions have been proposed or created, such as Banco Sur, the BRICs bank (the New Development Bank), and the Asian Infrastructure Investment Bank. However, most of all these regional arrangements include the participation of an IMF programme at some stage. They join a number of existing regional payments arrangements such as the Corporacion Andina de Fomento and the Latin American Reserve Fund (FLAR).

As yet, their potential remains unfulfilled. In an ambitious vision outlined before the economic crisis of 2007–2008 of last decade and before the coronavirus crisis of this one, the UN-DESA suggested: "Looking into the future, an organisational structure [...] could be conceived entailing the establishment of a dense network of multilateral, regional and sub-regional financial institutions to provide official financing, basically on a complementary basis.[1] [...T]his model could be extended to macroeconomic surveillance, again with regional institutions complementing multilateral ones, whereas regional arrangements might be especially suitable for macroeconomic policy coordination. Such a network of institutions would be more similar to federal arrangements, like those of the United States Federal Reserve Board, or the slightly less formal structure of the European Central Bank. Indeed, the post-war European experience of building financial cooperation, combined with growing macroeconomic surveillance, may offer some interesting lessons at the global level."

Despite these potentialities, existing regional financial arrangements among developing countries are only in an embryonic stage. The valuable role that regional reserve funds can play is illustrated by the Andean Reserve Fund, created in 1978, which became the Latin American Reserve Fund (FLAR) described in other chapters in this volume. Also, as described elsewhere in this volume, after the East Asian crisis, Japan had proposed the creation of an Asian monetary fund. Though the proposal was well received throughout the region, the idea was shelved owing to objections from outside the region. However, a more modest version was created in 2000, when the Association of Southeast Asian Nations

[1] Ocampo et al. (2006) prepared for the follow-up to the Monterrey Consensus.

(ASEAN)—China, Japan and the Republic of Korea—created a system of bilateral currency swap arrangements known as the Chiang Mai Initiative, as well as institutionalised meetings of finance ministers for policy dialogue and coordination.

6.1.2 *National and International Monetary Systems—Why Regional Financial Arrangements Have Emerged*

The reasons for the growth of Regional Financial Arrangements become clear when realising that the analysis of national financial systems is usually carried out on the basis of a closed national economy, and so must be adapted significantly to consider the international monetary system. It requires two types of adjustment. One is to take into account the impact of international trade on domestic incomes and financial conditions. Here external deficits lead to an increase in foreign borrowing and a surplus to an increase in foreign lending, in both cases to offset the external imbalance. This is the basic framework of the Bretton Woods adjustment system outlined above. IMF lending is required to provide the foreign borrowing when foreign lenders are unwilling to do so and the IMF adjustment programme is the recipe to return the country to surplus in order to repay the IMF and the foreign lenders. This was a reasonable characterisation as long as there were minimal foreign capital flows independent of trade financing. Indeed, the Bretton Woods system was predicated on this assumption.

However, after the 1970s crisis in the Middle East, private capital flows became dominant and created a second change in the analysis of the closed system. In the presence of open international capital markets, it was possible for the capital account to either offset or reinforce the current account balance. The size of international capital flows far exceeded the resources available to the IMF and the result was the introduction of floating exchange rates. However, the same problems of adjustment remained, but capital flows created the possibility of a much larger external imbalance when lenders continued to invest in a country despite a trade deficit. As a result, instability increased and the resolution of the imbalances occurred more frequently in the form of banking and exchange rate crises as foreign lenders pulled back.

In what follows it will be useful to conceive of the domestic and international systems as what might be called a "dual financial systems," or what is often presented as the difference between money and credit. For the national system, domestic money is the liability of the government (or gold) and credit the liability of the private financial system. At the international level, the "international" money is the US dollar (or gold), which is still the liability of the US government, and credit the liabilities of the other countries, whether of the government or the private sector. The former are the reserves and the latter the credits. In this way it is easy to see the ambiguous role of the US dollar under the Bretton Woods system as the reserves for the liabilities of US financial institutions and of the liabilities of the other nations in the international financial system. It is then obvious that the reserves that the US central bank creates to pursue the stability of US domestic financial institutions will be the same as the international reserves required for the stability of the liabilities of the other nations in the world. The instability and conflict inherent in the system are then caused by the fact that the objectives of the US Federal Reserve in creating US government money are directed towards the conditions only in the US economy and, as will be seen, will in general be at odds with the needs and financial stability of developing countries.

This conflict of interest has become even more visible in the current international financial environment in which the policies of zero interest rates (ZIRP) and quantitative easing (QE) that were introduced in the US in order to counter weakness and instability in the US economy have made capital flows to developing countries more attractive, producing an impact on domestic liquidity conditions that may conflict with those of domestic monetary authorities, and appreciation in exchange rates that may not be supportive of the competitiveness of domestic industry. When the US central bank indicated in May of 2013 that these policies might no longer be needed, the reversal in capital flows, collapsing exchange rates and growth slowdowns produced substantial disruption in developing countries as well as a collapse in commodity prices, which caused deterioration in both trade and capital accounts simultaneously.

It is thus sensible that developing countries should seek an alternative international financial architecture that is no longer based on this conflict of policy objectives created by the dual financial system, whether it is a fixed or a floating rate system. The question is what system should developing countries propose that will be more in their own interests? As will be noted below, the problems of diverse objectives across different countries were already present in the divergence between the post-war US economy and the conditions of the war-ravaged European combatants. While the US approach to post-war international financial reform relied basically on uniformity in performance of the members of the system as represented by roughly balanced external accounts over time, the UK government produced an alternative that would maximise the ability of countries in diverse stages of reconstruction to implement diverse domestic policies. That proposal was for an International Clearing Union, based not on gold or the US dollar, but on a national settlement currency or unit of account; instead of a stabilisation fund to lend countries the funds needed to stabilise their exchange rates relative to the dollar, it provided for automatic lending denominated in a notional unit of account from surplus to deficit countries to allow them to introduce coordinated stabilisation policies.

The International Clearing Union proposal drafted by Keynes was constructed around what he called the "banking principle," in contrast to the US position, which, as noted above, was based on a dual money and credit system. Instead of credit being built on a reserve base, Keynes argued that banks are primarily engaged not to produce substitutes for government means of payment, but rather to provide payment services. In short, the principle is that banks make payments on their clients' behalf, rather than providing their clients with means of payment. Since these payment services are achieved by means of netting debit and credit positions through a clearing system, they must be made in some standard of value that is a notional unit of account. As will be seen in more detail below, such a system eliminates the problems of an external currency or a fixed exchange rate between money and credit, and thus the instability that is associated with those systems is absent in a clearing-based system.

While Keynes's Clearing Union was not adopted by the Allied powers, nor even discussed at the Bretton Woods conference, a very similar system was introduced at the behest of the US and implemented by Triffin for the recipients of US Marshall Plan aid under the Economic Cooperation Administration. It is largely considered to have been a success, which suggests that it might have produced a more stable international financial architecture than the one that was actually introduced under the Bretton Woods agreements. Since then it has not been tried. But it is clear that it provides both the possibility of diverse national economic conditions and avoids the instability of a dollar-based system. It is thus here suggested that it is the most promising reform to meet the needs of developing countries.

In evaluating the possibility of a regional clearing arrangement that might better serve the interests of developing countries, it is necessary to assess first the drawbacks of the current dollar-based system for developing countries, then to investigate the importance of the banking principle that Keynes used as the basis for his clearing system. It is then necessary to evaluate the evidence and experience that is available from the actual experience of this principle on a regional basis: the European Payments Union.

As already mentioned, the Bretton Woods system did not survive the presence of increasing and increasingly volatile capital flows. These capital flows are a dominant source of the instability and linkage between US monetary policy and developing countries' monetary policy. Decisions will have to be made on how to deal with capital flows within the regional units and between the regional units and the rest of the world. This will be a crucial element of providing stability for clearing systems.

Finally, the proposal must deal with the relation between multilateral financial institutions, such as the IMF and the World Bank, and the regional financial institutions, as well as any potential problems that might arise in conjunction with the WTO's protocol on financial services.

6.2 Bretton Woods and Its Problems

Ever since Robert Triffin's 1950s prediction of the collapse of the Bretton Woods gold-dollar standard due to the internal contradictions of an international monetary system based on a national currency the developed world has been searching for a better financial architecture. It was more by necessity than decision that the world was forced to embrace floating exchange rates in the mid-1970s. And while there were acolytes of the free operation of markets in setting prices, the exchange rate soon appeared not to be one of them and international interest rate arbitrage flows quickly overwhelmed the impact of trade imbalances. As a result, the criticisms of the role of the dollar were not alleviated, but aggravated, by the Smithsonian Agreements and the decisions in the Jamaica Accord to abandon exchange rate stability as the major objective of the IMF.

Despite President Clinton's call for a new financial architecture in the aftermath of the 1997–1998 Asian financial crisis and the decision to proceed with the UN Financing for Development Conference, held in Monterrey some five years later, the "consensus" proposals were scarcely innovative and nearly all were built around an alternative to the dollar as international reserve currency. These ranged from greater use of the SDR to commodity reserve currencies. Since the SDR is composed of national currencies it really only multiplies the problem raised by the dollar. Commodity currencies simply take this problem to one remove since the commodities have to be valued in something, which in all likelihood would be the dollar (which would then return via a back door, so to speak). The basic problem is that while Triffin identified the inherent contradictions in the gold-dollar standard, this did not resolve the basic problems that Keynes has raised with any international standard. And most of the reform proposals were simply to substitute something in the place of gold that could be controlled. The decision to replace gold with the dollar did not reduce the problems of inequity and instability in the system, and Keynes's analysis of the international financial system suggests that substitution of gold or the dollar is not a viable remedy.

As Keynes pointed out, the international system under the gold standard was neither equitable nor stabilising: "[T]he main cause of failure of the freely convertible international metallic standard" was "that it throws the main burden of adjustment on the country which is in the debtor position on the international balance of payments" (Keynes, Vol XXV: 27). "[I]t has been an inherent characteristic of the automatic international metallic currency [...] to force adjustments in the direction most disruptive to social order, and to throw the burden on the countries least able to support it, making the poor poorer" (ibid.: 29). Indeed, the historical performance of the gold standard confirms this assessment. When debtor countries are faced with adjustment via credit restriction and declining domestic prices the pressure on the domestic financial system and the pressure of recession in incomes leads quickly to the suspension of the commitment to gold, while creditor countries resist the expansion of credit and the impact of higher levels of activity and pressure on prices by limiting convertibility and introducing counter-inflationary policies. While Keynes's criticism of the operation of the gold standard as being asymmetric and motivated by the perceived need of the UK to implement policies to maximise employment and prevent systemic deficiency of global demand that would make it a debtor country, his more fundamental critique is that it is a major destabilising element in the international system.

In addition, Keynes notes that the supposed coordination of the policies of the countries on an international standard "is to secure uniformity of movements in different countries—everyone must conform to the average behaviour of everyone else. [… T]he disadvantage is that it hampers each central bank in tackling its own national problems" (Keynes, Vol VI: 256). It is the uniformity of monetary and interest rates across countries facing very different domestic conditions produced by the existence of a convertible international standard, rather than the asymmetric adjustment, that produces the constraint on national monetary policy. Keynes also drew attention to "a further defect" in the supposed automatic coordination of economic adjustment under an international standard: "the remittance and acceptance of overseas capital funds for refugee, speculative or investment purposes" (XXV: 30), and in contrast to earlier periods "capital funds flowed from countries of which the balance of trade was adverse into countries where it was favourable. This became, in the end, the major cause of instability." His conclusion was that since "we have no security against a repetition of this after the present war […,] nothing is more certain than that the movement of capital funds must be regulated" (Keynes, Vol. XXV: 31).

This observation reprises Keynes's view of the importance of variable speeds of adjustment of financial and real variables as disruptive of any automatic adjustment process: "It is, therefore, a serious question whether it is right to adopt an international standard, which will allow an extreme mobility and sensitiveness of foreign lending, while the remaining elements of the economic complex remain exceedingly rigid. If it were as easy to put wages up and down as it is to put bank rate up and down, well and good. But this is not the actual situation. A change in international financial conditions or in the wind and weather of speculative sentiment may alter the volume of foreign lending, if nothing is done to counteract it, by tens of millions in a few weeks. Yet there is no possibility of rapidly altering the balance of imports and exports to correspond" (VI: 336).

Indeed, a characteristic of the post-Smithsonian Bretton Woods system has been the tendency for international capital to flow from debtor to creditor countries. This was first seen in Europe as speculative funds flowed to Germany forcing repeated exchange rate adjustments and in the global economy in the negative net flows of financial resources from developing to developed countries in the 1980s. Just as members of the euro area of the EU have not been spared financial instability with the single "inter-regional standard" replacing the Deutsche Mark, emerging markets countries are not likely to find a remedy to their complaints if the dollar is replaced with the SDR or an international reserve currency.

6.2.1 *The Bretton Woods System and Developing Countries*

As noted in Keynes's argument it is the existence of different economic conditions in different countries employing the common standard that makes the uniformity of an international money disruptive. (This is something that has recently been learned in the EU experiment with a common standard, the euro.) And the question of similarity of economic conditions was important in the contrasting approaches to the international architecture before the Bretton Woods conference. At the simplest level, this difference was between the US, which was little impacted by the war, and European combatants whose productive capacity had been decimated by the war. In the end it was decided to suspend the implementation of the Bretton Woods agreements and to create the International Bank for Reconstruction and Development (IBRD) to solve the problem of reconstruction in Europe. Only once the economies were again sufficiently similar would the stabilisation fund system come into operation.

Indeed, in the discussions over the post-war economic and financial structure, the debate was between those countries that were most interested in promoting local and global full employment and thus most likely to be in structural deficit—basically the UK—and a country that was experiencing positive expansion and what seemed to be a structural external surplus—the US. The debate was thus over the policies appropriate for eliminating these imbalances in the absence of what was believed to be the automatic mechanism of the gold standard.

The fear of the deficit countries was that the need to maintain stable exchange rates would require them to sacrifice full employment policy, whereas the surplus countries were more concerned about the inflationary impact of the measures that would be required to maintain exchange rate stability. Thus, the UK position proposed by Keynes was for a "symmetric" adjustment mechanism in which both surplus and deficit countries would be obliged to cooperate, whereas the US position proposed by Harry White was for a "stabilisation" fund in which the deficit country would be provided bridge financing to preserve exchange rate stability while introducing policies to reduce external imbalances.

But, while the problems created by the differing productive capacities of the US and Europe were at the centre of discussion, the difference between industrialised countries and primary producing countries were largely ignored until the Havana Conference and then they disappeared until the creation of UNCTAD in 1964. It is interesting that a similar debate over the role of developing countries in the international financial system to be designed at Bretton Woods never occurred.

Developing countries were not well represented at Bretton Woods; indeed, many were not yet in existence, and the question of the impact of the international financial system on development was hardly discussed except at the last minute with the addition of the last word to the title of the IBRD. There was no discussion of the implications for developing countries of the decision to promote stable exchange rates and to use the IMF's short-term stabilisation funds to employ policies to reduce or eliminate deficits. The implicit assumption behind the system was that members would, on average, have balanced external positions, because this is what would be required for maintaining exchange rate stability. This also implicitly applied to developing countries that would become members of the IMF.

In contrast, consideration of development policies was left primarily to UN agencies in the early post-war period. Their analysis of the problems that faced developing countries was based on the presumption of scarcity in domestic savings and financial resources. Thus, the problem of development was perceived as providing flows of financial resources from developed to developing countries. The first UN development decade (Stokke 2009) that set a growth objective of 5 per cent for developing countries therefore concluded that this would require a transfer of 1 per cent of developed country GDP to developing countries. The US programme of support for Latin America in the 1960s, the Alliance for Progress, was also predicated on inducing capital flows from the US to Latin America.

Few economists noted that this approach to development contradicted the principles of the Bretton Woods institutions because it would require sustained balance of payments surpluses in developed countries that corresponded to the capital outflows to developing countries—and conversely for developing countries to run balance of payments deficits that corresponded to the acquisition of industrial imports from developed countries. However, if international financial stability required stable exchange rates, this meant that the size of the deficits that could be run by developing countries would be limited by conditions of international financial stability and not by the needs of developing countries. Indeed, the very policies that would be required to preserve exchange stability would be designed to reduce the development possibilities of developing countries.

But the presumption of external equilibrium was not the only component of cognitive dissonance between development policies that were being proposed and conditions for international financial stability. When internal adjustment policies supported by IMF conditionality were unable to produce a reversal of external disequilibrium, countries were required to introduce currency realignment. Although Keynes argued that the new international system would require substantial exchange rate flexibility, his concerns—apart from granting countries the ability to adjust exchange rates within 10 per cent of parity without reference to the IMF and to introduce restrictions on trade under the scarce currency clause—were rejected (Skidelsky 2000).

However, the efficacy of devaluation in producing external balance was already known to require very precise elasticity conditions (summarised in the Marshall-Lerner conditions). Although it was not obvious that these conditions applied to developed countries—indeed, it was generally believed that the UK on the one hand and the reconstructing economies on the other did not satisfy the conditions—whether they would be satisfied in developing countries was never considered. It seems reasonable a priori that they would not have been met, and much of Prebisch's argument concerning the negative impact of the declining terms of trade were couched in terms of the impossibility of developing countries meeting those elasticity conditions.

The post-war international financial system was thus designed on the presumption of external equilibrium across countries, in which deficit countries would be primarily responsible for external adjustment through internal demand policies and, when that was not sufficient, to use exchange rate depreciation to reinforce the impact of contractionary fiscal policies. Conversely, international development policy was formulated on the presumption that sustained surpluses of the developed countries would be available to finance deficits of the developing countries in support of sustained expansion and the inapplicability of exchange rate adjustment as a measure of influencing external balances.

That these two visions of the post-war financial system were inconsistent does not seem to have occurred to the IMF, IBRD, or United Nations, each of which is respectively responsible for exchange rate stability and economic development. In this context, Prebisch's concerns can be seen as a recognition of this inconsistency, whereas the emergence of the Washington Consensus can be seen as a resolution of this cognitive dissonance in official policy by rejecting the need for any special conditions and policies for developing countries.

This internal inconsistency represented a major obstacle for developing countries and ignored a major problem: international debt. Because foreign exchange would be required to pay for the excess of imports of necessary consumption goods and capital goods over exports required for the development plans, these plans required positive net resource flows encouraged by early UN development policy. Over time, however, these flows generate debt service outflows that cause the current account deficit to increase unless the trade deficit is reduced to accommodate a fixed level of capital inflows and lead to a reduced impact on development. Alternatively, foreign capital inflows would have to increase to accommodate the rising current account deficit caused by the increased debt service payments on capital factor services accounts for any given level of the goods account deficit, leading to an ever-increasing level of external debt. Neither solution would be compatible with the stability of the international system conceived at Bretton Woods.

As Domar (1950) has shown, a development strategy based on net imports financed by foreign capital inflows can only exist with a stable ratio of debt to GDP if the interest rates paid for foreign capital are equal to or less than the rate of increase of lending by foreigners. If interest rates are higher than the rate of increase of inflows, the policy will eventually and automatically become self-reversing as the current account becomes dominated by interest and profit remittances that exceed capital inflows.

In the context of the cognitive dissonance between stability of the international financial system and development, it is interesting to note that the Domar conditions for a sustained long-term development strategy based on sustained external financing are equivalent to the conditions required for a successful Ponzi financing scheme. As long as the rate of increase in inflows from new investors in a pyramid or Ponzi scheme is equal to or greater than the rate of interest paid to existing investors in the scheme, there is no difficulty in maintaining the scheme. However, such schemes are eventually condemned to failure because of the increasing absolute size of the net debt stock. Domar's condition only refers to the ratio of debt to GDP, not its absolute size.

External financing cannot provide developing countries with a permanent development strategy unless the rate of increase of export earnings is equal to the rate of interest on the outstanding debt. However, if the foreign borrowing is not used for expenditures that create net foreign exchange earnings (it makes little difference if this is domestic infrastructure investments or purchases of basic or luxury consumption goods or military equipment), the country's development planning will be subject to maintaining the steady rate of increase in capital inflows and will become a hostage to international financial markets. But even if foreign borrowing is used to expand export potential, any external event that causes the rate of increase in inflows to fall off will create domestic instability and require domestic adjustments to reduce dependence on external resources, which usually leads to a financial crisis through failure to meet financial commitments. At the same time, to make foreign lenders confident in the country's ability to meet foreign commitments, policies that enhance the short-term ability to pay, such as building up foreign exchange reserves or reducing external dependence by reducing domestic growth to produce a stronger export performance and fiscal balance, must be implemented. However, these policies are also self-defeating from the point of view of positive development, because they either reduce the capital inflows that can be maintained on a permanent basis or reduce the growth of per capita incomes. External financing as a source of a long-term development strategy is thus a double-edged sword that must be managed judiciously if it is to contribute to development rather than becoming a source of persistent financial instability and crisis. The international financial system's prejudice in favour of limited external imbalances, however, is as much of an impediment.

Another alternative, given by Ohlin (1995), is to recognise that deregulated open competitive internal markets and sustained international capital inflows are neither necessary nor sufficient conditions for a successful development strategy. He noted that there is sometimes an indignant presumption that there should always be a net transfer to developing countries in order to help them to import more than they export. Behind this presumption there is the old idea that countries in the course of their development should be capital importers until they mature and become capital exporters. This, however, does not mean that they should receive positive net transfers, borrowing more than they pay in interest and dividends. If export performance and the returns on the use of foreign resources are adequate, foreign debts and investments can be serviced without the aid of new loans (Ohlin 1995: 3).

The bottom line is that the international financial system has to be capable of accepting sustained and substantial international imbalances to provide the funding of such scenarios, as well as allowing developing countries to practice policies that produce the required export earnings to generate the funds required to meet debt service and debt repayment. And here the discussion recalls the cognitive dissonance described previously, because the international financial system was designed to prevent the existence of such sustained imbalances and continues to promote and encourage policies to eliminate them.

The Bretton Woods framework for international trade and financial stability was thus predicated on application to developed countries at a similar stage of development and with similar productive structures. It implicitly precluded the implementation of any development strategy that relied on developing the manufacturing sector by imports from developed countries producing substantial international imbalances. This is because it was predicated on a rough balance in external positions over time to preserve exchange rate stability.

The presumption of exchange rate stability and the preclusion of dual exchange rates prevented developing countries from overcoming cost disadvantages in their nascent export sectors; in addition, the use of devaluation as a tool for eliminating external imbalances also worked against the ability of developing countries to develop the foreign exchange through exports that were necessary for financing the development of manufacturing.

The international financial system developed at Bretton Woods may have been appropriate for developed countries; it was a positive impediment to developing countries' attempts to embark on a strategy of industrial catching up.

6.3 The Banking Principle and Financial Institutions

To understand the difference between the US Stabilisation Fund and the UK Clearing House principle it is necessary to look at the institutional characteristics of the banking and financial system. The Stabilisation Fund is based on what may be termed an outside money system or a theory of banking based on the quantity theory as it was interpreted under the gold standard. Thus, the quantity of gold (or coin and currency) issued by the government is considered to be exogenously created without counterpart liabilities. The quantity of money can be increased in only three ways. The first is digging it out of the ground. The second is via external surplus under a fixed exchange rate system (or possibly a sticky price system) that generates claims on gold held in the rest of the world. The third is via the operation of fractional reserve banks. Here banks receive deposits of exogenously created "money" and issue their own liabilities as substitutes in a multiple determined by the reserve ratio. Thus, bank credit creation provides a substitute means of payment that increases the amount of outstanding purchasing power over and above that created by the government or the gold from the mines. This is the kind of system described in Hayek's (1937) *Monetary Nationalism* and the recognition that investment cannot be constrained by saving as long as the banks engage in multiple credit creation. It leads to the obvious recommendation that if stability is defined as investment being limited by voluntary saving then the money multiplier must be eliminated. This can only be done via 100 per cent reserve backing or other measures that limit money creation to the supply of saving. It is also the system that was recommended by Henry Simons and Irving Fisher. It is what Keynes referred to as a "real-wage" economy.

The alternative approach to the banking system that Keynes proposed was "the banking principle," which he defines as "[t]he necessary equality of debits and credits, of assets and liabilities. If no credits can be removed outside the banking system but only transferred within it, the Bank itself can never be in difficulties" (XXV: 44). This approach is based on a very different interpretation of money.

To understand this approach it is best to go back to Keynes's own definitions of money in the *Treatise on Money*, where he defines money as "that by delivery of which debt contracts and price contracts are discharged, and in the shape of which a store of general purchasing power is held," noting that money "derives its character from its relationship to the money of account, since the debts and prices must first have been expressed in terms of the latter." He goes on to note that from the money of account it is possible to distinguish: "Offers of contracts, contracts and acknowledgements of debt, which are in terms of it, and money proper, answering to it, delivery of which will discharge the contract or the debt [...] for many purposes the acknowledgements of debt are themselves a serviceable substitute for money proper in the settlement of transactions. When acknowledgements of debt are used in this way, we may call them bank money [...] an acknowledgement of a private debt, expressed in the money of account, which is used by passing from one hand to another, alternatively with the money proper, to settle a transaction. We thus have side by side State money or money proper and bank money or acknowledgements of debt" (Keynes, I: 2, 5).

Keynes is here distilling the results of a long tradition in banking: "A dealer in debts or credits is a Banker" (Hawtrey 1919: 4). Hawtrey is simply echoing McCleod's description of banking found in his *Theory of Credit* (1894). A similar account of the operation of banks can be found even earlier in Colwell's (1859) *The Ways and Means of Payment* that defines banking as "a system by which men apply their credits to the extinguishment of their debts. [...T]his is in direct contrast with the cash or money system, in which every article is either paid for in the precious metals at the time of delivery, or at some time afterwards. These two systems work side by side" (Colwell 1859: 188–189).

In this alternative payments system, "a class of men is formed, who make it their business to deal in these securities, or evidences of debt. If a banker or broker purchases the two notes given by the merchant and his customer, it is obvious that both receive the means from him to pay the notes of which he has become holder and owner. The Process of payment between them will be very simple, if the banker merely gives each of the two parties credit on his books for the proceeds of the notes purchased of them their respective checks on these credits pay off the whole indebtedness [...]" (ibid.). Thus, "banks become, in this way, substantially book-keepers for their customers" (ibid.: 9), and "[t]he books of the banks furnish, thus, a mode of adjustment by which the customers are enabled to apply their credits to the payment of their debts" (ibid.: 10), "[...n]o currency can be more suited to pay a man with than that which he has issued himself" (ibid.: 8).

Mitchell Innes (1914) provides a similar explanation of the operation of banks: "A credit cancels a debt; this is the primitive law of commerce. By sale a credit is acquired, by purchase a debt is created. Purchases, therefore, are paid for by sales. The object of commerce is the acquisition of credits. A banker is one who centralises the debts of mankind and cancels them against one another. Banks are the clearing house of commerce. [...t]he value of credit does not depend on the existence of gold behind it, but on the solvency of the debtor" (Innes 1914: 168).

Minsky also provides a similar view of the system at a more advanced level: "Banking is not money lending; to lend, a money lender must have money. The fundamental banking activity is accepting, that is, guaranteeing that some party is creditworthy. A bank, by accepting a debt instrument, agrees to make specified payments if the debtor will not or cannot. Such an accepted or endorsed note can then be sold in the open market. A bank loan is equivalent to a bank's buying a note that it has accepted" (1986: 258). But, for this system to function it requires that the bank debtors have access to bank deposits to liquidate the loan.

The implication of this approach was codified by the British financial journalist Hartley Withers who noted that "[m]ost of the money that is stored by the community in the banks consists of book-keeping credits lent to it by its bankers. It is usually supposed that bankers take money from one set of customers and then lend it to other customers; but in most cases the money taken by one bank has been lent by itself or another bank" (Withers 1906: 46), and that "the greater part of the banks' deposits consist, not of cash paid in, but of credits borrowed. For every loan makes a deposit" (ibid.: 51).

Thus, while unlimited purchasing power can be created from a fractional reserve banking system, and its destabilising properties controlled by limiting the creation by controlling reserves, this is not the explanation of Keynes's banking principle. In this approach the role of commercial banks is to "make payments" on behalf of their clients by organising an alternative payments system, rather than providing an alternative "means of payment" to their clients which allows them to make payments. The evolution of the banking system may thus be viewed as an evolution of how banks provide the bookkeeping function of netting client assets and liabilities, or what is more easily seen as a "clearing house" function for debts.

As Colwell notes, "[t]he credit system does not, then really furnish a substitute for money, so much as a model of dispensing with it" (Colwell, op. cit.: 193). Indeed, in this point of view the credit system is a financial innovation that "creatively destructs" the use of commodity or government money by economising and replacing it as a means of payment in the commercial transactions of the economy: "In all stages of commerce, we find there has been a constant effort to dispense entirely with the use of precious metals" (ibid.: 157). "[...I]ndividuals might have trouble, owing to particular circumstance, in meeting payments; but a whole class or body of men could not, unless from other causes, because the fund for payment could never be short, and interest upon credits could never go to a high rate."

The idea is easiest to see in terms of a clearing house system. As long as all debtors are members of the clearing and settled within it, there can only be individual divergences between debts and credits, but not for the system as a whole. Any divergences can be handled by means of internal clearing house credits, as was indeed the case in the regional "money centre" banks that participated in clearing houses in the US before the creation of the Federal Reserve. And this is precisely what Keynes defined as the banking principle—the offsetting of debits and credits without reference to an external means of payment at values determined in a unit of account.

It is difficult for the modern observer to appreciate this system, for in the modern financial system bankers accept liabilities from the private sector in exchange for the issue of their own liabilities that not only serve as means of making payment, but are "means" of payment because they are guaranteed redeemable at sight, and thus substitutes for State money. As Colwell notes, this is a guarantee that cannot be kept because "under our present system," bank liabilities are "required to be convertible at will into gold or silver. In point of fact they are not so convertible, and they cannot possibly be, as they amount at all times to a sum from ten to twenty times greater than any possible amount of gold and silver which would be available for such purposes. [...N]either the necessities of business, nor the demands of convenience, require to be convertible on demand[...] This requirement, as it operates, is one of the most mischievous blunders in modern times" (ibid.: 197–199). It is this instability the 100 per cent reserve requirement is meant to eliminate, but the clearing system provides an alternative, which Keynes translated from the national system to the international system.

Minsky also notes that the reason that banks are able to provide clearing via a system of sight redemption of its liabilities that so bothered Colwell: "In our system payments banks make for customers become deposits, usually at some other bank. If the payments for a customer were made because of a loan agreement, the customer now owes the bank money; he now has to operate in the economy or in financial markets so that he is able to fulfil his obligations to the bank at the due dates. Demand deposits have exchange value because a multitude of debtors to banks have outstanding debts that call for the payment of demand deposits to banks. These debtors will work and sell goods or financial instruments to get demand deposits. The exchange value of deposits is determined by the demands of debtors for deposits needed to fulfil their commitments. Bank loans, while ostensibly money-today for money-later contracts, are really an exchange of debits from a bank's books today for credits to a bank's books later" (Minsky 1986: 258). In simple terms, bank liabilities are held because businesses have debts denominated in those same liabilities and thus they extinguish those liabilities.

6.4 The Banking System and the International Level: Keynes' Clearing Union

As Keynes noted in his proposals for post-war international monetary reform, the fact that "the problem of maintaining equilibrium in the balance of payments between countries has never been solved since methods of barter gave way to the use of money and bills of exchange [...] has been a major cause of impoverishment and social discontent and even of wars and revolutions" (XXV: 21). His proposals for the post-Second War financial system sought a solution to the problem by avoiding the difficulties caused by the Treaty of Versailles, as represented in his first popular book, *The Economic Consequences of the Peace*. Indeed, it is difficult to understand any of the discussion of post-war international finance without reference to the financial problems of the Treaty of Versailles and the Dawes and Young committees dealing with German reparations and the debts of the Allies to the US.

Two fundamental principles emerged from problems caused by German reparations payments. The first was that reparations could only be achieved through net exports of goods and services, not by fiscal surpluses and financial transfers, and second that this could only be achieved if the recipient country was willing to open its domestic markets and accept an external deficit. The formulation of proposals for the post-war system was dominated by the need to make sure that the absence of these two conditions, which had led to volatile international capital flows and exchange rates, should not be repeated.

As Keynes's thinking evolved, a third fundamental principle gained ascendancy, "the banking principle" that we have discussed above, which as noted he defines as "[t]he necessary equality of debits and credits, of assets and liabilities. If no credits can be removed outside the banking system but only transferred within it, the Bank itself can never be in difficulties" (XXV: 44). As his thinking progressed, "the analogy with a national banking system is complete. No depositor in a local bank suffers because the balances, which he leaves idle, are employed to finance the business of someone else. Just as the development of national banking systems serves to offset a deflationary pressure which would have prevented otherwise the development of modern industry, so by carrying this analogy into the international field we may hope to offset the contractionist pressure which might otherwise overwhelm in social disorder and disappointment the good hopes of our modern world" (XXV: 75).

But as noted above, this principle did not refer to credit creation via the fractional reserve credit multiplier creation of bank deposit liabilities. It is not a pyramid of money approach; it was motivated by an application of his theory of liquidity preference and effective demand.

One of the initial solutions to the reparations problem that is relevant to the concerns of emerging markets because it took the role of developing countries into account was made by Hjalmar Schacht for an international "Clearing House" or International Settlements Bank (see Lüke 1985: 248) to Owen Young during the committee of experts that met in Paris in 1929. The idea behind the plan was to resolve the difficulty faced by the German industry in producing for export due to the loss of raw materials for its former colonies, and the difficulty in penetrating the export markets of its creditors. The clearing house was to make loans to developing countries in support of the provision of raw materials to Germany and to create markets in these countries for German exports. Schacht notes that his objective was "to take decisive action to strengthen German export trade in order to achieve a surplus. [...T]he economic history of the past decades had furnished convincing proof that loans should be used first and foremost to help the under-developed countries to make full use of their raw materials and gradually to become industrialised. Before the war the European capital markets had supplied the funds in connection with loans for the economic advancement of the under-developed South American and Balkan States and many other overseas territories. England, France, Germany, etc., had not been in need of foreign loans: on the contrary they had been creditors and suppliers of capital to under-developed countries. Germany was now an impoverished country and no longer able to make loans to others. If the Allies really wished to help her to meet her reparations liabilities they should grant loans to the under-developed countries, and thereby put the latter in a position where they would be able to purchase their industrial equipment in Germany. No useful purpose would be served by allowing Germany to compete in existing world markets against other European industrial states as she had hitherto done." This objective was never realised, but the proposal formed the basis for the Bank for International Settlements (BIS) with the reduced objective of managing reparations payments.

The reform plans that were discussed in the early 1940s were built on another of Schacht's schemes, the "New Plan" based on bilateral "Clearing Accounts." As economics minister he applied the "very simple principle that Germany must refrain from buying more than she could pay for, in order to prevent an accumulation of foreign debt which would make a proper trade balance still more difficult to establish in the future." Given that the creditor countries' "system of import quotas had closed markets to German goods" he sought "to find countries which would be willing to sell their goods not against payment in their own currency, but against […] German goods. […T]he best solution was the establishment of 'clearing accounts.' Foreign countries selling goods to us would have the amount of our purchases credited to their account in German currency, and with this they could then buy anything they wanted in Germany" (Schacht 1949: 80–81). Since Germany was in bilateral deficit with most countries this led to "blocked credit balances" of Reichsmarks, or what were called "Sperrmarks," that could only be used for specific types of payments—either to foreign exporters or bond holders, leading to a demand for German exports to release them. As Beyen (1951: 104–7) notes, creditor "governments had to square the account with whatever Germany was prepared to deliver; and they were inclined to do so because the German purchases solved their unemployment problem. There may be some exaggeration in the story that the Balkan countries had to buy mouthorgans none of its inhabitants care to play on, or aspirin in quantities that could have poisoned the whole populations […,] clearing agreements enabled the German government to 'modulate' its imports and exports and to adapt its international trade to its needs for rearmament."

Thus it was not Schacht's 1929 clearing house plan, but his system of bilateral clearing agreements that provided the blueprint for both the Keynes and White plans for a stable international financial architecture. Keynes's expressed these initial ideas for the post-war system in these terms: "The virtue of free trade depends on [it…] being carried on by means of what is, in effect, barter. After the last war laissez-faire in foreign exchange led to chaos" (XXV: 8). He noted in this regard that it was Dr Schacht that provided "the germs of a good technical idea. This idea was to […] discard the use of currency having international validity and substitute for it what amounted to barter, not indeed between individuals, but between different economic units. In this way he was able to return to the essential character and the original purpose of trade whilst discarding the apparatus which had been supposed to facilitate, but was in fact strangling, it" (XXV: 23).

But Keynes assured his critics, this "does not mean that there would be direct barter of goods against goods, but that the one trading transaction must necessarily find its counterpart in another trading transaction sooner or later" (ibid.: 18).

Keynes's proposal was based on the simple idea that financial stability was predicated on a balance between imports and exports, with any divergence from balance providing automatic financing of the debtor countries by the creditor countries via a global clearing house or settlement system for trade and payments on current account. This eliminated national currency payments for imports and exports; countries received credits or debits in a notional unit of account fixed to national currency. Since the unit of account could not be traded, bought, or sold it would not be an international reserve currency. The implication was that there would be no need for a market for "foreign" currency or reserve balances, and thus no impact of volatile exchange rates on relative prices of international goods or tradeable and non-tradeable goods. In addition, the automatic creation of credit meant that the UK would not be constrained by its non-existent gold reserves nor its non-existent dollar balances in financing its reconstruction needs for imports.

Since the credits with the clearing house could only be used to offset debits by buying imports, and if not used for this purpose they would eventually be extinguished, the burden of adjustment was shared equally—credit generated by surpluses had to be used to buy imports from the countries with debit balances. Alternatively they could be used to purchase foreign assets, foreign direct or portfolio investment, but the size of these purchases would be strictly limited by the size of the surplus country's credit balance with the clearing house. Once an agreed limit on the size of multilateral debits and credits for each country was reached—called its "quota"—penalties in the form of interest charges, exchange rate adjustment, forfeiture or exclusion from clearing would be applied and the outstanding balances would automatically be reduced. Although Keynes's initial proposals did not take developing countries into account, the subsequent drafts suggest that the interest charges on the credit and debit balances generated could be provided as additional credits to support the clearing accounts of developing "backward" countries (XXV: 120).

Another advantage that Keynes claimed for his plan was that it was multilateral in nature, in difference from Schacht's bilateral clearing agreements. It also avoided the problem of blocked balances and multiple exchange rates for different types of balance and different countries that had been prevalent within the exchanges under the bilateral agreements. Both of these attributes were considered to be primary objectives of any post-war arrangement and were also present in the US proposal and were expressly included in the Final Act Bretton Woods Agreements.

Given the historical experience of the negotiations and performance of the structure launched at Bretton Woods it would seem obvious that the aspects that emerging market economies find objectionable cannot be fixed by means of the policy proposals that they have put forward. It is the structure that has to be changed, and the structure of the Keynes proposal would seem to meet the criticisms more directly.

Under these more radical proposals there can be no currency wars, no wall of money, no interest rate arbitrage. Foreign investment by any country is limited by its global current account position. Indeed, there would be no need for discussion over the efficacy of capital controls, or whether they should be on inflows for outflows, or monitored by the creditor country central bank or the debtor country central bank. As Keynes had envisaged in his original proposal: "International capital movements would be restricted so that they would only be allowed in the event of the country from which capital was moving having a favourable balance with the country to which they were being remitted" (XXV: 16–17). Capital flows would extinguish foreign credits in the same way as imports and thus would only be "allowed when they were feasible without upsetting the existing equilibrium" (ibid.: 17) on external account.

Thus replacing the dollar with a non-national currency or the SDR will not eliminate the problems facing emerging markets. Neither will increased multilateral cooperation, even if that could be achieved. The creation of financial institutions governed by regional or other restricted groupings do create the most important possibility, but not in the form in which they are currently being discussed. The current proposals are primarily designed to escape the inadequate governance of the IMF and the World Bank and the dominance of the US in both the theory and practices of these institutions. In addition, as noted above, they usually take the IMF as the template and at some level of financial commitment impose IMF programme conditionality.

There is no reason why these institutions cannot be created on the template of the Keynes clearing unions, building on the bilateral swap agreements that many countries have already established. Thus the creation of a common currency for the members of the Banco Sur may not be the most sensible proposal, but the creation of a regional clearing union with a notional unit of account would provide a remedy to the problems faced by these countries. Indeed, Keynes had already considered this as a possibility: "One view of the post-war world which I find sympathetic and attractive and fruitful of good consequences is that we should encourage small political and cultural units, combined into larger, and more or less closely knit, economic units. Therefore, I would encourage customs unions and customs preferences covering groups of political and geographical units and also currency unions, railway unions and the like. Thus, it would be preferable if it were possible, that the members should, in some cases at least, be groups of countries rather than separate units" (XXV: 55). Thus, the currently proposed financial institutions could be cast in the form of clearing unions.

Indeed, there is already an historical experience of the operation of a regional clearing union in the European Payments Union which provided an integral part of the restoration of intra-European trade and payments to complement the Marshall Plan. This might provide a better template for the emerging markets initiatives than the IMF.

Aside from Latin American countries, few developing countries were present at Bretton Woods. India was still represented by Great Britain and the Chinese presence was apparently a question of American political expediency. Indeed, in the discussions of the clearing union there was virtually no consideration of developing countries. This was primarily because the concentration was on post-war reconstruction finance. It was only in the discussion of the collateral issues of commercial policy and commodity support schemes that development questions emerged. They were quickly separated from the financial discussions because they were considered a threat to rapid approval of the international financial reform.

Indeed, as noted above, only Schacht's original proposal for a clearing union directly concerned developing countries, but this was a source of financing German inputs of primary materials and a market for German exports rather than as a positive development agenda. The other proposal that took developing-country concerns into account, if only generally, was John H. Williams' (1949: 173) assessment of the post-war proposals that their "fundamental requirement is the maintenance of an even [external] balance, with only temporary fluctuations from it" (ibid.: 158) and that this presumes the same principle as the gold standard which was "based on the principle of interaction between homogenous countries of approximately equal size" (ibid.: 173). Recognising that different countries might require different currency schemes, his "key currency" proposal involves only the major "key" currencies. He raised the question of whether "the world needs a single, uniform system or a combination of different systems by consideration of the diversity of countries, and in particular the differences in their proportions of home and foreign trade." This line of reasoning leads directly to the needs of countries with different export compositions and the problems faced by countries with primary commodity dependence that was to be raised by Prebisch, Singer, Myrdal and others. For these countries may require sustained periods of external deficit (foreign finance of industrialisation) or external surplus (export-led development) which is directly contrary to the basic principle of equilibrium external balance as the key to international financial stability. The same is true of multiple exchange rates, which many economists have suggested may play a crucial role in policy to build a more balanced productive structure in developing countries (e.g., Kaldor 1964; Diamand 1978), but which are expressly excluded under Bretton Woods because of the experience of German rearmament.

Keynes's clearing union approach is just as deficient in this respect as the stabilisation fund approach and some special measures would have to be included to allow for developing countries to have relatively larger debit (or credit) balances and to eliminate the sanctions on such balances since they would be the result of a successful development policy. Otherwise countries that have used either import substitution or export-led growth strategies that are too successful could find themselves facing additional charges and pressure to reign in or adjust their successful policies in order to keep their external accounts within acceptable ranges. These special measures might include exemption on the size of balances and remission of the interest charges for developed country creditors and developing country debtors. Alternatively, the Bank could have been made a more development-centred institution and made an integral part of the IMF. Or, more simply, an alternative clearing union institution for developing countries could have been proposed. Clearly a balanced external account may be the most appropriate objective for the international financial stability of developed countries, but it certainly need not be so for developing countries. Indeed, multilateral institutions and the

UN have consistently argued for the transfer of resources from developed to developing countries in magnitudes of 0.7 per cent of developed country GDP, which would presumably generate interest charges on the resulting deficits and surpluses for the donor and recipient countries (cf. Kregel 2016).

6.5 The Experience of the European Payments System[2]

6.5.1 *The Return to Multilateral Settlement in Europe Under the Marshall Plan*

European reconstruction after the Second War was dominated by what came to be called "dollar scarcity," that is the availability of means of payment for the purchase of US goods necessary to rebuild the ravaged European productive structure. Although the IMF was instituted in 1944, it was precluded from financing capital expenditures such as those required for reconstruction and, further, none of the European countries were in a condition to meet the Article IV conditions requiring exchange convertibility for current account transactions necessary to access IMF stabilisation programmes. Thus, those critics of the new international financial architecture who had argued that it was designed for economic conditions that did not, and might not ever, exist were largely correct. The IMF was thus incapable of resolving the problem of the reconstruction of Europe via substantial imports from the US that were limited by dollar reserves, of which these countries had none. Even reliance on the development of trade among the recovering countries was inhibited by exchange rate instability for which the IMF could provide no remedy. Thus reconstruction was initiated on intra-European trade on the basis of bilateral exchange regimes between countries that were little different from those that had prevailed before the war and which the IMF was supposed to supplant. According to Guido Carli, then a Bank of Italy official responsible for exchange rate policy, despite the existence of the IMF principle of fostering multilateral trade: "Immediately after the war

[2] The historical description of the evolution of the post-war European settlements and payments systems and passages cited below are drawn principally from Carli (1958), Tew (1963), and Kaplan and Schleiminger (1989).

200 bilateral payments agreements had been established among European countries. A number of them reproduced the model experienced in Europe during the 'thirties.'" A survey of these bilateral payments agreements is given in the eighteenth annual report of the BIS (1948: 81): "They were usually concluded between governments, according to fairly uniform pattern: the central banks, as technical agents, supplied their own currency at a fixed rate of exchange against that of their partner up to a certain limit, which was often referred to as the 'swing,' since it was intended to afford room for minor fluctuations in commercial deliveries between the two countries; beyond the limit thus fixed settlements had generally to be made in gold or convertible currency."

"Countries with deficits tended to restrict imports from countries with surpluses to protect their scarce supplies of gold and convertible foreign exchange. In the course of 1947, effective credit or debit balances under existing payments agreements were tending to exceed the bilateral ceilings. Simultaneously there was an actual decline in the volume of intra-European trade and this was regarded as probably due to the progressive paralysis of the payments agreements." By October 1947 the "margins of credit under the agreements were almost exhausted. The need for greater margins of flexibility led to the November 1947 *Agreement on Multilateral Monetary Compensation* promoted by the Committee of European Economic Cooperation set up to implement the Marshall Plan."

According to Carli a "group of junior central bank officials—I was one of those—came to the conclusion that intra-European trade could be expanded by the institution of some system of multilateral compensation and multilateralisation of credits among European countries. What we were aiming at was a mechanism by which European countries having bilateral surpluses with other European countries could mobilise surpluses to offset deficits in order to keep payments in gold and convertible currencies at a minimum level. Following a meeting which took place in London in September 1947 coinciding with the annual meeting of the IMF, France, Italy, the Netherlands, Belgium, and Luxembourg signed a 5-nation agreement on multilateral compensation. The meeting was held at the bottom of the bunker situated in the neighbourhood of the British Parliament and it was where the British Cabinet met during the war. Our initiative was regarded with great suspicion by central bankers and particularly by the staff of the Bank for International Settlements (BIS). The dominant creditor position of Belgium among the European countries, and the limited number of participants in the scheme restricted the scope for compensation. Belgium was, inside the group of five countries, in the strongest position having available resources of coal, steel and copper. In negotiating trade agreements between Italy and Belgium, representatives of both countries struggled hard: on the Italian side to obtain export quotas as large as possible of essential raw materials from Belgium, and on the Belgian side to make such quotas conditional upon acceptance by Italy of imports of lettuce that quite honestly exceeded the absorption capacity of the Italian market. A memorable fight between Italian and Belgian negotiators became known at the time as the 'Battle of the Lettuce.'"

In order to make mechanisms of bilateral compensation inside Europe more effective it became increasingly evident that reserves in convertible currencies ought to be expanded. The only possibility was to dedicate to that aim part of the funds allocated by the US under the European Recovery Programme (ERP). This idea met some resistance by the American administration because the ERP had been approved by the American Congress to cover specific dollar deficits of European countries related to programmes of recovery of their economies. Another reason of opposition was that the Economic Cooperation Administration (ECA), an agency of the US Government set up to administer the ERP, was anxious to stimulate competition of European industries.

In October 1948, the 16 OEEC countries signed an agreement under which part of the ECA assistance to European countries was based upon the amount of each country's planned bilateral surplus with each of the other members. Recipients of conditional aid were required to provide drawing rights to each bilateral partner with whom they expected to have a surplus during a specified period. Thus each ERP country would receive drawing rights on the member countries with which they were expected to have a bilateral deficit, entitling them to incur a given amount of deficit without being required to pay gold. By this device nearly every country entitled to ECA aid both extended drawing rights to other members and received drawing rights from others. This was the beginning of what was to become the European Monetary Union (EMU) based on a system of multilateral clearing and creation of international credits to support the expansion of trade in the European recovery.

The participation of Britain in such a system was anomalous, in particular because of the existence of outstanding "sterling balances" represented by the credits that British Commonwealth countries had extended to the UK in support of the war effort. Since these credits were in sterling their value to the Commonwealth countries was dependent on the convertibility of sterling with the rest of the world. Thus these countries could claim priority on any British surplus with any of its trading partners. Since the UK had declined the US offer to resolve this problem within the negotiations over the creation of the IMF it remained as a bone of contention within Europe and an impediment to the return of sterling to convertibility.

It was against this background, Richard Kahn, one of Keynes's closest collaborators, proposed a "Discount Scheme" (Kahn 1949) that "provides for a multilateral clearing between the participating countries of payments resulting from current transactions. Over any interval of time some of the participants will accumulate credit balances and some debit balances in the clearing, these representing the accumulated balance of payments on income account of each country with all the other participants taken together. The algebraic sum of these credit and debit balances will always be zero. I come now to the essence of the Scheme. From time to time (e.g., at six-monthly or yearly intervals) these balances would be liquidated in dollars (or gold), the owners of the credit balances receiving dollars from the owners of the debit balances. But instead of such liquidation taking place at exchange parity (in which case the Scheme would be tantamount to the resumption of full convertibility by all the participants) it would take place on the basis of reckoning the European currencies at a discount in terms of the dollar. This discount, the same of course for all the European currencies involved, I shall call the 'European Discount.' It would be altered from period to period according to need, but it would be fixed at the beginning of each settlement period (or, perhaps better, a couple of months before) for the whole of that period, so that the authorities of each country could operate their economies with full knowledge of the value of intra-European exports, and of the cost of intra-European imports, passing between their own country and the other participants. The European Discount would not of course in any way apply to the rates of exchange at which transactions were effected between traders in the various countries. It would apply only to the settlement of net balances arising from intra-European trade. And such settlement would be definitive—the liquidation in dollars, on the basis of the Discount, would be complete. I do not attempt to estimate what this European Discount should be, either at present or over the next few years, but my guess is that at the present time (and with present rates of exchange—those of early September, 1949) a discount of rather less than 50 per cent would work out about right. The main advantages of a scheme of this kind can be summarised as follows:

a. It would enable trade inside Western Europe, and between Western Europe and the sterling area, to be provided with a multilateral instead of a bilateral basis. The advantage of full 'transferability' would be secured, without the disadvantages of full 'convertibility.'
b. In so far as participation in the Scheme was general, the obstacle to freer European trade represented by the gold points in certain payments agreements would be circumvented. Nevertheless, intra-European credit balances would still yield dollars (and if it were possible for, e.g., Belgium's favourable balance with the other participants to increase, under the operation of the Scheme, in proportion to the European Discount, Belgium's total dollar [or gold] receipts from the other participants would be maintained).
c. Resumption of normal economic relations would become a continuous process, instead of involving an abrupt break from a regime based on free gifts and interest-bearing loans by some European countries to others. The way to restoration of full convertibility would be open. As conditions became more normal, and in particular as exchange rates became readjusted to current needs, the European Discount could, and should, be progressively reduced. Its complete elimination would spell the restoration of full convertibility.
d. Additional countries could at any time join the Scheme (irrespective of whether or not they were recipients of Marshall Aid or covered by the European Recovery Programme).
e. The pattern of European trade would be free to develop under economic influences instead of being subjected to the strait-jacket of bilateralism (moderated somewhat by the system of transferable accounts), and of the preconceived estimates of civil servants, who, apart from other human failings, can never have been clear to what assumptions their estimates of trading balances were intended to relate.
f. In influencing the course of imports, the authorities of each country would exercise a preference for imports from Europe (and the sterling area) over imports costing dollars, such as it was the presumed

object of the Marshall Plan to encourage and the two actual Intra-European Payments Agreements have encouraged to only a very limited extent.

g. But, though costing less than their equivalent in dollars, additional imports from the other participating countries would by no means cost nothing. The European Discount would from time to time be fixed at such a rate as to give the stimulus to European trade that was wanted but not more than was wanted. So long as Europe's economic condition tends, by and large, towards the inflationary, there is a distinct limit beyond which it is undesirable to carry the stimulation of intra-European trade, which must to some extent carry with it a reduction of Europe's exports to dollar countries and a diversion of resources from important domestic uses.

h. The authorities of each country would be stimulated to assist, in so far as it was in their power to do so, exports to dollar destinations even at the expense of exports to European destinations. One of the anomalies of the present position is that it is morally embarrassing, and intellectually difficult, for a Minister or Civil Servant to advise on the relative desirability of these different destinations. How is the dollar export drive to be reconciled with the case for increasing trade within Europe? The European Discount would give the answer. And, here again, there would now be less danger that the 'closer economic integration of Western Europe' would simply result in a loss of dollar earnings.

i. At the same time the worship of dollar exports would not be carried *a outrance*. Additional exports to European destinations would also provide dollars, though not so many as the same amount of dollar exports. The fixing of the European Discount must to some extent be a matter of trial and error. It would have been fixed too low if the Scheme was showing signs of resulting at the settlement in excessive dollar payments by some participants to others, and if it gave an inadequate stimulus to the participants to buy from one another in preference to buying from outsiders. The Discount would have been fixed too high if the Scheme was found to give an excessive stimulus to European trade, at the expense of European exports to, and of European imports from, non-participating countries."

Thus, the scheme was primarily intended to provide for a flexible internal depreciation of the European currencies in order to increase competitiveness of intra-European exports relative to US imports.

6.5.2 *The European Payments Union as Part of the ERP*

Since US funding was required for settlement within any multilateral clearing, the US became more involved in the design of such schemes. During the second half of 1949, Paul Hoffman, in charge of the implementation of the ERP, proposed a scheme for a single market in Western Europe. Although it took decades before a Single European Act was agreed upon, European ministers responded by opening negotiations for the creation of the European Payments Union (EPU), which could be regarded as the forerunner of the "European System of Central Banks." Given the delays in operations of the IMF, the EPU was the first international monetary system to function effectively after the Second War and the first step on the road to economic integration of Western Europe.

The EPU was built on a multilateral settlements system for Europe that would eliminate quantitative restrictions on intra-European trade and provide a framework for dealing with balance of payments crises. Accounting trade surpluses and deficits were settled by crediting or debiting each member's clearing account. EPU credits covered any country's deficits with other EPU members, because each member agreed to accept EPU clearing credits in settlement of a credit against any other member. The bilateral positions were thus replaced by an EPU clearing balance. When a country's credit or debit surpassed a certain threshold, the excess had to be settled partly in gold. Schedules fixing the proportion of the monthly settlements to be made in gold by debtors and to be received in gold by creditors was based on a sliding scale with an increasing proportion by debtors as their cumulative deficits rose and receipt of a decreased proportion by creditors as their cumulative surpluses rose.

The liquidity of the payments system was secured by the members themselves through the automatic extension of credit within the stipulated limits and by the working capital of the EPU supplied by an ECA contribution of $350 million to be used whenever gold payments to creditor countries exceeded gold received from debtor countries.

The OEEC supplied the structure for the EPU. Its keystone was the Managing Board, independent experts elected by OEEC councils.

Although some held senior positions in the governments of the largest members of the system, they did not function on the EPU Board as government representatives and they could only offer recommendations to officials of member governments. The EPU offered the first multilateral credits conditioned on macroeconomic adjustments—based on Board recommendations on appropriate fiscal and monetary policies.

Richard Kahn noted the differences and similarities with his original scheme "for multilateral payments," in which "at regular intervals the balances of each participant with the other participants taken together (which must add up algebraically to zero) would be settled by transfers of dollars (or gold), after they had been reduced in value by the amount of the 'European Discount,' which could be altered from time to time. This settlement would be definitive—the liquidation in dollars, on the basis of the Discount, would completely discharge the outstanding credit and debit balances. Under the EPU, the members will extend lines of credit to the Union and have lines of credit extended to them by the Union. The extent to which these credits are to be utilised is determined by the accrued credit or debit balance of each member with the other members taken together, reckoned cumulatively from the date at which the EPU begins to function. The first tranche of credit or debit balances will carry with it no payment in gold. Of the subsequent tranches of credit balances, it appears that 50 per cent will be settled by the Union in gold as they accrue to a member. A member which has a growing debit balance with the Union will have to settle in gold 20, 40, 60 and 80 per cent of each successive tranche. It appears that an accrued debit balance which outstrips all the tranches will, if it grows any bigger, involve 100 per cent gold payments to the Union, but that no decision has been reached about the position of credit balances beyond the point at which all the tranches have been exhausted."

"My main quarrel with the EPU arises from the concept of 'creditor' and of 'debtor' countries. A 'creditor' country is a country which has a favourable balance of payments with the other members, even though its over-all balance is adverse. A 'debtor' country has an unfavourable balance with other members, but might conceivably have an over-all favourable balance. The philosophy of the EPU is based on the view that there is something wrong—in the sense of departure from equilibrium—in a country being either in a 'creditor' or in a 'debtor' position with the rest of Western Europe. The latitude which the Union will provide in either direction is represented by an aggregate lump sum, the amount of which is fixed irrespective of the period of time over which the Union has operated. If this ceiling had been conceded as an annual rate, the amounts of the possible credits and debits being renewed year by year, much of my objection would have disappeared, since a 'departure from equilibrium' in the EPU sense could then be financed under conditions which could remain steady through time. But the ceiling is a cumulative aggregate and not an annual rate. Once the ceiling has been reached the Union can offer no further help however much time is allowed to elapse. For this reason alone its days are probably numbered, but that is a poor consolation for the unsuitability of the arrangements, particularly as the dimensions of the maximum credits and debits are generous, thus rendering it probable that the Union will run for two or three years before revision becomes essential" (Kahn 1950: 307).

In this regard Raymond Mikesell (1948: 503) observed that "[i]n any regional or group multilateral payments mechanism there are three general problems to be solved: (1) the multilateral offsetting of net surpluses and net deficits arising out of bilateral trade between individual members of the group; (2) the settlement of net surpluses and net deficits of individual members with the group as a whole; and (3) the settlement of the net deficits or surpluses of the group as a whole with non-members. Although the clearing operation per se is confined solely to the first of these three problems, all three are closely inter-related and must be dealt with, if intra-group clearing is to be successful." Hirschman (1951: 49) provided a similar assessment: "As was true of all similar previous plans for multilateral clearing, the EPU project consisted of two distinct parts: (i) an offsetting mechanism and (ii) a settlement mechanism." However, he notes the divergence of views on the operation of the system between the UK and the rest of the recovering economies: "[T]he EPU project ran into serious trouble as the result of British opposition. During the session of the OEEC Council in January, Sir Stafford Cripps declared that the United Kingdom would be unable to accept substitution of the proposed clearing mechanism for the bilateral agreements involving sterling. He refused to accept an EPU that would supersede the existing bilateral agreements; rather, he favoured one that would function only after exhaustion of bilateral credit lines and would thus be superimposed upon the bilateral agreements as a 'lender of last resort.' At the same time, Sir Stafford declared that the United Kingdom could not agree to restrict its freedom of action with respect to quantitative restrictions on trade" (ibid.: 50–51).

These problems soon became evident in the EPU with respect to the limits placed on the size and method of settlement balances. The success of any clearing scheme depends on a relative balance in each member's trade with the other members' country, since an excessive imbalance in any one country compromises the value of the outstanding credits of the others. It is in such conditions that the ability of such schemes to provide adjustment credit becomes evident. Since Germany had suffered the most extensive war damage it was in the weakest position and, not surprisingly, in October 1950 a major payments crisis developed in the Federal Republic of Germany. As part of its reconstruction efforts it had fully liberalised 75 per cent of imports coming from EPU countries. Carli notes that "[u]nder my chairmanship the EPU Board decided to send to Germany two experts of high reputation to report on the degree of solvency of that country. It was our view and in particular my view that the EPU should provide a stand-by credit and should prevent by all means a crisis. The experts were required to report on the desirability of extending a stand-by credit to Germany instead of allowing this country to withdraw the policy of import liberalisation it had already implemented.

The programme the two experts brought back from their visits in Germany included:—rejection of policies of 'deficit financing' (an expression whereby they meant the Keynesian expression of 'deficit spending'); increase of indirect taxation to restrict consumption;—substantial credit restrictions in order to establish a better balance between domestic production and demand;—an increase in interest rates sufficient to promote the expansion of saving;—exchange controls to prevent speculative capital movements. The Board approved the plan and extended to Germany a stand-by credit of 120 million dollars and granted to Germany a *rallonge* of its quota of 180 million dollars to be utilised 2/3 in the form of credits and 1/3 in the form of dollar payments.

The programme proved to be a most impressive success and very shortly the external position of Germany reversed. The action taken by the Bank der Deutscher Lander was one of the most determined and consisted in the repeal of commercial bank credits of one billion DM in few months. At the end of the adjustment process Germany moved into the position of an extreme creditor and on several occasions was requested to provide extensions of credits to finance its surpluses."

In difference from Germany, "Italy started at the very beginning as a creditor country and in October 1951 advised the Minister for Foreign

Trade that Italy had already exhausted its quota and that member countries could be entitled to restrict imports from Italy. The decision of the Minister was to fully liberalise imports from EPU countries. It was a bold decision and contributed greatly to the renaissance of the Italian economy. It was made feasible because of the credit policies followed by the Bank of Italy in 1947 in order to mop up the huge purchasing power accumulated before."

"The positive side of the EPU experience may be summarised as follows: 1) the EPU was based on an agreement renewable on a fixed schedule and adaptable to changing conditions; 2) an independent Board of experts serving both the multilateral institutions and their respective governments; 3) regular monthly meeting of the members of the Board that included quarterly reviews of the situation of each participating economy; 4) agendas proposed by an international secretariat responsible for identifying the priority problems of the system; 5) authority for the members of the Board to recommend to governments policy adjustments essential to the continuity and integrity of the system; 6) before formulating recommendations in critical situations, meetings of the members of the Board with senior officials of the government at issue; 7) regular meetings of delegates of all participant governments, authorised to decide whether to adopt the recommendations of the members of the Board; 8) meetings of cabinet ministers to decide a limited number of major unresolved issues; 9) monthly surveillance by the members of the Board over the implementation of adjustment measures on which multilateral financing was conditioned.

At the end of 1958, the EPU was precipitously liquidated. Between 1958 and 1968 the international monetary system designed at the Bretton Woods conference in 1944 went into full operation. It could be described as a gold exchange standard in the process of becoming a dollar standard; the international cooperation aimed at making the transition as gradual as possible. The establishment of external convertibility for the European currencies at the end of 1958 was expanded to other currencies, including the Japanese yen, and was followed by the elimination of exchange restrictions on current payments and to some extent on capital transfers; adjustments of parities were limited to 'fundamental' disequilibrium in the balance of payments, in accordance with the objectives of the system created by the delegates to the conference."

6.6 A Central American Payments Union and a Proposal for Asia

The EPU is not the only example of a regional payments union that was actually introduced. The experience of European integration, initiated in the ERP and the creation of the EPU, provided a framework for regional integration that had long been under discussion for Latin America and led to attempts to emulate the European Economic Community through the Latin American Free Trade Area. Part of this emulation was an attempt to apply a settlement system or clearing union. The Centro de Estudios Monetarios Latinoamericanos (CEMLA), a research institute of Latin American central banks, commissioned Robert Triffin (as the intellectual father of the EPU) to provide a report on "A Latin American Clearing House and Payments Union" (Triffin 1962). Pierre Uri, who had collaborated with Myrdal and Kaldor in the UN Economic Commission for Europe, was also part of a mission to CEMLA on the same subject (Uri 1963). A report for CEMLA was also prepared by Keesing and Brand (1963), as well reports by Jorge Gonzalez del Valle, "Structure and Operation of the Central American Clearing House," and "The Financing of Intra-LAFTA Trade: Some Problems and Possible Approaches to Their Solution," by Professors Raymond Mikesell and Barry N. Siegel. These proposals were reviewed by the USAID Latin American office by Young (1965). The framework for a clearing arrangement was established at the end of 1965 by the central banks of the member countries (Argentina, Brazil, Chile, Colombia, Ecuador, Mexico, Peru, and Uruguay) of the Latin American Free Trade Association (LAFTA).

Triffin (1964: 15–16) also proposed "various possible alternative schemes for a Caribbean Payments Union" … "such a Caribbean Payments Union should be built upon two separate groups: 1. A Central American group, based on the commitments already incorporated in the Camara de Compensacion Centroamericana and the Acuerdo para el Establecimiento de la Union Monetaria Centroamericana, and composed of Guatemala, El Salvador, Honduras, Nicaragua and Costa Rica; 2. An Outer Caribbean group, composed, at the very least of Mexico, Venezuela, Colombia and Jamaica. The above listing of countries should not be regarded as exclusive. The absence of a Central Bank has constituted, up to now, the main obstacle to full participation by Panama in the Central American efforts at monetary integration, but ways and means should be sought to associate Panama with these arrangements. As for the Outer Caribbean group, it should certainly remain open to later accession by the Dominican Republic, Haiti, and hope fully Cuba when present political obstacles to such a step can be lifted. Judging from available trade estimates, however, it seems that Ecuador might well wish to participate, from the start."

Triffin (1967: 11–12) also served as an adviser to an initiative to set up a Clearing Union under the auspices of ECAFE. He recommended "a Clearing House among the central banks of the participating countries. This Clearing House would deal exclusively with its member central banks rather than with commercial banks or the public. Private traders would continue to deal with their own commercial banks, and the commercial banks would continue to undertake with their central bank only those operations which cannot be cleared directly among them through the market i.e. because of exchange control regulations, or because of imbalances between market demand and market supply requiring stabilization interventions by the central bank itself. Importers would thus buy from their own bank, and exporters sell to it the cheques, payment orders, etc. arising from intra–regional trade or ether transactions authorized by the exchange authorities. In view of the savings derived from the clearing system, however, exchange margins, banking charges and commissions on such intra-regional exchange transactions should be limited to lower levels than those prevailing on the sale or purchase of foreign currencies. The member currencies sold to a central bank by its own traders or commercial banks would be deposited by it to the clearing house and credited to its clearing account. Conversely each central bank could draw on its clearing account to obtain any member currency needed by it for sale to its own traders and banks. The Clearing would also debit each country's account for any amount of its currency deposited with it by another member, and credit it for any amount of its currency purchased from it by other members."

"The operations of central banks with the Clearing House would not, of course, balance from day to day. Daily transactions with the Clearing House would thus require the maintenance by each central bank of an adequate working balance and or credit line in its account."

In addition, Bhatt reports proposals for clearing arrangements and monetary unions in Africa and the Middle East, as well as for Asia (See *Economic and Political Weekly* 1970). The basic thrust of these proposals was as an adjunct to free trade areas and as a substitute or first step towards a common currency, thought to be necessary as a next step in

Table 6.1 Multilateral clearing and credit arrangements among developing Countries

Multilateral clearing and credit arrangements among developing Countries
A Clearing Arrangement

(a). Latin America and the Caribbean
1. Central American Clearing House (5), 1961
Costa Rica, El Salvador, Guatemala, Honduras and Nicaragua
2. Latin American Integration Association (LAIA) (a) Payments and Reciprocal Credits System (12), 1965
Argentina, Bolivia, Brazi,l, Colombia, Chile, Dominican Republic, Ecuador, Mexico, Paraguay, Peru, Uruguay and Venezuela
3. CARICOM Multilateral Clearing Facility (6), 1977
Barbados, Belize, East Caribbean Currency Authority, Guyana, Jamaica and Trinidad and Tobago.
(b) Africa
1. West Africa Clearing House (16).1975
Benin, Burkina, Cape Verde, Gambia, Ghana, Guinea, Guinea-Bissau, Ivory Coast, Liberia, Mali, Mauritania, Niger, Nigeria, Senegal, Sierra Leone and Togo.
2. Grand Lakes Economic Community's Monetary Arrangement (3), 1978
Burundi, Rwanda, Zaire
3. Central African Clearing House (5), 1979
Central African Republic, Congo, Gabon, United Republic of Cameroon and Zaire, Equatorial Guinea and Chad
4. Eastern and Southern Africa Clearing House (18) (o) 1981
Comoros, Djibouti, Ethiopia, Kenya, Lesotho,Malawi, Mauritius, Somalia, Swaziland, Tanzania, Uganda, Zambia, Burundi, Rwanda and Zimbabwe.
(c) Asia
1. Regional Co-operation for Development (RCD) Union for Multilateral Payments Arrangements (3), 1967
Iran, Pakistan and Turkey
2. Asian Clearing Union (7), 1974
Bangladesh, Burma, India, Iran, Nepal, Pakistan and Sri Lanka

trade integration. There were many arrangements across the developing world following the example of the EPU (See Table 6.1 from Kamara (1967:424).

6.7 Payments and Settlements Systems for Development: UNCTAD Early Beginnings

The EPU is not the only example of a regional payments union that was actually introduced. The experience and the application of regional payments schemes in support of developing countries was first raised at the 1964 UNCTAD Conference, which proposed the creation of an expert group whose report was not wholly favourable to the idea. At UNCTAD II (UNCTAD 1968), there were "further requests [of] the Secretary- General of UNCTAD: (a) To address a questionnaire to Governments on the problems in the establishment of different forms of multilateral payments arrangements between developing and socialist countries and also suggestions thereon and to prepare, for the group of experts mentioned below, a background study on the topics taking into account replies received from the countries concerned and having in view the report on Payments Arrangements among the Developing Countries for Trade Expansion" (u 1 1 TD/B/80/Rev. l, United Nations publication, Sales No.: 67.II.D.6).

In response to the report of the expert group it was proposed that "a framework can be provided by a Payments Union in which membership would be open to all developing countries and sub regional and regional unions and which would be linked with agreed trade liberalisation and expansion measures by member countries. Such a move would stimulate trade within the entire group of developing countries. To start with, this Union should have at least three countries as members from each region—Asia, Africa and Latin America.

Existing or proposed sub regional or regional unions can become members of the Union. Such developed countries as agree to the following conditions could participate in the Union as associate members:

a. They should give trade preferences to industrial exports from developing countries in their markets.
b. They should agree to provide annually one per cent of their GNP as net external assistance to developing countries.

Clearing arrangements with regard to all payments transactions subject to exchange control regulations of member countries on a multilateral basis would reduce the transaction costs in convertible currencies of their trade and thus result in net saving of real resources. The unit of account could be the US dollar of a given gold value. Credit facilities should be automatic and should relate only to incremental trade of member countries within the Union. For this purpose, countries with structural surpluses and deficits should be assigned appropriate 'initial position' based on last three years' experience and these 'positions' should be periodically revised. Thus, no distortion in trade patterns would result from the setting up of this Union. Terms and conditions governing credit facilities should be such as to stimulate intra-group trade without discriminating against trade of member countries with developed countries. Countries having a deficit would get automatically from the Union credit up to 10 per cent of their intra- group imports in the past three years; however, excepting the first credit tranche, in the other tranche 50 per cent of the deficits would have to be settled in hard currencies. The interest rate would rise with the duration of outstanding debt and persistent credit and debit balances for more than five years would be amortised by transfer of reserve assets among the member countries. These provisions would provide incentives for correcting payments problems within the group; they would also provide an incentive to increase exports to developed countries. Credit facilities would be available to member countries only if they adopt agreed measures of trade liberalisation and expansion. Surplus countries would grant credit to the Union up to 10 per cent of their exports in the past three years; excepting their first tranche credit, they would be paid 50 per cent in convertible currencies by the Union. The interest on outstanding credit balances would decline with increase in duration of such balances. Surplus countries would thus have an incentive to correct their payments surpluses. All accounts with the Union would be denominated in US dollar of a given gold value. Further, all members would be required to channel through the Union all payments to a defaulting member until such default is fully covered and met. (16) Thus, there would not be any exchange risk for the members and at the same time there would be exceptionally strong guarantee against default. There would arise occasions where the payment by the Union to the surplus countries would exceed its receipts from the deficit countries. For this purpose, the Union would require adequate working balances. Such working balances should be provided by each member agreeing to deposit 5 per cent of its gross foreign exchange reserves (excluding gold) with the Union. Such deposits would for all practical purposes form part of the reserves of the member countries and would be available for meeting payments deficits in proportion to their use of their other reserves. The member countries would face no serious risk or inconvenience because of the exchange guarantee and strong guarantee against default. These deposits would be more riskless than the member countries reserves in the form of convertible currencies. To meet situations where the reserves of the Union would be inadequate to meet its liabilities, the Union should be accorded membership status and drawing rights by the IMF. The Union, after some experience is gained and mutual confidence among members is established, could raise the deposit obligations of members from 5 per cent of their gross convertible currency reserves to 10 per cent and use these additional resources for short-term investment in member countries instead of lending them to developed countries. The initiative for setting up this Union should be taken by the Central banks of countries desirous of joining it. Initial discussion can start in a small group of ten or eleven Central bankers. This would ensure that the discussion would remain on a technical level. And in any case, the Union can operate only in co-operation and consultation with the member Central banks" (Bhatt 1969).

6.8 Intra-regional and Global Trade Balance and Potential for RFAs and Clearing Unions

As seen from the discussions of the Trade and Development Board, the use of clearing systems is not a new one. As in all such discussions, however, the intentions of proposals from the Board have had at their centre the interest of developing countries and in particular the use of such measures to remove impediments to trade among developing countries. As seen above, the 1968 proposals were for a group encompassing an inter-regional group of countries whereas the current proposals are directed towards regional groups or developing countries at similar levels of development.

It is thus important to identify the objectives that clearing is to provide. For example, Keynes's original proposal was to create freedom in countries' decisions on development strategies. It thus emphasised the symmetrical nature of the adjustment process based on multilateral discussion of policies and measures to ensure broad equilibrium in payments accounts. This was not only to prevent excessive credit creation and the perceived risk of inflation, but more importantly to assure credit countries that their credits would eventually be repaid. Thus the system of quota limits and the assessment of penalties when those limits were exceeded.

But, as Kahn pointed out in his original criticism of the EPU, these conditions have no clear meaning in the context of a regional agreement. There is no reason why there should be a rough balance on trade within the region and no reason to assess a penalty on excess debit or credit positions since a country may and indeed most frequently will be a regional debtor or creditor, but have a balance of the opposite sign on the global level. It thus makes little sense to apply quota limits or penalties on counties that exceed limits within the regional context, nor do the conditions on the proportion in which excess settlements should be paid in gold or convertible currencies.

Thus, in the present context, the return to multilateral trade, to currency convertibility, and economic recovery are not relevant objectives to be achieved from clearing. The elimination of the role of dollar balances and dollar financing of regional trade is the basic objective, and laying the groundwork for an eventual extension of the scheme to the entire developing world remains paramount. In this respect, what appears to have been a response to Kahn's observations by Hirschman appears most relevant. Hirschman (1951: 54–55) offers what appears to be a rebuttal of this position: "The EPU arrangement has frequently been attacked on the ground that it appears to place a particular premium on intra-European as distinct from over-all balance of payments equilibrium. It would seem indeed that, in the EPU, debtors and creditors are 'penalised' (by having to pay more and more gold or by having to grant more and more credit, respectively) the farther they move away from intra-European equilibrium regardless of what happens to their international accounts as a whole. This criticism calls for the following comments: It is a strange use of language to say that a debtor is 'penalised' when he is only made to pay his debts. It would be far more correct to say that an intra-European debtor obtains the special privilege of not having to settle in gold for a fraction of any intra-European debt he incurs; this privilege is granted primarily to promote the special effort that is being made to reduce trade barriers within Europe with the intent of creating a strong competitive European economy. It is true that it would hardly make sense for a country which is a net earner of dollars outside of Europe to receive a credit from EPU rather than to be required to settle its intra-European deficit fully in gold. But the EPU was conceived at a time when all its prospective members expected to continue to run dollar deficits for at least two more years." While none of these considerations appear relevant today, he goes on to note that, "[w]hile in general the EPU account of member countries starts at zero, those countries that are clearly expected to be net debtors or net creditors within Europe have been given 'initial positions' in the EPU that take account of this expectation. Countries which are expected to be debtors (Austria, Greece, Norway, Netherlands) start out in the EPU with a certain agreed creditor position, and therefore do not incur any obligation as long as their deficit remains within the scope of this initial credit. Presumed creditor countries (Belgium, UK, Sweden), on the other hand, start out with a debit which they have to work off before starting to secure any claim on the EPU. However, they receive a full dollar allocation from ECA for the initial debit position with which they are burdened in EPU.

In this rather artificial way, certain EPU countries are permitted to earn dollars directly through their European surpluses while others have officially sanctioned and freely financed intra-European deficits; this mechanism, a survival from the drawing rights of the Intra-European Payments Schemes, is no doubt cumbersome, but it at least must be recognised as an attempt at dealing with 'structural' surpluses and deficits in intra-European trade which are due to present dislocations or which can be expected to persist after the dollar problem has been solved." Hirschman is here referring to what was described above as "indirect" financing provided by the ERP to "seed" the EPU. Thus, in the present context, developing countries could provide the same role by granting to regional clearing groups additional credits from their global trading positions to expand the coverage of the clearing balances.

Since the creation of credit in substitute for external financial resources and the diminution of the use of the US dollar as the means of financing trade depend on the ability of groups of countries to provide internal credits, the actual trade positions of the members of any regional clearing system will be crucial to its viability. Thus, this section will present the current trade balances of the major regional developing country groupings. Since the idea of a clearing union is to eliminate the use of compensating capital flows to cover imbalances and to replace them with the extension of trade credits against country deficits, the appropriate feasibility statistic is the balance of commercial trade within groupings. Thus for each group we provide indications of the net balance of each member of the group to the group as a whole, as well as a measure of the intra-group trade (imports plus exports) relative to its total global trade and of the net balance of each member on its global trade. This allows comparison of group deficit countries with their global position and the importance of the group trade in its global trading position.

a. **BRICS**

For the BRICS member countries Brazil, China, India, Russia and South Africa, an important drawback of introducing a clearing system is the fact that the share of intra-BRICS trade is relatively low compared to members' trade with the rest of the world, although this is largely due to the position of China. Also, it is clear that China represents the classic case of a regional deficit country with a large global surplus. The same is true to a lesser extent for Russia. Thus, while there is little group credit balance (Brazil) to offset the deficit balances, there is really no logic in penalising China for its deficit position in the group when it has such a large external surplus. It should be China that provides credits to countries such as India or South Africa and indeed does this through its foreign investments in these countries.

b. **Mercosur**

Another trade area that might benefit from clearing is Mercosur—Argentina, Brazil, Paraguay and Venezuela—but this regional trading area suffers from the opposite problem from the BRICS with a large surplus country, Brazil. Thus there is no problem of providing credits to deficit countries, but the size of the deficits of the other countries is relatively small. At the same time, much like the BRICS, Mercosur suffers from the low share of intra-group trade in their global trading balances. Moreover, this position is further aggravated by the fact that globally, the countries in this group are in surplus in their trade balances.

c. **Latin American Integration Association (LAIA)**

To extend the range of countries beyond Mercosur, consider the larger Latin American grouping of the Latin American Integration Association (LAIA), the successor to the Latin American Free Trade Association.

This now comprises Argentina, Bolivia, Brazil, Chile, Colombia, Cuba, Ecuador, Mexico, Panama, Paraguay, Peru, Uruguay and Venezuela. In this grouping the major surplus countries are Brazil followed by Mexico and Argentina. But again, the overall balance in the region is close to balance with the exception of Venezuela and Chile, which suggests that this region could derive more benefit from a clearing system than in Mercosur, and a substantial reduction in the impact of dollar financing of its external imbalances.

Nonetheless, this group also suffers from the low share of intra-regional trade in its total trade, although it has recently been increasing. And much as in the case of Mercosur, indeed really as a result of the impact in the group of the major Mercosur countries, the region has a substantial overall surplus on its global trade.

d. **ASEAN**

ASEAN is probably the most important regional grouping, but it also suffers from the fact of having predominantly intra-group trade surpluses, thus providing the very few deficit countries with the possibility of funding their trade. Relative to other groupings, ASEAN has the advantage of having a much larger share of intra-group trade relative to its total trade, representing the greater regional integration which is being restored after the 1997 crisis.

But the group is also a global surplus for almost all countries with the exception of Philippines and Thailand, and for some periods, Vietnam. Of note in the ASEAN case is the extremely large surplus position of Singapore and the region would be a better candidate for clearing with the exception of Singapore. This transforms the group from an overall surplus position on intra-group trade to a deficit position.

e. **ASEAN + China, Japan and Korea**

Since Japan proposed an Asian equivalent for the IMF, it is appropriate to look at what that configuration might have brought, as well as to recognise the regional cooperation on monetary and financial matters between ASEAN and the three more-developed economies in the region—China, Japan and Korea. With the inclusion of these countries the region becomes a net deficit group on the basis of intra-regional trade, with China and Japan more than offsetting the impact of Singapore. But, with respect to global balances, the large Chinese surplus still dominates. A better idea of this dominance is given by the position of ASEAN + 2 without China. Japan then becomes the major deficit country along with Korea, and no one would argue that these countries need funding for their regional deficits, and indeed there are hardly any regional surpluses to offset them. If anything, it would be the global surpluses of the original ASEAN countries that would provide this source.

6.9 Dealing with Capital Flows

In the conditions of European recovery, the EPU did not have to deal with the problems of capital flows. Indeed, one of the basic presuppositions of the Bretton Woods system was that international capital flows would be intermediated by the multilateral financial institutions. As is now well known, private cross-border flows, which expanded dramatically in the aftermath of the October War in the Middle East, were a major factor in the demise of the stable exchange rate regime crafted at Bretton Woods. And capital flows and reversals, or sudden stops as they have come to be known, have created a scenario of frequent banking and exchange rate crises in developing countries in the 1990s and 2000s.

As Keynes pointed out in his original proposals for a Clearing Union, capital flows do not create a particular problem for such an arrangement since all capital transactions would have to pass through the clearing house and thus the size of flows would be limited by the relative clearing balances. Thus capital flows within the region would be limited in the same way by any limits set on debits and credit balances. Thus a creditor country could freely transfer funds to any country within the limits of its credit balance.

However, the same limits would not apply to transfers from non-members and would not be limited by the relative balances of the members of the regional union. Capital flows would then have an impact primarily on the current account balances of the member countries with the rest of the world. They could not jeopardise the operation of the clearing and settlement functions of these systems, while continuing to cause instability and volatility in trade and payments with the rest of the world. However, the exchange rates of currencies within the region would remain unaffected and this would make trade within the regional group more desirable since it would be undertaken at more stable exchange rates across currencies of the members of the clearing group.

Indeed, while the tendency to concentrate trade and payments within the region was initially thought to be one of the drawbacks of regional arrangements (since it contradicted the presumption in favour of free, multilateral trade and convertibility that the post-war world was seeking to restore), in the current environment these implication have a positive impact on developing countries and the proliferation of regional trading agreements makes regional unions well within the existing paradigms on trade integration.

6.10 Relations Between Regional Unions and the Rest of the World and the Multilateral Organisations

Any regional clearing union would have to determine how it interacted with the other regional groupings as well as with the multilateral financial institutions. This is a problem that was already present with the EPU. Hirschman (op. cit.: 52) notes with respect to the EPU that "it had become clear that the issue of EPU's relationship to the International Monetary Fund, which had caused much concern at an earlier stage, would be disposed of without too much trouble. By general agreement, the EPU would be governed largely by automatic rules and would function under the supervision of the OEEC, a body that can make decisions only by unanimous vote. This arrangement did not seem likely to result in a powerful supra-national monetary board whose authority would supersede that of the Fund. An interesting attempt has been made to avoid the paralysis that has often been exhibited by international bodies tied to the rule of unanimity. On a number of important issues that must be deferred for decision to the OEEC Council, the final EPU agreement provides for the procedure of the 'Special Restricted Committee.' This Committee is to consist of 'five persons chosen by lot from a list of persons nominated by each of the members for reasons of competence and standing.' When the issue to be decided is a dispute involving one or several specific countries, none of the Committee members may be a national of one of the parties to the dispute. The Committee is to make a report to the OEEC Council on the issue at stake and the Council will then make a recommendation or take a decision 'in the light of this report.' The intention of this procedure is to invest the Committee with a moral authority which will make for unanimous acceptance of its reports within the OEEC Council."

The attitude of the IMF vis-à-vis the EPU was one of perplexity if not of hostility. Some directors believed that the aim of multilateral clearing in

Europe was in accord with the Fund's objectives but other directors had misgivings. Would the European payments scheme help to lay the basis for an eventual convertibility of European currencies? Would a clearing arrangement not tend to postpone the solution to Europe's problems rather than to solve them? Since the Fund had taken a decision limiting Europe's members' access to the Fund's dollar reserves during the life of the ERP, some directors inquired about those projects featuring any assistance extended by the Fund in dollars. Would not a contribution from the Fund to clearing arrangements be counter to the Fund's ERP decision? What guarantee could there be that the Fund's commitments under the clearing arrangements proposed would not be excessive, using up in a few months resources which should be made available over several years? The attrition between the IMF and the EPU became more intense in the course of time. The EPU board showed uncertainties about German surpluses and British deficits from 1956 through 1958. Both countries needed substantial exchange rate adjustments; the IMF was jealous of its jurisdiction over exchange rates though it had no authority to initiate changes and the EPU was reluctant to challenge the IMF's jurisdiction.

In the case of Britain, the EPU lost leverage after the IMF and US provided two billion dollars, conditioned primarily on the withdrawal of the UK troops from Egypt. The UK took action that improved its overall balance of payments and increased its reserves, but these results were obtained by complete suspension of economic growth and the restriction of imports of all manufactures from the dollar area. In the case of Germany, the board's leverage was limited by Germany's willingness to extend increasing amounts of credit to the Union and by its lifting of trade and foreign exchange restrictions. These are among the events that contributed to the termination of the EPU. Meanwhile forces opposing the EPU gathered momentum: the Bank of England had opposed the EPU since its inception because in the EPU it saw the status of the sterling differing little from that of any other member country. Rightly or wrongly the Bank of England considered that times were ripe for making sterling convertible for non-residents and for terminating participation in the EPU. The German authorities wanted the DM to become convertible as the conclusion of their economic "miracle" and the free market policies to which they attributed the miracle.

At the same time, as already mentioned, most proposals for regional stabilisation funds work on the basis of an initial level determined at the regional level, and at higher levels of commitment require the borrower to participate in an IMF-sanctioned stabilisation programme, which is precisely what the automatic extension of credit under the clearing approach is supposed to avoid. Thus, these existing regional programmes substitute an IMF programme for the clearing union approach of applying a penalty to countries exceeding their surplus or deficit lending and borrowing limits. Again, there seems to be no reason to apply these limits on the basis of a country's intra-regional balance. The problem is a question of creditworthiness of the deficit-country recipient of surplus-country credits, but this problem could be more easily resolved by means of the application of a credit balance limit at the level of the regional clearing house and minimal charges on transactions, rather than on the basis of overall lending limits.

As for relations with the IMF, members of regional clearing unions would have no change in their position except that they would have a cushion available before having to go to the IMF for lending support. The IMF Articles, as well as the WTO, should be able to accommodate regional associations such as those described here.

6.11 Conclusion

Keynes's proposed Clearing Union was never seriously considered or its implementation discussed at Bretton Woods. However there is a full history of discussion and implementation of Clearing Unions at the regional level ranging from the post-War European Payments Union to the Central American Clearing Union to proposals for similar operations in Asia, Africa and the Middle East. Indeed, there is a greater wealth of experience on the regional level than on the international. Unfortunately, much of this history has been forgotten or ignored, in particular as it applies to the process of economic development.

Consideration of this historical experience shows that clearing unions were designed and proposed for a wide range of different objectives. Keynes's original proposal was designed to generate the maximum non-conditional financing for British reconstruction. Although there were limits on the amount of global credit creation in the proposal, the American's balked at the prospect of being the sole creditor in the system and placed tighter limits on quotas in White's Stabilization Fund proposal which became the blueprint for the IMF. As a result, Keynes quickly moved to support first a global currency within the US proposal, and when that failed to greater autonomous exchange rate flexibility.

The EPU on the other hand was designed to provide a more rapid means to return to convertibility and exchange rate stability among the European economies to encourage recovery in intra-European trade and to lighten the constraint of "dollar scarcity" since none of these countries qualified for IMF support. Again limitations on the creation of multilateral credits emerged from participants, in particular Belgium as a major creditor country, and the UK because of the outstanding problem of Commonwealth sterling credits. The EPU's eventual success required the use of Marshall Plan US dollar grants as seed funding to meet payments in excess of the imposed credit limits. It was nonetheless considered a technical and operational success and would have survived in the absence of British opposition. It served as a template for proposals for clearing systems in other regions.

With the IMF dominating payments systems among the major developed countries and the former EPU members, clearing union proposals were adapted to the needs of developing countries and UNCTAD played a major role in supporting these efforts along with external consultants many of whom had direct experience in the creation of the EPU. Robert Triffin, considered the father of the EPU as well as Pierre Uri who had served as a consultant with Myrdal and Kaldor at the Economic Commission for Europe were instrumental in providing expertise. Here the objectives were also an attempt to lighten the external constraint on developing countries and to encourage what is now called "South-South" trade. Since their major impact was to limit the use of the US dollar, international support for these proposals often depended on the position of the US government vis-a-vis the role of the dollar. When the dollar parity was under pressure in the late stages of Bretton Woods these systems were seen as a way to reduce pressure on the dollar, but once the system collapsed and moved towards freer international capital flows intermediated in dollars support waned and countries were encouraged to introduced market determined floating exchange rates. Clearing unions then came to be seen as weak constraints on government policies and uncompetitive support for developing country exports. Clearly there was no place for these schemes in the Washington Consensus.

Aside from the question of the size of the internal creation of credit in regional schemes and the problems caused by the pattern of imbalances—in the 1960s the share of developing countries regional trade tended to be much higher than after the introduction of modern globalisation of trade and payment in the 1980s—an important aspect of multilateral clearing is the use of a notional unit of account to represent credit and debit balances. Keynes proposed a number of different names for the unit of account in his proposal. In the EPU, since the IMF had been created on the basis of a dollar link to gold the reference became the US dollar and gold and the dollar were the accepted settlement currencies when country balances exceeded the stipulated quota limits. The same was true of most of the other proposals.

However, in the current context the proposed clearing union is not only to supplement the dollar as a settlement currency but to supplant it. This means using the dollar as the reference unit of account would be totally inappropriate. In addition, one of the problems to be resolved is the negative impact of volatility in the dollar exchange rate, making the dollar even more inappropriate for this purpose.

Alternatives to the use of the dollar as the reference unit of account could be the Special Drawing Right (SDR) which many countries have proposed as a substitute for the dollar, but with little success, due to both technical and practical difficulties. However, it could much more easily serve as reference unit and settlement currency in a regional scheme.

On the other hand, a basket of the currencies of the countries that participate in the scheme could be used. This could be at a fixed rate, or it could be free to fluctuate as the SDR responds to its adjustable composition and value. There is much to be said for keeping a fixed rate, but allowing for fluctuation would dampen the impact of dollar volatility on the one hand, and to provide a proxy for the "Discount" scheme that was proposed by Richard Kahn in the 1950s as an alternative to EPU.

As noted in the discussion of the statistics of trade balances of the various regional groupings, there is a problem created by the much wider dispersion of trade in the current environment due to globalisation and cross-border production linkages and capital flows. This suggests that the original proposals made in the UNCTAD discussions of the 1960s seeking a much broader composition of the members of the Clearing would be important. At the same time, the statistics suggests that the quota limits on individual country credits are much less important than they were in the Bretton Woods and EPU discussions. Indeed, if the objective is to replace the negative impact of the volatility of the US dollar and its dominant role in intermediating global capital flows these limits should be as high as possible.

References

Bank for International Settlements (BIS). (1948). *Annual Report for 1948.* Basle: Bank for International Settlements.

Bhatt, V.V. (1969). A Payments Union for Developing Countries, *Economic and Political Weekly* 4(1/2), January.

Beyen, J.W. (1951). *Money in a Maelstrom.* London: Macmillan.

Carli, G. (1958). The Return to Convertibility of the European Currencies, *Giornale degli Economisti e Annali di Economia*, Nuova Serie 47(11/12): 525–536.

Colwell, S.P. (1859). *The Ways and Means of Payment.* Philadelphia: Lippincott.

Diamand, M. (1978). Towards a Change in the Economic Paradigm Through the Experience of Developing Countries, *Journal of Development Economics* 5(1): 19–53.

Domar, E. (1950). The Effect of Foreign Investments on the Balance of Payments, *American Economic Review* 40(5): 805–826.

Dunkman, W. (1933). *Quantitative credit control.* New York, NY: Columbia University Press.

Economic and Political Weekly. (1970). Asian Clearing Union, Vol. 5(50), December 12: 1985

Fisher, I. (1936). *100% Money.* New York: Adelphi (Foreword by Robert Hemphill).

Hawtrey, R.G. (1919). *Currency and Credit.* London: Longmans Green.

Hayek, F.A. (1937). *Monetary Nationalism.* London: Longmans Green.

Hirschman, A. (1951). European Payments Union: Negotiations and the Issues, *Review of Economics and Statistics* 33(1): 49–55.

Innes, A.M. (1914). The Credit Theory of Money. *The Banking Law Journal* 31(January–December). Reprinted in *Credit and State Theories of Money: The Contributions of A. Mitchell Innes*, Edited by L. Randall Wray, Cheltenham, UK: Edward Elgar.

Kahn, R.F. (1949). A Possible Intra-European Payments Scheme. *Economica*, New Series, 16(64): 293–304.

Kahn, R.F. (1950). The European Payments Union. *Economica*, New Series, 17(67): 306–316.

Kaldor, N. (1964). Dual Exchange Rates and Economic Development, *Essays on Economic Policy* 2: 178–200.

Kamara, S. (1967). Exchange Rate Instability and Its Effects on the Functioning of the Clearing Houses, *Savings and Development*, 11(4) (1987): 423–435

Kaplan, J., and G. Schleiminger. (1989). *The European Union: Financial Diplomacy in the 1950s.* Oxford: Clarendon Press.

Keesing, F.A.G., and P.J. Brand. (1963). Possible Role of a Clearing House in the Latin American Regional Market, *International Monetary Fund Staff Papers* 10(3): 397–460.

Keynes, J.M. (1930). *A Treatise on Money*, Volume I, The Pure Theory of Money. Royal Economic Society Edition, Volume V. London: Macmillan.

Keynes, J.M. XXV. Activities 1940–44 Shaping the Post-War World: The Clearing Union, Vol. XXV. London: Macmillan for the Royal Economic Society, 1980.

Kregel, J.A. (2016). The Effective Demand Approach to Economic Development. In: R. Kattel, J. Ghosh, and E. Reinert (eds.), *Elgar Handbook of Alternative Theories of Economic Development*. Cheltenham, UK: Edward Elgar.

Lüke, R. (1985). The Schacht and Keynes Plans, *BNL Quarterly Review* 38(152): 65–76.

McCleod, H.D. (1894). *Theory of Credit*, Second Edition. London: Longmans Green.

Mikesell, R. (1948). Regional Multilateral Payments Arrangements, *Quarterly Journal of Economics* 62(4): 500–518.

Minsky, H.P. (1986). *Stabilizing and Unstable Economy.* New Haven: Twentieth Century Fund.

Ocampo, J.A, J. A. Kregel, and S. Griffith-Jones. (2006). *International Finance and Development.*

Ohlin, G. (1995). The Negative Net Transfers of the World Bank. In *International Monetary and Financial Issues for the 1990s*, vol. 5. New York, NY: UNCTAD.

Prebisch, R. (1950). *The Economic Development of Latin America and Its Principal Problems.* Santiago: United Nations Economic Commission for Latin America.

Schacht, H. (1949). *Account Settled.* Translated by Edward Fitzgerald. London: Weidenfield & Nicolson.

Skidelsky, R. (2000). *John Maynard Keynes fighting for Britain, 1937–1946.* London: Macmillan.

Stokke, O. (2009). *The UN and Development: From Aid to Cooperation.* Bloomington: Indiana University Press.

Tew, B. (1963). *International Monetary Cooperation 1945–63,* Seventh (revised) edition. London: Hutchinson University Library.

Triffin, R. (1957). *Europe and the Money Muddle.* London.

Triffin, R. (1962) "Una camera de compensacion y union det pagos LatinoAmericana." A report prepared for CEMLA. Available at http://archivo.cepal.org/pdfs/economicBulletin/S6600267.pdf.

Triffin, R. (1964). International Monetary Arrangements, Capital Markets, and Economic Integration in Latin America, typescript available in URI archives http://archives.eui.eu/en/fonds/190019?item=PU.T-285. Citation at pp. 125–6 of the archived document.

Triffin, R. (1967). Payments Arrangements Within The Ecafe Region, Yale University Economic Growth Center Paper No. 114, available in URI archive, op. cit. pp. 375 ff.

UNCTAD. (1964). Towards a New Trade Policy for Development. In *Proceedings of the United Nations Conference on Trade and Development*, vol. II, March 23–June 16, Geneva, Switzerland.

UNCTAD. (1968). Proceedings of the United Nations Conference on Trade and Development, Second Session. New Delhi, February 1–March 29, Volume I, Report and Annexes.

Uri, P. (1963).Les Problemes d'une Union de Paiements pour L'Americaine Latine. http://archives.eui.eu/en/fonds/189810?item=PU.G-10–77

Williams, J.H. (1949). *Post-war Monetary Plans and Other Essays*. Oxford: Basil Blackwell.

Withers, H. (1906). *The Meaning of Money*. London: John Murray.

Young, J.P. (1965). *Central American Monetary Union*. Guatemala: United States Department of State, USAID Regional

CHAPTER 7

Sovereign Wealth Funds and the South: Under-used potential for development and defense

Diana Barrowclough

7.1 Introduction

The burst of new Sovereign Wealth Funds is one of the major trends in international finance over the last decade and, as with the other mechanisms described elsewhere in this volume, it has the South at its core. So many new funds were set up in recent years that, at the time of writing, SWFs now hold some $7 trillion in assets. More than 64 out of the largest 80 funds, worth some $6 trillion on recent estimates, are owned by governments across the developing world. To give a sense of scale, this dwarfs flows of Foreign Direct Investment in 2019 of 1.39 trillion globally or 695 billion to developing countries (UNCTAD 2020).

D. Barrowclough (✉)
Division Globalization Development Strategies, United Nations Conference on Trade and Development, Geneva, Switzerland
e-mail: Diana.Barrowclough@unctad.org

D. Barrowclough et al. (eds.), *South–South Regional Financial Arrangements*, International Political Economy Series,
https://doi.org/10.1007/978-3-030-64576-2_7

SWFs typically play either a short-term, *defensive* role to build resilience against the instability of foreign reserves, fiscal and macroeconomic imbalance; or a long-term more *developmental* role of investing in structural transformation and providing a revenue stream for retirees and future generations. These two roles are moreover interdependent, in that SWF's longer-term investment strategies could potentially play an important stabilizing role in reducing vulnerability and building resilience in the domestic, regional and even global economy.

Whichever role dominates, SWFs now dwarf the traditional multilateral institutions set up decades ago to provide defensive and developmental finance (Table 7.1). The resources of the International Monetary Fund and the World Bank are measured in just billions of dollars as opposed to trillions. They are also perceived to be slower to act and burdened with unpopular conditionalities. This is not to say these multilateral lenders are no longer needed; quite the contrary. However, the new players are changing expectations and the terms of engagement[1]. This chapter argues that Southern-owned SWFs could play an important complementary role alongside Southern-led, defensive arrangements such as the FLAR, the Arab Monetary Fund (AMF), European Stabilization Mechanism and Chiang Mai Initiative in addition to the traditional lender of last resort, the IMF. They could also complement the work of national, regional and multilateral Development Banks, including the World Bank. As public investors, and moreover essentially Southern public investors, SWFs could play an important developmental role especially in regions and sectors where private investors remain reluctant to enter. This does not necessarily have to come at the expense of financial returns and could moreover create positive returns in the broader economic and social sense as well.

However, for this to happen, some shifts in approach and important policy support are still needed because although the world of SWFs has become increasingly 'Southern-led' it is not as yet particularly 'South–South' nor even oriented towards the South. It is not therefore as developmental is it could be and may rather be reinforcing existing imbalances. Rebalancing this could be beneficial for both their defensive and developmental roles as well as enhancing their complementarities with the Bretton Woods institutions and would contribute to a more diverse and competitive offering of global development finance.

[1] Including among others, Grabel (2017), Fritz and Muhlich (2014), Barrowclough and Gottschalk (2018), Kring and Gallagher (2019), Ocampo (2014), and UNCTAD (2015).

The structure of the chapter is as follows. Part 1 is a brief mapping, showing recent trends in SWFs and how these fit into the broader landscape of South–South finance. Part 2 sets out the background context, positing the rise in SWFs as a response to global imbalances and frustrations with the current international financial architecture and desire for a 'voice' more commensurate with their economic weight. Part 3 looks at how SWFs work in practice, showing how different SWF asset allocations reflect their defensive and developmental roles and how these changed in part following the global financial crisis of 2007–2008. A health warning though—as many authors have noted (Kunzel et al. (2011) and Inderst and Steward (2014) (among others) data on SWFs and their asset allocation decisions is extremely scarce, so this chapter should be seen as raising issues for discussion more than providing definitive answers. Part 4 asks how SWFs could do more to help build resilience and reduce vulnerability. Part 5 concludes with a few practical policy suggestions.

7.2 SWF Trends Within the Broader Landscape of SS Mechanisms

Sovereign Wealth Funds are typically categorized as stabilization funds, saving funds, pension funds or reserve investment funds, but in fact the phrase is a catch-all that can include any dedicated, state-owned investment vehicle funded by budget surpluses, regardless of their purposes or investment strategies. SWFs can vary greatly—from Venezuela, Chile and Algeria's stabilization funds that are designed to give governments' fiscal resilience in the face of price or currency shocks; to the Persian Gulf's many long-standing funds for investing surplus oil dollars to provide for future generations when oil reserves are depleted; and India and Saudi Arabia's large surpluses of foreign reserves. As shown in Figure 7.1, they now exist in all regions of the developing and developed world and have considerable firepower. Even in regions where funds are smaller or fewer (such as Africa), they can still have a significant impact if other sources of finance are lacking (Fig. 7.2).

SWFs are usually financed from foreign exchange surpluses earned from the export of commodities such as oil and minerals (more than half of all world SWFs according to the African Development Bank). They can also be set up from revenues earned by other sources of the balance of payments surpluses such as merchandise trade (China), official foreign currency operations, foreign reserves held by the Central Bank or

Table 7.1 SWFs, the IMF and World Bank compared

Sources of finance		*Total value (assets or loans, latest data)*	*Value or share (voting rights) accruing to transition and developing countries+*	*Value or share currently invested in or lent to transition and developing countries*
SWFs	Sovereign fund, existing assets owned directly by local or national Government—used both to stabilize currencies and balance of payments and make investments.	$7 trillion	86%	10–25%
IMF	Multilateral lender to rebuild foreign reserves and balance of payments and stabilize currencies	$201 billion committed; $77 billion currently drawn down	45%	100%
World Bank IBRD	Multilateral lender of development finance	Loans outstanding total $184 billion	44%	100%

Sources Author estimates on SWFs derived from swfinstitute, annual reports and cited articles; voting rights estimated as % of total assets and estimate owned by developing countries equal to $6 trillion. IMF voting quotas from list updated 19 March 2019, lending committed as of Feb 2019. WB data IBRD Annual Report June 2018. Countries categorised following UN classification

fiscal surpluses earned through privatization sales (Chile), among others. Whatever their source, the point is that the national governments decided to manage these surpluses separate from the foreign reserves that were otherwise being managed by Central Banks (who may also use investment Funds or independent managers). Typically, the funds are established by a special Act of Government, often a year or two before the fund is initiated. Reflecting the fact there is no universally agreed definition, some countries have in place mechanisms that are like SWFs in all but the name.[2]

[2] Other mechanisms with similar functions to SWFs but which are not SWFs also exist in many countries. Timor-Leste's Infrastructure and Human Capacity Development Fund is a multi-year account rather than an institution with its own organizational structure,

Region	Assets (billion USD)
Sub-Saharan Africa	17
Latin America	65
North America	158
Asia-Pacific	2,638
MENA	2,981
Europe	1,123
Central Asia	194
TOTAL	**7,176**

Region	Assets (billion USD)
Developed countries	1,194
Developing countries	5,982
TOTAL	**7,176**

Fig. 7.1 Assets under management by Sovereign Wealth Fund by region of Fund Owner (*Source* Author estimate using data from SWF institute, 2018)

Fund endowment takes many forms, including regular or ad-hoc injections of capital, depending on the state of the balance of payments and fiscal balance; or one-off start-up payments after which funds are expected to rely on their own returns. Bolivia's FINPRO (Fund for Productive Industrial Revolution) borrows reserves from the Central Bank, whereas Brazil's Fund for Fiscal Stabilization and Investment is allocated funds from Treasury.

Regardless of how funds are initially financed, the fact remains that they are public assets (national or sub-national) with a public objective. Countries have chosen very different ways to run them, with some choosing a high degree of public monitoring and involvement and others much less.

staff and buildings. The difference between a State-Owned Development Bank and a SWF could be a moot point, depending on how returns are allocated. Not all countries with large current account surpluses have SWFs (Germany). In Switzerland and Japan, large external surpluses are intermediated through the private sector rather than through SWFs.

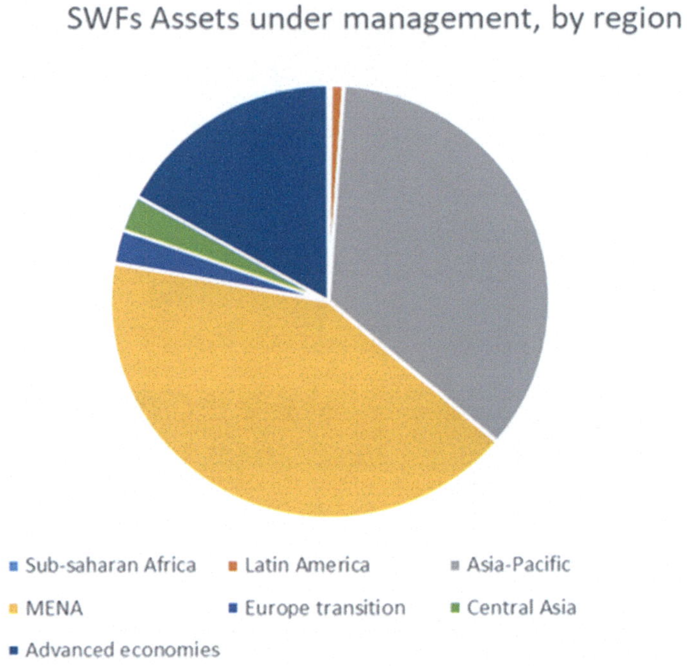

Fig. 7.2 SWFs are unevenly distributed around the world (*Source* Author using data from swf institute, 2018)

Some are set up as independent entities; others are run within Central Banks, Ministries of Finance or the Prime Minister's office. Norway's fund, for example, is managed within the Central Bank, on behalf of the Ministry of Finance.

While the creation of SWFs has been especially marked in recent years (Figure 7.3), they are not a new phenomenon and have long been used for macroeconomic stabilization purposes or to finance public service and infrastructure needs. A few of today's active Funds date back several centuries[3]; several were established in the 1950s (the Kuwait Investment

[3] The Permanent School Fund was established in Texas, United States, in 1854 to fund public education. It currently manages $37.7 billion assets (annual report 2014 $31 billion). The Texas Permanent University Fund, established in 1876, manages $17.2 billion. The Fund supplements tax revenues to invest in and pay for public education.

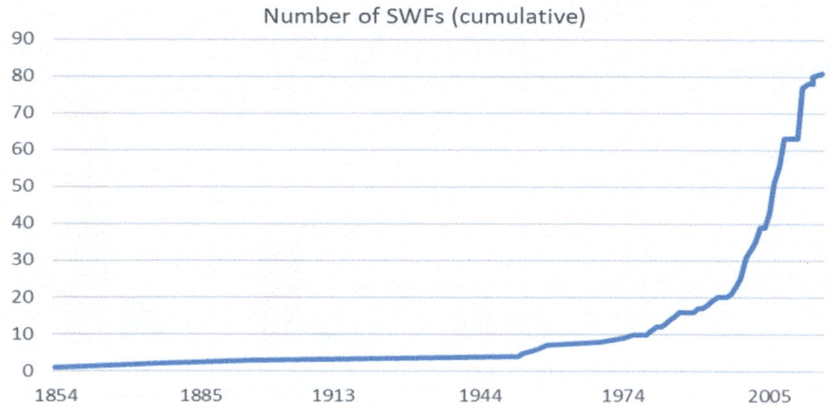

Fig. 7.3 Number of SWFS existing today, by year of establishment 1854–2016

Authority and the Kiribati fund in the Pacific Islands). In the 1970s many oil-exporting countries in the Middle East established Funds for the first time and the Temasek SWF that is credited with developing Singapore was established in 1974, initially financed through proceeds from privatization sales. Despite this early beginning, nonetheless, their rapid use really intensified from the 1980s and especially from 2000, related to the emergence of extremely large current account surpluses in many commodity-based developing countries, as well as some key non-commodity exporting developing countries (especially in East Asia). As many as 55 new SWFs were established between 2000 and 2016 alone, compared to just 14 funds for the longer period of the years 1981–1999. Of these 55 new funds, 47 are based in developing and transition economies (Figure 7.4).

7.3 South–South SWFs Respond to Systemic Challenges in the International Monetary and Financial System

The burgeoning of Southern-led SWFs is part of a broader context whereby developing countries have been designing and implementing their own mechanisms to respond to long-standing imbalances and limitations of the international financial and monetary system. The need for

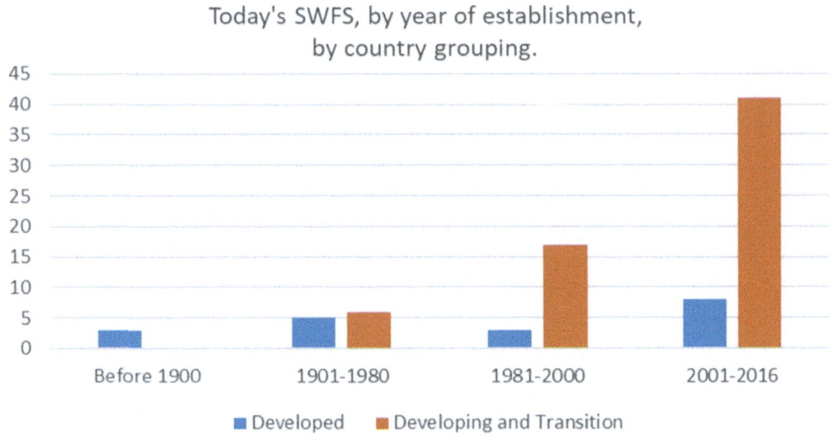

Fig. 7.4 Numbers of SWFs existing today, by year, by region (*Source* Author estimate, using data from swfinstitute.org)

ways to protect fiscal revenues from shock was clear for countries that experienced the Latin American and Asian crises of the 1990s and were forced to impose so-called structural adjustments as a condition to receive IMF assistance. These involved severe retrenchment of the public sector, job cuts, privatization of state assets and other reductions in fiscal expenditure but did not produce the recoveries promised: GDP typically fell much more sharply than envisaged and fiscal debts remained stubborn for years, and investment remained low with the private sector reluctant to enter; not to mention the civil and political costs of unemployment, reduced social benefits and lost human and physical capital (see UNCTAD 2012, among others[4]).

At the same time, the need for cover did not go away; in many senses developing countries' vulnerability to external shocks over which they had little control rather increased. With de-regulated and liberalized financial markets, followed by Quantitative Easing in the advanced economies following the 2007–2008 crisis, a glut of capital flooded world markets, much of it short-term 'carry-trade' destined even if only temporarily for developing countries. These ebbs and flows can reverse abruptly as monetary and financial conditions in the advanced countries change, bringing

[4] EG http://cepr.net/images/stories/reports/IMF-voting-shares-2016-04.pdf.

havoc in terms of interest rates and exchange rates and largely irrespective of conditions in or needs of developing countries (Fig. 7.5).

In order to build resilience and a buffer, those countries that could sought new strategies. Accumulating large foreign exchange reserves is one form of self-insurance and first line of defence against external shocks (albeit an expensive strategy with high opportunity costs). Another was to establish bilateral or regional currency arrangements such as SUCRE and SMP, to reduce exposure to third currencies such as the US Dollar and to promote inter-regional trade in local currencies. Others were to create reserve pools and credit swaps that make short-term finance available without having to resort only to the IMF.

Another strategy was to establish Sovereign Wealth Funds, drawing upon surplus foreign reserves when countries had them and investing them strategically. If oil or copper prices fall sharply, risking government revenues, the fund would liquidize some of its assets in order to re-stock government budgets and ensure fiscal balance. If exchange rates changed sharply the fund would sell some investments to intervene on currency markets, buying or selling the domestic currency or buying and selling bonds.

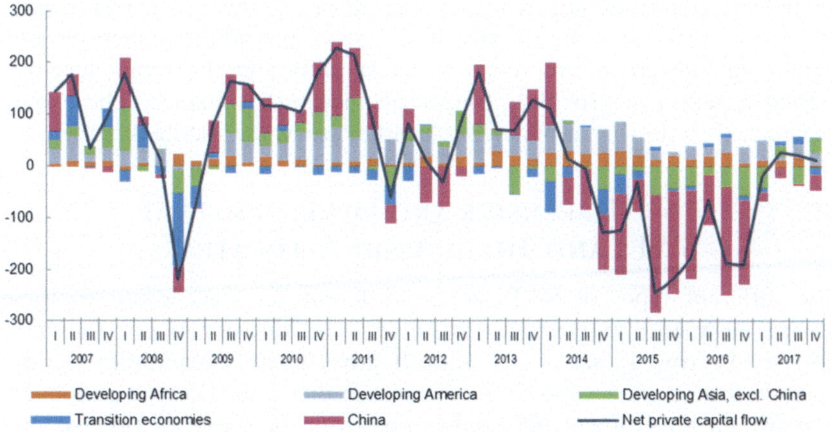

Fig. 7.5 Why build resilience? Capital markets are highly volatile and reverse abruptly (*Blns current dollars*) (*Source* UNCTAD, Financial Statistics Database based on IMF, Balance of Payments database; and national central banks)

At the same time, parallel processes were taking place in the world of long-term development finance. Developing countries again turned to their own institutions, beefing up existing national development banks and creating new ones, to support developmental investments at home and in the region (such as Brazil's National Bank for Economic and Social Development (BNDES), China's Development Bank (CDB) and South Africa's Development Bank of Southern Africa (DBSA)), and then to new Southern-led multilateral banks and funds such as the Asian Infrastructure Investment Bank (AIIB) as well as long-standing ones such as the Islamic Development Bank (See Barrowclough and Gottschalk 2018). These number in the hundreds and have firepower that far exceeds the traditional lender of last resort, the World Bank. Some of the Southern-owned Sovereign Wealth Funds also fit into this category, being specifically mandated to provide long-term finance for development for the country or its region. For many this is oriented to infrastructure but some are broader with a remit that includes strategic industrial investment and small and medium enterprises.

To sum up these processes, as developing countries faced disappointment in both the long-term developmental and the short-term crisis management aspects of the international monetary and financial system, many were able to design their own institutions to meet their own needs. SWFs potentially straddle the two functions of providing a defensive and stabilizing bulwark against crisis and instability and the more developmental function of providing long-term investment finance. The extent to which they do this in practice is another story, as described below.

7.4 Defensive and Developmental SWFs and Their Asset Allocations

The different types of SWFs act in different ways according to their sources of finance and objectives (Table 7.2). Macroeconomic stabilization funds (row 1) set up to smooth government expenditure against revenue shocks are necessarily short-term in their time horizon and invest primarily in government bills and bonds from their own or other countries, cash, gold or other highly liquid assets.[5] They are unlikely to hold

[5] Cash includes current accounts and other cash-equivalent instruments, debt securities including bills, notes and treasury bonds and corporate bonds (Kunzel et al. 2011).

Table 7.2 Categories of Sovereign Wealth Funds—defensive and developmental roles

Objective of SWF	*Risk preferences*	*Time horizon*	*Portfolio structure*	*Selected examples*
1. Macro or fiscal stabilization funds (e.g. to offset commodity price volatility)	Depends on the fiscal budget. Usually quite conservative	Short-term	Mostly highly liquid, holding government bills and bonds, cash, gold or other liquid assets. Unlikely to invest in long-term assets such as equities and infrastructure.	Alaska Permanent Fund, Azerbaijan State Oil Fund, Abu Dhabi Investment Authority, Bahrain Reserve Fund, Brunei Investment Agency, Kuwait Investment Authority, Kazakhstan National Fund, Russian Federation Reserve Fund, Chile Economic and Social Stabilization Fund, Mexico Oil Revenue Stabilization Fund, Nigeria Stabilization Fund, Timor-Leste Petroleum Fund, Trinidad & Tobago Heritage & Stabilization Fund, Venezuela, Algeria and others

(continued)

Table 7.2 (continued)

Objective of SWF	*Risk preferences*	*Time horizon*	*Portfolio structure*	*Selected examples*
2. Strategic development, Counter-cyclical investment	Variable	Medium-term	Mixed, including some medium-long term and illiquid, transport, energy, communications as well as bonds etc.	France Fonds Stratégique d'Investissement, now Bpifrance Participation, Italy cdp equity
3. Public pension funds	Medium risk return profile	Long-term	Tend to hold equities (as hedge for wage growth)	Chile Pension Fund, NZ Superannuation Fund Norway Pension Fund
4. Savings funds	Higher risk-return profile	Long-term	Bonds, Equity and other alternatives with low liquidity such as real estate, infrastructure	Botswana Pula Fund, Kiribati Revenue Equalization Fund, Nigeria Infrastructure fund, India, Saudi Arabia, Persian Gulf countries
5. Foreign exchange reserve funds	Higher risk profile	Long-term	Some weight towards equity and other alternatives with low liquidity but may need to keep some liquidity as well in case of short-term imbalances	Government of Singapore Investment Corporation, Korea Investment Corporation, China Investment Corporation

Source Author, derived from swfinstitute.org; IMF (2014); Kunzel et al. 2011; Annual Reports of Funds, and others equities and even less likely to hold 'alternative investments' such as real estate or infrastructure. Their spending rules need to permit fast liquidation of assets at short notice.[6]

There are many very large funds in this category. They are needed especially for commodity-dependent countries because a shock to the resource price (or the US dollar) will quickly impact on government revenues, and it is usually caused by something completely outside the control of the country itself. These shocks often necessitate borrowing to meet unanticipated shortfalls in the budget. Moreover, this usually means borrowing internationally, and at times when the cost of borrowing is high; it may not even be possible for the poorest countries generally shut out of global capital markets. The macroeconomic flow-on effects can be painful—the demand shock being transferred to a scaling back of investment, production and employment. Households stop spending. Governments are under pressure to make cuts just at the time when their counter-cyclical role as spender of last resort is most needed to boost aggregate demand. Any monetary policy options will likely have limited effectiveness, and currency depreciation can add to the woes assuming the country has few other exports, or that they are not particularly responsive to the exchange rate. Moreover, countries with a pegged exchange rate (the majority of oil exporters) cannot depreciate their currency anyway, leading to foreign exchange liquidity shortage if not actual insolvency. The SWF therefore needs to act quickly to restore fiscal balance and potentially foreign exchange balance as well.

Chile's Economic and Social Stabilization Fund (ESSF), for example, withdrew funds in 2009 to help the government take a counter-cyclical position, maintaining and even increasing spending to stimulate the economy and protect growth following the global financial and economic turbulence. It withdrew $9.3 billion out of the fund (a bold move as this represented almost half the total, which was $20.2 billion), using the majority for a stimulus plan to compensate for the sharp drop in demand. This included an ambitious programme of public investment as well as subsidies to the poorest households, worth almost 3% of total GDP. A smaller portion of the drawdown was used for debt repayment and to maintain the pension fund. 'At a time when many countries faced restrictions to credit, Chile was able to finance its fiscal programme almost

[6] They should also include a mechanism for recapitalizing the fund when prices rise again (Venables and Wills (2016).

exclusively out of its own resources', cites the Annual Report for 2009.[7] It has made subsequent withdrawals over recent years but never on the same grand scale: withdrawing around $475 m during each of the three years from 2014 to 2016 in order to finance the contribution to the Pension Reserve fund. At the same time, reflecting the difficult environment, it has also made no fresh contributions into the fund for the last six years.[8]

Such funds are essentially defensive in nature and have some similarities to the stabilization role played by the managers of Central Bank reserves and regional liquidity funds such as FLAR, where members have paid up capital that remains deposited in the Fund, pooled with other members and managed by that institution. There is little research on how these different institutions interact in practice but anecdotal evidence suggests there are both formal and informal discussions between regional fund and national SWF managers as they must be aware of and take account of each other's actions (e.g. in currency and bond markets), while maintaining their specific identifies and specializations. It should be an advantage for countries to have access to both a SWF and a regional reserve fund, because even while reserve funds can provide liquidity very promptly and without conditionalities, this is still a loan that needs to be repaid, with some interest, as compared to drawing down on a SWF that is already financed and hence the cost is rather in opportunity foregone rather than an interest rate to be repaid.

While this is still an ongoing research question, preliminary evidence suggests that countries with their own SWFs would be less likely to call upon liquidity support from their regional reserve fund. In Latin America, three of the four countries with both stabilization SWFs *and* membership of the regional foreign liquidity fund FLAR were less likely to use FLAR compared to members that did not have the benefit of a sovereign wealth fund.[9] Peru, with a well-resourced SWF mandated to ensure fiscal stability, the Fondo de Estabilizacion Fiscal (FEF), has not borrowed from FLAR since 1991 despite the volatility of prices in its main exports of copper and silver that sent shock waves to government revenues. On the other hand, in 2015 the FEF transferred $1.3 billion US dollars to Treasury to supplement the government's budget, and again in 2017

[7] Annual Report on Sovereign Wealth Funds 2009, Ministry of Finance, Chile.

[8] Annual Report Sovereign Wealth Funds 2017, Ministry of Finance, Chile.

[9] Bolivia, Colombia, Peru and Venezuela.

it transferred another $1.9 billion. These amounts were relatively small compared to the Fund's total capacity (in 2017 Peru's FEF had some $8.3 billion total assets) but large compared to the total firepower of FLAR. Nonetheless, in 2015 no other member was borrowing from FLAR and so the capacity for a loan was presumably available had it been requested. A few years later however the situation had worsened. By 2017 Peru's stabilization needs would have been well beyond FLAR's capacity especially since three other members borrowed that year (Costa Rica, Ecuador and Venezuela had loans totaling $1.8 billion). Hence Peru's national sovereign wealth fund appears to have been an important complement for the region, as well as an asset for the country.

In a similar vein, Bolivia, with a SWF financed through export earnings of silver and natural gas has not borrowed from the regional reserve fund since 2002, despite the volatility of metals prices; while Colombia (with a SWF based on oil) last borrowed from it in 1999. Other members of the fund that do not have the benefit of SWFs have called for support much more frequently. Moreover, a fiscal stabilizing SWF has a broader remit in the sense that shocks to government budgets can come from other quarters not just those related to foreign reserves.

By comparison, other SWFs are mandated not so much defensively but with a wider developmental remit. This can include building up capital resources for future generations (rows 2–4) or investing to support the changes in underlying economic structure needed for transformation and long-term development. Such Funds are more likely to make long-term investments such as in infrastructure, or they may simply just chase high returns in equities or real estate in already well-established markets and advanced economies. Unlike the stabilization funds, they tend not to create such highly liquid portfolios dominated by cash, bills and other easily sold-assets. Chile's two funds offer a useful comparison: in 2017, the fund designed to provide long-term pension revenues (PRF) held almost 16% of the total portfolio in equities whereas the fiscal stabilization fund ESSF had only 8% in this category. Nonetheless, this does not absolve them from potential exposure and vulnerability to shock, because many of these long-term investments will be in foreign countries and so there can still be a significant exposure to currency or interest rate volatility. This can prompt crises of foreign liquidity and balance of payments if these investments yielded essential foreign currency revenue, have contingent or actual foreign exchange liabilities, or if the currency exposure is hedged in derivatives markets. So, the need for stabilization does not disappear with a longer-term horizon[10]. Similarly, loans to developing country from the World Bank window the International Bank for Reconstruction and Development (IBRD), currently total outstanding some $184 billion, are for the most part in US dollars (78%) or euros (20%), thereby bringing exposure to currency movements.

In practice therefore the different types of Funds and mandates are inter-related and complementary whether they have ***developmental*** or and ***defensive*** strategies. This can also of course be a positive and virtuous cycle, unlike the more negative one described above. Developmental factors such as the underlying economic structure of a country fundamentally affects its structure of production, the diversity or vulnerability of its economic base, the nature and volumes of its imports and exports, and hence its exposure and vulnerability to exchange rate volatility (especially the US Dollar) and other sources of external shocks against which defence is needed. Reflecting this, new funds recently set up in advanced countries suggest that since the economic crisis the concept of ***stabilization*** has broadened beyond the narrow view of creating a buffer against external price shocks. It is now more of a hybrid category that includes both building in resilience and growth-potential through counter-cyclical support to aggregate demand as well as a longer-term structural and transformative development sense.[11]

[10] Some Funds cross over both short- and long-term classifications—such as Norway's which recently changed name from the Petroleum Fund to the Government Pension Fund, even though it is not a pension fund in the traditional sense because it is financed through oil profits rather than through pension contributions. Similarly, a Canadian fund established in 1976 in part financed from oil revenues changed focus and is now less directed to economic development and more to savings and investment, reflecting demographic changes at home.

[11] France's Strategic Investment Fund, established in 2008 to support French firms, was created with an initial endowment of 40 billion euros and owned 49% by the government of France and 51% by the Caisse des Depots et Consignations, the state-owned group charged to invest in development projects that serve the economic development of France. In 2013 it was integrated into Bpifrance, now Bpifrance Participations and is described as an investment bank not a fund. A similarly counter-cyclical purpose lead to Ireland's National Pensions Reserve Fund and Miscellaneous Provisions Act 2009, which requires investments to be made into credit institutions when needed to remedy a serious disturbance in the economy, or to prevent potential serious damage to the financial system or instability. Ireland's National Pensions Reserve Fund changed its name in 2013 to Ireland Strategic Investment Fund, reflecting its new focus on domestic investments. Italy's Strategic Fund was established in 2011 to invest in healthy and profitable strategic

For example, infrastructure is a real asset (as opposed to a financial one) that has short-term defensive and macroeconomic stabilizing benefits (such as being less reliant on the export or import of foreign exchange denominated commodities) in addition to long-term capital appreciation and a stream of revenues to support a government's pension liabilities or savings funds. There are other ways infrastructure can benefit the balance of payments and fiscal stability. For one, most infrastructure projects are dependent on government investment or under-writing alongside any private sector role. Public investment is typically significantly cheaper than private from the outset (worth a 3–4 per cent premium for debt finance on international capital markets, according to the UK National Accounts Office, and maybe more in developing countries). Hence there can be a saving in capital costs as well as some congruence of objectives if public SWFs invest alongside Development Banks and other actors. Secondly, even when the private sector does finance infrastructure, it typically involves debt in a foreign denomination—opening the door to foreign liquidity problems and more later if the project does not go as well as planned. So, there are many interlinkages between long-term developmental finance and the short-term stabilization roles for SWFs. This does not mean that all funds can play all roles, but rather than they are complementary.

7.5 Southern-Led But Not Southern-Oriented. Could SWFs Be More Developmental?

Although the world of SWFs is massively Southern-led, it is not particularly Southern-oriented, and this is a missed opportunity for development. Apart from a few exceptions, most of the Funds owned by developing countries do not invest much if at all in developing countries or regions. They have done little to change the long-standing pattern whereby capital flows to developing countries remain highly volatile, and net outflows exceed inflows by a lot (Fig. 7.6).

UNCTAD secretariat, based on national accounts data and Global Financial Integrity, Financial Flows and Tax Havens (2015)

Italian companies that needed capital injection in order to grow and be competitive on a global scale.

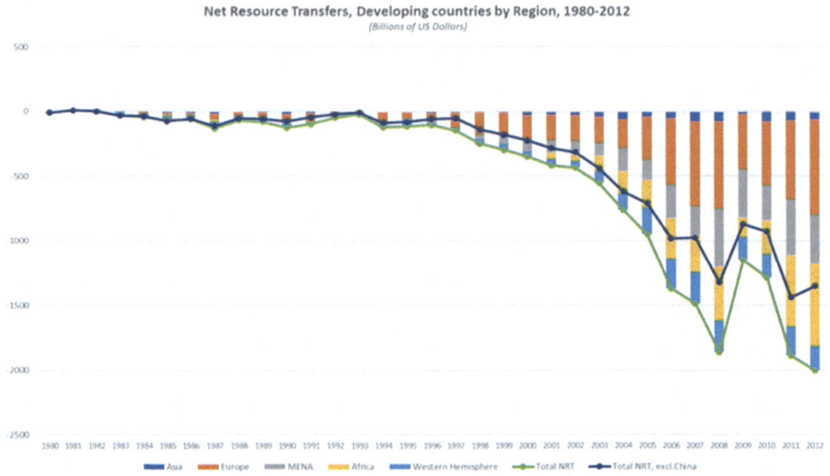

Fig. 7.6 Developing countries export more capital to the rest of the world than they receive

Fewer than half of the world's SWFs publish reports of their activities (Bauer 2018), but on the basis of the limited information available, in terms of location choices, the bulk of investment from all SWFs goes to developed economies and global financial markets (swfinstitute 2018). The United States and the United Kingdom received the lion's share, dwarfing sharply all other recipients. Advanced economies accounted for 6 of the top 7 host countries, with the exception being China (which ranked number three) and Europe accounts for almost one quarter of total SWF investments. This picture is reinforced by a recent survey[12] of 52 SWFs managing total assets apparently worth some \$5.7 trillion (to put this in perspective, the sum is on a par with the collective output of United Kingdom and Germany combined). Survey respondents noted that only 9% of the total portfolio was allocated to emerging markets, let along considering the broader category of developing countries. Another survey found that while most respondents already invested in or were interested in investing in Western Europe (93%) or North America (69%), only 24% were interested in Latin America, 12% in Africa and the Middle East (IPE

[12] Survey Invesco Global Sovereign Asset Management Study (2015).

and Sterling 2013). This confirms previous reports that fewer than 14% of international investors target emerging markets over the next 12 months (Inderst and Steward 2014: 14). Reflecting this at the level of individual deals, some of the biggest Southern SWF deals have been to the north—including high-profile acquisitions of financial institutions and banks.[13]

Changing to a more Southern orientation would mean investing more at home, or at least in the region. This is happening, but to a relatively small extent. Some funds have always invested domestically[14] and domestic holdings constituted around 16% of total investments over a sample of 60 SWFs, including some pension funds (Truman 2011). However, infrastructure deals tend to have been limited to the largest funds, such as the Libyan Investment Authority (total assets under management $53.3 billion of which around 7% believed to include investment in infrastructure throughout Africa, and the Qatar Investment Authority ($80 billion AUM and with $400m investment plans in infrastructure in South Africa). From a more developmental perspective, smaller funds could also be very beneficial especially in countries where capital formation is low and other sources of long-term investment funds marginal.

The picture of current allocation decisions is also not encouraging in terms of sectors. South–South investment may replicate the focus on finance and real estate seen in the rest of the world—such as Singapore's Temasek purchases in Indian bank ICIC and Tata Sky; Kuwait Investment Authority's investment in Chinese banking; Abu Dhabi Investment Authority's purchases of Egypt's EFG Hermes and Malaysian land projects. On the other hand, survey evidence shows that slightly more than half of all SWFs currently invest in infrastructure.[15] However even

[13] Some of the biggest SWF deals have been from the south to the north—including high-profile acquisitions of financial institutions and banks such as Barclays, Morgan Stanley, Merrill Lynch, Citigroup and UBS by SWFs from by Singapore, China, Kuwait and Korea. These purchases were broadly welcomed as the Funds were seen as having long-term horizons that made them less sensitive to ongoing market volatility—as compared to the protectionist concerns that blocked previous investments in non-financial activities such as Dubai and US ports, or China and a US oil company (Griffiths-Jones and Ocampo 2008).

[14] Including Funds from the eighteenth century in the United States, New Zealand Superannuation Fund, Singapore Temasek and more recently France.

[15] (34% investing directly and 50% investing both directly and through third-party funds (Inderst and Steward 2014: 27; and a similar finding in Preqin 2012). It can also be a

then, there continues to be a focus on energy, transport and telecommunications—which are already most likely to attract private sector or PPP investors—and in middle income or advanced economies rather than the poorest.[16] Moreover, commitments are likely to be small. The Inesco survey (2015) cited above found that out of the total AUM in the survey of $4 trillion, only around 2% (around $80 billion) was directed to infrastructure—an incredibly small proportion given the need and given the potential benefits to be created. Also, of this total only 17% was allocated to emerging markets (and this is not even considering other developing or least developed countries). Size was an important determinant of funds' willingness to make infrastructure investments, and respondents claimed that because infrastructure involved high sunk costs and transactions costs to get started, only large-scale projects were really worth their attention. This meant a focus on global rather than regional or local projects.[17]

Changing to a more Southern orientation would mean either investing more at home, or in one's region; and investing more in transformative activities that would help build true resilience and strength for the longer term. One reason that few funds have invested locally is that traditionally this was not considered appropriate, if the Funds' main objectives were to sterilize large export surpluses, stabilize the economy against volatile commodity or currency swings, and save for future generations. Funds in Abu Dhabi, Botswana, Chile, Ghana, Kazakhstan, Norway and Timor-Leste are explicitly not allowed to invest domestically.

However, the issue deserves to be reappraised—not least because of the persistent investment gap in developing countries and the low returns on investments elsewhere. There can be an irony that SWFs investing in

significant weighting in their portfolios—the Singaporean SWF Temasek and GIC have between 10–12% of total assets in infrastructure (OECD 2016: 23).

[16] Transport is sometimes favoured in PPPs because it offers relatively straightforward mechanisms for charging for the service through tolls and SWFs similarly favour transport. Angola's SWF set up a dedicated $1.1 billion infrastructure fund and identified transport infrastructure (alongside hospitality) for its potential to generate a high yield, citing potential returns above 10% per year on a ten-year investment horizon (Economist 28 February, 2015). Chinese funds signed with the African Union for a network of high-speed railways to link all countries on the continent.

[17] Small funds, with AUM less than $10b, allocated 1.2% of AUM in infrastructure. Larger projects ($10–$100b) allocated 0.7% of AUM to local infrastructure and 1.3% to global infrastructure. The largest funds (greater than $100b), allocated 0.5% to home infrastructure and 1.5% to global infrastructure.

advanced economies are receiving a lesser rate of return than would be realized closer to home, even without incorporating broader measures of social or human benefits of that investment.

It used to be that countries planning to invest more domestically were low and middle-income countries typically looking for ways to address their large infrastructure deficit. Now this may be starting to change, thanks to shrinking aid flows, tighter long-term financing and the fact that for many developing countries, both current and future returns at home are expected to be higher than those on global markets. Some also hope using SWF investment at home could contribute to improving the quality of public spending, by encouraging crowding-in of investors. Well performing SWFs that have long invested at home include Singapore's Temasek fund that holds around 25% domestically as well as the New Zealand Superannuation Fund which holds 17% of its assets at home. France's Strategic Investment Fund, established 2008, has a different priority to make strategic investments in French firms to prevent them from being bought at discounted prices by foreign investors, through participation and investment in innovative enterprises with a long-term investment horizon. There is more support for the view that domestic investment should particularly be the priority in capital-poor developing countries, even for SWFs with a stabilization mandate, and reflecting this, many funds have been established in recent years with the purpose of domestic, greenfield infrastructure investments.[18]

Venables and Wills (2016) for example argue that few occasions justify investment offshore for countries that are not capital poor. For long-run savings funds, the need to generate long-run capital accumulation can likely be better met by investing in and growing the domestic economy than by accumulating assets abroad. If the country's absorptive capacity is limited, or if domestic investment needs to be staggered in order to be efficient, then offshore investment can be justified but only on a temporary basis, a kind of 'parking' of resources before they are put into their real use, not as an end to itself. Only Funds that are explicitly designated for stabilization purposes have a strong argument for investing abroad,

[18] This includes some Gulf funds, Kazakhstan's Samruk Kazyna and Malaysia's Kazanah. Angola (Fundo Soberano de Angola), Azerbaijan, Equatorial Guinea, Iran, Kuwait, Mongolia, Nigeria, Papua New Guinea and Russia. Others are in the making, including Colombia, Morocco, Mozambique, Sierra Leone, Tanzania, Uganda and Zambia (Gelb et al. 2014).

according to the authors but even this stance could presumably be softened in the case where investment in diversifying the economy in the long-term would also be a stabilization measure. Moreover, even when there are good arguments for investing offshore, this could be more directed locally or at least to one's region rather than to distant advanced economies.

This is not to say there are no risks of investing at home (Bauer 2015). Investing in large domestic development projects may provoke the Dutch disease that most commodity-based funds were set up to avoid. If governments transfer excess foreign reserves into a fund, then transfer that money back into the economy through domestic investment or spending, the macroeconomic objective of sterilizing capital inflows could be undermined.

Domestic investment through SWFs may also undermine the public financial management systems, if Fund managers go around the political budget process, avoiding proper project appraisals, procurement and monitoring and authorizing investments that would not normally have been approved by the government and which could even undermine other projects and plans. It can be difficult to separate SWF's domestic investment decisions from political interference and elite capture (Gelb et al. 2014) and even if transparency is increased, the fact that Funds are authorized to support investments with a low commercial return in favour of a public return, opens the door to subjective decision-making that is difficult to monitor—especially since SWF processes are traditionally very opaque compared to budgetary decision-making which is usually overseen by the legislative process or discussed in the media. This risk is even higher in cases where SWF activities are not publicly disclosed—which is the case in more than 50 per cent of the cases examined by the Natural Resource Governance Institute (Bauer 2015).

Finally, financial and developmental mandates require very different forms of expertise. Sovereign Wealth Fund managers may be experts in financial matters but probably do not have the technical capacity to judge or manage an infrastructure project.

7.6 Looking to the Future

SWFs are a significant new actor in the international financial landscape and are largely—as with the other mechanisms described in this volume—Southern-led. They bring with them massive firepower that far exceeds the resources available to the traditional lenders of last resort and are helping to rebalance the 'voice' of the South to be more commensurate with its economic weight. They can provide extra liquidity and resilience in response to shocks that complements other regional or global reserve mechanisms. Those that invest locally or regionally can potentially directly transform and diversify economies, complementing regional and global development banks, and in turn reducing the exposure and vulnerability to shocks. The very act of creating a SWF seemingly has indirect benefits,[19] even before they do anything.

However, capital is only one of the inputs needed and SWFs may not be appropriate for all countries. Some countries are still in relatively early stages of developing legislative practices and policies to manage revenues, with Funds far from transparent in terms of asset allocation processes. This is in fact a complaint made of many SWFs not just those in low-income countries. In some countries, lack of transparency has led to constant political wrangling between federal governments and states, expropriation and corruption and investment strategies that favour short-term goals at the expense of longer-term maximization of returns (Bernstein et al. 2013).

On top of this, countries that are new to SWFs face internal risk management issues including operational and financial risks, which are already difficult in some of the advanced economies with long histories and much experience of these issues, and so would be expected to be even higher in new organizations in countries that are new to the practice and where regulatory or oversight mechanisms are less well established. There are also practical problems of how to manage strategically and technically, when funds are so large that entering or exiting markets is cumbersome and can sharply change prices.

Moreover, this chapter has argued that even with funds that are long-standing and with good reputations, we have not yet seen their full potential for development in part because even though they are Southern-led that are not particularly Southern-oriented. There are limited examples of SWFs investing in other Southern countries, especially those that lack the capacities to develop their own funds. One might argue that rather than

[19] As Nigeria discovered, when its credit rating was raised by Moody's to Ba3 after its establishment of a SWF (Whitehead 2012). This in turn eased Nigeria's ability to raise funds on international markets and at cheaper borrowing costs.

set up a SWF, in some cases it would be just as good to better capitalize a country's Development Banks.

However, there are encouraging examples where SWFs have helped countries to fulfil their aims of stabilizing the fiscal balance, resisting the negative shocks of exchange rate volatility and providing long-term revenues and investments for the future. This is encouraging and indicates that much could be done to benefit more from the potential offered by SWFs. One suggestion is to focus their long-term investments more in Southern countries and in developmental sectors. Another is to share the stabilization role more broadly, including with countries that lack the capacity to establish their own Funds. There are examples already where Funds have pooled with other investors[20] in physical investments and this could be extended to the resilience cover provided by stabilization funds, especially for countries that are trade partners.

Towards this end, SWFs could take on board some of the lessons from Development Banks that have articulated relatively modest targets for performance[21] that recognize there is a trade-off between securing commercial type rates of return vis-à-vis the lower rates are associated with a more developmental, social modality of investment. The goal would be to avoid either duplicating the task of central government budget setting (for investment in education and hospitals, etc.) as well as avoiding crowding out the private sector—leaving a small segment of projects with close-to-but-not-quite market rates of return (Gelb et al. 2014). Similarly, pooling across countries or to special partners could also be extended to the shorter-term fiscal stabilization role, especially for example to neighbouring countries where a fiscal shortfall could provoke cuts in demand and a fall in trade.

One reason that few funds appear to think like this is that most are not managed locally but rather are outsourced to foreign banks, such as UNS Global, Goldman Sachs and Credit Suisse (Masamba 2014). They cannot be expected to have the local knowledge or sensitivities that are often claimed to support south–south investment. This may happen naturally as

[20] E.g. Nigeria Infrastructure Fund's cooperative agreements with General Electric, the Africa Finance Corporation and the International Finance Corporation (see Rice and Blas 2013).

[21] These include achieving a minimal return that exceeds inflation (Finaciera Rural of Mexico, Credit Bank of Turkey); generating a rate of return that equals or exceeds the government's long-term borrowing costs (Business Development Bank of Canada).

SWFs are setting up satellite offices in international financial centres or in places where they have major investments (Bortolotti 2013: 14). On the other hand, it seems that often SWFs invest a sizeable proportion of their portfolios through subsidiaries that are registered in low-tax environments such as Mauritius and the Cayman Islands (BAFFI 2014: 7), suggesting a rather limited view of the integrated nature of today's economy. The question of whether SWFs are contributing to illicit flows relating to tax havens has not been explored empirically but this would be an obvious development irony if it is depleting fiscal revenues from governments to which they are due.

At present there is no special south–south forum for discussing experiences of Southern-led SWFs and their role but this could be a useful creation—following the lead for example of the global forum International Working Group of Sovereign Wealth Funds (See http://www.ifswf.org/pr/pr24.pdf). This would enable also a forum for better communication between SWFs and Development Banks, as well as the regional reserve funds; as well as encouraging further expansion of the Santiago Principles to improve the transparency of SWF investment decision-making processes. It would also enable the kind of inter-regional planning that is needed for larger scale investments in infrastructure for example where many countries need to co-ordinate together. The main factor constraining this and other forms of collaboration is that—in common with many other aspects of international relations—Funds are considering only national interests and not regional or global ones. This may even be explicitly part of their fiduciary duty and mandate. However, as long as developing countries eschew investment at home and in the global South, this potential will be limited. The FLAR offers an encouraging example where member countries have realized the strengths and benefits of co-operating together, contributing an agreed upon portion of their surplus reserves into a pool for all members to use. Why not a regional SWF to complement it as well? (Table 7.3)

Table 7.3 Sovereign Wealth Funds

Country	*Fund Name*	*Assets (billion USD)*	*Established*	*Source of funds*
Sub-Saharan Africa				
Angola	Fundo Soberano de Angola	5	2012	Oil
Botswana	Pula Fund	5.7	1994	Diamonds and minerals
Equatorial Guinea	Fund for Future Generations	0.08	2002	Oil
Gabon	Sovereign Wealth Fund	0.38	1998	Oil
Ghana	Ghana Petroleum Funds	0.45	2011	Oil
Mauritania	National Fund for Hydrocarbon Reserves	0.3	2006	Oil
Mauritius	Sovereign Wealth Fund	3	(in talks)	N/A
Nigeria	Nigerian Sovereign Investment Authority	1.35	2012	Oil
Senegal	Fonds Souverain d'Investissements Stratégiques	1	2013	Non-commodity
Latin America				
Bolivia	Fondo para la Revolución Industrial Productiva	1.2	2012	Silver, natural gas
Brazil	Fundo Soberano do Brasil	5.3	2008	Non-commodity
Chile	Economic and Social Stabilization Fund	15.2	2007	Copper
Chile	Pension Reserve Fund	7.9	2006	Copper
Mexico	Fondo Mexicano del Petroleo	N/A	2014	Oil
Mexico	Mexico Stabilization Fund	6	2000	Oil

(continued)

Table 7.3 (continued)

Country	*Fund Name*	*Assets (billion USD)*	*Established*	*Source of funds*
Panama	Panama Sovereign Wealth Fund	1.2	2012	Non-commodity
Peru	Fondo de Estabilización Fiscal	9.2	1999	Non-commodity
Trinidad and Tobago	Heritage and Stabilization Fund	5.5	2000	Oil
Falkland Islands, UK	Oil Development Reserve	13.1	2012	Oil
Venezuela	Fondo para la Estabilización Macroeconómica	0.8	1998	Oil
North America				
Canada	Alberta Heritage Saving Trust Fund	17.5	1976	Oil
USA	Alabama Trust Fund	2.5	1985	Oil and gas
USA	Alaska Permanent Fund Corporation	53.9	1976	Oil
USA	Louisiana Education Quality Trust Fund	1.3	1986	Oil and gas
USA	New Mexico State Investment Council	19.8	1958	Oil and gas
USA	North Dakota Legacy Fund	2.4	2011	Oil and gas
USA	Texas Permanent School Fund	37.7	1854	Commodity
USA	Texas Permanent University Fund	17.2	1876	Oil and gas
USA	Permanent Wyoming Mineral Trust Fund	5.6	1974	Mineral
USA	West Virginia Future Fund	0	2014	Commodity
Asia-Pacific				

(continued)

Table 7.3 (continued)

Country	*Fund Name*	*Assets (billion USD)*	*Established*	*Source of funds*
Australia	Australian Government Future Fund	95	2006	Non-commodity
Brunei Darussalam	Brunei Investment Agency	40	1983	Oil
China	China-Africa Development Fund	5	2007	Non-commodity
China	China Investment Corporation	652.7	2007	Non-commodity
China	National Social Security Fund	236	2000	Non-commodity
China	SAFE Investment Company	547	1997	Non-commodity
Hong Kong, China	HKMA Investment Portfolio	400.2	1993	Non-commodity
Indonesia	Government Investment Unit	0.34	2006	Non-commodity
Kiribati	Revenue Equalization Reserve Fund	0.6	1956	Fishing licenses
Republic of Korea	Korea Investment Corporation	84.7	2005	Non-commodity
Malaysia	Khazanah Nasional	41.6	1993	Non-commodity
Mongolia	Fiscal Stability Fund	0.3	2011	Mining
New Zealand	New Zealand Superannuation Fund	21.8	2003	Non-commodity
Papua New Guinea	Sovereign Wealth Fund	N/A	2011	Gas
Singapore	GIC Private Limited	320	1981	Non-commodity
Singapore	Temasek Holdings	177	1974	Non-commodity
Timor-Leste	Timor-Leste Petroleum Fund	16.6	2005	Oil and gas
Vietnam	State Capital Investment Corporation	0.5	2005	Non-commodity
MENA				

(continued)

Table 7.3 (continued)

Country	*Fund Name*	*Assets (billion USD)*	*Established*	*Source of funds*
Bahrain	Mumtalakat Holdings	10.5	2006	Non-commodity
Algeria	Fonds de Régulation des Recettes	50	2000	Oil
Iran, Islamic Rep. of	National Development Fund of Iran	62	2011	Oil and gas
Iraq	Development Fund for Iraq	18	2003	Oil
Kuwait	Kuwait Investment Authority	548	1953	Oil
Libya	Libyan Investment Authority	66	2006	Oil
Oman	Oman Investment Fund	6	2006	Oil
Oman	State General Reserve Fund	13	1980	Oil and gas
Qatar	Qatar Investment Authority	256	2005	Oil and gas
Palestine	Palestine Investment Fund	0.8	2003	Non-commodity
Saudi Arabia	Public Investment Fund	5.3	2008	Oil
Saudi Arabia	SAMA Foreign Holdings	757.2	1952	Oil
UAE	Abu Dhabi Investment Authority	773	1976	Oil
UAE	Abu Dhabi Investment Council	90	2007	Oil
UAE	Emirates Investment Authority	15	2007	Oil
UAE	International Petroleum Investment Company	68.4	1984	Oil

(continued)

Table 7.3 (continued)

Country	*Fund Name*	*Assets (billion USD)*	*Established*	*Source of funds*
UAE	Investment Corporation of Dubai	175.2	2006	Non-commodity
UAE	Mubadala Development Company	66.3	2002	Oil
UAE	Ras Al Khaimah Investment Authority	1.2	2003	Oil
Europe				
France	Fonds Stratégique d'Investissement	25.5	2008	Non-commodity
Ireland	National Pensions Reserve Fund	27.4	2001	Non-commodity
Italy	Fondo Strategico Italiano	6	2011	Non-commodity
Norway	Government Pension Fund Global	882	1990	Oil
Russian Federation	Russian Direct Investment Fund	13	2011	Non-commodity
Russian Federation	National Welfare Fund	79.9	2008	Oil
Russian Federation	Russia Reserve Fund	88.9	2008	Oil
Central Asia				
Azerbaijan	State Oil Fund of the Republic of Azerbaijan	37.3	1999	Oil
Kazakhstan	Samruk-Kazyna	77.5	2008	Non-commodity
Kazakhstan	National Fund of the Republic of Kazakhstan	77	2000	Oil, gas and metals
Kazakhstan	National Investment Corporation	2	2012	Oil
Turkmenistan	Turkmenistan Stabilization Fund	N/A	2008	Oil and gas

Source Author's estimates, derived from swf institute, OECD (2018), Annual Reports and others

References

BAFFI (2017), Dealing with Disruption: IFSWF Annual Review 2017. Centre for Applied Research on International Markets, Banking Finance and Regulation, University of Bocconi, Italy.

BAFFI (2014), Towards a New Normal, Sovereign Wealth Fund Annual Report 2014, Centre for Applied Research on International Markets, Banking Finance and Regulation, University of Bocconi, Italy.

BAFFI (2013), The Great Reallocation, Sovereign Wealth Fund Annual Report 2013, Centre for Applied Research on International Markets, Banking Finance and Regulation, University of Bocconi, Italy.

Barrowclough and Gottschalk (2018), Solidarity and the South: Supporting the New Landscape of Long-term Development Finance. UNCTAD Research Paper No. 24, UNCTAD/SER.RP/2018/6.

Bauer A (2015), Six Reasons Why Sovereign Wealth Funds Should Not Invest or Spend at Home. Natural Resource Governance Institute, April 2015.

Bauer A (2018), How good are SWFs at investing? Natural REsource Governance Institute., 13 June 2018.

Bernstein S, J Lerner and A Schoar (2013), The Investment Strategies of Sovereign Wealth Funds, *Journal of Economic Perspectives* 27(2), Spring 2013.

Bertaut C (2014), Sovereign Wealth Funds: Evolution and Outlook, Board of Governors of the Federal Reserve System, American University Conference on The Contributions and Impact of Sovereign Wealth Funds, October 2014.

Bortolotti (2013 and subsequent years), SWF Annual Report, Sovereign Investment Laboratory, Bocconi University, Milan.

Fritz B and L Muhlich (2014), Regional Monetary Cooperation in the Developing World, Taking Stock. UNCTAD.

Gelb A, S Tordo, H Halland, N Arfaa and G Smith (2014), Sovereign Wealth Funds and Long-term Development Finance: Risks and Opportunities. Policy Research Working Paper No. 6776, World Bank. Washington, DC.

Grabel I (2017), *When Things Don't Fall Apart: Global Financial Governance and Developmental Finance in an Age of Productive Incoherence*. Cambridge, MA: MIT Press.

Griffiths-Jones S and JO Ocampo (2008), *The Future of National Development Banks*. Oxford: Oxford University Press.

Inderst G and F Steward (2014), Institutional Investment in Infrastructure in Emerging Markets and Developing Economies. Public-Private Infrastructure Advisory Facility, World Bank, Washington DC.

IMF (2019), IMF Members' Quotas and Voting Power and IMF Board of Governors, 19 March 2019.

IPE and Sterling (2013, 2015), Institutional Infrastructure Survey 2013, 2015. London, Investment and Pensions Europe and Stirling Capital Partners.

Kogod School of Business (2014), Proceedings, the Contributions and Impact of Sovereign Wealth Funds, Meeting Proceedings, American University, Washington, DC, October 9, 2014.

Kring WN and KP Gallagher (2019), Strengthening the Foundations? Alternative Institutions for Finance and Development, *Development and Change* 50(1): 3–23. International Institute of Social Studies.

Kunzel P, Y. Lu, I. Petrova and J Pihlman (2011), Investment Objectives of Sovereign Wealth Funds—A Shifting Paradigm, IMF Working Paper WP/11/19.

Masamba M (2014), SWFs, a race worth joining to unlock Africa's hidden potential? Polity, 11 June 2014.

Ocampo JA (2014), Reforming the international monetary and financial architecture. Fredrich Ebert Stiftung, Dialogue on Globalization.

OECD (2016), *Large Pension Funds Survey*. Paris: OECD.

Preqin (2012), Special Report, Sovereign Wealth Funds. Prequin: London, UK.

Rice, X and B Javier (2013), Nigeria SWF Makes Maiden In-vestment. *Financial Times*, September 16. http://www.ft.com/intl/cms/s/0/d0751b26-1ee8-11e3-b80b-00144feab7de.html#axzz2qII7WFoF.

Salas R, D Camacho and YM Alzamora (2018), El Fondo de Estabilizacion Fiscal en el Peru Mondea Politica Fiscal, June 2018.

Sovereign Wealth Fund Institute website and database (2018).

Sovereign Wealth Fund Institute (various years), Sovereign Wealth Fund Rankings. Available at http://www.swfinstitute.org/sivereign-wealth-fund-rankings.

Truman EM (2011), Sovereign Wealth Funds: Is Asia Different? Working Paper 11-12, Peterson Institute, Washington, DC.

UNCTAD (2015), Making the international finance architecture work for development. Trade and Development Report. United Nations: Geneva and New York.

Venables AJ and S Wills (2016), Resource Funds: Stabilizing, Parking and Inter-Generational Transfer, *Journal of African Economics* 25, AERC, Supplement 2: ii20–ii40.

Chile SWF fund. http://www.hacienda.cl/english/sovereign-wealth-funds/economic-and-social-stabilization-fund/financial-situation/market-value.html.

Annual Report (2017 and 2009), http://www.hacienda.cl/english/sovereign-wealth-funds/annual-report/annual-report-sovereign-wealth-funds.html.

http://www.oecd.org/daf/fin/private-pensions/2016-Large-Pension-Funds-Survey.pdf.

Peru

https://www.mef.gob.pe/contenidos/english/investor_relations/Strategy_2019_2022.pdf.

http://www.bcrp.gob.pe/docs/Publicaciones/Revista-Moneda/moneda-174/moneda-174-07.pdf.
Bolivia
https://medios.economiayfinanzas.gob.bo/MH/documentos/2016/agosot/Presentacion_16_9_2016.pdf.
Whitehead E (2012), The Rise of the African SWF, This is Africa, 22 December 2012.
World Bank (2018), Annual Report of the IBRD and IDA. http://pubdocs.worldbank.org/en/474791538065340369/211296v2.pdf.

CHAPTER 8

Toward a Regional Financial Architecture: The East Asian Experience with a Focus on Defense

Mah Hui Lim

8.1 Introduction

The Asian regional financial architecture in place today has two goals—defensive and developmental—supported by three pillars. These are (i) regional forums for closer policy dialogue and coordination; (ii) a liquidity support fund (the CMIM) with an institution for economic surveillance (AMRO), and (iii) the development of local currency and regional bond markets. This chapter focuses in particular on the defensive elements[1] and has four main sections. The first briefly reviews the background and limitations of the traditional international financial architecture. The second

[1] This is a shortened and revised version of a longer paper initially prepared for UNCTAD that examined the role of bond markets and long-term development or credit banks as complementary pillars of the regional financial architecture. It also draws upon the discussion in UNECA (2011); and discussions at international conferences and workshops in South Africa and Ecuador (2017).

M. H. Lim (✉)
Penang, Malaysia
e-mail: limmahhui@gmail.com

D. Barrowclough et al. (eds.), *South–South Regional Financial Arrangements*, International Political Economy Series,
https://doi.org/10.1007/978-3-030-64576-2_8

examines the roots of the Asian Financial Crisis of 1997/1998 and subsequent impacts of International Monetary Fund (IMF) rescue packages to the region and shows how this led to the emergence of an Asian regional financial architecture. Section three introduces the initiatives and mechanisms adopted to prevent or reduce the occurrence of future crises, and the management of such crises, including a brief overview of the process of regional forums and debate that lead to the emergence of today's institutions. Focusing in turn on crisis prevention and crisis management it includes examination of exchange rate mechanisms and a particular focus on the role of capital flows coordination. Section four highlights the need to supplement these efforts with the promotion of regional and national long-term development or credit banks as another pillar of the regional financial architecture, and the limitations of other mechanisms such as regional bond markets. Section five, concludes the paper reminding of the basic lessons learned—which include most importantly the need to retain policy tools, regulate the financial system, and control capital flows.

8.2 East Asian Responses to the Breakdown of the Traditional International Financial Architecture

Banking and financial crises have occurred with higher frequency and greater intensity following the increasing globalization in the post-Bretton Woods international financial system. The last and most severe since the 1929 Great Depression was the Global Financial Crisis of 2007. Asia underwent a similar experience in 1997/1998. It was the failure of the traditional international architecture to help Asia resolve the crisis that prompted efforts to create an Asian regional financial architecture.

The 1945 signing of the Bretton Woods agreement was the world's first attempt to establish an international financial architecture. Its aim was to manage monetary policies between countries in order to promote financial and monetary stability and economic growth.

The main concerns of the Bretton Wood agreement were: how to avoid the monetary chaos of the inter-war period and to replace the floating exchange rate with a more stable exchange rate system for the world; how to correct global balance of payment imbalances; and how to finance and resuscitate the war-damaged economies of Europe. New rules, procedures, and institutions were set up to achieve these goals.

To manage the international financial and monetary systems, a new fixed exchange rate system was established in which countries agreed to peg their currencies to the US dollar that in turn was pegged to gold at the rate of $35 per ounce. The IMF was tasked to manage this new system and be the keeper of the rules. IMF approval was required for any change in exchange rate in excess of 10% of the peg. It also pledged to provide liquidity support to countries experiencing balance of payment difficulties, as well as providing the forum for consultation and cooperation among governments.

The Bretton Woods system worked for a couple of decades, mainly to the advantage of U.S., the issuer of the dollar reserve currency, until it broke down in 1971 when the U.S., faced with persistent balance of payment deficit and dwindling gold reserves, abandoned the conversion of dollar into gold at the agreed rate. The breakdown of the Bretton Woods system and the reintroduction of flexible exchange rate, coupled with the ascent of neoliberal policies ushered in an era of financial and monetary instability again. Domestically, the industrial and financial sectors were deregulated and liberalized. Internationally, the U.S. and IMF pushed countries to dismantle barriers to free capital flows. Capital started to flow freely in and out of countries, corporations spread their wings abroad and became foot-loose, banks started to internationalize their operations with greater portion of profits derived from overseas operations. Financial deregulation and liberalization led to a litany of financial crises in the 1980s and 1990s. First was the Latin American debt crisis in the 1980s; followed by Mexico in the mid-1990s. Then it was Asia and Russia that suffered their most severe crisis in the late 1990s.

8.3 Asia's Financial Crisis and the Emergence of Regional Financial Architecture

The roots of the Asian Financial Crisis (AFC) of 1997/1998 were many. They included huge inflow of speculative foreign capital into Asia attracted by arbitrage opportunities and abetted by a pegged exchange rate regime; misallocation of capital and financial mismanagement resulting from excessive liquidity; rapid deregulation and liberalization of the financial sector without stronger supervision; an explosion of corporate and financial borrowings that were short term and denominated in foreign currencies.

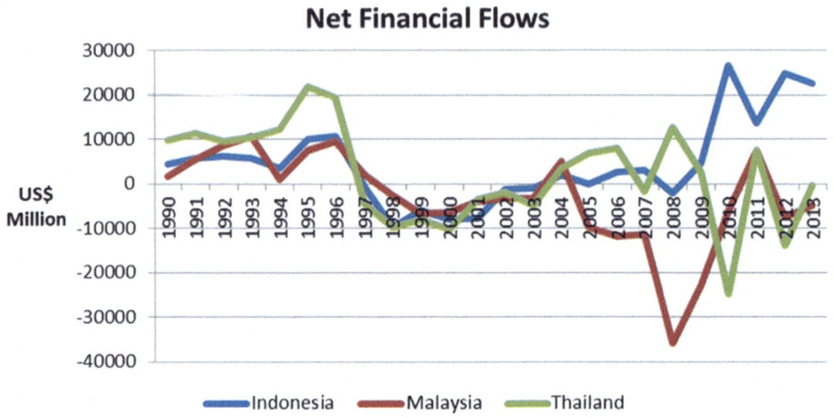

Fig. 8.1 Net Financial (Capital) Flows for three ASEAN countries, 1990–2013 (*Source* ADB Key Indicators for Asia & Pacific 2010, 2014)

The Asian crisis was not the boom and bust of a normal business cycle, but rather, one associated with speculative and erratic financial flows. Starved by low interest rates in developed countries, funds flowed into Asia searching for higher yields. Private capital flows into emerging markets reached $256 billion by 1997 compared to $42 billion in 1990 (Krugman 2009: 79).[2]

Figure 8.1 shows the massive influx of capital (the sum of net direct, portfolio, and other investments) into three Southeast Asian countries before 1997 and the equally large outflow during the crisis. Net financial (capital) flows into Thailand reached US$20 billion in 1996 and turned negative $10 billion in 1998, a swing of $30 billion. Similarly, in Indonesia and Malaysia, the swings were too massive for the economies to absorb.

The drastic reversal of capital flows led to a dramatic fall in currencies that ballooned foreign currency debt and bankrupted corporations and banks alike. The Thai baht plunged from 25 baht to 50 baht per dollar and the Indonesian rupiah from 2500 to 15000 per dollar at the height of the crisis in 1998. What began as a currency crisis in Thailand in July 1997 soon spread to other countries like Indonesia, Malaysia, and even South

[2] All $ are in US dollars, unless otherwise specified.

Korea and spilled over to the real economy. Indonesia and Thailand were the hardest hit—banks and corporations collapsed, the economy shrunk and unemployment soared—and suffered an output loss of 40% of GDP. The fiscal costs of the crisis were estimated at 55% of GDP for Indonesia and 35% for Thailand (Caprio et al. 2003).

The response of international financial institutions and non-Asian countries to the Asian Financial Crisis (AFC) was timid at best and negative at worse. At the G7-IMF meeting in September 1997, Japan proposed to set up an Asian Monetary Fund to assist Asian countries suffering balance of payment difficulties to be funded by Asian countries of which Japan was willing to be the largest contributor. Both the United States and the IMF strongly opposed this Fund on the argument that it would encourage moral hazard. Most probably the reason was the US did not want to set a precedent where regional cooperation or blocs could assert some degree of independence. Hence the Asian Monetary Fund never saw the light of the day (Masaki 2007; Lipscy 2003).

Instead, the IMF provided rescue packages to Thailand, Indonesia, and South Korea and, as usual, imposed its one-size-fits-all solution and conditions on the crisis-affected countries even though the causes of the AFC were quite different from that of the Mexican financial crisis. Unlike Mexico, the Asian governments did not over-borrow; it was mainly the private corporations and financial institutions that had crushing debt, many of which were short term and in foreign currencies leading to a double mismatch in currency and maturity. The IMF imposed over 100 conditions on South Korea and Indonesia as part of its rescue packages many of which were only remotely related to the immediate causes of the crisis. What rescued the Korean economy was the rollover of short-term debt by foreign lenders. But the IMF took this golden opportunity to totally reform and restructure the Korean economy according to its neoliberal framework.

In the case of Indonesia, the medicine given by IMF aggravated the economic ills of the country. The hike in interest rate to over 10% per annum did not stem the deluge of capital outflow (as evident in Fig. 8.1); or the decimation of the rupiah that lost over 80% of its value; instead it smothered the economy as borrowers suffered crushing debt from high interest payment and ballooning principal repayment resulting from currency depreciation. It took over five years for Indonesia to recover. Malaysia also initially followed the IMF prescription but, within a few months, reversed course and implemented anti-cyclical as well as non-conventional monetary and fiscal policies that included capital control measures. These measures helped its economy to recover within two years without any assistance from the IMF.

Among the hard lessons Asian countries learned from the Asian financial crisis was the need to pull up their own boot straps; to lessen their dependence on the international financial institutions and Western countries; and to strengthen regional cooperation and resources to deal with financial crisis. The failure of the existing international financial system to deal with the Asian crisis thereby provided the impetus for Asian nations to search for an alternative regional financial architecture.[3]

The other impetus for greater regional financial and monetary cooperation is market considerations. While European economic and financial integration was driven more by political motives, Asian cooperation and integration is more market-driven. Asian intra-regional trade and investment flows have risen over the years. Asian intra-regional trade was 54% of total trade in 2014; its intra-regional foreign direct investments accounted for 51% of total investments received in 2012. See Fig. 8.2. Asia's intra-regional portfolio investments are less developed, making up only 15% of total portfolio assets and 20% of total portfolio liabilities in 2013 (ADB 2014a: 43). The development of an Asian regional financial architecture would facilitate more trade and investments.

8.4 Asian Initiatives in Regional Financial Architecture—Overlapping Systems

An international financial architecture should address a number of key issues such as: the role of the US dollar as the predominant international reserve currency; the current global account imbalances and the accumulation of reserves; the exchange rate regimes of countries; regulation of national financial systems; and governance of the international financial institutions (UNECA 2011:21). The failure of the traditional international financial architecture to adequately address these issues

[3] Prior to this, there was no structure or forum in Asia to deal with regional financial issues, except for EMEAP (forum for central bankers of ASEAN and other Asian countries) set up in 1991 that became active after the AFC.

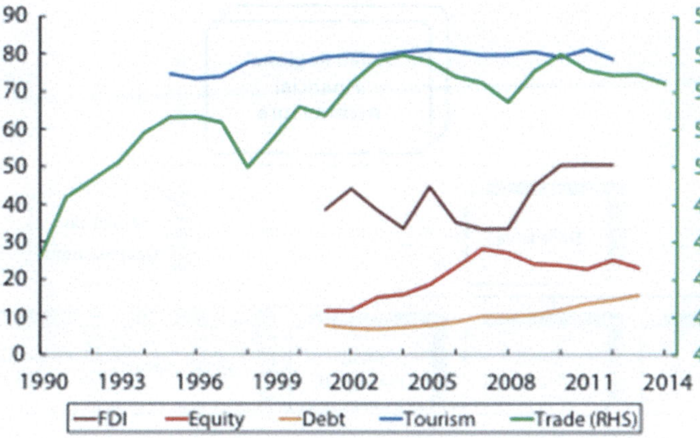

Fig. 8.2 Intra-regional Asia Integration Indicators (% of total) (*Source* ADB 2014a: Fig. 1)

prompted countries to develop their own regional financial architecture. A regional financial architecture consists of two partially overlapping parts—a regional financial system and a regional monetary system.

There are two broad objectives for greater regional financial and monetary cooperation—defensive and developmental. The purpose of the defensive objective is to cooperate and pool resources together to overcome regional economic and financial crises, while the developmental purpose is to establish policies and institutions to promote greater economic integration and higher growth in the region.

The defensive mode of a regional financial architecture can be further broken down into three areas—crisis prevention, crisis management, and crisis resolution (Kuroda and Kawai 2003). The regional financial and monetary forums and institutions created after the AFC fall are primarily for defensive purpose (Fig. 8.3).

8.5 Crisis Prevention Mechanisms

The Asian crisis showed that contagion within a region can happen and spread rapidly; and relying on outside help is risky. The region should establish its own crisis prevention mechanisms.

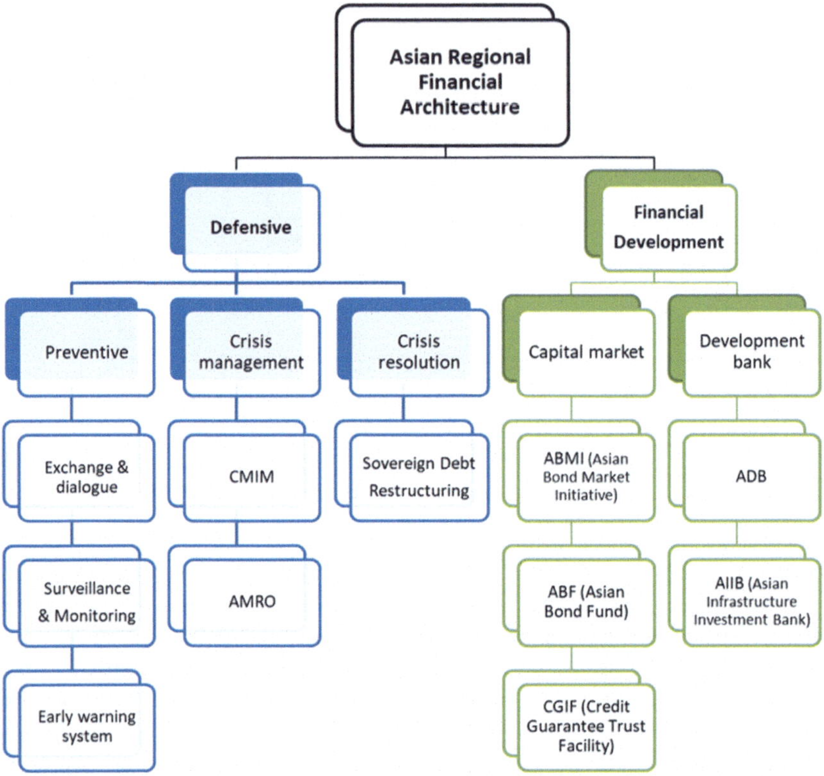

Fig. 8.3 The two pillars of Asian regional finance—development and defense

Developing and strengthening a regional financial system at the most basic level involves setting up a network for policymakers to engage in regular information exchange, policy dialogue, and cooperation. This enables countries to better understand each other's economic objectives, policies, and problems, to avoid unnecessary conflict, and to coordinate policies on common issues. The next level entails the establishment of economic surveillance and early warning systems for member countries, a closer monitoring of national and regional economic conditions, and cultivation of peer review and pressure to maintain strong macroeconomic fundamentals.

8.5.1 *Forums to Foster Greater Cooperation*

To date many regional forums and institutions have been set up in East Asia for the above purposes. We shall focus only on the main ones: ASEAN+3 Finance Ministers Meeting; ASEAN Surveillance Process (ASP), Executives' Meeting of East Asian and Pacific Central Banks (EMEAP), and AMRO (ASEAN+3 Macroeconomic Research Organization).

8.5.2 *ASEAN+3FM*[4]

With the outbreak of the AFC, ASEAN+3 leaders got together in December 1997 to discuss regional economic and financial issues and to establish mechanisms for resolving the financial crisis. Within the ASEAN+3 leaders grouping, the ASEAN+3 Finance Ministers (ASEAN+3FM) group spearheads financial and monetary cooperation among the member countries. Its aim is to strengthen policy dialogue, coordination and collaboration on common financial, monetary, and fiscal issues. This forum has four main parts: (i) Economic Review and Policy Dialogue (ERPD); (ii) the Chiang Mai Initiative (CMI); (iii) the Asian Bond Markets Initiative (ABI); and (iv) the ASEAN+3 Research Group. For a while, the region's crisis prevention and resolution process was handled mainly by finance ministries, with some participation from central banks. In May 2012, the ASEAN+3 FM group took a significant step and upgraded its composition to officially include central bank governors of 13 member countries (plus Hong Kong).

8.5.3 *ASEAN+3 ERPD (Economic Review and Policy Dialogue)*

The first meeting of ASEAN+3FM was held in April 1999 on the sidelines of the ADB annual meeting in Manila. They focused on three issues—setting up a platform for exchange of information and policy dialogue; providing regional liquidity support; and development of regional bond market.

In the following year, they set up the ASEAN+3 Economic Review and Policy Dialogue (ERPD) for the purpose of strengthening economic

[4] ASEAN refers to the Association of Southeast Asian Nations that was originally set up in 1967 and consisted of the five founding countries—Indonesia, Malaysia, Philippines, Singapore, and Thailand. Eventually it expanded to 10 countries to include Brunei, Kampuchea, Laos, Myanmar, and Vietnam. The Plus 3 countries refer to China, Japan, and Republic of Korea.

and financial cooperation through information exchange and policy dialogue. It focuses on assessing macroeconomic conditions globally, regionally, and nationally; provision of information on policy changes; financial market development including exchange rates, interest rates, foreign exchange reserves; exchanging views on risk management and early warning systems; monitoring capital flows; strengthening banking and financial systems; and providing an Asian voice in the reform of international financial architecture (Kawai and Houser 2007:5).

The finance ministers meet annually, usually at the ADB annual meetings, while the deputy finance ministers and central bank deputies meet bi-annually to present development in their own countries and to exchange views on global, regional and country economic and financial development. But no peer review is undertaken. International financial institutions like the ADB and IMF participate and provide input to facilitate the dialogue.

The ERPD process is important because it is a regional liquidity support system, like the CMI. To work, member countries must have knowledge of and feel comfortable about the macroeconomic strengths and weaknesses of each other. Hence the tasks of information exchange, surveillance, and monitoring are vital. The ERPD must be able to assess correctly the economic and financial risks of each country and the region and recommend policies to minimize these challenges; the ERPD and CMI are thus mutually dependent. At the 2005 ASEAN+3FM meeting a decision was made to integrate the ERPD process into the CMI framework and to strengthen its capacity. Kawai and Houser (2007: 10–11) suggest three modalities of operation for the ERPD process—information sharing, peer review and pressure, and due diligence for potential borrowers.

8.5.4 ASEAN Surveillance Process (ASP)

The 2nd ASEAN Finance Ministers' Meeting in February 1998 agreed to set up the ASEAN Surveillance Process (ASP) with the following objectives: (i) to strengthen cooperation through exchange of information on economic and financial matters; (ii) to provide a mechanism for peer review and early warning system to enhance economic and financial stability; (iii) to highlight policy options to prevent and manage crisis; (iv) to monitor and discuss global development that impact regional stability.

Key achievements include: establishment of a dedicated unit at the ASEAN Secretariat to conduct regional surveillance; establishment of national surveillance units in selected countries (Indonesia, Cambodia, Lao PDR, Philippines, Thailand, and Viet Nam); capacity building training programs for ASEAN finance and central bank officials on regional economic monitoring and surveillance, conducted by the Asian Development Bank (ADB); conduct of technical studies and policy papers on finance and economic issues (e.g., fiscal sustainability, banking and corporate restructuring, and monitoring of capital flows. The major weaknesses of ASP program are: the quality and extent of data collected and shared; the peer review process compromised by a reluctance of ASEAN member countries to be critical of each other under the ASEAN principle of non-interference; the ASP lacking authority and resources to do a comprehensive job (Anas and Atje, 2005).

8.5.5 Executives' Meeting of East Asian and Pacific Central Banks (EMEAP)

EMEAP is the forum for central banks of 11 economies in Asia to promote exchange of information and cooperation on monetary and financial matters. The countries are the five original ASEAN countries plus six others—Australia, China, Hong Kong (territory of China), Japan, Republic of Korea, and New Zealand. Although set up in 1991, its first central bank governors' meeting was held only in 1996 where two decisions were made: to hold an annual meeting of central bank governors and to set up working groups to study financial development, and strengthen the primary functions of central banks in bank supervision, bank payment, and settlement systems.

After the crisis, EMEAP took a more active role in building stronger regional monetary and financial monitoring. In 2007, it set up the Monetary Financial Stability Committee (MFSC) composed of deputy governors and their staff to handle regional monetary and financial monitoring, and also to perform activities such as risk and crisis management and resolution.

EMEAP is an active promoter of Asian regional bond markets. Its first important policy was the establishment of the Asian Bond Market Initiative. It launched the first Asian Bond Fund (ABF1) in June of 2003 harnessing the official reserves of Asian governments. The EMEAP bought US$ 1 billion of US dollar bonds issued by sovereign and quasi-sovereign institutions in eight EMEAP countries (Japan, Australia, and New Zealand were excluded) as a step to promote cooperation among the regional central banks. The success of ABF1 led to the launching of ABF2 in December 2004 that was implemented in April 2005. This time local currency bonds equivalent to US$ 2 billion were issued by sovereign and quasi-sovereign entities in EMEAP countries. The ABF2 consists of two parts: a Pan-Asia Bond Index Fund investing in local currency-denominated bonds; and a Fund of Bond Funds that invests in eight single-market funds (Yap 2007: 15–16; Jang 2011: 14–15).

8.5.6 ASEAN+3 Macroeconomic Research Organization (AMRO)

Despite the 2005 decision to enhance and integrate ERPD activities into CMI, the ERPD process remained largely a means of examining country-specific macroeconomic conditions and has limited, if any, surveillance, monitoring, and peer review capability. Furthermore, it does not have full-time research staff to do independent review of the macroeconomic and financial health of each member country; nor does it have a secretariat to provide logistic support. Recongnizing such shortcomings, the ASEAN+3 FM decided in 2009 to start a separate institution to perform the functions of surveillance and monitoring to support the CMI that was moving from a series of bilateral swap arrangement to a multiteralized swap agreement—the Chiang Mai Initiative Multilateralisation (CMIM).

AMRO is the culmination of the surveillance and monitoring process for ASEAN+3. It was officially established in Singapore in April 2011 as an independent regional surveillance unit to monitor and analyze national and regional economies, to contribute to early detection of risks, and recommendations for remedial actions. It serves primarily to support the CMIM decision-making, although it is not the secretariat for the CMIM.

It prepares quarterly reports on the economic health of each member country and the ASEAN+3 region. During the period of financial crisis, it assesses the economic and financial condition of the member country requesting assistance from CMIM, monitor the disbursement, use, as well as the compliance to conditions for the use of the funds.

The members of AMRO consist of the 27 finance ministries and central banks of the ASEAN+3 countries and its organization structure is made up of an executive committee, an advisory panel, and a managing director. Four years into its operation, slightly over a dozen economists staff AMRO. Being a nascent organization, AMRO is working with other regional and international financial institutions to build up its capacity.

AMRO plays a critical role in the success of CMIM, particularly as the CMIM is a self-managed pool of reserve fund. This means that the contributions of each member country to the reserve fund is still managed by each country and not consolidated into a single pool. What has been multilateralized is the application process for accessing the funds, not the disbursement. i.e., instead of accessing swap lines bilaterally, the applicant accesses a central pool of reserves.[5] But it is possible that a member may not contribute its share for a specific application if it feels uncomfortable about the creditworthiness of the applicant country.

Presently, 40% of the usage of CMIM's swap line is subject to IMF conditionality and 60% is not. Hence, all the more reasons that AMRO has to provide high quality and accurate assessment of CMIM's potential borrowers. The due diligence function should be done "through the lens of potential creditors—to ensure that the borrowing country will make appropriate policy adjustment, restore financial stability and health, and be able to repay short-term loans provided during a crisis time" (Kawai and Houser 2007: 21).

It has been suggested that AMRO should introduce a Regional Monetary Unit (RMU) that would provide a benchmark for member countries to target their currencies. This would aid in its surveillance activities and help countries avoid engaging in competitive devaluation (Rana 2012). A survey conducted for the ASEAN Secretariat found that over two-thirds of ASEAN+3 opinion leaders felt that AMRO should provide the calculation for the RMU and even CMIM's drawings be denominated in RMU (Rana 2012).

8.5.7 Exchange Rate Mechanisms

Large swings in capital flows and differences in exchange rate regimes have caused wild swing in exchange rates. It used to be that exchange rates are driven by trade flows. But today, it is short-term speculative flows, like carry-trades, rather than trade flows, that drive currency fluctuations. For many Asian countries that are dependent on trade and investment,

[5] Interview with Benhua Wei, the first director of AMRO.

exchange rate stability is desirable and can promote greater regional trade, investments, and growth.

With increasing intra-regional trade and investments, there is a greater case for regional exchange rate coordination and stability to reduce foreign exchange rate misalignment, competitive devaluation, and trade protectionism.

With the AFC and the collapse of the informal pegged exchange regime in Southeast Asia, countries initially floated their currencies, and later adopted different exchange regimes, ranging from fixed rate (Malaysia for several years), to managed floats in Thailand, Singapore, and Malaysia (later period), to almost free-floating regimes in Indonesia and the Philippines. It is hard to tame exchange rates if capital accounts are open and large swings in short-term flows abound.[6]

While hardly any economist today is calling for a single currency system in East Asia like the euro for the European Union, some have proposed greater cooperation and coordination in exchange rates in the region. One way is set to up a benchmark for currencies in East Asia, such as an Asian Currency Unit (ACU) or Asian Monetary Unit (AMU), to measure if a country is strong or weak against this currency. The ADB has done considerable work in possible computation of an ACU or AMU made up of a weighted average of the currencies of the ASEAN+3 region. Eichengreen (2006) has suggested that an ACU can act as a parallel currency, operating alongside national currencies. An ACU can be used for trade, investment, issuance of regional bonds, and lending purposes.

Ogawa and Shimizu (2011) computed the AMU Deviation Indicators for currencies of each East Asian country from January 2001 to June 2010. They recommended the AMU as a measure of whether a currency is overvalued or undervalued. Huge deviations from the AMU can signal large capital inflows or outflows or a beggar-thy-neighbor policy. They also suggested the AMU act as the peg for East Asian currencies for a managed float system. Kuroda and Kawai (2007) suggest a regional exchange rate mechanism to stabilize intra-regional exchange rate and to avoid competitive devaluation. Kawai (2009) also favors an Asian Currency Unit mechanism.

Exchange rate cooperation is hobbled by several difficulties. The first is the heterogeneous exchange rate regimes practiced by the countries, each

[6] South Korea lost US$60 billion of foreign reserves in a matter of months trying to defend the won in 2008–2009.

with its own monetary priorities. Second, it is hard to tame exchange rates if capital accounts are relatively open and large swings abound. A sizeable and well-managed regional liquidity support fund is needed to provide timely liquidity assistance to countries under speculative attack. Finally, significant political differences exist among the Asian countries and this impacts currency behavior just as much as technical ones. Hence the issue of regional exchange rate coordination remains mainly at a theoretical level with little, if any, appearing in the agenda of an East Asian regional financial architecture. There is no indication that politicians and policymakers are keen to push it.

8.5.8 Capital Flows Control Coordination

If one objective of an international and regional financial architecture were to promote financial stability, then one mechanism that could contribute to this would be for countries to manage or regulate capital flows. But this goes against the underlying foundation of the post-Bretton Wood international financial architecture. The theoretical assumption of this international financial architecture is that free market is the way to promote growth, employment, and prosperity. The system must guarantee free flow of capital, trade, and investments; and greater financial liberalization and integration with global financial markets. The challenge facing developing countries is simply to build deeper and more liquid financial markets to cope with the forces of globalization.

Yet evidence from the AFC shows free capital flow and financial liberalization contributed to financial instability. Rapid inflow of "hot money"—short-term portfolio and other investments flows—brought about asset bubbles, over-lending and overheating of the economy, and caused large and harmful appreciation of currencies. When the bubbles burst, there was massive capital outflow that led to large devaluations, bankruptcies of companies and banks, unemployment and recession.

China was spared the AFC because its domestic financial system and its capital account were not liberalized; capital flow was tightly regulated and there was no massive speculative capital inflow. Its integration into the global financial system was still at an infant stage.

Southeast Asian countries, on the other hand, started to liberalize its financial systems in the early 1990s and became subjected to the volatility of free capital flows. Capital gushes in when economic growth is strong and rush out in times of crisis creating booms and bursts. Countries like

Indonesia and Thailand, following the IMF's advice, used market mechanisms like raising interest rates to stem capital outflow, but to no avail. Instead, the currencies and economies of these countries went into a free fall during the AFC.

One country that went against the IMF prescription, after a brief period of following it, was Malaysia. Initially, Malaysia followed the IMF prescription of raising interest rates, floating the ringgit, and cutting public expenditure. The economy contracted 14%, the stock market plunged 70% and the ringgit dropped to its lowest to US$1 = RM 4.9.

By mid-1998, Malaysia changed course. [7] It introduced counter-cyclical fiscal and monetary policies domestically, and capital controls externally. The central bank gradually reduced interest rates from 6 to 9%; statutory reserve requirements were also lowered from 13.5 to 4%; and non-performing loan definition changed back to six-month arrears from three-month.

Selective capital control measures were introduced that were strongly opposed by the IMF. To discourage speculative trading, a one-year moratorium on repatriation of proceeds from sale of securities was imposed on foreigners. Ringgit loans to non-residents banks and securities companies were stopped. Offshore ringgit deposits and trading were banned. Conversion of ringgit to other countries was controlled except for trade and foreign direct investment purposes. Malaysians were required to obtain the central bank's approval for purchase of foreign currencies for the amount in excess of RM 10,000 equivalent. Instead of allowing for free float, the ringgit was pegged at RM3.80 to US$1.

Pegging the ringgit and other capital control measures allowed Malaysia to lower interest rates to stimulate the economy without worrying about capital flight or currency volatility. When the economy started to recover in 1999, capital and currency controls were gradually relaxed and finally removed years later. In February of 1999, the one-year moratorium on repatriation of profits from share sale was replaced by a 10 percent exit levy on the sale proceeds on a graduated scale.

Today upon looking back at these capital control measures, even the IMF has reluctantly accepted that they were effective in aiding the rapid recovery of Malaysia's economy. The IMF has also recently slightly shifted

[7] For more details, see Khor (2011), and Lim and Goh (2012).

its position from a rigid no to capital controls to a qualified and cautious nod (Ostry et al. 2011).

Another Southeast Asian country that used capital controls in more recent times was Thailand. In December 2006, it imposed an unremunerated reserve requirement (URR) on foreign inflow of short-term funds. "All foreign transactions, except those related to trade in goods and services, repatriation of investment abroad by residents and FDI, were required to deposit 30% of foreign exchange with [Bank of Thailand] BOT as an unremunerated reserve requirement (URR). 30% of capital will be refunded after funds have remained within Thailand for a period of one year. If funds are repatriated before one year, only two-third of the amount will be refunded" (Jongwonich et al. 2011). This led to a stock market collapse, forcing the monetary authorities to exempt the stock market from the rule. The URR requirement on other foreign investments was slowly removed starting in 2007. Now, the main capital control measures of Thailand are prudential regulations on foreign borrowings by banks and rules and regulations limiting financial institutions from borrowing baht or providing baht to non-residents.

More recently, rounds of quantitative easing in the U.S. have led to massive capital inflows into emerging market economies. In two years between 2010 and 2012, searching for higher yields, investors poured $3.6 trillion into emerging markets (Xie 2015).

This led to rapid appreciation of their currencies, threatening their exports and financial stability. Among the countries, affected, South Korea in October 2010 considered introducing several measures to stem speculative capital inflows and currency appreciation. These included reimposing taxes on foreign purchases of local government bonds, a withholding tax on interest income, as well as a 20% capital gains tax on foreigner purchases of local bonds aimed at protecting the country from sudden swings in capital flows (Oliver 2010; Kong and Frangos 2010). In November, South Korea reintroduced the 14% tax on foreign purchases of local bonds (Oliver et al. 2010).

The experience of the above countries shows the difficulties of imposing capital controls on their own. Thailand and South Korea had to reverse some of their policies in the face of opposition and severe market reaction.[8] Since asset bubbles are the result of rapid and massive capital inflows, the regulation of capital inflow should be a more effective way to prevent financial crises. Regulating capital flow is more about managing and minimizing the negative effects of a financial crisis that has already happened.[9]

When countries try to impose such controls on their own, the result is capital flows to other countries, transferring the bubble to other parts of the system. The results could probably have been different and more effective if there was greater coordination on capital controls. Since East Asia is one of the fastest growth regions, a coordinated action may not lead to massive outflows from the region. But there is little, if any, effort made in the ASEAN+3 present regional financial architecture to strengthen cooperation in the area of capital controls.

Instead, most of the emphasis is placed on macro-prudential regulations. Some of these prudential rules that comprise capital controls are:

a. Limits or higher capital requirements on loans to unhedged foreign borrowings
b. Ceilings on foreign derivatives positions
c. Limits and regulation on short-term foreign debt
d. Limits on aggregate foreign exchange liabilities
e. Loan-to-value (LTV) limits on property loans.

Instead of controlling speculative capital inflows, several Asian countries have instead relaxed and encouraged outflow of capital for residents investing abroad as a means to counter capital inflows. Some economists favor this approach (see Gochoco-Bautista et al. 2010). But Akyuz (2009) is critical of this and pointed out the risks. Countries have little control over capital that has flowed abroad and such capital is unlikely to be reversed during periods of panic and massive capital outflows when sentiments are negative.

[8] The withholding tax exposed the friction in Korea. The tax was dropped in early 2009 and Kang Man-soo had to step down as finance minister over his weak won policy (Oliver et al. 2010).

[9] Malaysia soldiered on with controls on capital outflow for a few years and gradually removed control measures as the economy improved.

8.6 Crisis Management

Once a financial crisis starts it can spread quickly to other sectors and countries unless properly managed as was shown in the AFC. Right policy responses and timely and adequate provision of liquidity support are crucial in managing and containing crises. The AFC experience demonstrated that international support for managing the AFC was timid at best and negative at worst. The U.S. and IMF blocked regional efforts to start a regional financing arrangement and instead they provided rescue packages with too many conditions and prescribed wrong policies that worsened the crisis. This led the East Asian countries to find alternative arrangements at regional cooperation.

8.6.1 *Chiang Mai Initiative (CMI)*

The most important mechanism for crisis management that the East Asian countries established was the regional financial arrangement. This happened in May 2000 where at the sideline of the ADB annual meeting, the ASEAN+3FM initiated the Chiang Mai Initiative (CMI). This was a regional arrangement consisting of bilateral swaps and repurchase agreements among its members to assist member countries facing balance of payment liquidity problems. The CMI had two components, the existing ASEAN Swap Arrangement, ("ASA") and the new Bilateral Swap Arrangements ("BSA").

The ASA was set up in 1997 as short-term liquidity support for member countries facing balance of payment difficulties. The initial size of the facility was only US$ 100 million and increased to US$1 billion for the CMI. The BSA is a new facility with the Plus 3 countries, available to countries with temporary international liquidity problems in the form of swap of US dollars with the domestic currencies of the borrowing countries in the form of a repurchase agreement. The two countries will, after a predetermined period, return the original amount of the currencies they swapped with to each other. There was a stipulation in the BSAs that 10% of the agreed amount could be utilized without any linkage to an IMF program for 180 days. The rest can be used only under a current or impending IMF program.

The CMI has undergone many increases in size and changes in structure since its inception in May 2000 (see Sussangkarn 2010). By May 2004, 16 BSAs were signed totaling US$36 billion and the amount of

ASA increased to $2 billion in 2005. By May 2007 the amount of BSA rose to $75 billion. An important decision was made in May 2007 to agree in principle to convert the BSAs of CMI into a multilateralized self-managed reserves pool governed by a single contract. Thus, the idea of Chiang Mai Initiative Multilateralization (CMIM) was born; but it was only two years later in December 2009 that the actual agreement was signed and the program took effect in March 2010. In May 2012, another milestone was reached when the fund size was increased to $120 billion, and the IMF de-linked portion raised from 20% to 30%. In July 2014, the CMIM was further strengthened when the total size doubled to $240 billion, the CMIM Precautionary Line (CMIM-PL), which is designed on the model of PPL program within the IMF to prevent a financial crisis, was adopted and the IMF de-linked portion increased to 40%.

Table 8.1 shows the latest data on the CMIM swap lines effective July 2014. The Plus 3 countries contribute 80% of the total swap lines with China + Hong Kong accounting for 32%, Japan 32%, and Korea 16%. China and Japan have drawing rights of up to 50% of their contributions, while Korea has drawing rights of 100% of its contribution. The five original ASEAN countries each contribute 9.1% of the fund with drawing rights of 2.5 times their contributions. The remaining ASEAN countries have much smaller financial contributions but with drawing rights of 5 times their contributions.

Even though the CMI was in operation during the Global Financial Crisis of 2007–09, member countries like South Korea and Indonesia that ran into liquidity problems in 2009 did not access the CMI swap lines. Instead Korea obtained a $30 billion bilateral swap from the U.S., while Indonesia sought a swap line with Japan after it failed to secure one from the U.S.

Why didn't these member countries make use of the CMI arrangements? While we may never know the real reasons, it is likely due to the inadequate amount of swap line available and the 80% IMF linked conditionality at that time. Both Indonesia and Korea had bad experience with the IMF during the AFC when they were slapped with over 100 conditions linked to the IMF rescue package. It is very possible they do not wish to undergo the same experience. Also, the amount of financing was inadequate.

In the Korean case, even though it had $260 billion of foreign reserves in 2009, $60 billion was spent within a matter of months trying to defend the won, without much success. It was the $30 billion bilateral swap

Table 8.1 Chiang Mai Initiative Multilateralization Arrangement, 2014

Contributions, Maximum Arrangement Amount and Voting-Power Distribution (After the amendement of the CMIM)

	Financial Contribution				Purchasing Multiple	Maximum Arrangement Amount	Basic Votes	Votes based on Contribution	Total voting power	
	USD (billion)		(%)			USD (billion	(no. of votes)	(no. of votes)	(no. of votes)	(%)
China	76.80	China (excl. HK) 68.40	32.0	28.50	0.5	34.20	3.20	68.40	71.60	25.43
		Hong Kong, China 8.40		3.50	2.5	6.30	0.00	8.40	8.40	2.98
Japan	76.80		32.00		0.5	38.40	3.20	76.80	80.00	28.41
Korea	38.40		16.00		1	38.40	3.20	38.40	41.60	14.77
Plus 3	192.00		80.00			117.30	9.60	192.00	201.60	71.59
Indonesia	9.104		3.793		2.5	22.76	3.20	9.104	12.304	4.369
Thailand	9.104		3.793		2.5	22.76	3.20	9.104	12.304	4.369
Malaysia	9.104		3.793		2.5	22.76	3.20	9.104	12.304	4.369
Singapore	9.104		3.793		2.5	22.76	3.20	9.104	12.304	4.369
Philippines	9.104		3.793		2.5	22.76	3.20	9.104	12.304	4.369
Vietnam	2.00		0.833		5	10.00	3.20	2.00	5.20	1.847
Cambodia	0.24		0.100		5	1.20	3.20	0.24	3.44	1.222
Myanmar	0.12		0.050		5	0.60	3.20	0.12	3.32	1.179
Brunei	0.06		0.025		5	0.30	3.20	0.06	3.26	1.158
Lao PDR	0.06		0.025		5	0.30	3.20	0.06	3.26	1.158
ASEAN	48.00		20.00			126.20	32.00	48.00	80.00	28.41
Total	240.00		100.00			243.50	41.60	240.00	281.60	100.00

Source Bank of Thailand 2014

extended by the U.S. that stemmed the outflow of funds.[10] Under the CMI quota, Korea could access only a total of $18.5 billion bilateral swap lines in 2009, of which only 20%, i.e., $3.7 billion, would be free from IMF conditionality. It is unlikely that Korea would want to repeat the same experience with the IMF during the AFC.

8.7 Conclusion

The post-Bretton Woods international financial system marked by financial deregulation and liberalization resulted in free capital flows and floating exchange rate system for many countries. Volatile capital flows have heightened financial instability and led to financial crises in many parts of emerging market economies. The failure of the current international financial architecture to assist Asia resolve the AFC in the late 1990s, particularly the objection by the US and IMF to establish an Asian liquidity support fund, pushed these countries to find a regional solution to the problem.

The Asian regional financial architecture has two goals (defensive and developmental objectives) and three pillars—regional forums for closer policy dialogue and coordination; a liquidity support fund (the CMIM) with an institution for economic surveillance (AMRO); and the development of local currency and regional bond market.

Under the defensive objective, the ASEAN+3 countries set up mechanisms for crisis prevention, management, and resolution. These included establishing a regional network and forums among political leaders and policymakers to promote better exchange of information and policy dialogues; more effective economic surveillance and early warning systems, and cultivation of peer review and pressure to maintain healthy macroeconomic fundamentals. With frequent and regular meetings among the countries' finance ministries and central banks' officials, considerable progress has been made. The most visible and significant achievements in this area are the establishment of the Chiang Mai Initiative Multilateralization (CMIM) fund and the ASEAN+3 Macroeconomic Research Organization (AMRO). The first is a $240 billion multilateral swap arrangement among the ASEAN+3 economies to provide liquidity support to member countries with balance of payment problems. The

[10] Subsequently, Japan and China each also provided $30 billion of bilateral swap to Korea.

second is the economic research and surveillance organization to monitor the economic health of member countries and the region, and to provide logistic support to the CMIM. AMRO plays a critical role for the success of the CMIM fund; the more it is able to build up its capacity and credibility, the more the region is able to wean itself from IMF conditionality when accessing CMIM funds.

Large swings in capital flows cause exchange rate volatility and financial instability. Mechanisms for enhancing exchange rate cooperation can reduce pressures for competitive devaluation, and capital controls coordination can lower capital flows volatility, particularly in the management of excessive capital inflows. These should form part of the toolkit in a regional financial architecture. However, there is little effort made in these two areas as many of the Asian countries are more inclined to promote freer capital flows and deeper integration with the global financial system.

In terms of the developmental objective in Asia's regional financial architecture, most of the effort is toward developing local currency bond markets to tap the large amount of foreign reserves held by Asian countries and to promote closer regional financial integration. In their zeal to promote bond markets, the risks of greater financial instability associated with capital markets are overlooked. We propose that attention be given to develop another pillar of a regional financial architecture, i.e., the establishment of long-term regional and national development banks as a means to promote stable and long-term growth with less risk of volatile capital flows.

References

ADB (Asian Development Bank). AsianBondsOnline Website.

ADB (2010a). Key Indicators for Asia and Pacific.

ADB (2010b). ASEAN+3 Forum Discusses Harmonizing Asia's Bond Markets. September 28, 2010. http://www.adb.org/news/asean3-forum-discusses-harmonizing-asias-bond-markets. Accessed June 14, 2015.

ADB (2014a). Key Indicators for Asia and Pacific.

ADB (2014b). Asian Economic Integration Monitor, November.

Akyuz, Yilmaz (2009). Exchange Rate Management, Growth and Stability: National and Regional Options in Asia. Asia Pacific Trade and Investment Initiative. Colombo. UNDP Regional Centre for Asia Pacific. September.

Akyuz, Yilmaz (2015). "Internationalization of Finance and Changing Vulnerabilities in Emerging and Developing Economies. Research Paper 60, January. South Centre, Geneva.

Anas, Titik and Raymond Atje (2005). Economic Surveillance and Policy Dialogue in East Asia. Report prepared for ASEAN Secretariat, Jakarta.
Bank Indonesia (IFS). Indonesian Financial Statistics. Accessed June 16, 2015.
http://www.bi.go.id/en/statistik/seki/terkini/eksternal/Contents/Default.aspx.
Bank Negara (MSB). Monthly Statistical Bulletin. Accessed June 16, 2015.
http://www.bnm.gov.my/index.php?ch=en_publication_catalogue&pg=en_publication_msb&mth=4&yr=2015&lang=en.
Bank of Thailand (2014). The Amended Chiang Mai Initiative Multilateralisation (CMIM) Comes into Effect on 17 July 2014. Press Release 28/2014. https://www.bot.or.th/Thai/PressAndSpeeches/Press/News2557/n2857e.pdf. Accessed June 4, 2015.
Bhattacharya, Biswa Nath (2011). Bond Market Development in Asia: An Empirical Analysis of Major Determinants. ADBI Working Paper Series, No. 300, July.
BNDES (Brazilian Development Bank) website. http://www.bndes.gov.br/SiteBNDES/bndes/bndes_en/Institucional/The_BNDES_in_Numbers/.
Bordo, Michael D., Angela Redish and Hugh Rockoff. (2011). Why Didn't Canada Have a Banking Crisis in 2008 (OR in 1930, OR 1907, OR...)? Working Paper 17312, National Bureau of Economic Research. http://www.nber.org/papers/w17312.
Caprio, Gerard, Daniela Klingebiel, Luc Laeven and Guillermo Noguera (2003). Banking Crises Database. Washington, DC., World Bank. October.
Cargill, Thomas F. and Shoichi Royama (1988). *The Transition of Finance in Japan and the United States: A Comparative Perspective*. Hoover Institute, Stanford University.
CGIF. Credit Guarantee and Investment Facility. http://www.cgif-abmi.org/about/contributors. Accessed June 4, 2015.
CGIF (2014). Progress Report. Available at http://www.cgif-abmi.org/datas/pdf/CGIF_Progress%20Report%202014_20150520%20Final.pdf. Accessed June 4, 2015.
Eichengreen, Barry. (2006). The Parallel Currency Approach to Asian Monetary Integration. *American Economic Review* 96(2): 432–436.
FT (Financial Times) (2015). Markets. Malaysia's Ringgit Hits 9-year Low http://www.ft.com/intl/fastft?q=Malaysia%27s+Ringgit. June 8.
Gochoco-Bautista, Maria S., Juthathip Jongwanich, Jong-Wha Lee (2010). How Effective Are Capital Controls in Asia? ADB Economics Working Paper Series No. 224, October.
Hakansson, N (1999). The Role of a Corporate Bond Market in an Economy and in Avoiding Crises. Research Program in Finance. Berkeley, CA: Institute of Business and Economic Research, UC Berkeley

Herring, R. and N. Chatusripitak (2000). The Case of the Missing Market: The Bond Market and Why It Matters for Financial Development. Paper presented at The Asian Development Bank Institute / Wharton Seminar, on Financial Structure for Sustainable Development in Post-Crisis Asia. Tokyo. May 26.

Ho, Daniel (2011). "F" for Ethics in Business Schools: Ho Kwon Ping in Straits Times, July 25, p. B15.

IMF (International Monetary Fund). International Financial Statistics.

Jang, Hong Bum (2011). Financial Integration and Cooperation in East Asia: Assessment of Recent Developments and Their Implications. IMES Discussion Paper Series No. 2011-E-5. Bank of Japan, February. Available at http://www.imes.boj.or.jp.

Jongwonich, Juthathip, Maria Socorro Gochoco-Bautista, Jong-Wha Lee. (2011). When Are Capital Controls Effective? Evidence from Malaysia and Thailand. ADB Economics Working Paper Series No. 251, March 2011.

Kawai, Masahiro (2009). The Role of an Asian Currency Unit for Asian Monetary Integration. Asian Development Bank Institute, 9 September.

Kawai, Masahiro and Cindy Houser (2007). Evolving ASEAN+3 ERPD: Towards Peer Reviews or Due Diligence? ADB Institute Discussion Paper No. 79, September

Keynes, John M (1936). *The General Theory of Employment Interest and Money.* London: Macmillan.

Khor, Martin (2011). Financial Policy and Management of Capital Flows: The Case of Malaysia. *TWN Global Economy Series* (16).

Kong, Kanga and Alex Frangos (2010). Korea Moves to Impose New Capital Controls. *The Wall Street Journal*, November 18.

Krugman, Paul (2009). *The Return of Depression Economics and the Crisis of 2008.* New York: W.W. Norton.

Kuroda, Haruhiko and Masahiro Kawai (2003). Strengthening Regional Financial Cooperation in East Asia. PRI Discussion Paper Series, No. 03A-10, May 2003.

Lim, Mah Hui and Goh Soo Khoon (2012). How Malaysia Weathered the Financial Crisis:
Policies and Possible Lessons. In *How to Prevent the Next Financial Crisis: Countries Lessons from Country Experiences of the Global Financial Crisis.* Edited by Aniket Bhushan. Ottawa: The North-South Institute.

Lim, Mah Hui and Joseph Anthony Lim (2012). Asian Initiatives at Monetary and Financial Integration: A Critical Review. Research Papers No. 46, South Centre, Geneva.

Lim, Mah Hui and Lim Chin (2010). *Nowhere to Hide: The Great Financial Crisis and Challenges for Asia.* Singapore: Institute of Southeast Asian Studies.

Lim, Wing Hooi (2015). Set up MSME Bank, Please. The Star, SMEBiz, May 11.

Lipscy, P.Y (2003). Japan's Asian Monetary Fund Proposal. *Stanford Journal of East Asian Affairs* 3(1): 93–104.

MAS (Monetary Authority of Singapore) (2007). *Asian Financial and Monetary Integration: Challenges and Prospects*. Singapore: Monetary Authority of Singapore.

Masaki, Hisane (2007). Asian Monetary Fund? 10 May 2007. http://english.ohmynews.com/articleview/article_view?at_code = 409447asp.

Ogawa, Eiji and Junko Shimizu (2011). Asian Monetary Unit and Monetary Cooperation in Asia. Asian Development Bank Institute Working Paper Series No. 275, April 2011.

Oliver, Christian (2010). S. Korea Considers More Capital Controls. *Financial Times*, October 27.

Oliver, Christian Oliver, Song Jung-a, and James Lamont (2010). South Korea to Reimpose Tax on Bonds. *Financial Times*, November 18.

Ostry, Jonathan D., Atish R. Ghosh, Karl Habermeier, Luc Laeven, Marcos Chamon, Mahvash S. Qureshi, and Annamaria Kokenyne (2011). Managing Capital Inflows: What Tools to Use? IMF Staff Discussion Note, SDN/11/06, April 5, 2011.

Park, Yung-Chul and Daekeun Park (2003). Creating Regional Bond Markets in East Asia: Rationale and Strategy. Paper presented at the Second Annual Conference of PECC Finance Forum, Hua Hin, Thailand, July 8–9.

Patrick, Hugh (1994). The Relevance of Japanese Finance and Its Main Bank System. In *The Japanese Main Bank System: Its Relevance for Developing and Transforming Economies*. Edited by Aoki, Masahiko and Hugh Patrick. New York: Oxford University Press.

Poo, Chermaine (2013). Financing for SMEs. The Star Online, September 27.

Rana, Pradumna B (2012). Monetary Integration in ASEAN+3: The Next Steps. East Asia Forum, May 25.

Sussangkarn, Chalongphob (2010). The Chiang Mai Initiative Multilateralization: Origin, Development and Outlook. ADBI Working Paper Series, No. 230, July.

Tett, Gillian (2014). Emerging Markets Repent of 'Original Sin'. *Financial Times*, April 18.

UNECA. (U.N. Economic Commission for Africa) (2011). Reform of International Financial Architecture and Policy Implications for Africa. Policy Research Paper, No. 1.

Wikipedia. Accessed June 10, 2015. https://en.wikipedia.org/wiki/Asian_Infrastructure_Investment_Bank.

Xie, Ye (2015). Capital Controls. June 1. Accessed June 10, 2015. http://www.bloombergview.com/quicktake/capital-controls.

Yap, Josef T (2007). Ten Years After: Financial Crisis Redux or Constructive Regional Financial and Monetary Cooperation? Discussion Paper Series No. 2007-05, June. Philippines Institute for Development Studies.

CHAPTER 9

Alternatives to the International Monetary Fund in Asia and Latin America: Lessons for Regional Financial Arrangements

William W. Grimes and William N. Kring

9.1 Introduction

Global economic governance is in a state of flux. In addition to a profusion of regional and multilateral trade agreements, a variety of new institutions for the provision of short-term liquidity and long-term development finance have emerged over the past few decades. The 2008 financial crisis reinvigorated interest in establishing such non-traditional institutions, whether as alternatives or as complements to the existing order. This was evidenced by the emergence of the New Development Bank, the Contingent Reserve Arrangement (CRA)—both created by the BRICS (Brazil, the Russian Federation, India, China and South

W. W. Grimes
Frederick S. Pardee School of Global Studies, Boston, MA, USA

W. N. Kring (✉)
Global Development Policy Center, Boston University, Boston, MA, USA
e-mail: wkring@bu.edu

D. Barrowclough et al. (eds.), *South–South Regional Financial Arrangements*, International Political Economy Series,
https://doi.org/10.1007/978-3-030-64576-2_9

Africa)—and the Asian Infrastructure Investment Bank, as well as by the introduction of innovations in existing institutions.

This chapter presents a comparative analysis of the background, governance and economic impacts of two existing short-term liquidity mechanisms, the Chiang Mai Initiative Multilateralization (CMIM) and the Latin American Reserve Fund (hereinafter referred to by its better-known Spanish acronym, FLAR—Fondo Latinoamericano de Reservas). We find that the structures of regional financial institutions as well as the amount of resources available to member countries are contingent on regional dynamics, the economic characteristics of members, and members' reluctance to approach the IMF for short-term balance-of-payments support. This study offers an up-to-date assessment of the two RFAs, based primarily on on-site interviews with their respective staff members, regional government and central bank officials, and scholars. Those interviews, conducted in 2016, revealed how, in the wake of the 2008 financial crisis, RFAs advanced efforts to improve their internal research capacity, develop strategic alliances, and increase the resources available to their members.

The CMIM and the FLAR offer two very different models of regional liquidity facilities. This chapter describes and analyses these differences by investigating their histories, credit facilities and institutional governance and procedures. It finds that the capabilities of these two mechanisms have been defined not only by size, but also by the quality of the institutions and procedures they have developed. The FLAR, as a result of its well-developed organization and procedures, as well as an extensive track record (with numerous financial operations undertaken over its 38-year history), has earned greater credibility than the as yet untested CMIM. As a result, the CMIM continues to borrow credibility from the IMF through explicit linkages in fund disbursements and conditionalities even as it continues to develop its functional capabilities.

Finally, the chapter highlights some key lessons for existing and future regional reserve mechanisms. In comparing the structures of the CMIM and the FLAR in conjunction with member countries' reserve levels, it notes that establishing a network of swaps is a mechanism that can enable much higher commitments of funds than transferring money to an independently managed fund. As such, it may be one viable way to enhance the lending capacity of the FLAR and other future mechanisms. We also observe that, in contrast to the CMIM, in which there is a clear asymmetry in the size of members and their degree of vulnerability, the FLAR

Table 9.1 CMIM membership

	Countries
Current ASEAN members	Brunei Darussalam, Cambodia, Indonesia, Lao People's Democratic Republic, Malaysia, Myanmar, Philippines, Singapore, Thailand, Viet Nam
Plus 3 members	China, Japan, Republic of Korea

is much more symmetrical in its governance and activities. Indeed, most members have borrowed from the FLAR, including the largest contributors. The degree of asymmetry among members of a liquidity facility appears to have a considerable influence on its governance and activities. For a regional group of relative equals such as the FLAR, this has led to a borrower-led dynamic in which member countries share a sense of pride of ownership of the institution, which has contributed to a perfect record of repayments.

9.2 Origins and Evolution of the CMIM and the FLAR

9.2.1 The Evolution of the Chiang Mai Initiative Multilateralization

The CMIM and its predecessor, the Chiang Mai Initiative (CMI), were established by the members of the Association of Southeast Asian Nations plus China, Japan and the Republic of Korea (ASEAN+3) to provide these countries with liquidity support in the event of a currency crisis (Table 9.1).[1] These economies realized the pressing need for a regional contingent reserve arrangement following the 1997–1998 Asian financial crisis. When first Thailand, then Indonesia and finally the Republic of Korea were forced by payments crises into negotiating stand-by agreements (SBAs) with the IMF, the limitations of the existing liquidity regime were laid bare. First, all three countries needed significantly more access to reserves than were permitted under existing IMF rules, which limited drawings to a maximum of 255 per cent of a given member's quota. As a result, they had to resort to constructing ad hoc packages

[1] Much of the history outlined here is drawn from Grimes 2009 and 2012.

requiring commitments from a variety of governments and international financial institutions to ensure that there were sufficient funds to end the crises in each of the countries. For example, of the Republic of Korea's total package of $58.4 billion (including second line of defence), the IMF provided only $9.1 billion (Kim 2006). Negotiation of non-IMF commitments, however, contributed to greater uncertainty and delay in assembling the packages.

Second, the conditionalities imposed on the crisis-affected countries were widely criticized for being not only misdirected, but also overly extensive, intrusive and deflationary.[2] In particular, critics pointed to what they saw as a "cookie-cutter" approach that applied conditionalities developed over decades in Latin America and Africa—where repeated currency crises had been attributed to low savings, weak export competitiveness and lax fiscal policy—to economies in East Asia that were export-oriented and fiscally responsible.

A first regional solution was proposed in the midst of the crisis, several weeks after Thailand's package was agreed, when the Japanese Government mooted the creation of an Asian Monetary Fund (AMF). While details of the proposal were never officially released, reports stated that it would be a regional bailout fund of $100 billion, half of which would be committed by Japan, which would disburse funds rapidly with minimal or no conditions imposed on economies experiencing currency crises. However, the idea was soon abandoned in the face of opposition from the IMF and the United States Government, as well as hesitation by China and some regional economies (Sakakibara 1998; Katada 2001; Lee 2008; Grimes 2009; Kawai 2015).

While many observers saw IMF and United States opposition as stemming from concerns that they would lose influence over East Asian governments, the stated reason was concerns over moral hazard.[3] Moral hazard has long been understood to be a potential problem for insurance or bailout regimes, from the individual level all the way to the global

[2] There are many scholarly and popular journals that make this argument. The IMF's own review (IMF 2003) offers perhaps the best account of the rescue packages' flaws, although it understandably chooses not to level a wholehearted attack on the IMF as an institution, as does Stiglitz (2002), for example.

[3] Kawai (2015: 6), for example, takes at face value the moral hazard concern, while Lee (2008) argues strongly that United States resistance to the AMF proposal was political in nature.

level. Indeed, a stated rationale for intrusive IMF conditionality was to reduce moral hazard. Currency crises, and thus the design of liquidity facilities, are particularly challenging from the point of view of managing moral hazard. For open economies such as those in East Asia, currency crises and their contagion effects can occur quickly, necessitating the rapid provision of liquidity. Further, to deter speculative attacks or capital flight, there must be a high degree of certainty among investors that a rescue will occur when needed. However, while effective crisis management and prevention necessitate a liquidity provision facility that will be able to deliver large amounts of reserves rapidly and with certainty, those attributes also reduce the costs to member-country policymakers of pursuing risky macroeconomic policies. Thus, in order to prevent fiscal and monetary mismanagement, liquidity facilities may choose to attach conditions to their disbursements, whether in the form of *ex ante* conditions (pre-conditionality) or *ex post* conditions.

9.2.1.1 Creation of the CMI

The Chiang Mai Initiative, which was agreed by the ASEAN+3 finance ministers in May 2000 (see ASEAN+3, 2000), constituted a more cautious and incremental approach to regional institution-building than the AMF proposal. The amount of the fund started small (nominally $40 billion distributed across eight members), but increased over time. Unlike with the AMF proposal, there was no overt United States opposition to the CMI, apparently because, by the time it was established, the gap between United States and East Asian interpretations of the Asian financial crisis had narrowed considerably (Grimes 2006). However, there was growing concern about the potential for moral hazard among Japanese and Chinese policymakers, which the CMI agreement sought to address. In contrast to the original conception of the AMF, the CMI was set up as a network arrangement in which China, Japan and the Republic of Korea entered into bilateral swap agreements (BSAs) with each other and with each of the five original ASEAN economies (Indonesia, Malaysia, Philippines, Singapore and Thailand). In addition, the original CMI absorbed the existing (small) ASEAN Swap Agreement.[4]

From the beginning, the CMI was asymmetric, with clear distinctions between likely creditors and likely borrowers. In particular, Japan—then

[4] See Hill and Menon (2012),one of the few to offer even minimal details on the ASEAN Swap Agreement.

the largest economy in the region, with the largest foreign exchange reserves and the only widely used international currency—offered leadership, both conceptually and practically. Until 2005, the BSAs were not standardized across the ASEAN+3: while most were reciprocal, some were one-way commitments, and often, even the two-way BSAs were not symmetrical in terms of amounts pledged; most were denominated in dollars, but some of China's were in renminbi (RMB). Moreover, according to published reports (although the full texts of the BSAs were not released), some carried preconditions, including a requirement for a minimum level of foreign exchange reserves.[5]

The other key institutional characteristic of the CMI was its reliance on the "IMF link," which acted as a constraint on the release of the bulk of pledged funds. This meant that only after beginning good-faith negotiations with the IMF could a country facing a currency crisis request the full amount of funds pledged by its BSA counterparts. Initially, only 10 per cent of BSAs were "delinked," rising to 20 per cent in 2005, and subsequently to 30 per cent when the CMI Multilateralization (CMIM) agreement took effect in 2010. However, even at 30 per cent, delinked funds would likely be insufficient to prevent a crisis in an open East Asian economy. Thus, for all practical purposes, IMF approval was a necessary (but not sufficient) trigger for activation of CMI swap lines. In effect, the CMI was set up as a supplement to the IMF, not as a rival. Adding to the complexity of the arrangement and to uncertainty for potential borrowers, the activation of swap lines remained, legally, at the discretion of partner countries.

9.2.1.2 From the CMI to the CMIM

The CMI underwent several modifications over time, including a substantial increase in committed funds (to over $80 billion) that was agreed in 2005. After the global financial crisis of 2008, however, the ASEAN+3 introduced a series of ambitious revisions that substantially changed the nature and potential impact of the arrangement. That crisis offered several lessons for the ASEAN+3 members (Grimes, 2011; Hill and Menon, 2012; Kawai, 2015). First, the global crisis and the subsequent Greek/euro-zone crisis demonstrated that the potential scale of bailouts had increased dramatically. Second, the Republic of Korea nearly ran out

[5] See Grimes (2009) for the most complete account of the workings of the original CMI.

of dollar liquidity in October 2008, even though its economic fundamentals were strong and it held approximately $250 billion in official reserves. To address the shortfall, it did not seek to draw on CMI or existing central bank swap lines with China and Japan; rather, it arranged a dollar swap line with the Federal Reserve Bank of New York (Chey 2012; Kawai 2015). Although it subsequently increased its RMB and yen swap lines with China and Japan, these were never drawn upon. Third, the Greek crisis revealed the limitations of surveillance in preventing crises.

In December 2008, with the global financial crisis continuing to expand, the ASEAN+3 finance ministers held the first of several meetings that eventually led to an agreement in 2009 to "multilateralize" the CMI swap network as a formal reserve pooling arrangement, to increase the total financial commitment to $120 billion, and to establish the ASEAN + 3 Macroeconomic Research Office (AMRO) (ASEAN+3 2009). The new arrangement also expanded membership to include the other ASEAN countries (Brunei Darussalam, Cambodia, the Lao People's Democratic Republic, Myanmar and Viet Nam). In 2012, the CMIM members further agreed to increase the total commitment to $240 billion and reduce the share of IMF-delinked funds to 30 per cent of the maximum swap amount, while also introducing a new facility known as the Precautionary Line (CMIM-PL) and renaming the existing crisis line as the Stability Facility (CMIM-SF) (ASEAN+3 2012). Thus, within the space of a few years from the start of the global crisis, the ASEAN+3 members agreed to a tripling of resources and introduced three major institutional innovations. So far, however, this has not altered two basic characteristics of the original CMI set-up: the IMF link and the principle of self-management of funds.

9.2.2 The Latin American Reserve Fund

Despite its repeated use since its inception, the FLAR is far lesser known than its Asian counterpart, the CMIM, which has not activated its swap lines, so far. When the Andean countries that designed the FLAR were negotiating the terms of a potential reserve mechanism in the 1970s, there were no guarantees that a consensus would be forged and a mechanism instituted. The leadership of the central bank in Colombia, the region's largest economy, was not necessarily convinced of the need for

Table 9.2 Evolution of FLAR membership

	Countries
Founding members of the Andean Reserve Fund, 1978–1991	The Bolivarian Republic of Venezuela, Colombia, Ecuador, the Plurinational State of Bolivia and Peru
New members of the FLAR, 1991 to the present	Costa Rica (1999), Uruguay (2009) and Paraguay (2015)

an Andean regional liquidity mechanism.[6] While officials at the Colombian Ministry of Finance and Public Credit believed the institution would benefit the country, central bank officials struggled to conceive of a situation in which Colombia would need to borrow from such a fund.[7] Ultimately, Colombian officials were persuaded, and the Andean Reserve Fund (ARF), the FLAR's immediate predecessor, was created. (For the evolution of FLAR membership, see Table 9.2.) The initial sceptics saw the Fund as a means to secure and promote highly integrated intraregional trade in instances of economic shock by providing swift access to liquidity funds. This would obviate the need for member countries to restrict imports or take other extreme measures.

Approximately a decade later, the Andean countries decided to expand the membership of the FLAR to include all Latin American countries so as to diversify its members' economies and increase the capital base of the mechanism. While there have been informal discussions regarding the addition of new members—ranging from smaller economies such as Honduras, to much larger economies such as Argentina, Brazil and, Mexico—the transformation of the ARF into the FLAR has not expanded membership to the degree that was initially anticipated or desired by the member states. In contrast, the Development Bank of Latin America (CAF, the acronym for its Spanish name, Corporacion Andina de Fomento), a regional development bank, has expanded its membership base significantly more than FLAR to become the leader of development financing in the region.

[6] Authors' interviews (in August 2016) with those involved in discussions on the creation of the Andean mechanisms.

[7] Ironically, Colombia utilized the mechanism four times.

A major objective of the ARF was to create a mechanism more attuned to the difficulties of the adjustment processes and "better adapted to the conditions of the economies and political structure of the countries in the region" (Perry 2015: 197). The Andean countries desired access to funds that would be disbursed more rapidly than those from the IMF, and without the harsh conditionalities often associated with IMF loans. The three main objectives of the FLAR are articulated in Chapter 1 of its Constitutive Agreement[8]:

i. To provide support to member countries via credits, and guaranteeing third-party credits during balance-of-payments crises.
ii. To improve the investment conditions of international reserves of member countries.
iii. To facilitate harmonization of the exchange, monetary and financial policies of member countries.

The primary focus of the FLAR since its founding has been to provide balance-of-payments support through loans to member countries. In this respect, the FLAR is an example of a successful "regional reserve pooling arrangement that acts largely as a credit cooperative" (Grabel 2013: 9). Although historically most of the FLAR's resources have focused on providing support to member countries in the form of credit, it has also increasingly "helped to manage the reserve portfolios of member countries and other public sector institutions" (Ocampo 2015: 160). Additionally, while the third objective of the FLAR—to facilitate harmonization of the exchange, monetary, and financial policies of member countries—has been marginal, it, nevertheless, facilitates dialogue, which remains potentially important. While harmonization is unlikely, as the policy regimes of member countries vary—for example, Ecuador is dollarized while Colombia and Costa Rica use inflation targeting—the FLAR can continue to serve as a forum for dialogue between policymakers of the member countries, allowing them to share their respective experiences and knowledge.

[8] See: http://flar.net/about_us/objetivos.

9.3 Key Features and Products of the CMIM and the FLAR

9.3.1 Key Features of the CMIM

The institutional design of the CMIM has several distinctive features.[9] First and foremost, it is a multilateral reserve pool. However, neither "multilateralization" nor "reserve pool" are well-defined terms. In the CMIM, as in the CMI, members' "financial contributions" are commitments to dedicate a specified portion of their foreign exchange reserves to the regional liquidity facility. No funds are transferred until the CMIM is activated, and they never go through a common pool. Multilateralization in the context of the CMIM means that: (a) activation procedures are conducted through a single contract rather than through non-standardized BSAs, although reserves are still transferred bilaterally; (b) financial contributions are agreed multilaterally; and (c) activation of CMIM swaps is voted upon by the members, with votes weighted primarily based on their respective financial contributions (see Table 9.3 for further details). Because the IMF link remains in effect, and delinked funds are unlikely to be sufficient to prevent a currency crisis in the region, the CMIM Stability Facility (CMIM-SF, as the main facility has been renamed) can effectively only be used as a bridge and/or supplement to an IMF-led rescue package.

A second novel feature of the CMIM is AMRO, established in 2011 as a means of monitoring financial and economic conditions in regional economies and making recommendations to the CMIM members.[10] Its creation was the outcome of discussions dating back to at least 2005, relating to the need for an effective surveillance mechanism to further reduce and perhaps eventually eliminate the IMF link (Kawai 2005; Takagi 2010). AMRO was initially set up as a limited partnership under Singapore law in order to allow the rapid hiring of staff, setting procedures, carrying out surveillance and providing policy advice to the

[9] This section draws from interviews, published works (Grimes 2009, 2011, 2012, 2015; Siregar and Chabchitrchaidol 2013; Pardo and Rana 2015), ASEAN+3 finance ministers' statements and other official documents from the AMRO website (http://www.amro-asia.org).

[10] Much of the discussion of institutional and procedural characteristics of AMRO is based on interviews with AMRO officials, government and central bank officials, and scholars, in research trips to Tokyo and Singapore in June, July and August 2016.

Table 9.3 CMIM credit facilities

Credit facility	*Maturity*	*Percentage of permissible swap amount*	*Interest rate*	*Approval requirements*
CMIM-PL (delinked from IMF)	6 months, renewable (2 years maximum)	30	IMF lending rate, plus 0.15 per cent commitment fee	Two-thirds of total CMIM members' votes
CMIM-PL (IMF linked)	1 year, renewable (2 years maximum)	70	IMF lending rate, plus 0.15 per cent commitment fee	Following notification from IMF; two-thirds of total CMIM members' votes
CMIM-SF (delinked from IMF)	6 months, renewable (2 years maximum)	30	IMF lending rate	Two-thirds of total CMIM members' votes
CMIM-SF (IMF linked)	1 year, renewable (3 years maximum)	70	IMF lending rate	Following notification from IMF; two-thirds of total CMIM members' votes

Source ASEAN + 3 Macroeconomic Research Office

members. In February 2016, it was officially chartered as an international organization based on a treaty signed by its members.

The CMIM-PL is a third innovative feature of the CMIM. The Republic of Korea's resort to emergency swap lines from the New York Federal Reserve Bank in 2008 was a wake-up call for ASEAN+3 members. Although that country did not face a currency crisis, it nevertheless sought access to dollar liquidity to manage the needs of its banking system and thus effectively prevent a crisis of the sort that it had experienced in 1997. However, it also demonstrated that the CMI—which was designed to function as a bridge or a supplement to an IMF SBA—was poorly designed to deal with the needs of a well-managed and open economy such as that of the Republic of Korea, which could become the victim of contagion through no fault of its own. The CMIM-PL has attempted to fill that gap in a manner analogous to the IMF's Precautionary and Liquidity Line (PLL) (Grimes 2015; Kawai 2015).

Finally, the CMIM is also notable for its uncertain relationship to a set of parallel swap lines (Grimes 2015). Outside the CMIM, China, Japan and the Republic of Korea have entered into BSAs with other member countries (see Table 9.4). Several are very large; for instance, the Japan-Indonesia BSA was increased in 2013 to $22.76 billion, which is equivalent to Indonesia's maximum swap amount under the CMIM, while the RMB-denominated China-Indonesia BSA was increased in 2015 to the equivalent of approximately $20 billion. These BSAs have an ambiguous relationship with the CMIM, but have major potential effects on the regional financial system. They also differ considerably among themselves. Japan's are all dollar-denominated swap lines and (according to interviews) are expected to be activated only in tandem with the CMIM swap line activation. China's and the Republic of Korea's BSAs are denominated in renminbi or Korean Republic won (KRW), and the principles for activation and use are not publicized.

Table 9.4 Bilateral swap agreements among ASEAN + 3 participants

Countries	*Date*	*$ billion*
China-Indonesia	20 Nov. 2015	20
China-Republic of Korea	27 June 2013	57
China-Malaysia	8 Feb. 2012; renewed 18 April 2015	29
China-Singapore	15 Mar. 2016	45
China-Thailand	22 Dec. 2014	11
Japan-Indonesia	12 Dec. 2013	22.76
Japan-Republic of Korea	12 June 2012	Expired Feb. 2015; under negotiation since 27 Aug-2016
Japan-Philippines	15 Oct. 2014	12
Japan-Singapore	13 Dec. 2013	3
Republic of Korea-Indonesia	12 Oct. 2013	10
Republic of Korea-Malaysia	26 May 2014	4.5

Note Japan's BSAs are in dollars; China's and the Republic of Korea's BSAs are in their own respective currencies

Source Japanese Ministry of Finance, Bank of Korea, Liao and McDowell 2015

9.3.1.1 FLAR Credit Facilities

The FLAR's loans are intended primarily for providing liquidity support to countries facing balance-of-payments difficulties, and the loan amounts are in proportion to their paid-in capital. This is accomplished through four official mechanisms outlined in Table 9.5.

A fifth mechanism, treasury credit, is not currently operational. FLAR currently has paid-in capital of $2.764 billion and subscribed capital commitments of $3.609 billion (Table 9.6).

For balance-of-payments loans and liquidity, funds are only extended to member countries' central banks, and need to be approved by the FLAR's Board of Directors and the Executive President respectively. The other mechanisms have also been used, but to a much lesser extent.

While the capitalization of the FLAR is smaller than that of the CMIM, for most of the FLAR's history, from 1978 to 2013, its lending to member countries has exceeded that of the IMF with the exception of the period 1989–1993 if the Bolivarian Republic of Venezuela is excluded (Ocampo 2015: 160). Excluding IMF loans to the Bolivarian Republic of Venezuela during that period, the FLAR's lending was 25 per cent higher than that of the IMF; it disbursed loans amounting to $5.324 billion, compared with IMF disbursements of $4.37 billion. If the Bolivarian Republic of Venezuela is included, during the period

Table 9.5 FLAR official credit facilities as of 2016

Credit facility	*Maturity*	*Interest rate*	*Approval*
Balance of payments	3 years with 1 year grace period for amortizations	3-month LIBOR* plus 300–400 basis points	Board of Directors
Liquidity	1 day to 1 year	3-month LIBOR plus 170–230 basis points	Executive President
External public debt restructuring	3 years with 1 year grace period for amortizations	3-month LIBOR plus 300–400 basis points	Board of Directors
Contingency Loan	1 day to 6 months, renewable	3-month LIBOR plus 140–190 basis points	Executive President
Treasury	1 day to 30 days	Not operational	Executive President

Note *LIBOR – London Interbank Offered Rate
Source http://flar.net/lineas_credito.php

Table 9.6 Access limits to credit facilities, by country

Member country	*Subscribed capital ($ million)*	*Paid-in capital ($ million)*	*Access to balance-of-payments credit*	*Access to external public debt restructuring credit*	*Access to liquidity credit*	*Access to contingency credit*	*Access to treasury credit*
			As a percentage of paid-in capital				
Bolivia (Plurinational State of)	328.1	245.3	260	155	100	200	200
Colombia	656.3	490.6	250	150	100	200	200
Costa Rica	328.1	423.6	250	150	100	200	200
Ecuador	328.1	245.3	260	155	100	200	200
Paraguay	328.1	244.9	250	150	100	200	200
Peru	4 656.3	490.6	250	150	100	200	200
Uruguay	328.1	245.8	250	150	100	200	200
Venezuela (Bol. Rep. of)	656.3	490.8	250	150	100	200	200
Total	3 609.4	2 876.9					

Source FLAR, May 2017

1978–2013 the IMF approved loans of $8.011 billion compared with the FLAR's loan commitments of $6.701 billion and disbursements of $5.617 billion. In the post-crisis period (2008–present), the FLAR has lent its members $1.52 billion more than the IMF (Table 9.7). The FLAR issued five loans for a total of $2.25 billion, while the IMF approved one precautionary SBA, to Costa Rica, in the amount of $735 million for balance-of-payments purposes, and Colombia has access to the IMF's

Table 9.7 FLAR and IMF loans to FLAR member countries ($ million)

	FLAR loans approved	*IMF loans approved*
Pre-2008 financial crisis (1978–2007)	4 622	8 011
Post-crisis (2008–2016)	2 252	261.6

Source FLAR and IMF, July 2017

flexible credit line (FCL).[11] However, Costa Rica has never drawn against the precautionary SBA and Colombia has not drawn on the FCL.[12]

The fact that members have resorted to the FLAR rather than the IMF at certain periods, and that, during its existence, it has provided more financing than the IMF to Colombia, Costa Rica and Ecuador, demonstrates the mechanism's capacity, potential, and success. However, despite the success of the FLAR in supporting smaller member States, an evaluation of its current level of capitalization reveals that it would be unlikely to meet the needs of its larger members (Titelman et al. 2014). This does not mean that the larger members do not benefit from FLAR support: its credit facilities help member countries "avoid a severe contracting in intraregional trade flows" (Ocampo 2015: 163). This is because of the implicit quid pro quo among the FLAR member countries: in exchange for loans from the FLAR, the borrowing member country agrees not to restrict trade with the other members. Further, interviews with officials from member countries indicate that the FLAR has a variety of unofficial mechanisms, some of which it has used in the past.

One of the hidden, yet ever-present, tools of the FLAR is the peso andino, a reserve asset issued to the FLAR's original members. Upon request and for a short term, member countries can swap pesos andinos at the FLAR for dollars. While Costa Rica, Paraguay and Uruguay do not hold pesos andinos, Colombia, Peru and the Bolivarian Republic of Venezuela have 20 million pesos andinos on each of their central banks' balance sheets, and Bolivia and Ecuador have 10 million each. The FLAR is still technically obligated to exchange pesos andinos for dollars at a rate of 1:1 for a period of up to six months, with interest. However, as some member countries' officials stated in interviews, despite the presence of pesos andinos on the balance sheets of most members' central banks, the FLAR does not encourage their use. Despite this consensus view, the peso andino could play a valuable role in providing rapid liquidity via a

[11] The FLAR issued three balance-of-payments loans to Ecuador in the amounts of \$480 million (2009), \$515 million (2012) and \$617.58 million (2014), and to the Bolivarian Republic of Venezuela in the amount of \$482.5 million (2016). It also issued a liquidity loan to Ecuador of \$156.46 million (2016).

[12] The IMF also issued \$364 million to Ecuador in 2016 as emergency assistance through the Rapid Financing Instrument, but this was not for balance-of-payments support.

swap with a member country, potentially allowing a member to overcome various types of economic pressures more rapidly.

The peso andino is no longer used, partly because the FLAR did not issue it to countries that joined the Fund more recently, but also because, as reported by FLAR officials, it has become redundant. Swapping pesos andinos for dollars serves the same purpose as a liquidity loan and it also undergoes the same approval process via the FLAR's Executive President. However, some member countries have used peso andino swaps in the past to gain additional time to repay other FLAR obligations. Such moves tie up FLAR resources, thus limiting the agility of the institution. Therefore, for a wider adoption of the peso andino, the FLAR would need to increase its capital base. Following the example of the CAF, seeking more deposits from member countries, and perhaps also non-member countries, is one possible approach to increasing the FLAR's capital.

In addition to calls from some members for the FLAR to become more flexible and issue more types of credits, both FLAR staff and those involved in its formation consistently assert that the Fund needs more capital. Among members, staff and founders, two camps have emerged. One camp, comprising the FLAR's staff and some member countries, asserts that the mechanism needs more resources and members to improve its capacity to deal with regional crises. The other camp, comprised of some member country officials, disagrees that more members are needed in order to obtain more resources. Many member countries' central bank officials noted that the FLAR could easily leverage its AA credit rating to raise additional resources to lend to member States. There are also other means of increasing its financial resources. For example, the CMIM swap network could be one model to follow, as suggested by the extent of members' reserves that could potentially be pooled (see Table 9.8). Also, as one member country's official suggested in an interview, the FLAR could more aggressively seek deposits from non-member central banks to bolster its balance sheet and increase its resources, following the example of the CAF.

9.4 CMIM and FLAR Governance Compared

In addition to providing alternative means of financing for member countries in their respective regions, the CMIM and the FLAR represent alternative models of institutional governance for regional financial institutions, though their relationship with the existing Bretton Woods

Table 9.8 Member countries' reserves and FLAR deposits as of 2016

	FLAR paid-in capital, 2016 ($ million)	*FLAR capital as a percentage of reserves, 2016*	*Reserves, 2015 ($ million)*	*Total reserves in months of imports, 2015*	*Reserves as a percentage of GDP, 2015*
Bolivia	241.1	1.79%	13 049.6	12.22 months (2014 data)	40.86
Colombia	482.3	1.04%	46 222.9	7.53 months	12.26
Costa Rica	352.8	4.59%	7 833.93	4.74 months	14.55
Ecuador	241.2	6.92%	2 487.3	1.16 months	3.45
Paraguay	240.7	3.61%	5 938.4	5.57 months	21.60
Peru	482.3	0.79%	61 594.9	14 months	30.16
Uruguay	241.6	1.38%	15 633.9	13.02 months	30.67
Venezuela (Bol. Rep. of)	482.5	2.38%	15 625.3	3.13 months	5.46
Total	2764.5		4550.23		

Source FLAR and World Bank Open Data

institutions varies. This section first compares the decision-making process of the CMIM and the FLAR against that of the IMF by analysing the institutional structure of these respective organizations, such as allocation of voting rights and procedures, the composition of their boards, and their appointment processes. It then explores their programmatic governance in the key areas of macroeconomic monitoring, policy guidance and research. Finally, it compares the governance of CMIM and FLAR loans with that of the IMF by analysing the conditionality associated with loans, the design of loans, debt seniority and monitoring.

9.4.1 CMIM Governance, Membership and Commitments

The CMIM is a multilateral agreement, not a fund. Members pledge to provide certain amounts of dollars from their foreign exchange reserves under particular (but not fully specified) conditions, and according to a predetermined formula. The maximum commitments of members vary from $60 million to $76.8 billion (Table 9.9). Voting shares are a combination of 3.2 "basic votes" per member plus their committed funds

Table 9.9 CMIM contributions and voting shares

Countries	*Financial contribution*		*Purchasing multiple*	*Maximum swap amount*	*Basic votes*	*Votes based on member's contribution*	*Total voting power*	
	($ billion)	*Share (Per cent)*					*Total votes*	*Per cent*
Plus three	192	80		117.3	9.6	192	201.6	71.59
Japan	76.8	32	0.5	38.4	3.2	76.8	80	28.41
China	76.8	32	0.5	38.4	3.2	76.8	80	28.41
Korea (Rep. of)	38.4	16	1	38.4	3.2	38.4	41.6	14.77
ASEAN	48	20		126.2	32	48	80	28.41
Indonesia	9.104	3.793	2.5	22.76	3.2	9.104	12.304	4.369
Thailand	9.104	3.793	2.5	22.76	3.2	9.104	12.304	4.369
Malaysia	9.104	3.793	2.5	22.76	3.2	9.104	12.304	4.369
Singapore	9.104	3.793	2.5	22.76	3.2	9.104	12.304	4.369
Philippines	9.104	3.793	2.5	22.76	3.2	9.104	12.304	4.369
Viet Nam	2	0.833	5	10	3.2	2	5.2	1.847
Cambodia	0.24	0.1	5	1.2	3.2	0.24	3.44	1.222
Myanmar	0.12	0.05	5	0.6	3.2	0.12	3.32	1.179
Brunei Darussalam	0.06	0.025	5	0.3	3.2	0.06	3.26	1.158
Lao People's Dem. Rep.	0.06	0.025	5	0.3	3.2	0.06	3.26	1.158
Total	240	100		243.5	41.6	240	281.6	100

Note Hong Kong (SAR China) accounts for $8.4 billion of China's total contribution and 8.4 votes in this table. Its votes cannot be exercised except with the Chinese Government's permission. If Hong Kong (China) must draw from the CMIM, its purchasing multiple is 2.5. Its drawings are not IMF linked, as it is not a member of the IMF
Source ASEAN + 3 Macroeconomic Research Office

(financial contribution). ASEAN members cumulatively account for 20 per cent of financial contributions and 28.41 per cent of voting shares, while the "+3" members (China,[13] Japan and the Republic of Korea)

[13] China's overall financial contribution and voting share is formally split between the People's Republic of China and Hong Kong (China), reflecting a compromise between China and Japan over shares. However, Hong Kong does not vote independently from China. To reduce unnecessary complication, this report refers to the combined role of the Peoples' Republic of China and Hong Kong (China) as "China."

account for the remaining 80 per cent of financial contributions and 71.59 per cent of voting shares.

Each member is assigned a "purchasing multiple" that helps to determine the maximum amount it can draw in the event of a currency crisis. For example, Japan has a purchasing multiple of 0.5 and a financial contribution of $76.8 billion, so it would be entitled to draw a theoretical maximum of $38.4 billion. The Philippines (like other ASEAN-5 members)[14] has a purchasing multiple of 2.5 and a financial contribution of $9.104 billion, so it could draw up to $22.76 billion. Those members with the largest financial contributions have the lowest purchasing multiples, and those with the lowest financial contributions have the highest purchasing multiples. This reflects, in part, the clear distinction between likely creditors and likely borrowers.

The implications of the CMIM's system of "self-management" differ in at least two important ways from those of the FLAR, which is an independently managed fund. First, if a contributing CMIM member is under financial duress, there is an opt-out clause whereby it may be exempted from its contractual obligation to contribute. Moreover, in the CMIM, the amount of each member's required financial contribution is unaffected by investment performance. In contrast, in an independently managed fund, disbursement is automatic once the decision has been made to do so, as funds have already been transferred out of the member's foreign exchange reserves. Second, the value of an external fund can vary based on the market performance of investments.

In many respects, the largest economies have a disproportionate responsibility within the CMIM. In particular, China and Japan have the highest financial contribution and the lowest purchasing multiples. In turn, they also have the largest voting shares, each holding 28.41 per cent of the total votes. However, voting shares are weighted somewhat towards the ASEAN members, since a voting share is the sum of the financial contribution and "basic votes" (the latter of which are equal for all members). Thus, the total ASEAN voting share is 28.41 per cent (not coincidentally identical to the individual shares of China and Japan), although the total ASEAN financial contribution is only 20 per cent.

[14] The ASEAN-5 are the five original ASEAN members (Indonesia, Malaysia, Philippines, Singapore and Thailand), which are also the region's largest (on a nominal basis) and most open economies.

9.4.2 *The FLAR's Organizational Structure*

To a certain extent, the institutional structure of the FLAR resembles that of the IMF (Table 9.10). The IMF has a Board of Governors comprising

Table 9.10 Organizational structures of the CMIM, FLAR and IMF

CMIM	*FLAR*	*IMF*
• ASEAN + 3 finance ministers comprise ministerial level decision-making body	• Comprised of the Executive Director, Representative Assembly, Board of Directors, and Department of Economic Studies	• Comprised of a Managing Director, the Executive Board and Board of Governors. Executive Board is composed of 24 seats with some seats reflecting 4 or more countries
• Deputy finance ministers comprise executive level decision-making body	• One country/one vote.	• Countries are assigned quotas based on economic size and characteristics as calculated by the quota formula
• All non-operational decisions require consensus in ministerial level decision-making body	• Three quarters of directors and governors must be present, and of these, three quarters must approve debt restructuring and liquidity loans. No formal linkage to the IMF	• No formal linkage to the FLAR
• Swap activation and renewal require two-thirds majority of voting shares by executive level decision-making body • Votes are based on a combination of "basic votes" and financial contribution • No more than 30 per cent of borrowing limits can be activated without cooperation with the IMF		• Some issues require 85 per cent majority vote.

ministers of finance or central bank heads, an Executive Board and a Managing Director. Similarly, the FLAR has a Representative Assembly comprising the finance ministers from each member country, a Board of Directors made up of the central bank governors of each member country and an Executive President. However, the FLAR's structure differs from that of the IMF in a number of important ways. First, voting rights in the FLAR are equally distributed across member countries. Each member of both the Representative Assembly and the Board of Directors has a single, equal vote. The FLAR's Executive Board is also balanced, with one seat/one vote per country, whereas that of the IMF is comprised of 24 members representing 189 countries with votes weighted by financial contribution. As a result, large economies such as the United States have a full seat, while most other "countries are grouped into constituencies representing four or more countries. The largest constituency comprises 24 countries."[15]

Further, for decisions on liquidity credits, the FLAR strives for consensus; a minimum of three quarters of the directors and governors must be present to deliberate, and of those present, three quarters need to vote in favour of a decision for it to pass. Certain issues, such as increasing capital, modifying credit limits or altering the terms of the FLAR agreement require a supermajority of 80 per cent. As opposed to the IMF, where voting power is based on quotas largely related to economic size, the governance of the FLAR is "independent of capital contributions," giving it, what the FLAR believes, a comparative advantage vis-à-vis the IMF in constructing loan packages (Velarde 2015: 150). The FLAR argues that the equal voting approach to fund governance "provides the opportunity for a more balanced decision-making system, which is agile and less prone to political influence" (Garcia 2015: 160). The factors contributing to the FLAR's agility are discussed in Sections 4.4 and 4.6 below, but include the equal weighting of member countries' votes and limited conditionality. According to interviews, the principles of equality and regional solidarity give the FLAR's activities considerable political legitimacy.

Some scholars and FLAR member countries' representatives argue that if the FLAR's lending capacity were to be increased through a larger

[15] See IMF Governance Structure at: https://www.imf.org/external/about/govstruct.htm.

membership base, it could become a more influential regional mechanism (Ocampo and Titelman 2012; Titelman et al. 2014). On its face, this seems a reasonable proposal; for instance, Costa Rica had to seek a precautionary loan through an SBA with the IMF in 2009 for $735 million instead of borrowing from the FLAR, in part because the most it could borrow from the FLAR was $600 million. On the other hand, if more resources were made available through the inclusion of larger countries such as Brazil and Mexico, it would likely undermine one of the core tenets of the FLAR's success, namely equality of the members. Because all of the members currently have equal voice and representation, there is a shared sense of ownership and responsibility among member countries that "has in practice been expressed in [FLAR's] solid position as senior creditor" (Titelman et al. 2014: 21). As a result, no member country has ever failed to pay back a FLAR obligation, and the fund maintains an AA credit rating, which is the highest rating in the region. If the FLAR were to sacrifice its equitable membership and voting structure to accommodate a larger regional member, it would likely undermine the way the agreement is governed.

Unlike other regional alternatives, such as the CMIM and the European Stability Mechanism, the FLAR largely lacks formal linkages to the IMF. This practice is rooted in the experience of Bolivia, which suffered from a balance-of-payments crisis in the early 1980s. Its loans from the IMF were cancelled because it was not in complete "compliance with the term of the letter-of-intent" (Morales 2015: 227). A few years later, when Bolivia needed further assistance, it found "the IMF's resources were insufficient, being limited by the small quota Bolivia had in this institution" (ibid.). Further, the loans from the IMF were not only very slow to originate, but were also accompanied by harsh conditionalities imposed on the borrowing country (ibid.). However, in May 2015, the FLAR concluded an agreement with the IMF to facilitate the addition of smaller member countries in Latin America to the FLAR by reducing entry costs. The IMF agreed to allow *future* smaller country members to count paid-in capital at the FLAR as a portion of their international reserves with the IMF.

While it has been pointed out that there are some benefits to IMF loans,[16] many member countries "are reluctant to request one due to

[16] Interview with Carlos Giraldo, FLAR's Director of Economic Studies.

the strong conditionality attached to [its] financial assistance programs" (Velarde 2015: 147). The FLAR is designed to respond to this shortcoming by offering loans that provide "rapid and timely access to resources" (ibid.) and limit the indirect costs of conditionality that accompany IMF loans. Despite the lack of formal linkages, the FLAR staff members frequently engage with the IMF by attending IMF meetings and hosting IMF staff periodically.

9.4.3 ASEAN + 3 Macroeconomic Research Office (AMRO) and Programmatic Governance in the CMIM[17]

AMRO was established in 2011 and formally became an international organization in 2016. Its articles of incorporation are publicly available (ASEAN+3 2016), and from 2017 onwards, it will issue annual reports that will include important data such as revenue and expenditures. Prior to 2016, the AMRO was incorporated as a limited partnership in Singapore. As such, it was not required to make those data public, and in fact did not do so. According to interviewees, AMRO has two main budgetary sources. One is annual levies on its members, with the total decided by consensus and then apportioned by share of total financial contribution. This is apparently insufficient to meet the needs of the organization and its expanding responsibilities. Consequently, a significant (albeit not publicly available) portion of the budget is made up of additional, voluntary payments from some members, primarily China and Japan. The Monetary Authority of Singapore also offers substantial assistance in the form of space and information technology (IT) support.

AMRO is headed by a Director, who is hired by the CMIM members' finance ministers. Below the Director, are a chief economist and two deputy directors (Administration; CMIM, Strategy, and Coordination). Surveillance, which is carried out by professional economists organized under five group heads, is arranged both along country lines and by function (e.g. financial stability, fiscal policy). By internal practice, no group head is in charge of surveillance of their own country. There are no field offices, and all AMRO personnel are based in Singapore. In principle, all

[17] AMRO is a new and understudied organization. This paper appears to represent the first scholarly description of its organizational and procedural characteristics. Since AMRO has not yet issued its first publicly available annual report, this study relies heavily on interviews with current and former AMRO officials.

AMRO employees are hired on an individual basis by AMRO, although in practice a few are seconded by their home governments or central banks.

AMRO has four main roles: surveillance, acting as a de facto CMIM secretariat (producing and maintaining records for the Asean + 3 finance ministers), designing packages for swap activation and providing technical assistance for members. The bulk of its surveillance function involves consultations with members that parallel IMF Article IV consultations, although they are less extensive and are kept confidential. Also, the Director formally briefs the CMIM finance ministers (annually) and deputies (semi-annually) during their Economic Review and Policy Dialogue (ERPD), along with the IMF regional representative and the President of the Asian Development Bank (ADB). The AMRO Director also attends the meetings of the EPRD.

Building on its surveillance responsibility, AMRO has also been tasked with making recommendations to the CMIM finance ministers regarding size and conditions for swap activation. While this function has never been tested, AMRO has been building procedures and expertise to develop its capabilities in this area. According to policymakers and analysts who believe in the importance of eventually eliminating the IMF link, AMRO's ability to turn its economic analysis into viable support plans objectively, effectively and without political interference from members is the key hurdle to surmount (Kawai 2005; Takagi 2010). So far, this goal has not been met, but it remains a major topic for discussion.

Finally, technical assistance takes two forms. One is essentially providing guidance to some developing-country members on economic data collection and analysis. Of more direct importance to the CMIM mechanism is AMRO's role in planning for activation of CMIM swap lines. A major tool in this area of responsibility has been "test runs" (simulations) involving members and some external actors. For example, an important finding of one test run was that not all members had accounts at all other members' central banks, which would have created a major hitch for swap activation if this problem had not been discovered through the simulation. In October 2016, AMRO ran its first test run involving IMF-linked funds, and thus included the IMF in the exercise as well as its own members and the New York Federal Reserve.

9.4.4 *Programmatic Governance of the FLAR*

The FLAR's programmatic governance is best understood by comparing it with that of the IMF (see Table 9.11). One of the key elements of the IMF's programmatic governance is its economic surveillance, monitoring, and consultations, also known as Article IV consultations, conducted with member countries, typically on an annual basis. IMF staff members visit member countries for discussions covering "exchange rate, monetary,

Table 9.11 Programmatic governance of AMRO, FLAR and IMF

	CMIM (AMRO)	*FLAR*	*IMF*
Programmatic governance (e.g. macroeconomic monitoring, general policy recommendations, research production)	• AMRO conducts informal consultations with member countries on a regular basis; results are not publicly disclosed	• FLAR conducts informal consultations with member countries on a regular basis	• IMF conducts Article IV consultations with member countries
	• In case of a request for funds, AMRO will design and recommend a package (size, facility, conditions) to decision-making bodies.	• Results of surveillance/consultations are not publicly disclosed	• Results are publicly shared and disseminated
	• Limited internal research capacity at current stage of development	• Limited internal research capacity, but enhanced by regional proximity and a new strategic alliance with AMRO	• Robust internal research capacity and large research staff
	• AMRO leaders attend IMF annual meetings	• FLAR representatives attend annual IMF meetings	
	• Strategic partnerships with the FLAR, IMF and ADB	• Strategic partnerships with the CMIM, BIS, and other Regional Financial Arrangements.	

fiscal and financial policies, as well as macro critical structural reforms" (IMF 2016). Following the completion of this process, member countries usually agree to the publication of a press release highlighting "the view of the Board, as well as the Staff Report and accompanying analysis" (IMF 2016). Finally, the IMF also has a robust research department that continually produces research findings.

While IMF consultations are quite public, the FLAR (like AMRO) conducts its consultation less formally and more confidentially with members. Officials from the FLAR visit member countries and generate internal reports on the state of their economy, foreign exchange reserves, exchange rate, and fiscal and monetary policies. They also evaluate the likelihood of the member country's need for credit in the near future. There is an agreement between member countries and the FLAR to not publish this information and to keep it private between the central banks, Representative Assembly, and the Board of Directors, but to keep it private between the central banks, the Representative Assembly and the Board of Directors.

Although the FLAR's surveillance is not public and is not as extensive as the IMF's, nor as extensive as the IMF's, it does frequently provide technical advisory services to central banks and other regional institutions. In addition, it has been working on bolstering its policy guidance and research capacity, as evidenced by the strategic alliance it maintains with the Bank for International Settlements (BIS) and, as of 2016, with AMRO. These organizations maintain a dialogue and share their respective experiences over surveillance and research. These relationships also guide the FLAR in strategically planning the further development of its surveillance process and macroeconomic policy guidance. This is an important goal, as regional mechanisms like the FLAR may be better equipped than the IMF to address "region-specific problems and risks, given that they possess an abundance of local knowledge" (Eichengreen 2015: 137).

While the FLAR does not publish reports on macroeconomic oversight, unlike the IMF with its Article IV consultations, FLAR officials have suggested that press releases can be a powerful tool for deterring speculators or assuring creditors. Specifically, former FLAR staff and officials noted that they have the ability to attempt to deter speculators by releasing announcements confirming that a member country has access to certain amounts of credit facilities at the FLAR.[18] Indeed, in 2008 and 2009 the FLAR strategically informed markets publicly through communications of the credit lines available to member countries.

Finally, another important point of programmatic governance concerns investment of the FLAR's resources. It takes an orthodox approach to such investment, mimicking "that of central banks."[19] And it strives for significant liquidity and security by investing in AA and AAA rated securities. However, as seen in the most recent financial crisis, this does not always prevent losses: the FLAR suffered losses on investments in highly rated assets that lost money, such as mortgage-backed securities. Indeed, it is worth noting that the FLAR would have suffered net losses in 2009 and 2010 had it not earned interest on its loans to Ecuador. Disagreements over fund management persist, with some regional policymakers disapproving of the FLAR's purchase of mortgage-backed securities instead of buying the bonds of member countries' central banks. This has resulted in tension between those members who wish to see the FLAR invest paid-in capital in more orthodox, high-quality, liquid investments, and other members who favour investment in the sovereign bonds of member States.

9.4.5 CMIM Project Governance: Decision-Making and Swap Activation

Decisions within the CMIM regarding institutional issues are made on the basis of consensus among the members. This includes, for example, all decisions about membership, financial contributions and procedures. Meetings, whether at the ministerial (Ministerial Level Decision-Making Body) or working levels (Executive Level Decision-Making Body), are chaired by representatives from the current ASEAN+3 co-chairs. There are two annually rotating co-chairs, one each from ASEAN and from the +3.

Decisions regarding swap activation require a supermajority of two-thirds of voting shares. Since no single member holds a third or more of voting shares, no single country can exercise veto power. In many cases, it is assumed that discussions and votes concerning swap activation

[18] Author interviews at FLAR in August 2016.

[19] Author interviews at FLAR in August 2016.

will be carried out electronically rather than in person, given the confusion and potential for contagion inherent in currency crises. According to interviews, members have agreed that votes may be counted cumulatively by the co-chairs, rather than requiring all finance ministers (or their representatives) to be simultaneously present, whether in person or online.

The decision to activate swaps considers several elements:

i. The total amount to be disbursed. The amount will depend on three factors: the request itself, an analysis by AMRO staff as to how much money is needed to address a particular crisis,[20] and whether the request is for funds that are subject to the IMF link or only to delinked funds. The amount that each member contributes is determined by its relative share among those members that will be contributing. (Due to the opt-out clause, this may be fewer than 12 members, even if only one economy is requesting an activation of swaps.)

ii. Whether funds are to be accessed under the Precautionary Line (CMIM-PL) or the Stability Facility (CMIM-SF). CMIM-PL funds are more attractive than CMIM-SF funds, as they come with fewer conditions attached, although their maximum duration is shorter (see Table 9.3). However, members cannot draw funds under the CMIM-PL if they are considered to be in crisis; also, AMRO (and/or the IMF) must agree that they satisfy the CMIM-PL's preconditions of sound economic management. There is some subjectivity in both these judgements, which may create significant pressure on AMRO from both borrowers and creditors.

iii. Whether to draw IMF-linked funds. Many members may prefer only to draw IMF delinked funds, either because of the domestic political stigma attached to resorting to the IMF or because they expect AMRO's conditions will be more lenient than those of the IMF. However, it is difficult to imagine any crisis or other contingency where 30 per cent of any borrowing country's maximum swap

[20] For the time being, AMRO is likely to have to rely on IMF guidance, as it lacks the institutional resources and experience to independently determine the needs of a requesting member. It is also likely, even going forward, that in at least some cases, CMIM funds will be provided along with IMF funds, whether via a precautionary and liquidity line or a stand-by arrangement.

amount would be sufficient on its own. The CMIM finance ministers, after receiving AMRO's recommendation, are empowered to reject a request for an amount they consider insufficient to address the crisis or contingency.

iv. Conditions. In principle, the CMIM finance ministers might also decide, on AMRO's recommendation to attach conditions that a member must fulfil in order to receive CMIM funds. In practice, it is likely that IMF-linked funds will simply piggyback on IMF conditions. AMRO and the CMIM ministers would be solely responsible for imposing conditions on delinked funds.

Although the CMIM is a "multilateralized" version of the CMI, the basis of liquidity provision is still bilateral swaps. Each member that is contributing to liquidity support must authorize the Federal Reserve Bank of New York to credit the receiving country's dollar account with the agreed amount from its own dollar reserves. Simultaneously, the receiving country's central bank will credit each contributing country's local-currency account with an amount of the local currency that is equivalent to the dollar credits in New York. The interest rate that the receiving country must pay on the dollar credit is the official IMF lending rate in effect at that time.

9.4.6 FLAR Project Governance

The best way to understand project governance at the FLAR is to draw a comparison with the IMF's short-term mechanisms aimed at alleviating balance-of-payments crises. These include SBAs, the Stand-by Credit Facility (SCF), the Rapid Credit Facility (RCF) and the Rapid Financing Instrument (RFI). The FLAR contingency, liquidity and balance-of-payments credit facilities are designed to address similar issues. The maximum duration of the IMF facilities, such as the RCF, can range from one year to as many as ten years. The interest rate of loans in the form of special drawing rights (SDRs) is currently 1.050 per cent, and the IMF has seniority as a creditor, a fact that is recognized by markets.[21] Finally, these loans are often accompanied by the requirement that a member

[21] See IMF Rates Query at: http://www.imf.org/external/np/fin/data/queryoutput.aspx?origin=imf-finances (accessed 16 September 2016).

country sign an agreement to commit to a variety of conditions, such as privatizations or austerity measures.

In contrast, the FLAR has shorter term mechanisms that have a maximum duration of three years. Interest rates are calculated using an internal formula, and are steeper than those of the IMF, typically around the three-month LIBOR plus 300–400 basis points (Table 9.4). However, these rates are significantly lower than the rates at which the member countries could typically borrow in private capital markets, provided the country has access to private capital at all. The FLAR enjoys de facto seniority status as a creditor because "the degree of involvement and a sense of belonging of its members [has] guaranteed the total and timely reimbursement of loans" (Corvalan 2015: 273). So far, no FLAR member country that has borrowed has ever failed to honour its obligations.

The FLAR does not attach the same amount of conditionality to its loans as the IMF.[22] That said, there is both explicit and implicit conditionality associated with FLAR loans. A major conditionality explicitly stated in its covenant is that member countries must not impede trade by instituting trade barriers. Explicit conditionality is dependent on a number of factors, but can include a mandated fiscal surplus (Rosero 2014: 75). Nonetheless, such conditions are substantially less burdensome than those imposed by the IMF.

When a country seeks a loan, it contacts the FLAR's economic team and the Executive President, leading to discussions about the country's macroeconomic conditions, its plans to address the issues and its credit needs. While these discussions progress, the member country submits a formal request for credit and a detailed macroeconomic plan to the Division of Economic Studies, which is responsible for reviewing the macroeconomic conditions of member countries. This division assesses the extent to which the stated goals are attainable and conducive to the country's economic recovery and its ability to repay its debt obligations. This analysis is then submitted to the Executive President who can either approve or refuse the request for the loan (for liquidity and contingency loans) or present the plan to the Board of Directors for a vote (for balance-of-payments and debt restructuring loans).

[22] For more details, see Copelovitch 2010, Vreeland 2007, Ban and Gallagher 2014, Broome 2015, Ban 2015, Chwieroth 2010, and Grabel 2011.

The amount of capital available to member countries varies in proportion to their paid-in capital (see Table 9.6). Depending on the circumstances, these loans can be disbursed within as short a period as one week for liquidity support purposes.[23] Debt refinancing can take as long as four to eight weeks. The interest charged on the different mechanisms listed in Table 9.4 and the spread are determined by the FLAR's Asset and Liability Committee, which evaluates external financing conditions in international markets. While IMF officials may visit countries where there are ongoing IMF loan programmes as often as quarterly for monitoring, FLAR officials visit member countries with FLAR loans approximately twice a year to monitor progress towards economic stability. Officials also hold monthly telephone conferences with the officials in the borrowing country.

A comparison of project governance between the FLAR and the IMF shows that the FLAR is much more agile and, in the experience of those interviewed, faster in responding to member countries' requests for funds. In addition, it imposes significantly fewer conditions on member countries, and has never denied a loan request by a member country, so far. However, the interest rate is higher than that of the IMF, which suggests that FLAR members attach greater value to its flexibility and lack of conditionality. Overall, the approach of the FLAR is deeply embedded in the creditor–debtor dynamics of the institution. (Paraguay and Uruguay, which recently joined the FLAR, are the only members not to have borrowed from it.) Member countries feel a sense of shared ownership and responsibility, which leads them not only to support each other, but also to repay the loans extended by this mechanism (Table 9.12).

9.5 Assessing the Economic Impacts of the CMIM and FLAR

This section analyses the impacts of the CMIM and FLAR on member countries. First, it considers the economic effects of the CMIM on member countries, and outlines potential issues that could arise in the event that the swaps are activated. It then looks at the FLAR's overall activities and at aggregate economic data for member countries through

[23] Author interview with FLAR staff, August 2016.

Table 9.12 Project governance of the CMIM, FLAR and IMF compared

	CMIM	*FLAR*	*IMF*
Project governance (e.g. conditionality, design and debt seniority, monitoring)	• No swap activation to date	• Never denied a loan	• Has five mechanisms to alleviate balance-of-payments and liquidity problems
	• Conditionality attached to IMF-linked funds based on IMF conditionality	• Limited conditionality; sense of shared ownership and conditionality has resulted in 100 per cent repayment track record	• Approval can depend on historic economic track record and adherence to IMF conditionality on other loans
	• Conditionality for delinked funds to be determined by AMRO (methodology pending)	• Maturity ranging from 1 day to three years	• Pre-lending conditions for many credit facilities
	• Preconditions as basis for CMIM-PL approval and disbursement	• Implicit conditionality noted in charter; member countries must not impede trade in the event of a crisis	• Maturity ranges from 1 year to 10 years
	• Maturity ranging from 6 months to 3 years • Uses IMF lending rate.	• De facto preferred credit status for debt seniority	• Interest rate of 1.05 per cent (as on 15 Sept. 2016) • Seniority of debt rooted in market sentiment.
	• A CMIM-PL programme can be changed to a CMIM-SF programme at the discretion of the executive body • Seniority of debt unclear, but use of swaps aims to reduce risk		

an evaluation of lending volumes and a comparison of members' paid-in capital and their reserves. It also compares total disbursements of the FLAR with those of the IMF. In addition, a post-crisis FLAR loan and a post-crisis IMF loan are compared using a variety of metrics for illustrative purposes.

9.5.1 *Impacts of the CMIM*

Given that neither the CMI nor the CMIM has ever been activated, it is not possible to gauge their economic effects. It is plausible that currency crises in East Asia have not occurred since the establishment of the CMI because investors have been reassured that the regional arrangement would allow members to defend their currencies against attack. However, there is no direct evidence to support this contention, and indeed it is not clear whether the CMIM is sufficiently well-known among currency traders and asset managers investing in the region.

An alternative way to observe the perceived efficacy of the CMIM is to try to determine whether member countries have changed their behaviour as the amounts that they can draw from it have increased. One way to measure this is by considering foreign exchange reserves of the CMIM countries (particularly those with relatively open capital accounts). As seen in Fig. 9.1a, there is little evidence that CMIM countries are choosing to reduce the amount of their foreign exchange reserves, which would suggest that they still rely on self-help rather than on the pledges of their partners. For example, Indonesia has the lowest level of reserves relative to nominal GDP among the major CMIM economies. As Fig. 9.1b shows, however, neither the expansion of available funds that accompanied the creation of the CMIM in 2010 nor the subsequent doubling of funds in 2012 appear to have had an impact on Indonesia's foreign reserve holdings.

As noted, it is not possible to gauge the actual effectiveness of the CMIM until a member has drawn on it or East Asia has been tested in a real crisis. However, there are at least four ways in which serious problems could arise in the event of an activation of the CMIM:

1. Operational issues. It is possible that activation of swaps could be slowed or prevented by lack of standardized procedures, cyber-security problems and/or domestic laws. Test runs have already

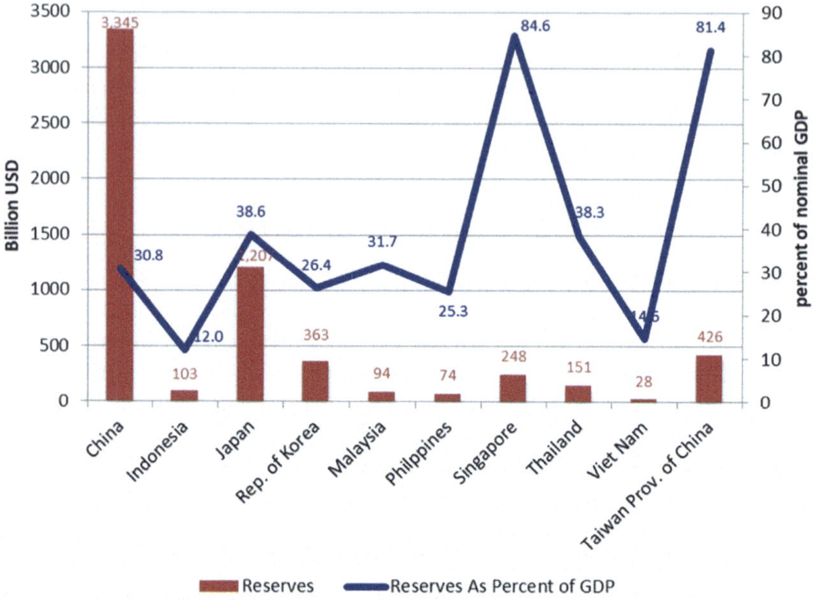

Fig. 9.1 a Foreign exchange reserves of the major CMIM members, end 2015 (*Source* IMF, national central banks; Note: Taiwan Province of China is added for comparison, as it is an economy that does not have access to either the IMF or the CMIM)

identified a number of procedural issues, and they will remain a valuable tool for finding solutions to these potential problems.

2. Disputes over whether to invoke CMIM-PL or CMIM-SF. There may be cases in which members that are not in crisis but do not strictly meet precautionary line criteria will seek to draw on the PL rather than the SF for domestic political reasons. It cannot be predicted how either AMRO or CMIM ministers would respond, but efforts to reduce uncertainty in this regard by clarifying procedures, and ongoing communication will be imperative.
3. Disagreement over IMF link. As noted above, some members may seek to avoid borrowing from the IMF, whether for domestic political reasons, to avoid conditionality, or to avoid being downgraded in international bond markets. In principle, this could be prevented

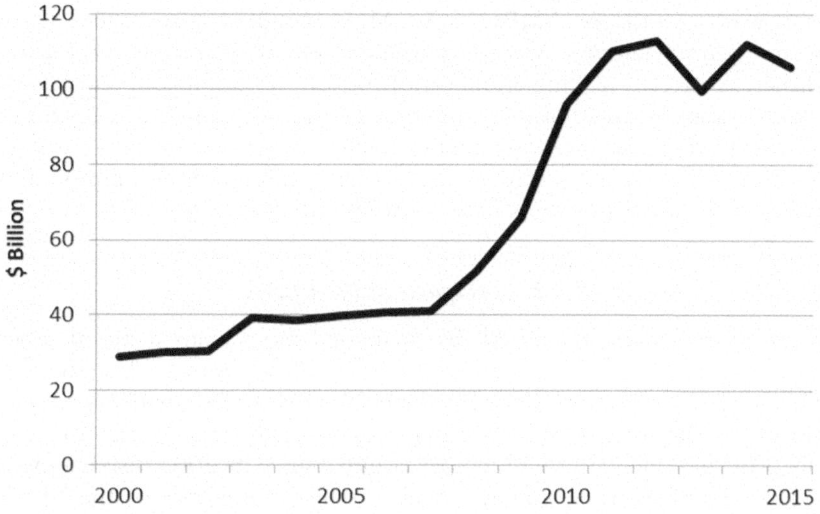

Fig. 9.1 **b** Indonesia's foreign exchange reserves, 2000–2015 (*Source* Bank Indonesia (central bank])

if AMRO were to formulate convincing and consistent methodologies for determining the necessary size of a package. Since this challenge could take some time to overcome, it is likely that CMIM ministers will choose to rely on the IMF's judgement in many such instances.

4. Interactions with parallel BSAs. The existence of large, parallel BSAs may lead some members to seek bilateral help in a crisis or contingency, rather than going through the CMIM process, or at least as a way of avoiding IMF-linked funding (Grimes 2015). China, Japan and the Republic of Korea would need to make clear their criteria for activating BSAs and how the funds obtained through those swaps can be used. For example, will the People's Bank of China convert RMB swaps to Indonesia or to the Republic of Korea into dollars, or will they only be usable to settle RMB trade? Without such clarification, there is a risk of moral hazard or a lack of effective coordination between China, Japan and the Republic of Korea.

Thus, a major task for AMRO and CMIM members is to reduce these remaining uncertainties. According to interviews with current and former officials, AMRO is making significant progress in outlining an agenda to reduce technical uncertainties and to improve its analytical capabilities and ability to make recommendations. However, some of these uncertainties need to be addressed by leaders, and differences of opinion and preferences among members pose a continuing challenge.

9.5.2 *Impacts of the FLAR*

As previously noted, the FLAR has extended more loans to its member countries than the IMF at various intervals throughout its history, and indeed significantly more since the financial crisis. In fact, with the exception of an SBA with Costa Rica that was never disbursed, the IMF has only provided one loan to a member country since its 2006 disbursement of $126.3 million to Uruguay, which was not a member of the FLAR at the time. As Fig. 9.2 shows, over the past decade, the IMF has made no short-term balance-of-payments-type disbursements to FLAR member countries. This has not been because of a lack of need in the region, as evidenced by the extensive disbursement of FLAR funds, amounting

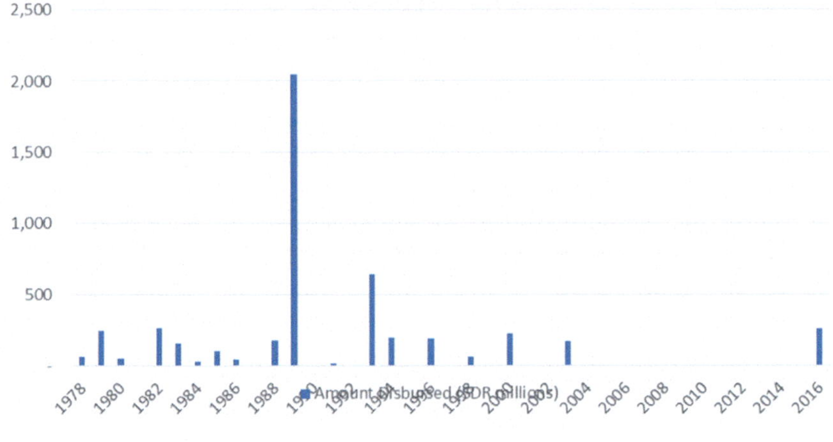

Fig. 9.2 IMF lending to FLAR member countries, 1978–2016 (*Source* IMF)

to $2.74 billion, during this period, although the vast majority of those credits were extended to Ecuador.[24]

An analysis of the composition of the FLAR's disbursements of paid-in capital demonstrates that the greatest demand has been for balance-of-payments support, with $4.97 billion disbursed from 1978 to 2016 (Table 9.13). The FLAR has also provided significant liquidity support in the amount of $2.74 billion. So far, since the creation of the FLAR, Ecuador has accounted for 51 per cent of the Fund's disbursements, whereas Bolivia, Colombia, Peru and the Bolivarian Republic of Venezuela have each accounted for between 9 and 13 per cent. Among its newest members, Costa Rica (1999) accounts for a mere 1.83 per cent, while Uruguay (2009) and Paraguay (2015) have not yet drawn any funds at all.

As previously noted, some authors (e.g. Agosin and Heresi 2011; Agosin 2012; Rosero 2014) have called for an increase in FLAR membership to include larger countries, such as Brazil and Mexico, and for the establishment of stand-by lines of credit. Ocampo and Titelman (2012) have called for "swap arrangements among the region's countries and with extra-regional central banks, and eventual access to IMF credit lines and even SDR allocations." However, such proposals overlook two key points. First, the FLAR's success is deeply embedded in its members' shared sense of equal ownership and responsibility towards the fund. This important dynamic would be jeopardized if a larger regional partner were to join the membership ranks and demand a change to the FLAR's hallmark governance principle of one country, one vote. Second, linkages with the IMF would further undermine member countries' sense of shared ownership of the FLAR and its provision of alternative credit to member States with minimal conditions attached.

Instead, the best solution possibly lies somewhere in the middle. An updated analysis (2014 data) of FLAR member countries' paid-in capital to reserves reveals that most of the FLAR members have very robust reserves—many multiples of their contributions to the FLAR (Fig. 9.3). Their total reserves amounted to nearly $168.386 billion. If the FLAR

[24] The FLAR issued four balance-of-payments loans to Ecuador, for $400 million (2005/2006), $480 million (2009), $515 million (2012) and $617.58 million (2014) and one balance-of-payments loan to the Bolivarian Republic of Venezuela for $482.5 million (2016). It also issued a liquidity loan to Ecuador for $156.46 million (2016).

Table 9.13 FLAR versus IMF credits to member countries, 1978–2016 ($ million)

Original members	*Liquidity*	*Balance-of-payments*	*Debt restructuring*	*Contingency*	*Total FLAR disbursements*	*Percentage of total FLAR disbursements*	*IMF disburse-ments*
Bolivia (Plurinational State of)	779.00	153.00	0.00	0.00	932.00	10.91	998.00
Colombia	560.00	229.00	0.00	375.00	1 164.00	13.63	0.00
Ecuador	856.46	3 200.58	300.00	0.00	4 357.04	51.02	1 159.00
Peru	519.00	636.00	0.00	0.00	1 155.00	13.52	2 213.00
Venezuela (Bol. Rep. of)	23.00	753.50	0.00	0.00	776.50	9.09	3 642.00
New members							
Costa Rica	0.00	0.00	156.00	0.00	156.00	1.83	0.00
Paraguay	0.00	0.00	0.00	0.00	0.00	0.00	0.00
Uruguay	0.00	0.00	0.00	0.00	0.00	0.00	0.00
Total	**2 737.46**	**4 972.08**	**456.00**	**375.00**	**8 540.54**		**8 012.00**

Source IMF and FLAR

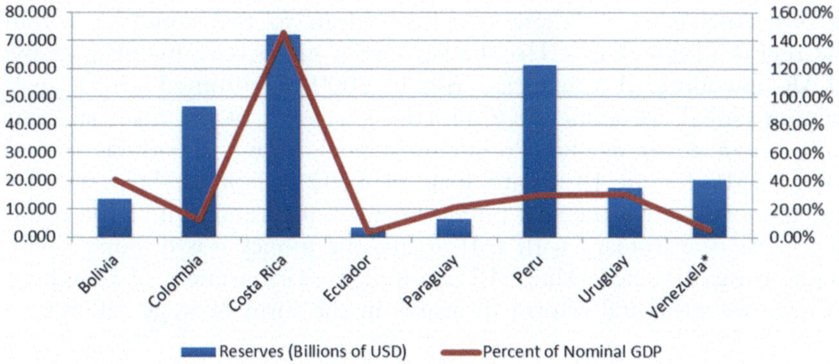

Fig. 9.3 FLAR member countries' paid-in capital and reserves as a percentage of GDP, 2016

were to focus on establishing swaps between itself and member countries' central banks, as well as administering and overseeing swaps between member countries' central banks, it would have sufficient resources to meet the demands of even its largest current member States. Further, if the fund were to revive the concept of the peso andino, it could set up a multilateral swap network as illustrated in Fig. 9.4.

To better understand the potential of the FLAR as an alternative to the IMF as a source of funding, it is useful to consider a comparison

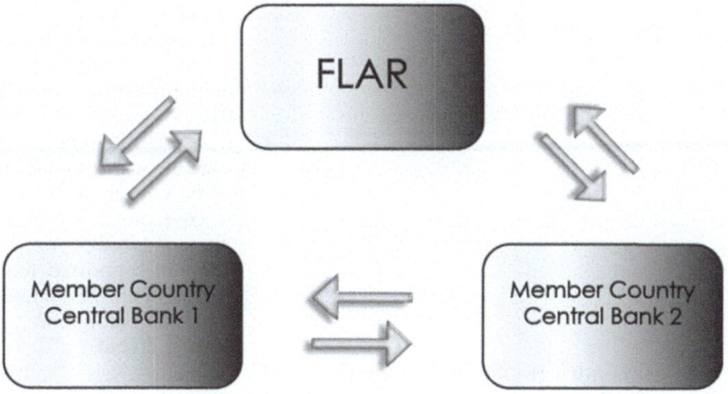

Fig. 9.4 Possible FLAR swap network

of post-crisis loans by these two institutions to two countries within the region (Table 9.14). Honduras, once a prospective member of the FLAR, encountered a financial crisis in 2009. Confronted with a challenging global economic environment as a result of the financial crisis and a *coup d'état* against President Manuel Zelaya, Honduras turned to the IMF for an 18-month loan of $202 million to help stabilize the economy, strengthen its public finances and rebuild investor confidence. As is customary with IMF loans, the money was disbursed with many strings attached. The IMF required the Government of Honduras to institute structural reform measures in the form of wage ceilings, as

Table 9.14 Post-crisis loans of the FLAR and IMF compared

	FLAR loan to Ecuador, 2016	*IMF loan to Honduras, 2010*
Loan size	$156.46 million	$202 million
Loan term	3 months	18 months
Loan type	Liquidity credit	SBA/SCF
Seniority	Implicit senior creditor status	Implicit senior status resulting from market conventions
Conditions	**Implicit conditionality:** • Borrower must not prevent trade with member countries **Explicit conditionality:** • Borrower must repay FLAR in full for capital and interest within five days of receipt of the first disbursement of the CDB loan	**Explicit conditionality:** • Monthly reporting of fiscal, monetary, external debt and other data. • Implementation of structural reform measures, including wage ceilings • Fiscal consolidation to rein in current spending and "help create space for increasing anti-poverty spending and public investment." (IMF, 2010) • "Resolute adherence to the program of fiscal consolidation will be critical to the success of the government's economic strategy." (Ibid.) • IMF staff supported request because of the "Strength of the authorities' economic program."(Ibid.)
Interest rate	3-month LIBOR (.64 per cent) plus 195 basis points	0.5 per cent

Note For IMF, 2010, see: https://www.imf.org/external/pubs/ft/scr/2010/cr10322.pdf

well as "growth-friendly fiscal consolidation... to rein in current spending and help create space for increasing anti-poverty spending and public investment" (IMF press release 10/374, 2010).

Ecuador, the largest borrower from the FLAR over the past decade, most recently has struggled with falling oil prices, an appreciation of the real exchange rate and increases in international interest rates. While the country secured a $2 billion loan from the China Development Bank (CDB) in early 2016, it required a bridge loan until it received its first disbursement. Accordingly, it requested a liquidity credit of $156.46 million from the FLAR for a term of 90 days. Apart from the implicit conditionality on all FLAR loans, whereby member countries cannot impede intraregional trade, the only other condition was that Ecuador would have to repay the liquidity loan once it received the disbursement from the CDB. Ecuadorian officials noted in interviews that, unlike the IMF loan to Honduras, there is no invasive conditionality attached to FLAR loans, including its 2016 bridge loan to Ecuador.

9.6 Lessons from a Comparison of the FLAR and CMIM

A comparison of the FLAR and CMIM demonstrates significant differences between the two mechanisms (Table 9.15). That said, they are both long-standing regional alternatives to the IMF, and, as such, hold important lessons in terms of fund size, moral hazard/conditionality, certainty and efficiency and solidarity. Below are some key lessons for other emerging reserve pooling arrangements:

1. The structure and capabilities of a regional liquidity facility should reflect the characteristics and needs of the member economies.
   a. Facilities for economies that are very open to trade and capital flows need to be much larger than ones that cater to less open economies.
   b. Economies that are similar to each other in size and vulnerability may benefit from an independently managed revolving fund.
   c. In asymmetric groups (by size or vulnerability), a fund with varying financial commitments and voting weights can provide significantly more resources than one with equal contributions and voting.

Table 9.15 Comparison of the CMIM and FLAR

	CMIM	*FLAR*
Size	$240 billion	$2.76 billion
Number of members	13	8
Distribution of voting rights	Based primarily on share of financial contribution, combined with unweighted "basic votes" for each member	One country, one vote. Weighted paid-in capital contributions do not affect funds available for lending.
IMF linkage	70 per cent of maximum borrowing limit	• Minimal linkage • For future small-country members, the IMF can consider their FLAR paid-in capital as international reserves
Services for members	Structural facilities, precautionary line, surveillance, design of SF and PL packages, technical assistance	Balance-of-payments loans, liquidity, external public debt restructuring, contingency loans, international reserve guidance and monetary policy guidance/harmonization
Research capacity	• In process of building research capacity • Current staff of 35–40 economists, mostly focused on country surveillance plus limited functional surveillance (e.g. financial stability)	• Moderate internal research capacity by the Division of Economic Studies. • Strategic alliance with AMRO and the BIS.
Approval process	**IMF-delinked:** AMRO proposes package; must be approved by two-thirds majority of total votes **IMF-linked:** Following consultation with IMF, AMRO proposes package; must be approved by two-thirds majority of total votes	**Liquidity/contingency:** Approval by Executive President **Balance of payments/external public debt restructuring:** Approval by Board of Directors
Repayment track record	N/A	100 per cent

2. A variety of facilities and services can benefit participating economies.

    a. Precautionary or liquidity lines may prevent balance-of-payments crises and trade disruptions.

b. Longer term stability facilities can substitute for, or supplement, IMF packages.
c. Clear procedures for both types of facilities can benefit members by improving the speed and ease of disbursement, and reducing the incentives for capital flight when reserves are drawn down.

3. An effective and autonomous surveillance and monitoring body is necessary to ensure informed decision-making regarding preparation for and use of the funding facilities.

   a. If either autonomy or capability cannot be provided by a regional body, delegation to a third party (e.g. the IMF or a regional development bank) might be the best way to ensure effectiveness and reduce moral hazard.

4. Liquidity facilities should seek to eliminate uncertainty regarding the provision of funds.

   a. The FLAR's credibility derives from its track record, quality of personnel and procedures, regional solidarity and capital that is already "paid in."
   b. In the CMIM, credibility derives from the simplicity of the mechanism, the enormous dollar reserves of the leading members, planning and test runs (since it has no track record), and quality of personnel.

5. If members have low credit ratings, external management of funds can contribute to effectiveness.
6. There may be trade-offs between size and solidarity.

   a. The FLAR is a smaller, more integrated unit in which solidarity is high, but resources are modest. While some members have been calling for its expansion to include larger members, such as Mexico or Brazil, in order to increase the FLAR's capital, this would alter the current principle of equality of members and sacrifice the equality that has undergirded solidarity since the FLAR's inception.
   b. In contrast, the CMIM is defined by asymmetry. While the asymmetry means more resources, it also gives China and Japan a preponderance of influence.

7. Regional liquidity facilities can be seen as a kind of scalable exit option for economies that are dissatisfied with the IMF's emergency liquidity facilities. Those RFAs that are able to expand their resources to meet members' needs, can create a credible exit option from IMF funding and conditionality. Having such an option may increase members' voice within the IMF and give them more say in determining the conditions attached to IMF lending.

    a. The FLAR could be scaled up to more directly displace the role of the IMF in the region through increases in paid-in capital, the establishment of swap arrangements between member countries (as in the CMIM), the issuance of debt under its AA credit rating, and/or seeking deposits from non-member central banks.
    b. The CMIM is designed in such a way that credit facilities, of which currently 70 per cent are linked to IMF programmes, could be further, or even completely, delinked from IMF rules and regulations. It would also be relatively easy to increase resources or change purchasing multiples to boost the amount of funds available to economies in need. Already, the existence of non-CMIM BSAs could render the IMF peripheral to a crisis in South-East Asia.
    c. Regional groups that wish to reduce their dependence on the IMF for liquidity support and policy advice could benefit from following one of these strategies.

References

Agosin M (2012). Un Fondo Monetario Latinoamericano: Dimensiones Requeridas y Modalidades. Paper presented at the FLAR Annual Conference, Cartegena, 22–23 July 2012.

Agosin M and R Rodrigo Heresi (2011). Hacia un Fondo Monetario Latinoamericano.In: *Papers and Proceedings of the 2010 FLAR International Conference*, Cartagena, 10 March 2010.

ASEAN + 3 (2000). Joint Ministerial Statement of the ASEAN + 3 Finance Ministers Meeting, Chiang Mai, 6 May 2000. Available at http://www.amro-asia.org/services/view_file.aspx?f=/Files/Communiques/ASEANplus3/AFMM3_ChiangMai20000605.

ASEAN + 3 (2009). Joint Media Statement: Action Plan to Restore Economic and Financial Stability of the Asian Region, February. Available at http://www.amro-asia.org/services/view_file.aspx?f=/Files/Communiques/ASEANplus3/AFMM3_Phuket20090222.

ASEAN + 3 (2012). Joint Statement of the 15th ASEAN + 3 Finance Ministers and Central Bank Governors' Meeting, (Manila Statement), 3 May. Available at http://www.mof.go.jp/english/international_policy/convention/asean_plus_3/20120503.pdf.

ASEAN + 3 (2016). Agreement Establishing ASEAN + 3 Macroeconomic Research Office. Available at http://www.amro-asia.org/services/view_file.aspx?f=/Files/About%20AMRO/Legal%20Documents/AMRO-Agreement-website-upload.

Ban C (2015). Austerity Versus Stimulus? Understanding Fiscal Policy Change at the International Monetary Fund since the Great Recession. *Governance* 28(2): 167–183.

Ban C and K Gallagher (2014). Recalibrating Policy Orthodoxy: The IMF since the Great Recession. *Governance* 28 (2): 121–146.

Broome A (2015). Back to Basics: The Great Recession and the Narrowing of IMF Policy Advice. *Governance* 28(2): 147–165.

Chey Hyoung-kyu (2012). Why Did the US Federal Reserve Unprecedentedly Offer Swap Lines to Emerging Market Economies During the Global Financial Crisis? Can We Expect Them Again in the Future? GRIPS Discussion Paper 11–18. Available at http://www.grips.ac.jp/r-center/wp-content/uploads/11-18.pdf.

Chwieroth J (2010). *Capital Ideas: The IMF and the Rise of Financial Liberalization*. Princeton, NJ: Princeton University Press.

Copelovitch M (2010). *The International Monetary Fund in the Global Economy: Banks, Bonds and Bailouts*. Cambridge: Cambridge University Press.

Corvalan J (2015). Paraguay in the FLAR. In: G Perry (Ed.), *Building a Latin American Reserve Fund: 35 Years of FLAR*. Bogota, Pan-American Formas e Impresos SA: 265–276.

Eichengreen B (2015). Regional Financial Arrangements and the IMF. In: G Perry (Ed.), *Building a Latin American Reserve Fund: 35 Years of FLAR*. Bogota, Pan-American Formas e Impresos SA: 131–141.

Garcia LE (2015). Financial Institutions for Regional Integration. In G Perry (Ed.), *Building a Latin American Reserve Fund: 35 Years of FLAR*. Bogota, Pan-American Formas e Impresos SA: 49–62.

Grabel I (2011). Not Your Grandfather's IMF: Global Crisis, 'Productive Incoherence,' and Developmental Policy Space. *Cambridge Journal of Economics* (35): 805–830.

Grabel I (2013). Financial Architectures and Development: Resilience, Policy Space and Human Development in the Global South. Occasional Paper,

United Nations Development Programme, Human Development Office, New York.

Grimes WW (2006). East Asian Financial Regionalism in Support of the Global Financial Architecture? The Political Economy of Regional Nesting. *Journal of East Asian Studies* 6(3): 353–380.

Grimes WW (2009). *Currency and Contest in East Asia: The Great Power Politics of Financial Regionalism.*

Grimes WW(2011). The Future of Regional Liquidity Arrangements in East Asia: Lessons from the Global Financial Crisis. *Pacific Review* 24(3): 291–310

Grimes WW (2012). Financial Regionalism after the Global Financial Crisis: Regionalist Impulses and National Strategies. In: W Grant and G Wilson (Eds.), *The Consequences of the Global Financial Crisis: The Rhetoric of Reform and Regulation*. Oxford: Oxford University Press, 88–108.

Grimes WW (2015). East Asian Financial Regionalism: Why Economic Enhancements Undermine Political Sustainability. *Contemporary Politics* 21(2): 145–160.

Hill H and J Menon (2012). Financial Safety Nets in Asia: Genesis, Evolution, Adequacy, and Way Forward, ADBI Working Paper Series no. 395, Asian Development Bank Institute, Tokyo.

IMF (2003). The IMF and Recent Capital Account Crises: Indonesia, Korea, Brazil. Report of the Independent Evaluation Office. Available at https://www.imf.org/external/np/ieo/2003/cac/pdf/all.pdf.

IMF (2016). *IMF Surveillance.*

IMF Surveillance, at http://www.imf.org/en/About/Factsheets/IMF-Surveillance.

Katada S (2001). *Banking on Stability: Japan and the Cross-Pacific Dynamics of International Financial Crisis Management*. Ann Arbor, MI: University of Michigan Press.

Kawai M (2005). East Asian Economic Regionalism: Progress and Challenges. *Journal of Asian Economics* (16): 29–55.

Kawai M (2015). From the Chiang Mai Initiative to an Asian Monetary Fund. ADBI Working Paper 527, Asian Development Bank Institute, Tokyo. Available at http://www.adbi.org/working-paper/2015/05/20/6612.chiang.mai.asian.monetary.fund/.

Kim K (2006). The 1997–98 Korean Financial Crisis: Causes, Policy, Response, and Lessons. Paper presented at the High-Level Seminar on Crisis Prevention in Emerging Markets, organized by the IMF in Singapore 10–11 July 2006. Available at http://www.imf.org/external/np/seminars/eng/2006/cpem/pdf/kihwan.pdf.

Lee YW (2008). *The Japanese Challenge to the American Neoliberal World Order*. Redwood City, CA: Stanford University Press.

Liao S and D McDowell (2015). Redback Rising: China's Bilateral Swap Agreements and Renminbi Internationalization. *International Studies Quarterly* 59(3): 401–422.

Morales JA (2015). Bolivia in the History of FLAR. In: G Perry (Ed.), *Building a Latin American Reserve Fund: 35 Years of FLAR*. Bogota, Pan-American Formas e Impresos SA: 225–234.

Ocampo JA (2015). FLAR and Its Role in the Regional and International Financial Architecture. In: G Perry (Ed.), *Building a Latin American Reserve Fund: 35 Years of FLAR*. Bogota, Pan-American Formas e Impresos SA.

Ocampo JA and D Titelman (2012). Regional Monetary Cooperation in Latin America. Paper presented at the CAF/FLAR 2012 Conference in Cartagena 22–23 July 2012.

Pardo RP and PB Rana (2015).Complementarity Between Regional and Global Financial Governance Institutions: The Case of ASEAN + 3 and the Global Financial Safety Net. *Global Governance* 21(3): 413–433.

Perry G (2015). The Future of FLAR. In: G Perry (Ed.), *Building a Latin American Reserve Fund: 35 Years of FLAR*. Bogota, Pan-American Formas e Impresos SA: 175–192.

Rosero L (2014). Reserve Pooling of International Reserves: The Latin American Reserve Fund in perspective. *Latin American Policy* 5(1): 62–86.

Sakakibara E (1998). *Kokusai kin'yû no genba: Shihonshugi no kiki o koete* (The arena of International Finance: Moving Beyond the Crisis of Capitalism). Tokyo: PHP Shinsho.

Siregar R and A Chabchitrchaidol (2013). Enhancing the Effectiveness of CMIM and AMRO: Selected Immediate Challenges and Tasks ADBI Working Paper Series No. 403, Asian Development Bank Institute, Tokyo. Available at http://www.adbi.org/files/2013.01.17.wp403.enhancing.effectiveness.cmim.amro.pdf.

Stiglitz J (2002). *Globalization and Its Discontents*. New York: WW Norton.

Takagi S (2010). Regional Surveillance for East Asia: How Can It Be Designed to Complement Global Surveillance? ADB Working Paper Series on Regional Economic Integration, No. 50, Asian Development Bank, Manila. Available at https://www.adb.org/sites/default/files/publication/28524/wp50-regional-surveillance.pdf.

Titelman D, C Vera, P Carvallo and E Pérez Caldentey (2014). A Regional Reserve Fund for Latin America. UN ECLAC Financing for Development, Series No. 244, Economic Commission for Latin America and the Caribbean, Santiago, Chile.

Velarde J (2015). Financial crises and protection mechanisms: Perspectives for the FLAR. In: G Perry (Ed.), *Building a Latin American Reserve Fund: 35 Years of FLAR*. Bogota, Pan-American Formas e Impresos SA: 143–152.

Vreeland James R (2007). *The International Monetary Fund: Politics of Conditional Lending*. New York: Routledge.

CHAPTER 10

Conclusion

Diana Barrowclough and William N. Kring

10.1 South–South Financial Cooperation for Resilience and Development—Getting to the Next Level

The chapters in this volume have described some of the extraordinary trends in south–south financial cooperation of the last decade, with a particular focus on what could be called defensive mechanisms aimed to deal with liquidity crises and foreign exchange stresses. Whether as stand-alone institutions and mechanisms or whether as part of something broader and deeper—perhaps the first step toward full regional integration—these new mechanisms to meet official liquidity needs and to support new investment programs have changed the landscape and

D. Barrowclough (✉)
Division Globalization and Development Strategies, United Nations Conference on Trade and Development, Geneva, Switzerland
e-mail: Diana.Barrowclough@unctad.org

W. N. Kring
Global Development Policy Center, Boston University, Boston, MA, USA
e-mail: wkring@bu.edu

D. Barrowclough et al. (eds.), *South–South Regional Financial Arrangements*, International Political Economy Series,
https://doi.org/10.1007/978-3-030-64576-2_10

the terms of engagement forever. Developing countries have choices and, with these, a voice, that did not seem to exist in the previous decades. However, despite the many and real successful initiatives described in these pages, there is still much to be done and much caution still remains as to what has really been achieved. Without providing too much of a dampener, it is important to note that the current set-up cannot be called a global financial safety net—because the many different initiatives that have been described are not global, nor do they provide a guarantee of safety. New concerns about the extent to which climate change could provoke a "climate Minsky moment" (Carney 2015) of massive financial upheaval have just added one more concern to what was already a limited support system; continued imbalances and tensions regarding the world's dependence on the US Dollar remain another.

The fact is that actual financing for resilience and development is still largely insufficient. Traditional sources do not seem able to ramp up finance as they might be expected to help meet the global challenges for a safer, more inclusive, fairer, and sustainable world. Critical gaps remain, in areas such as concessional finance (critical for least industrialized countries (LICs), financing for dealing with shocks, especially natural disasters (affecting above all small state developing islands) which are becoming even more frequent and destructive; and the link between short-term finance of the kind discussed here and longer-term finance that is needed to support long-standing essential needs such as water, transport, and electricity. There is now a new urgency to scale up both emergency and long-term finance and direct it in a developmental manner.

Questions that remain include—what is still missing to strengthen south–south finance? Is it political will, more institutions and more coordination, as described in Mah Hui Lim's chapter on the political economy of developments in East Asia? Should the institutions engage more with the existing Bretton Woods institutions—and can those institutions reform sufficiently to make this something that developing countries actively want to do?

10.1.1 Strengthening Regional and Inter-regional Integration

Strengthening regional and inter-regional integration requires addressing both the "push" factors that have encouraged developing countries to integrate more closely in recent decades and the "pull" factors. Both gathered steam in the years following the global financial crisis of 2007–2008, but for many developing countries, this simply intensified a trend toward south–south integration that had been proceeding for several decades already. Push factors include the frustrations with the limitations and failures of the global financial architecture and traditional multilateral lenders; the lackluster economic performance and sluggish demand from northern economies in the post-crisis years; and a reappraisal of developing countries' experience in global value chains and other forms of global trade. As long as the global financial architecture remains unreformed and developing countries do not feel sufficiently supported in times of economic crisis or for long-term developmental needs, and as long as global trade appears uncertain, then it is to be expected that regional integration will strengthen, if only as a default reaction.

Alongside this, the pull factors that were already encouraging southern regional integration will likely continue, however they need to be better supported in order to be more inclusive and sustainable. This book has described well the important formation of pools of foreign reserves that can be called upon in times of balance of payments crisis including the Arab Monetary Fund (AMF), the Latin American FLAR, or Asia's Chiang Mai Initiative Mechanism CMIM. There continues to be growing interest in these mechanisms. However, at the same time these RFA's cover is unbalanced and many countries miss out. Larger members of regional pools can never be assured of sufficient liquidity in times of distress. In the last years both Ecuador, a relatively small economy member of FLAR, and Argentina one that some considered too large to join, have sought recourse with the IMF. In the Arab Monetary Fund only three members can be assured their needs will be fully met.

At the same time as this, credit swaps are becoming an increasingly important addition to the international financial landscape. Recent research carried out by Fritz and Muhlich find that for the 50 member countries of the south–south mechanisms FLAR, AMF, CMIM, and the Eurasian EFSD, short-term support from their regional arrangements was relied upon 219 times over the years 1976–2015, while the IMF was used 117 times—but, that in the most recent years, bilateral swaps between southern countries have been even more important. This raises new questions because just as reserve fund groupings do not exist in all parts of the developing world, nor can all members of regional groups be supported at the same time (especially for countries that are very large), and swaps are not an option open to all countries. In fact, swaps are probably an option only for a very small minority of countries and maybe not those that need it most. A small group of countries has the potential to "shop around" between Fund, bilateral swaps, and RFAs; some are too large for their RFAs but can potentially rely on bilateral swaps, and others are too small to be able to attract a swap but can be sufficiently covered by their RFAS. None could handle the shock of systemic crisis where many countries in the same region were hit at once. Thus, for most the only option remains the IMF and at present, that continues to mean accepting policy packages that are heavily conditional (Kentikelenis et al. 2016).

Hence it is by no means the case that these arrangements can handle the next big wave of crises—shocks and spillovers can be of a very large scale and highly detrimental; the capital reversals and currency fluctuations are driven by global factors out of the control of most national governments; and their size and degree of interconnectedness is extreme.

Therefore, while the new south–south mechanisms are extremely significant and relevant, reform of the multilateral financial architecture and its institutions remains an essential priority in order to meet the needs of all countries. Supporting south–south efforts to boost fiscal capacity and clamp down on tax "caves" will be a big help for this, given the trillions of dollars that are being diverted from developing country governments; but again, this will also require support at a global level, with regulations that have real teeth. In another vein, support for the south–south flanking policies such as interregional industrial cooperation (e.g. Latin America's pharmaceutical procurement agreement) and cross-border regulation and planning mechanisms for infrastructure are other obvious proactive factors to help strengthening regional integration because they will encourage regional production, consumption, and trade. Finally, support for boosting capacity and expertise in national governments is needed, as well as in financial institutions, in order to help countries better take advantage of the new opportunities that are emerging.

10.1.2 Principles of Solidarity

The RFAs and payments mechanisms described in this volume have many elements that are diverse and different but all share the grounding value and principle of Solidarity. One manifestation of this is the idea that all members should have a voice, and potentially an equal one irrespective of whether the country is most likely to be a creditor or a lender, or economic size or weight. In numerous meetings of RFAs and south–south development banks organized by the authors, this concept has been cited as part of the DNA of the institutions. But the trend of bilateral swaps discovered by Fritz and Muhlich are creditor driven and recipients depend on the goodwill or political willingness of just one partner nation—a very different dynamic from being part of a pool made up by multiple members who could always be creditors or debtors.

In practice only the FLAR holds the principle of one-member one-vote and historical experience does suggest that (with just one or two exceptions), all members can be borrowers just as often as lenders. In the CMIM votes are distributed according to the proportions of capital pledged with big differences between the larger richer economies and lower income ones. Some countries are not especially likely to be borrowers. This difference is also seen in the European Stability Mechanism (ESM) where one or two countries have very large voting shares. (Germany with 1,900,248 and France with 1,427,013 as compared to Portugal's 175,644 or Ireland's 111,454.)

However, the role of "voice" can be experienced even with differential voting especially when compared to the alternative of the institution not being there in the first place. None of the 22 members of the Arab Monetary Fund[1] are members of the G20 and so the AMF remains an important mechanism for voice; as with the FLAR, with also no members in the G20. Of the CMIM only four are members of G20 (China, Indonesia, Japan, and South Korea) meaning that the institution potentially offers small countries an important forum in which to share experiences and to be an alternative voice to the global institutions.

Additionally, questions remain about the practical ways in which emerging alternative southern-led institutions can co-exist with the existing multilateral institutions. As explored in Grimes and Kring's chapter, some RFAs such as CMIM, are designed to work in collaboration with the IMF through explicitly linked funds. In contrast, the FLAR is not designed to work with the IMF and only informally collaborates with the Fund. The ways in which RFAs collaborate with each other and the Fund will have serious implications for the governance of the global financial safety net. On the one hand, the presence of viable alternatives

[1] Jordan, United Arab Emirates, Bahrain, Tunisia, Algeria, Djibouti, Saudi Arabia, Sudan, Syria, Somalia, Iraq, Oman, Palestine, Qatar, Kuwait, Lebanon, Libya, Egypt, Morocco, Mauritania, Yemen, Comoros.

to the IMF provides developing countries with other alternatives to the IMF. However, IMF efforts to engage with RFAs could constrain the autonomy of RFAs if the IMF seeks to standardize lending standards or conditionality. Thus, while the RFAs and the IMF should strive for more substantive engagement, the comparative advantages of the RFAs and other southern-led mechanisms identified in this book should be safeguarded.

10.1.3 Broadening the Scope of Analysis and Advice

The G-20 Principle No. 5 urges that "*Consistency of lending conditions should be sought to the extent possible in order to prevent arbitrage and facility shopping, in particular as concerns policy conditions and facility pricing.*" However, these choices are what developing countries want. In intergovernmental meetings of the United Nations, developing country representatives and policymakers say they want real alternatives in the financial architecture. In only the second ever UN Conference on South–South Cooperation in forty years, held in Buenos Aires last year, country delegates debated and agreed an official statement that renewed their underlying principles. It said that "*developing countries tend to share common views on national development strategies and priorities,*" reflecting "*proximity of experience*" (Clause 13); and that they should "*develop country-led systems to evaluate and assess the quality and impact of south-south programmes,*" including thereby support from the RFAs (clause 25).

Hence the fact that RFAs are an alternative to the historical Bretton Woods institutions is one of their reasons for being. The FLAR may be small by global standards but it is valued because it has provided essential support to its members 46 times in 40 years, providing liquidity fast and without conditionalities. Similarly, the search for diversity and alternative choices lies at the birth of the CMIM—its members had a deep-rooted desire to never again experience having no choices of where to turn to, during the Asian crisis of the 1990s. The fact that countries appreciate having another kind of "voice" is further apparent in the recent decision that the European Stability Mechanism is not subsumed within the general legal framework of the European Community. The ESM was established at the height of the European sovereign debt crisis, outside the European Community framework by an intergovernmental treaty. It is a permanent rescue mechanism aimed at safeguarding the financial stability of the euro area.[2] In late 2017, the European Commission proposed to transform it from being an intergovernmental body into a European Monetary Fund (EMF) under EU law, shifting power away from the Member States. However, the proposal met considerable resistance and one year later it at the 2018 Euro Summit it was decided to maintain the ESM's intergovernmental character. This is one way in which it may maintain the ability to have an independent and alternative voice.

Having this kind of legislative respect for different internal voices is important because it can be difficult to adopt an alternative view within long-standing institutions. They are slow to change—steering like supertankers not racing yachts. Even during the crisis of 2007–2008, the teams of economists and managers carrying out Article IV consultations and advising on liquidity support to countries in dire straits did not take on board lessons learned from the failure of austerity-policies during crises more than one decade earlier and highlighted by their own internal evaluators. Article IV consultations are still the main vehicle through which the IMF carries out surveillance activities today and the new loans continued to contain conditionalities related to domestic economic policy, public employment levels, and sale of public assets (Kentikelenis et al. 2016) while also setting fiscal targets "based on over-optimistic assumptions about the pace of economic recovery, leading inevitably to fiscal underperformance," and "over-optimistic assumptions about the pace of revival of private investment" (IMF 2013). The cost of the gap is shown in the introduction to this volume. It is surely not a coincidence that the CMIM and ESM were established in the wake of such disappointments.

There are some encouraging signs of multiple views emerging, including the latest advice from the former chief economist of the IMF, Olivier Blanchard, that capital controls should be part of the toolbox of monetary policy, or most recently that Japan should forget about balancing its budget and run deficits for the indefinite future as the only way to avoid unemployment (Harding 2019).[3] This is encouraging.

On the other hand, a broader range of views is needed from other institutions as well. Credit Ratings Agencies which play an essential role in global capital markets—and whose judgments could spark a run that

[2] It has supported Greece, Ireland, Portugal, Spain and Cyprus, enabling them to stay in the Euro. With a paid in capital of 80 billion euros, it is one of the largest IFIs in the world.

[3] https://www.ft.com/content/ab57a006-7d07-11e9-81d2-f785092ab560.

could put countries into foreign liquidity distress—show little divergence in their analyses or views. These views are typically very mainstream, as shown for example in the strong convergence between their ratings of credit-risks and the World Bank's "east of doing business" indexes (UNCTAD 2016). One could argue that this is to be expected in the sense that the CRA is simply reflecting the general view, like a Keynesian beauty contest where the goal is to select the winner that most people would pick, however it reinforces the need for genuinely differentiated research approaches and assumptions, and different points of view. Thinking can be cyclical just as much as can be capital flows and the creation of credit. The rapid industrial transformers of Asia have benefitted greatly from designing their own views and taking an alternative path—the challenges of the present moment justify the continued push to create credible and robust southern-led alternatives.

References

Barrowclough (2019), Strengthening the International Financial Safety Net with South-South Principles of Analysis, Alternatives and Choice (May 2019) paper written for BU Policy Note, W Kring and W Grimes (Eds), Leading by Design: Lessons for CMIM-AMRO for the Global Financial Safety Net.

Carney M (2015), Breaking the tragedy of the horizon, climate change and financial stability. Speech by the Governor of the Bank of England and Chairman of the Financial Stability Board. London 29 September.

European Parliament (2019), Establishment of a European Monetary Fund. http://www.europarl.europa.eu/thinktank/en/document.html?reference=EPRS_BRI(2019)635556.

Eminent Persons Group (EPG) (2018), Making the Global Financial System Work for All, G-20 Eminent Persons Group. https://www.globalfinancialgovernance.org/assets/pdf/G20EPG-Full%20Report.pdf.

Gao H and K Gallagher (2019), Strengthening the International Monetary Fund for Stability and Sustainable Development. G20-T20 Japan 2019 Briefing Note.

G20 (2011), G20 Principles for Cooperation Between the IMF and Regional Financing Arrangements http://www.g20.utoronto.ca/2011/2011-finance-principles-111015-en.pdf.

G-24 (2018), Intergovernmental Group of Twenty-Four on International Monetary Affairs and Development. Washington, IMF. https://www.imf.org/en/News/Articles/201.

Harding R (2019), Top Economist says Japan should learn to love budget deficits, Financial times 23 August 2019.

IMF (2013), External Evaluation of the Independent Evaluation Office, IMF.
Kentikelenis A, T Stubbs and L King (2016), IMF Conditionality and Development Policy Space, 1985–2014, *Review of International Political Economy* 23(4).
Kring, W and K Gallagher (2019), Strengthening the Foundations? Alternative Institutions for Finance and Development, *Development and Change* 50(1 Special Issue): Beyond Bretton Woods: Complementarity and Competition in the International Economic Order, January 2019: 3–23.
Truman (2018), IMF Quota and Governance Reform Once Again. Peterson Institute for International Economics, *Policy Brief*: 18–19.
UNCTAD (2016), *Trade and Development Report, 2016: Structural Transformation for Inclusive and Sustained Growth*. New York and Geneva: United Nations Publication.

Index

D. Barrowclough et al. (eds.), *South–South Regional Financial Arrangements*, International Political Economy Series,
https://doi.org/10.1007/978-3-030-64576-2

The manufacturer's authorised representative in the EU is Springer Nature Customer Service Centre GmbH, Europaplatz 3, 69115 Heidelberg, Germany. If you have any concerns regarding our products, please contact ProductSafety@springernature.com

Printed and bound by CPI Group (UK) Ltd, Croydon, CR0 4YY
30/09/2026
02225700-0013